Roland Haratsch

Customized Graphical User Interfaces

Roland Haratsch

Customized Graphical User Interfaces

A Client-Server Architecture for Customized Graphical User Interfaces on the Client Side

Südwestdeutscher Verlag für Hochschulschriften

Impressum/Imprint (nur für Deutschland/ only for Germany)
Bibliografische Information der Deutschen Nationalbibliothek: Die Deutsche Nationalbibliothek verzeichnet diese Publikation in der Deutschen Nationalbibliografie; detaillierte bibliografische Daten sind im Internet über http://dnb.d-nb.de abrufbar.
Alle in diesem Buch genannten Marken und Produktnamen unterliegen warenzeichen-, marken- oder patentrechtlichem Schutz bzw. sind Warenzeichen oder eingetragene Warenzeichen der jeweiligen Inhaber. Die Wiedergabe von Marken, Produktnamen, Gebrauchsnamen, Handelsnamen, Warenbezeichnungen u.s.w. in diesem Werk berechtigt auch ohne besondere Kennzeichnung nicht zu der Annahme, dass solche Namen im Sinne der Warenzeichen- und Markenschutzgesetzgebung als frei zu betrachten wären und daher von jedermann benutzt werden dürften.

Verlag: Südwestdeutscher Verlag für Hochschulschriften Aktiengesellschaft & Co. KG
Dudweiler Landstr. 99, 66123 Saarbrücken, Deutschland
Telefon +49 681 37 20 271-1, Telefax +49 681 37 20 271-0
Email: info@svh-verlag.de
Zugl.: München, TU, Diss., 2009

Herstellung in Deutschland:
Schaltungsdienst Lange o.H.G., Berlin
Books on Demand GmbH, Norderstedt
Reha GmbH, Saarbrücken
Amazon Distribution GmbH, Leipzig
ISBN: 978-3-8381-1758-4

Imprint (only for USA, GB)
Bibliographic information published by the Deutsche Nationalbibliothek: The Deutsche Nationalbibliothek lists this publication in the Deutsche Nationalbibliografie; detailed bibliographic data are available in the Internet at http://dnb.d-nb.de.
Any brand names and product names mentioned in this book are subject to trademark, brand or patent protection and are trademarks or registered trademarks of their respective holders. The use of brand names, product names, common names, trade names, product descriptions etc. even without a particular marking in this works is in no way to be construed to mean that such names may be regarded as unrestricted in respect of trademark and brand protection legislation and could thus be used by anyone.

Publisher: Südwestdeutscher Verlag für Hochschulschriften Aktiengesellschaft & Co. KG
Dudweiler Landstr. 99, 66123 Saarbrücken, Germany
Phone +49 681 37 20 271-1, Fax +49 681 37 20 271-0
Email: info@svh-verlag.de

Printed in the U.S.A.
Printed in the U.K. by (see last page)
ISBN: 978-3-8381-1758-4

Copyright © 2010 by the author and Südwestdeutscher Verlag für Hochschulschriften Aktiengesellschaft & Co. KG and licensors
All rights reserved. Saarbrücken 2010

Abstract

This thesis treats the generation of customized graphical user interfaces for restricted client devices, which are mainly characterized by severe limitations in terms of processing power, available memory, and input/output interface. Since the late 1990s devices like mobile phones, PDAs, etc. have proliferated in the consumer and embedded market. In the beginning, these limited devices could hardly access Web content and other network services on the application layer, since the Internet technology and its provided services like the World Wide Web (WWW) have originally assumed networked clients with sufficient system resources. Whereas the industry has mainly concentrated on drastically increasing the hardware capabilities of such handheld devices, the approach of this thesis takes particularly the severe hardware restrictions into consideration. The attempt to save hardware resources as much as possible has become an essential part of the emerging initiative called Green Computing. As a result, this thesis proposes a uniform client-server architecture that enables a wide variety of client-devices to access Web content, from very low-end devices like wristwatches to mobile phones and even high-end workstations. The generation of graphical user interfaces for restricted clients with small displays imposes technical as well as ergonomic challenges. This thesis focuses on the technical aspects.

On the client side, a new and low-level binary format for describing graphical user interfaces is presented. This format is independent of any particular layout design and takes into account from scratch the different rendering and display capabilities of the restricted client devices by allowing user interface descriptions of different complexity. This new format does not depend on other formats and technologies. In addition, a new virtual machine, called Client Virtual Machine (CVM), is introduced which runs on the client device. The main tasks of the CVM are to communicate with the server, called CVM packet server, and to interpret the received CVM packets, which contain the user interface descriptions. The main design goal of the CVM is a simple and modular architecture so that small and restricted client devices can implement it without large efforts. In contrast to the recent developments in the area of handheld, mobile, and embedded devices, which came along with rising costs for their development and manufacturing, the CVM focuses particularly on very cheap client devices for the mass market to keep the per-unit manufacturing costs as low as possible.

On the server side, an exemplary framework for the generation of client-specific user interfaces is presented. After a client request, client-specific user interfaces are generated from an abstract user interface description and from the obtained profile data about the client capabilities such as screen dimensions, memory size, etc. The service providers can decide on their own how they create appropriate CVM packets for the requesting clients. This thesis proposes a technical platform that leaves the service providers as much flexibility and also responsibility in layout-related and other ergonomic issues as possible.

For the client-server communication a simple application protocol, called the CVM packet transfer protocol (CPTP), is proposed. It runs on top of the transport layer and is a very "thin" counterpart to the HTTP protocol, which is used in the WWW. Mainly, it consists only of a few protocol methods for requesting and delivering CVM packets and for sending profile data about the client capabilities.

The proposed concepts do not depend on Java-, XML-, or WAP-based technologies. They have been implemented in the C programming language and are demonstrated by several examples.

Contents

1 Introduction   **1**
- 1.1 Problem 1
- 1.2 Client-Specific Service and Content Adaptation 3
- 1.3 Thesis Scope — Client-Specific Graphical User Interfaces 5
- 1.4 Related Work — Overview 6
- 1.5 Summary of the Chapters 10

2 Proposed Client-Server Architecture — Overview   **12**
- 2.1 Main Components of Interactive Network Services 12
- 2.2 Client Side 13
    - 2.2.1 User Interface Description Format 13
        - 2.2.1.1 Compactness vs. Scalability 14
        - 2.2.1.2 Declarative vs. Operational 20
    - 2.2.2 Client Virtual Machine (CVM) 24
- 2.3 Server Side 25
- 2.4 Communication Protocol 29

3 Client Virtual Machine (CVM)   **31**
- 3.1 Core 32
    - 3.1.1 Data Types 32
    - 3.1.2 Operation Modes 33
    - 3.1.3 Register Stack 34
    - 3.1.4 Memory 36
        - 3.1.4.1 Data and Code 37
        - 3.1.4.2 Stack 38
        - 3.1.4.3 Heap 41
    - 3.1.5 Error Handling 41
        - 3.1.5.1 Error Processing 41
        - 3.1.5.2 Error Codes 42
    - 3.1.6 Event Handling 45
        - 3.1.6.1 Event Processing 46
        - 3.1.6.2 Event Registers 47
        - 3.1.6.3 Special Events 48
        - 3.1.6.4 Event Codes 49
    - 3.1.7 History Buffer 52
    - 3.1.8 Bookmarks Menu 56
    - 3.1.9 Interval Timer 57
    - 3.1.10 Runtime Behavior 58
- 3.2 Visual 75

		3.2.1	Graphics State	76
		3.2.2	Graphics Primitives	78
		3.2.3	Fonts	79
	3.3	Keyboard, Mouse		81
	3.4	Network		82
	3.5	Libraries		83
	3.6	Home Menu		86
	3.7	CVM Profile		89
	3.8	CVM Packet		93
	3.9	Instruction Set		98
		3.9.1	Overview	99
		3.9.2	Reference	100
	3.10	Implementation Notes		117
	3.11	Related Work		123
4	**CVM Packet Transfer Protocol (CPTP)**			**127**
	4.1	Message Format		127
	4.2	Protocol Methods		128
	4.3	Implementation Notes		131
	4.4	Example		131
5	**CVM Packet Server (CVMPS)**			**135**
	5.1	Abstract User Interface Description (AUI)		135
		5.1.1	Concrete Syntax	136
		5.1.2	Abstract Syntax	147
		5.1.3	Builtin Functions	148
		5.1.4	Example	149
	5.2	Session Manager		154
		5.2.1	Session Data	155
		5.2.2	Main Loop	156
	5.3	Service Generator		159
		5.3.1	Fixed Part of the Service Instance	160
		5.3.2	Generated Part of the Service Instance	161
	5.4	CVM Packet Generator		163
	5.5	CVM User Interface (CVMUI)		166
		5.5.1	Global Structure	166
		5.5.2	Page	170
		5.5.3	(Single-Line) Text	177
		5.5.4	Text Paragraph	179
		5.5.5	Text Box	182
		5.5.6	Hyperlink	187
		5.5.7	Button	192
	5.6	Implementation Notes		198
6	**Conclusions**			**202**
	6.1	Summary		202
	6.2	Results		204
	6.3	Future Work		205

Contents iii

A	Notations	206
	A.1 Miscellaneous	206
	A.2 Context Free Grammars	207
	A.3 Data Types	208
	A.3.1 Syntax of Data Type Definitions	208
	A.3.2 Data Access	210
	A.3.3 Example	212
	A.4 Code Templates	212

B	CVM Assembler (CVMA)	216
	B.1 Syntax	216
	B.2 Data Types	222
	B.3 Macros	224
	B.4 Builtin Functions	227
	B.5 Implementation Notes	232
	B.6 Examples	234

C	CVMUI Library (CVMUI Lib)	249
	C.1 libMisc.cvm	249
	C.2 libGui.cvm	251
	C.3 libGui3D.cvm	255
	C.4 libGuiTxtSmp.cvm	256
	C.5 libGuiTxt3D.cvm	256
	C.6 libGuiTxpSmp.cvm	256
	C.7 libGuiTxp3D.cvm	256
	C.8 libGuiHlk.cvm	257
	C.9 libGuiHlkSmp.cvm	257
	C.10 libGuiHlk3D.cvm	259
	C.11 libGuiIxt.cvm	260
	C.12 libGuiIxtSmp.cvm	262
	C.13 libGuiIxt3D.cvm	264
	C.14 libGuiBtnSmp.cvm	265
	C.15 libGuiBtn3D.cvm	267

D	CVM Packet Server: Example	272
	D.1 Generated Part of the Service Instance	272
	D.2 Generated CVM Packets	274
	D.2.1 Without Customization	274
	D.2.2 With Customization	295

Bibliography	324
Index	329

List of Figures

1.1 Common Internet Scenarios with Different Types of Clients 2
1.2 Software Requirements of a WWW Client 3
1.3 Simplified Client-Server Architecture for Client-Specific Service and Content Adaptation 4
1.4 J2ME: High-Level Architecture 8

2.1 Different Levels of Abstraction for User Interface Components 14
2.2 Simple User Interface Example 14
2.3 Modular Architecture of the CVM 25
2.4 Client-Server Session 26

3.1 CVM Modules and Functional Units 31
3.2 CVM Core: Functional Units 32
3.3 Procedure Stack Frame 40
3.4 Example of a Client-Server Session 55
3.5 History Buffer Behavior of an Exemplary Client-Server Session 56
3.6 CVM Screen Shot 1: `homeMenu.cvm` 86
3.7 CVM Screen Shot 2: `homeMenu.cvm` 87
3.8 CVM Screen Shot: `fibTimer.cvm` 122

4.1 CPTP Example Session 132

5.1 CVM Screen Shot: AUI Page p0 from `registration.aui` 149
5.2 CVM Screen Shot: AUI Page p1 from `registration.aui` 150
5.3 generateAuis: Structure of the output tree *genAuis* 165

List of Tables

3.1 Comparison: JVM ↔ CVM 125
D.1 Customized CVM Packets: `registration.aui`, CVMUI pages for AUI page p0 296
D.2 Customized CVM Packets: `registration.aui`, CVMUI pages for AUI page p1 297

Chapter 1

Introduction

1.1 Problem

New Consumer Devices as Networked Clients   The growing popularity of the World Wide Web (WWW) [92] and the proliferation of small, network enabled, and embedded consumer devices since the late 1990s, e.g., mobile phones, PDAs, hand-helds, set-top boxes, in-car computers, etc., have imposed new challenges on our network and user interface technology. Besides, new network services have emerged in the fields of E-Business and E/M-Commerce in addition to the classical network services like WWW, Email, Telnet [63], FTP [64], etc. In particular, M-Commerce aims at customers with mobile devices.

Traditionally, the access to Web content and other network services was limited to general purpose computers such as PCs or high-end workstations. In general, these are bound to a fixed place and are supplied with the typical system resources, e.g., a powerful processor, sufficient memory and secondary storage, monitor, mouse, keyboard, etc. With the new consumer devices, however, there has emerged a growing demand to access Web content and other network services with any — possibly mobile, wireless, and embedded — device, as illustrated in Figure 1.1 (page 2). A very common use case might be surfing the WWW with a mobile phone or an in-car computer.

Constrained System Resources   Restricted consumer devices are often dedicated to a special purpose and therefore do not have the hardware and software capabilities as general purpose computers have. The typical limitations of the first consumer devices can be summarized as follows:

- Low processing power: e.g. 1-10 MIPS

- Small memory: e.g. 128-512 Kbytes RAM, 0.5-1 Mbytes ROM

- Network connection often wireless and intermittent with limited bandwidth (e.g. 9600 bps or less), often no TCP/IP [69], high latency, etc.

- Restricted input capabilities: limited keyboard with a few input buttons, no mouse, possibly a touchscreen instead of a keyboard, possibly acoustic input via microphone, etc.

1. Introduction

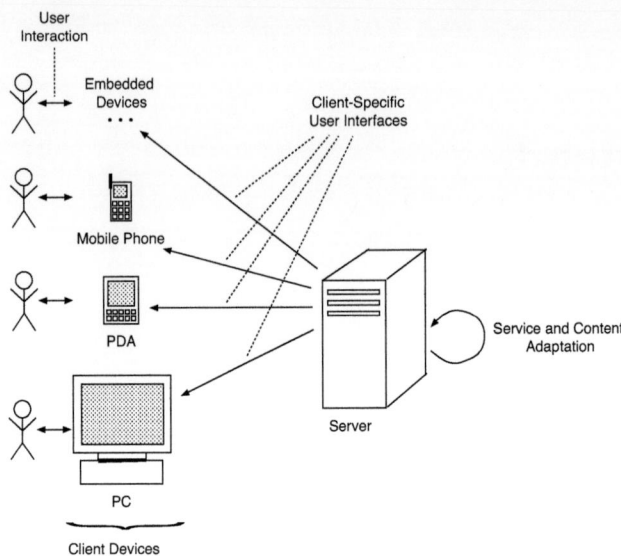

Figure 1.1: Common Internet Scenarios with Different Types of Clients

- Restricted output capabilities: small display with low resolution (e.g. 50x30, 100x72, 150x100 dots), restricted colors (e.g. mono color) and character fonts (e.g. only single font), possibly acoustic output via speaker, etc.
- Restricted power consumption, often operating with battery power

The capabilities of the consumer devices — particularly in terms of processing power, memory size, network bandwidth, battery life, etc. — have increased drastically since their appearance until today, however along with rising costs for their development and manufacturing. Therefore, the restricted capabilities still remain an issue particularly for very "thin" and low-cost devices on the consumer and embedded mass market. For example, typical "thin" clients might be in-car computers in the automotive industry, networked home appliances such as fridges, or wearables like wristwatches. In addition, the attempt to save hardware resources as much as possible has become an essential part of the emerging initiative called Green Computing [37].

Need of Client-Specific Adaptation of Network Services Apart from other involved technical problems relating to mobile, wireless, and ad-hoc networks [68, 82, 61, 83] and to embedded systems [9], the problems due to the limited system resources of the restricted client devices have to be approached as well, because the entire Internet technology and its provided network services originally have not been designed for different types of clients with constrained capabilities. Instead, the service providers have assumed general purpose computers as clients with sufficient system resources such as PCs or workstations. For example, Figure 1.2 (page 3) shows the software requirements of a WWW client. Nowadays, a WWW client is supposed to process protocol and data formats like

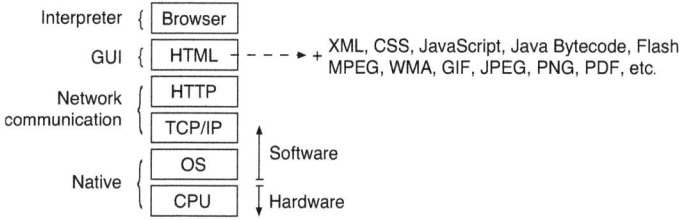

Figure 1.2: **Software Requirements of a WWW Client**

HTTP [10], HTML [65] and other XML [16]-based formats, CSS [12], JavaScript [27], Java bytecode [42], PDF [5], and several graphics, audio, and multimedia formats like GIF [29], JPEG [39], PNG [1], MP3 [46], WMA [93], MPEG [47], and Flash [28] for images, sounds, movies, and animations. Clearly, a restricted consumer device hardly can manage this variety of quite complex data formats.

To make network services accessible to the restricted client devices, a client-server architecture is required that adapts a requested network service to the particular hardware and software capabilities of the client device. Adaptation of network services can be performed on all layers of the ISO/OSI [81] protocol stack. For example, on the application layer mainly (user-)interactive network services are concerned. These are network services where the user of the client device is directly involved in the events of the network service. Here a so-called *user agent* runs on the client device which manages the communication with the server, makes the received server responses with the help of user interfaces visible or audible on the client device, and provides facilities for the user to interact. The WWW is an example of an interactive network service. Here, the browser software, e.g., Microsoft Internet Explorer or Mozilla Firefox, represents the user agent and displays the downloaded HTML documents on the client's screen. The user can scroll within the downloaded HTML document and follow hyperlinks via mouse clicks.

In addition to the client capabilities, the user of the client device should also be able to report his or her preferences when requesting a particular interactive network service. For example, the user might set a certain language, turn the sound off/on, or deactivate the reception of images.

1.2 Client-Specific Service and Content Adaptation

In general, data like HTML documents, images, etc., are involved in interactive network services. These resources are widely called *content*. Service adaptation usually involves content adaptation, as well. A common example of content adaptation is the filtering of HTML documents. Complex HTML markup elements, e.g., <TABLE>, <FRAME>, or images might be replaced by simpler markup elements or alternative representations, or they might be stripped off. Another example is the conversion of related data formats, e.g.:

- HTML [65] (WWW [92]) ⟷ WML [56] (WAP [54])

- JPEG [39] ⟷ GIF [29] ⟷ PNG [1]

- WAV [47] ⟶ WMA [93], MP3 [46]

- color image ⟷ gray scale image ⟷ mono color image

- written text ⟷ spoken language

The conversion of the communication protocols HTTP [10] (WWW) ⟷ WSP [57] (WAP) is also an example of service adaptation.

Simplified Architecture and Requirements A simplified client-server architecture for client-specific adaptation of interactive network services is illustrated in Figure 1.3 (page 4). Service and content adaptation is performed by the server or some proxy[†]. On

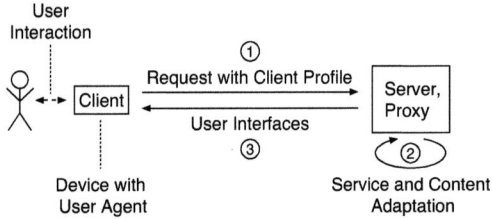

Figure 1.3: **Simplified Client-Server Architecture for Client-Specific Adaptation of Interactive Network Services**

the one hand, this reduces network bandwidth, because the client does not receive data, e.g., images, which it might discard. And network bandwidth is particularly in wireless networks a scarce resource. On the other hand, a restricted consumer device might not be capable of performing resource-intensive tasks such as service or content adaptation. However, server or proxy side adaptation requires that the client reports its hardware/software capabilities and current user preferences within a so-called *client profile* during a request (step 1) to the server or proxy. For this purpose a suitable format for the client profile as well as a communication protocol for efficient service and content negotiation are required. Service and content adaptation (step 2) can be carried out in three different ways, each one with growing complexity:

- **Selection:** The server or a proxy might always keep several versions available and, when there is a client request, select the one which best fits to the constraints given in the client profile. For example, a Web server might choose between several HTML and possibly WML document versions of a particular Web site.

- **Transformation:** The server might keep only one reference version permanently and transform it *dynamically*, i.e., when there is a client request, into a client-specific version. For example, a Web server might transform an XML [16] or HTML document

---

[†]Commonly, a proxy is an intermediary application that acts both as a server and a client. Incoming requests from other clients can be served internally or passed to other servers with possible translations.

into a suitable WML document. The XML based tree transformation language XSLT [22] might be used for such transformations.

- **Generation:** Finally, the server might keep an abstract description of its offered network service and content and generate dynamically a client-specific client-server session with adapted content. This requires, among other things, a language for describing network services, user interfaces, and content abstractly. The client-server architecture that is proposed in this thesis is based on the generative approach and will be discussed in more detail later on.

The adapted content is then sent to the client (step 3). In an interactive network service, the user agent of the client device presents the received content as a user interface. For example, in the WWW the HTML markup language is used as the description format for the user interface, whereas the browser software renders the HTML document and displays it on the screen of the client device. Considering the different rendering and display capabilities of the consumer devices, the description format for the user interfaces is a main issue. For example, the WAP Forum [54] has developed the less powerful markup language WML [56] for the wireless consumer devices.

In addition, the presentation of user interfaces on small displays also leads to major challenges in the fields of layout design and therefore might involve ergonomic factors. For example, one important question might be, how information can be rendered ergonomically on a small display to make it as much *readable* as possible. On the other hand, it might also be important, how visual information and its inherent logical structure, which is for example given by an HTML document, can be transformed best into spoken language.

1.3 Thesis Scope — Client-Specific Graphical User Interfaces

The topic of client-specific network service and content adaptation is very large and can be discussed at all levels of the ISO/OSI [81] reference model with all kinds of different content formats and client devices.

Therefore, this thesis mainly focuses on interactive network services on the application layer. Particularly, it deals with the generation of client-specific client-server sessions and graphical user interfaces (GUIs) from abstract user interface descriptions. Because of the large diversity of today's and future consumer devices, the proposed thesis mainly addresses devices with a graphic display for the output and with a keyboard and optionally a mouse for the input. However, other devices, e.g., devices with acoustic input and output, are taken into consideration as far as to enable enhancements towards these devices without substantial changes in the proposed ideas of this thesis.

The conversion of related multimedia, image, or other content formats and the conversion of written text or graphical user interfaces into speech for acoustic output are not covered here. Below the application layer a reliable network transport service, like TCP/IP [69] in the Internet, is assumed. How such a transport service is established in mobile, wireless, and ad-hoc networks is not covered here, either.

Finally, the proposed thesis only deals with the technical aspects regarding the generation of client-specific client-server sessions and graphical user interfaces, but it does not address layout-related or other ergonomic issues to avoid unnecessary restrictions. Rather, it proposes a technical platform that leaves service and content providers as much flexibility and also responsibility in layout-related and other ergonomic decisions as possible.

1.4 Related Work — Overview

A lot of working groups, many of them from the industrial sector, have early addressed the topic of providing interactive content and services for restricted client devices. Here, only the most important activities are introduced briefly:

World Wide Web Consortium (W3C) The World Wide Web Consortium (W3C) [92] has several working groups that deal with the description format for documents and user interfaces in the World Wide Web (WWW):

XHTML Basic The modularization of XHTML, XHTML 1.1 [6], decomposes XHTML 1.0 [60], which is the successor of HTML 4.01 [65], into functional subsets called *modules*. The module XHTML Basic [8] is specifically designed for Web clients such as mobile phones, PDAs, pagers, set-top boxes, etc., that do not support the full set of XHTML features. Mainly, XHTML Basic contains markup elements for basic text (including headings, paragraphs, and lists), hyperlinks and links to related documents, basic forms, basic tables, images, and meta information. However, it does not support style sheets, scripting, and frames.

XML, CSS, XSL The XML [16] working group of W3C pursues a separation of *content* and *layout*. In contrast to HTML documents which contain both content and layout information, the XML documents only contain logically structured content. As the XML elements have no intrinsic presentation semantics, layout has to be provided by additional style sheets, e.g., CSS [12] or XSL [2].

A CSS style sheet document is sent together with the XML document to the client device. On the client device a rendering engine, which understands CSS, formats and displays the XML document according to the style directives given in the CSS style sheet. As CSS is a quite powerful and complex style sheet language, a subset of CSS has been defined, called CSS Mobile Profile [95], which is tailored to the needs and constraints of mobile devices.

XSL consists of the tree transformation language XSLT [22] and a set of formatting objects and properties XSL-FO [2]. The XML document is first transformed with a given XSLT style sheet document into the resulting document. The client then renders and displays the resulting document. Note that the resulting document does not necessarily need to comply to XSL-FO. It may as well have any other XML-like format that is understood by the client. The tree transformation can be performed on the server or on the client side. If it is performed on the server side, then only the resulting document is sent to the client. Otherwise, both the XML and the XSLT style sheet documents are sent to the client. However, a resource-constrained client device might not be capable to perform such a resource-intensive task such as tree transformation. With the use of XSL an existing XML document might serve as a reference which is transformed dynamically to other XML documents that suit the client capabilities.

1.4. Related Work — Overview

XForms The XForms [24] working group of W3C deals with the next generation of Web forms which can be used with a wide variety of platforms including desktop computers, hand-helds, information appliances, etc. The XML-based language XForms describes user interfaces declaratively, i.e., not operationally, and on a quite high, i.e., abstract, level.

Composite Capabilities/Preferences Profiles (CC/PP) The CC/PP working group [90] of W3C has developed the Composite Capabilities/Preferences Profiles (CC/PP) framework [66] [49]. It consists mainly of an RDF [44] and XML [16] based format for describing the hardware and software capabilities of the client device and its user preferences, the CC/PP Profile [40], and an exchange protocol for content negotiation between client and server, the CC/PP Exchange Protocol [53]. The client sends its CC/PP profile within the request to the service provider. The service provider can use this information to customize its provided service or content, before it replies to the client. The vocabulary of the CC/PP profile is designed to be broadly compatible with the UAProf specification [59] from the WAP Forum [54]. It includes information about the hardware platform (e.g. vendor, model, class of device, screen size, etc.), the software platform (e.g. operating system, level of HTML, CSS, JavaScript, Java, and WAP support, etc.), and about an individual application (e.g. browser, etc.) of the client device. The CC/PP exchange protocol is based on the HTTP Extension Framework [48]. Note that HTTP is the assumed underlying protocol but the CC/PP framework might also be transportable over other protocols.

In the meantime the CC/PP working group has closed and its work moved to the Device Independence working group [91].

Wireless Application Protocol Forum (WAP) The Wireless Application Protocol Forum (WAP) [54] has specified a network protocol stack and an application framework for wireless consumer devices. Among others, they have developed WSP [57], WML [56], and WMLScript [58] which are, roughly speaking, the counterparts of HTTP, HTML, and JavaScript in the WWW respectively. In addition, the WAP Forum has also developed a core vocabulary, UAProf [59], for mobile devices, which complies with the CC/PP profile format of W3C. UAProf describes the hardware and software characteristics of the client device as well as the type of network to which the client device is connected. It defines attributes for the components "HardwarePlatform", "SoftwarePlatform", "NetworkCharacteristics", "BrowserUA", "WapCharacteristics", and "PushCharacteristics".

In the meantime, the WAP Forum has consolidated into the Open Mobile Alliance (OMA) [55] and no longer exists as an independent organization. However, the specification work from WAP continues within OMA.

Java 2 Platform, Micro Edition (J2ME) Sun Microsystems has grouped its Java technologies [77] into three editions with each aiming at a particular area in computing industry: the Java 2 Enterprise Edition (J2EE) for enterprises, the Java 2 Standard Edition (J2SE) for the desktop computer market, and the Java 2 Micro Edition (J2ME) [74] for the consumer and embedded device market. The high-level architecture of J2ME is illustrated by figure 1.4 (page 8).

For the host operating system only a minimal operating system is assumed that manages the underlying hardware. Support for separate address spaces or processes, guarantees about real-time scheduling or latency behavior, etc., are not required.

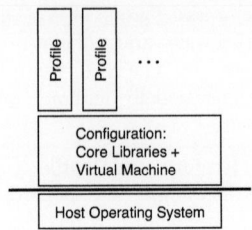

Figure 1.4: **J2ME: High-Level Architecture**

The configuration layer consists of a customized virtual machine and a minimal set of core Java class libraries available for a particular category of device. Devices of a particular category have similar characteristics in terms of memory budget and processing power. Currently, there are two configurations: the Connected Device Configuration (CDC) [72] and the Connected Limited Device Configuration (CLDC) [73]. CLDC is the smaller of the two configurations and designed for mobile devices with very little memory (measured in Kbytes) and processing power such as mobile phones, two-way pagers, personal digital assistants (PDAs), etc., whereas CDC is designed for fixed devices that have more memory (at least 2 Mbytes) and processing power such as TV set-top boxes, in-vehicle telematics systems, etc.,

The profile layer is implemented upon a particular configuration and provides additional APIs which are more domain specific for a particular family of devices. For instance, the Mobile Information Device Profile (MIDP) [78] operates on top of the CLDC configuration. Devices of a particular family have much more similar characteristics than devices of a particular category, i.e., a family is a refined subset of a particular category. For a particular configuration more than one profile might exist and a device can support multiple profiles at a time.

As a result, the modular and scalable J2ME architecture is mainly defined in a model with the following (software) layers built upon the host operating system of the device: a customized virtual machine, core and broad-range APIs provided by a particular configuration, and more specific APIs provided by profiles.

Connected Limited Device Configuration (CLDC)   CLDC [73] has been developed by Sun Microsystems in collaboration with major consumer device manufacturers since 1999. The devices targeted by the CLDC Specification have the following general characteristics:

- At least 192 Kbytes of total memory budget available for the Java platform, i.e., at least 160 Kbytes non-volatile memory for the virtual machine and CLDC libraries and at least 32 Kbytes of volatile memory for the virtual machine runtime and object memory (i.e., the heap space)

- 16/32-bit processor

- Low power consumption, often operating with battery power

1.4. Related Work — Overview

- Network connection often wireless, intermittent, and with limited bandwidth

The underlying Java virtual machine is the K Virtual Machine (KVM) [79]. The KVM is derived from the standard Java Virtual Machine (JVM), but designed from the ground up for small-memory, limited-resource, and network-connected devices. The "K" in KVM stands for "kilo", i.e., memory budget is measured in kilobytes. The KVM includes the execution of byte code, automatic garbage collection, and multi-threading. On the Java language and virtual machine level all central aspects are maintained with the following restrictions:

- No finalization of objects (i.e., `Object.finalize()`), no asynchronous exceptions, no user-defined class loaders, no thread groups and daemon threads, and no Java Native Interface (JNI)
- Limited set of error classes

CLDC contains classes that are identical or a subset of the corresponding standard J2SE classes, e.g., from the packages `java.lang.*`, `java.util.*`, `java.io.*`, and it contains additional classes outside J2SE which are specific to CLDC and inside the package `javax.microedition.*`.

CLDC does not cover application management (installation, launching, deletion) and user interface functionality (user interface components and event handling). These features have to be addressed by profiles implemented on top of the CLDC.

Mobile Information Device Profile (MIDP) The MIDP is designed for mobile phones, PDAs, and similar devices. Mainly it provides Java APIs for user interfaces, network connectivity, local data storage, sound, timers, and application management. The devices targeted by the MIDP Specification should have the following minimum hardware characteristics:

- Visual Output: screen size: 96x54, display depth: 1 bit, pixel shape (aspect ratio): approximately 1:1
- Input: one-handed keyboard or two-handed keyboard or touch screen
- Memory:
  - 256 Kbytes of non-volatile memory for MIDP implementation, beyond what's required for CLDC.
  - 8 Kbytes of non-volatile memory for application-created persistent data
  - 128 Kbytes of volatile memory for the Java runtime (e.g. Java heap)
- Networking: two-way, wireless, possibly intermittent, with limited bandwidth
- Sound ability

Other Some other activities like [11], [19], [25], [94], [84], [13], [23], etc., concentrate more on the layout-related and ergonomic aspects of content adaptation and presentation, which is performed on the server/proxy-side. For the description of user interfaces they rely on existing XML-based formats like HTML [65] and WML [56].

1.5 Summary of the Chapters

This section gives a summary for each chapter to come:

2 Proposed Client-Server Architecture — Overview This chapter gives an overview of the proposed client-server architecture that enables the generation of client-specific user interfaces for restricted client devices within the context of interactive network services on the application layer. It motivates the main ideas but does not go too much into details.

First, the main components of interactive network services are listed. Then, it is discussed which user interface description format is most suitable for client devices with different and restricted capabilities. In particular, the requirements of scalability, compactness, and functionality are addressed and it is discussed whether the description format should be declarative or operational. Thereby, different levels of abstraction are considered. As a result, a new virtual machine, called the Client Virtual Machine (CVM), is introduced that runs on the client device and serves as an interpreter for the new description format. On the server side a framework is presented where client-specific user interfaces with the new description format are generated and sent as CVM packets to the requesting client. For the client-server communication a simple application protocol, called the CVM packet transfer protocol (CPTP), is introduced briefly.

Reading this chapter is sufficient to get the basic idea of this thesis. The next chapters discuss the involved components of the proposed client-server architecture in detail.

3 Client Virtual Machine (CVM) This chapter specifies in detail the CVM and serves as a reference for any CVM implementor. The specification focuses mainly on the behavior and special characteristics of its modules and functional units by avoiding unnecessary restrictions that are implementation specific. This chapter specifies also the CVM profile and the CVM packet format. The CVM profile format is used by the CVM when it reports its capabilities and user preferences to the CVM packet server during a request. The CVM packet format is the new user interface description format and represents the binary executable format for the CVM. At the end of this chapter the main differences between the CVM and the JVM/KVM virtual machines from Sun Microsystems are outlined.

4 CVM Packet Transfer Protocol (CPTP) This chapter specifies in detail the CPTP protocol which manages the client-server communication between the CVM and the CVM packet server. The CPTP protocol runs on top of the transport layer and is a very "thin" counterpart to the HTTP protocol which is used in the World Wide Web. At the end of this chapter an exemplary CPTP session is demonstrated.

5 CVM Packet Server (CVMPS) This chapter specifies an exemplary server-side architecture for the CVM packet server. The CVM packet server processes the client requests and generates session instances and CVM packets that are optimized for the individual client capabilities. The exemplary CVM packet server consists of the following components:

1.5. Summary of the Chapters

- An abstract user interface description language (AUI) has been developed to specify interactive network services on the application layer. It provides language constructs to specify the client-side user interface components as well as language constructs to embed code for state-dependent actions that are executed on the client and server side. Client-side actions are specified in CVM assembler whereas server-side actions can be specified in any common programming language.

- The session manager processes all incoming client messages and stores the data that are involved during the client-server sessions.

- The service generator generates the client-specific service instance from a given AUI description and CVM profile.

- The CVM packet generator generates customized CVM packets from a given AUI description and CVM profile. These CVM packets are called CVM user interfaces. A CVM user interface may contain all parts of the requested AUI page or only a smaller subset.

6 Conclusions This chapter summarizes the main results and outlines perspectives for future work.

A Notations This appendix contains a description of the used notations.

B CVM Assembler (CVMA) This appendix specifies the CVM Assembler. Its syntax is used for the generated code samples throughout this thesis.

C CVMUI Library (CVMUI Lib) This appendix contains an exemplary implementation of the CVMUI library. The CVMUI library contains constant and function definitions that are imported by CVMUI programs.

D CVM Packet Server: Example This appendix contains the C and CVMA source code of the generated service instance and the CVM packets of an AUI description for an exemplary network service.

Chapter 2

Proposed Client-Server Architecture — Overview

On the client side, different levels of abstraction for describing graphical user interfaces are discussed and a new description format for it is presented. This format takes into account from scratch the limited display capabilities of the restricted consumer devices and thus enables scalability, i.e., "thinner" client devices may receive simpler user interface descriptions. A new virtual machine, called Client Virtual Machine (CVM), runs on the client device and serves as the user agent. It interprets and displays the received user interface descriptions.

On the server side, client-specific user interfaces and client-server sessions are generated from abstract user interface descriptions.

The communication between the client and the server is managed by a new and simple application protocol, called CVM packet transfer protocol (CPTP).

As already said in the introduction of this thesis, the proposed architecture for the generation of client-specific user interfaces mainly deals with the technical, but not layout related or other ergonomic aspects. As the basic ideas of the proposed client-server architecture are independent of any particular layout design, the service providers gain as much flexibility and also responsibility in layout-related and other ergonomic decisions as possible when creating user interfaces for restricted clients with limited capabilities.

2.1 Main Components of Interactive Network Services

First, the essential components that are necessary to implement interactive network services on the application layer will be summarized:

The server contains the control logic of the network service, manages the involved content, and supplies the client with user interfaces to be displayed. The control logic defines the course of the network service. A network service might consist of several phases. Between the phases client-server communication takes place to exchange data. In general, the control logic can be implemented by an (unrestricted) state machine. The involved content might be any data, e.g., text documents, forms, images, databases, etc., and is packed into user interfaces. The main task of a client is — apart from sending its request to a server for a particular network service — to display the received user interfaces on the client device. Therefore it needs a runtime environment or interpreter which is frequently also called browser or user agent. At last, a protocol is required for the client-server communication on the application layer.

The WWW is an example of an interactive network service on the application layer. However, in the traditional WWW the above components are not clearly separated: On the one hand, HTML [65] — possibly enriched with JavaScript [27] and Java [36] code — is used as the user interface description format on both the server and the client side. On the other hand, parts of the control logic, for instance the handling of status and error messages, are specified in the HTTP [10] communication protocol, instead.

2.2 Client Side

On the client side mainly a user interface description format is needed which suits the different capabilities and limitations of the networked clients and thus enables scalability.

2.2.1 User Interface Description Format

In general, a graphical user interface consists of several user interface components, where each user interface component is characterized mainly by its graphic appearance and event semantics. The event semantics is usually defined by an event table which specifies for each event type, e.g., a mouse click, a sequence of actions to be executed after the user has triggered an event of that type. However, some components of a user interface might not have any event semantics, e.g., a paragraph of simple text or an illustrative image. These non-interactive components are mainly used for informational or stylistic purposes. For reasons of generality they are referred to in this thesis as (non-interactive) user interface components as well.

Requirements The user interface description format for networked clients with different and restricted capabilities must meet the following requirements:

1. *Scalability:* The user interface description format must be as general and scalable as to be displayable by current and future client devices with different capabilities, especially by small and restricted consumer and embedded devices. Ideally, its appliance should also be suitable for general purpose computers with sufficient system resources such as PCs or workstations.

2. *Compactness:* The user interface description format must allow compact encodings of user interfaces to reduce network bandwidth during transport from the server to the client.

3. *Functionality:* The user interface description format should provide equal functionality and be as powerful as the current technologies that are used in the Internet nowadays such as HTML [65], JavaScript [27], and — to some extent — Java [36], because otherwise additional technologies are needed for more complicated and dynamic tasks. This is the case with HTML which often includes JavaScript or Java code for dynamic tasks.

2.2.1.1 Compactness vs. Scalability

To meet the requirements of *scalability* and *compactness*, a compromise must be found between different levels of abstraction which are illustrated in figure 2.1 (page 14). The

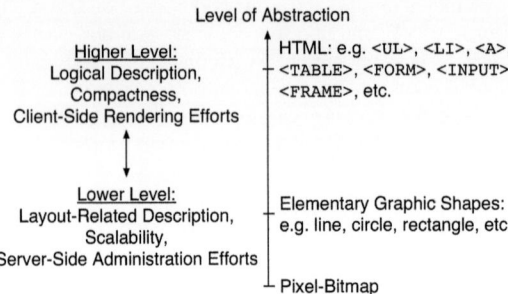

Figure 2.1: **Different Levels of Abstraction for User Interface Components**

more abstract the user interface components are, the more compact the user interface description becomes. But then less scalability can be achieved.

The different levels of abstraction will be discussed in more detail with the help of an example of a simple user interface that is shown in figure 2.2 (page 14). This user interface

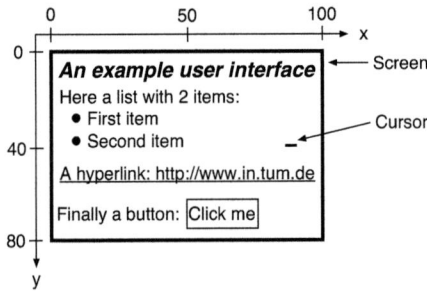

Figure 2.2: **Simple User Interface Example**

example begins with a title on the top. Then an unnumbered list with two list items follows. The next line represents a hyperlink to a WWW site at the given URL [26]. The last line begins with some text and finishes with a button. The current cursor position is indicated here by a narrow horizontal line. It depends on the peripherals of the client device how the user can control the cursor. As most consumer devices have limited input capabilities, some kind of arrow keys of the limited keyboard must be used for this task instead of a mouse which is usually only available on general purpose computers such as PCs or workstations. Apart from the cursor this user interface contains two interactive components: the hyperlink and the button. The user can activate such an interactive object by first moving the cursor into the geometric region of the object and then pressing

2.2. Client Side

some kind of Enter key on the keyboard. The activation of the hyperlink results in a new client request for the WWW site at the explicitly given URL. After the button is pressed, any actions can be performed and are not specified here in more detail. In the following discussion, this user interface will be described with respect to different levels of abstraction.

High-Level Components A high-level user interface component does not predefine a specific layout presentation. Instead, the user agent which displays this user interface component can choose a particular layout presentation. The only formatting constraint is that its appearance reflects to the user intuitively what kind of user interface component it is. For example, a button should look like a button. In addition, a high-level user interface component may be of any complexity and might consist of several sub-components. For example, a list usually consists of several list items, a table usually consists of several rows which in turn consist of several columns each, or a form usually consists of several input fields, buttons, etc. Typically, the default event semantics of a high-level user interface component is predefined implicitly without an explicit event table.

The markup language HTML [65] is an example of a high-level language for describing user interfaces because it has several high-level markup elements such as <UL>, <LI>, <A>, <TABLE>, <FORM>, <INPUT>, <FRAME>, etc. For example, an unnumbered list can be described in HTML with the markup element <UL>. Its list items are described each with the markup element <LI> and listed as children inside the parental <UL> element. The <A> element is used for hyperlinks. An input form is expressed by the <FORM> element and its subcomponents, called controls, can each be specified with the <INPUT> element. The type attribute of the <INPUT> element then specifies the control type, which might be a button, a text input field, etc. A button, for example, is expressed with the type attribute value "button". In general, the default event semantics of an interactive HTML element is implicitly predefined. Additional event semantics must be specified with the help of a scripting language such as JavaScript [27]. The corresponding scripting code is embedded into the HTML document. For example, the scripting code for the actions on a button click can be provided by the value of the onclick attribute of the corresponding <INPUT> element. The rendering of a high-level markup element into a particular layout presentation on the display of the client device is performed by the browser which runs on the client device and interprets the downloaded HTML document. Therefore, the browser determines the graphic appearance of a high-level markup element. In the course of time, however, similar representations for most markup elements have emerged for the common browsers like the Microsoft Internet Explorer or Mozilla Firefox. The above user interface can be specified in HTML as follows:

```
<HTML>
<HEAD>
  <TITLE>An example user interface</TITLE>
  <META http-equiv="Content-Script-Type" content="text/javascript"/>
</HEAD>
<BODY>
  <FONT face="Helvetica" size="3" color="black">
    <FONT size="+1"><I><STRONG>An example user interface</STRONG></I></FONT>
    <P>Here a list with 2 items:
      <UL>
        <LI>First item
```

```
        <LI>Second item
      </UL>
      <A href="http://www.in.tum.de">A hyperlink: http://www.in.tum.de</A>
      <FORM action="http://somesite.com/handle" method="post">
        Finally a button:
        <INPUT type="button" value="Click me"
               onclick="/* Here comes the JavaScript code */"/>
      </FORM>
    </P>
  </FONT>
</BODY>
</HTML>
```

The benefit of a high-level description language like HTML is that its language constructs allow quite compact descriptions of user interfaces, which is good to keep network bandwidth low. But on the other side, the client-side rendering efforts rise, because the client has to interpret these abstract user interface elements and perform the formatting into a particular layout presentation. Because of the complexity of some user interface components, this task might impose a lot of effort for the client. Therefore, a resource-limited client can hardly process complex user interface elements. The only way for a resource-limited client then is to omit user interface components with higher complexity. In terms of HTML, only a subset of its markup elements, which excludes elements like <TABLE>, <FORM>, <INPUT>, <FRAME>, etc., can be processed by a resource-limited client. Content adaptation then would rather become a matter of content filtering. As a result, because of its lack of scalability, a high-level description language for user interfaces like HTML is not suitable for limited client devices.

Pixel Bitmap Image If user interfaces are described on a lower level, more scalability and flexibility can be achieved for their adaptation. The lowest level for describing a particular user interface component might be a pure pixel bitmap that represents the image of its graphic appearance and an explicit event table that defines the event semantics. Then, the whole user interface description is an image whereas each user interface component occupies a particular geometric area inside the image. The event table defines the corresponding event semantics for each geometric area of the image that belongs to an interactive user interface component. Then, the above user interface can be described exemplarily in a C-like syntax [20] as follows:

```
char pixel_bitmap[] =
{
  /* Byte array which encodes the image of the user interface
     as a pixel bitmap. */
}

void event_table()
{
  if ( /* Arrow left key pressed ? */ )
    { /* Move cursor left. */ }
  else if ( /* Arrow right key pressed ? */ )
    { /* Move cursor right. */ }
  else if ( /* Arrow up key pressed ? */ )
```

2.2. Client Side

```
{ /* Move cursor up. */ }
else if ( /* Arrow down key pressed ? */ )
{ /* Move cursor down. */ }
else if ( /* Enter key pressed ? */ )
{
  if ( /* Current cursor position inside of rectangle
        [(5, 50), (90, 60)] ? */ )
  {
    /* Action code for the hyperlink: a new WWW request
       with the URL "http://www.in.tum.de". */
  }
  else if ( /* Current cursor position inside of rectangle
             [(50, 65), (80, 75)] ? */)
  { /* Action code for the button: application specific ... */ }
}
}
```

For reasons of brevity and clearness this description concentrates only on the essential parts. In addition, some sections are expressed informally within comments. The user interface description consists of two main parts: First comes the byte array (`pixel_bitmap[]`) that encodes the image of the user interface as a pixel bitmap. Next comes the event table (`event_table()`). The event table defines the corresponding actions for each event type, e.g., Enter key pressed, and the xy coordinates of the current cursor position. If the cursor position falls inside the geometric region of an interactive element while the user triggers an event of a particular type, then the corresponding actions are executed. Here, the geometric region of the hyperlink is defined by the rectangle with the (x, y) corners (5, 50) and (90, 60), and the geometric region of the button is specified by the rectangle with the corners (50, 65) and (80, 75). The event table and its actions must be encoded in a language format that the client device understands.

The main benefit of this approach is that the client does not need to render the graphic description of the user interface into a particular layout presentation because it is already encoded as a pure pixel bitmap image.

However, this approach also results in serious problems: First, the transport of bitmap images from the server to the client wastes too much network bandwidth, because bitmap images are quite huge even for small displays. If each pixel point is specified using the 24-bit RGB color model [70], then the whole size of the user interface description, which consists of the pixel bitmap and the event table, exceeds 100x80x3 = 24000 bytes. In comparison, the equivalent HTML description of the above user interface only requires approximately 700 bytes. In spite of the rapid developments in the area of wired and wireless network technology to provide more bandwidth, e.g., UMTS [87], network bandwidth might always be a limited resource. Compact image encoding formats like GIF [29], JPEG [39], etc., might help to reduce bandwidth requirements but not sufficiently. In addition, the client device then would have to perform some processing to decode the image.

Another problem is that user interaction is very hard to implement this way, because a user interface component might change its appearance when the user interacts with it. For example, the shading of a button might change when it is pressed or the color of a hyperlink might change after it has been visited by the user. A more complex example might be an editable text field which updates synchronously the contents of its text field while being edited by the user. In addition, the cursor — which is also part of the image — changes its position when the user presses one of the arrow keys. Whenever the user interface components change their appearance, the client — if we assume that it does not perform any rendering of the user interface — has to send an appropriate notification message to the server and wait for an updated image that reflects the new state of the user interface. The server, on the other side, has to keep track of the current state of the client-side user interface and send the updated image to the client after each received notification message. Thus, each user interaction leads to additional network traffic and might cause a network overload. In addition, the server has to do a lot of administration tasks. After each user interaction, it has to process a notification message and deliver the image that reflects the current state of the user interface.

It becomes clear that this approach cannot be implemented practically. This approach reduces the rendering efforts of the client to a minimum, but the bandwidth requirements and server-side administration efforts are immense. Therefore, more capabilities of the client are required to decrease the bandwidth requirements and server-side administration efforts.

Elementary Graphic Shapes The previously discussed approaches are extreme in nature. The first one describes a user interface from a very abstract and logical view without a strict relation to a particular layout presentation. The second approach defines a user interface by a pixel bitmap image and an explicitly defined, coordinate-based event table. Apart from the pixel point — which is the most elementary and unsplittable graphic object at all — the second approach does not assume any other or even higher-level components to form the graphic appearance of a user interface.

As a result, a compromise between these two extreme approaches might be elementary user interface components that are low level enough to serve as building blocks for more complicated user interface objects, but still allow compact descriptions of user interfaces. Besides text, the building blocks are elementary graphic shapes that occur frequently in user interfaces components such as lines, circles, rectangles, etc.

For example, the above user interface can be described with these elementary graphic shapes in an XML-like syntax [16] as follows:

```
<paint fontName="Helvetica" fontStyle="normal" fontSize="14pt" color="black">
  <text x="5" y="12" fontStyle="bold italic" fontSize="17pt"
        string="An example user interface"/>
  <text x="5" y="25" string="Here a list with 2 items:"/>
  <circle x="10" y="30" radius="3" fill="true"/>
  <text x="20" y="35" string="First item"/>
  <circle x="10" y="38" radius="3" fill="true"/>
  <text x="20" y="43" string="Second item"/>
  <text x="5" y="55" string="A hyperlink: http://www.in.tum.de"/>
  <line x1="5" y1="57" x2="85" y2="57"/>
  <text x="5" y="72" string="Finally a button:"/>
  <rect x1="50" y1="65" x2="80" y2="75"/>
  <text x="55" y="72" string="Click me"/>
</paint>
<eventTable>
  <!-- entry for the hyperlink: -->
```

2.2. Client Side

```
<entry x1="5" y1="50" x2="90" y2="60" type="Enter key pressed" action="..."/>
<!-- entry for the button: -->
<entry x1="50" y1="65" x2="80" y2="75" type="Enter key pressed" action="..."/>
</eventTable>
```

The names of the markup elements and attributes should be self-explanatory. This user interface description consists of two main sections. The first section is enclosed by the markup element `<paint>` and defines the visual appearance of the graphical user interface. The second section is limited by the markup element `<eventTable>` and contains the event table. By default, each child element inherits the attribute values of its parent element, if it does not overwrite them. For example, the first occurring `<text>` element in the above user interface description inherits the `fontName` attribute of the parental `<paint>` element, whereas it overwrites the parental `fontStyle` and `fontSize` attributes. The child elements of the `<paint>` element represent elementary graphic shapes which serve as building blocks. For example, the `<text>` element prints out the string that is given by its `string` attribute on the display at the coordinate position that is given by its `x` and `y` attributes. The `<line>` element draws a line that starts at the coordinate position given by the `x1` and `y1` attribute values and ends at the position given by the `x2` and `y2` attribute values. Each `<entry>` element defines the corresponding actions for a particular user event. If the type of the user event matches the value of the `type` attribute and the current cursor position falls into the rectangular area that is limited by the corners (`x1, y1`) and (`x2, y2`), then the client device executes the sequence of actions given by the value of the `action` attribute. For this the sequence of actions must be encoded in a language that the client understands.

In the following discussion, the building block idea is demonstrated by comparing particular sections of this user interface description with the equivalent sections of the corresponding HTML description: The lines

```
<circle x="10" y="30" radius="3" fill="true"/>
<text x="20" y="35" string="First item"/>
<circle x="10" y="38" radius="3" fill="true"/>
<text x="20" y="43" string="Second item"/>
```

build the unordered list which is expressed in HTML with

```
<UL>
  <LI>First item
  <LI>Second item
</UL>.
```

The lines

```
<text x="5" y="55" string="A hyperlink: http://www.in.tum.de"/>
<line x1="5" y1="57" x2="85" y2="57"/>
...
    <!-- entry for the hyperlink: -->
<entry x1="5" y1="50" x2="90" y2="60" type="Enter key pressed"
       action="..."/>
```

build the hyperlink which is expressed in HTML with

```
<A href="http://www.in.tum.de">A hyperlink: http://www.in.tum.de</A>.
```

The lines

```
<rect x1="50" y1="65" x2="80" y2="75"/>
<text x="55" y="72" string="Click me"/>
...
    <!-- entry for the button: -->
<entry x1="50" y1="65" x2="80" y2="75"
       type="Enter key pressed" action="..."/>
```

build the button which is expressed in HTML with

```
<FORM action="http://somesite.com/handle" method="post">
...
  <INPUT type="button" value="Click me"
         onclick="/* Here comes the JavaScript code */"/>
</FORM>.
```

In order to relieve the client from the task of performing layout computations, this user interface description explicitly contains the absolute xy coordinate positions for each user interface component. A mixture of relative and absolute xy coordinates might also be used. The formatting and assignment of the xy coordinates is performed by the server. As a result, the client can draw instantly the elementary graphic shapes without large rendering efforts.

Here, a pixel point is used as the measuring unit for the xy coordinates. However, as the dimension of a pixel point generally varies between different screen types of the client devices, an absolute and platform-independent measuring unit such as the Big Point or shortly Point (pt) might be used as well. The size of a Point equals to 1/72 inch and is widely used as the typographic unit in computer industry.

As this user interface description is only a little larger than the equivalent HTML description, this approach satisfies the two requirements of *scalability* and *compactness*. However, this user interface description does not specify how the cursor is controlled. In addition, this approach does not address the issue, which programming language might be used to encode the actions of the interactive components, either. These topics are discussed next.

2.2.1.2 Declarative vs. Operational

The third requirement of *functionality* leads to the question whether the user interface description should be declarative[†] or operational. Declarative means that the user interface is described without control-flow language constructs. In combination with high-level user interface components with default event semantics quite compact user interface descriptions can be achieved. HTML is an example of a declarative language. However, a declarative language reaches its limitations, when dynamic aspects of the user interface need to be specified explicitly such as individual and application-specific event semantics of particular interactive user interface components, because it is very difficult to describe actions, which are operational by nature, in a declarative way. HTML, therefore, has to include code

---

[†]The term *descriptive* is occasionally used as a synonym for the term *declarative*.

2.2. Client Side

written in another operational language, e.g., JavaScript [27], for these tasks. To avoid the dependence on another operational language the user interface must be described in an operational manner. Besides, an operational language can be interpreted by the client more directly and easier than a declarative language. Using this approach, a particular user interface description is a program for a virtual user interface machine, which is here called the *Client Virtual Machine* (CVM). Then, the above user interface might be described operationally in a C- and assembler-like syntax exemplarily as follows:

```
/* application specific variable declarations */

  /* xy position and length of cursor */
  int xPos = 0, yPos = 0, lenCursor = 10;

  /* state of the hyperlink */
  boolean isVisited = false;

  /* state of the button */
  boolean isCurrentlyPressed = false;


/* paint procedures */

  /* entry point for execution */
  main:
    call paintUserInterface
    call paintCursor
    abort

  /* paint procedure for the user interface */
  paintUserInterface:
    setcolor black
    setfont Helvetica, bold italic, 17    /* name, style, size */
    text 5, 12, "An example user interface"    /* x, y, string */
    setfont Helvetica, normal, 14
    text 5, 25, "Here a list with 2 items:"
    circlefill 10, 30, 3    /* x, y, radius */
    text 20, 35, "First item"
    circlefill 10, 38, 3
    text 20, 43, "Second item"
    call paintHyperlink
    text 5, 72, "Finally a button:"
    call paintButton
    ret

  /* paint procedure for the hyperlink */
  paintHyperlink:
    if (isVisited == false)
      { setcolor blue }
    else
      { setcolor red }
    text 5, 55, "A hyperlink: http://www.in.tum.de"
```

```
    line 5, 57, 85, 57     /* x1, y1, x2, y2 */
    setcolor black
    ret

  /* paint procedure for the button */
  paintButton:
    if (isCurrentlyPressed == false)
      { setcolor green }
    else
      { setcolor red }
    rectfill 50, 65, 80, 75    /* x1, y1, x2, y2 */
    setcolor black
    rect 50, 65, 80, 75    /* x1, y1, x2, y2 */
    text 55, 72, "Click me"
    ret

  /* paint procedure for the cursor */
  paintCursor:
    line xPos, yPos, xPos + lenCursor, yPos
    ret


/* event semantics */

  /* event attributes */
  int deviceCode, eventCode, eventPars[];

  /* global event handling procedure */
  eventTable:
    if (deviceCode == KEYBOARD)
      {
      if (eventCode == PRESSED)
        {
        /* eventPars[0] contains the key code */
        if (eventPars[0] == LEFT_KEY  &&  xPos > 0)
          {
          xPos = xPos - 1
          call paintUserInterface
          call paintCursor
          }
        else if (eventPars[0] == RIGHT_KEY  &&  xPos < XMAX)
          {
          xPos = xPos + 1
          call paintUserInterface
          call paintCursor
          }
        else if (eventPars[0] == UP_KEY  &&  yPos > 0)
          {
          yPos = yPos - 1
          call paintUserInterface
          call paintCursor
```

2.2. Client Side

```
      }
      else if (eventPars[0] == DOWN_KEY   &&   yPos < YMAX)
      {
        yPos = yPos + 1
        call paintUserInterface
        call paintCursor
      }
      else if (eventPars[0] == ENTER_KEY)
      {
        if (xCursor >= 5   &&   xCursor <= 90   &&
            yCursor >= 50  &&   yCursor <= 60)
          {
          isVisited = true
          call paintHyperlink
          /*
          Further instructions for the actions after the hyperlink was
          pressed.
          */
          }
        if (xCursor >= 50   &&   xCursor <= 80   &&
            yCursor >= 65   &&   yCursor <= 75)
          {
          isCurrentlyPressed = true
          call paintButton
          /*
          Further instructions for the actions after the button was
          pressed.
          */
          }
      }
    }
    else if (eventCode == RELEASED   &&   eventPars[0] == ENTER_KEY   &&
             xCursor >= 50   &&   xCursor <= 80   &&
             yCursor >= 65   &&   yCursor <= 75)
    {
    isCurrentlyPressed = false
    call paintButton
    }
}
```

This program consists of three sections: a section for application-specific variable declarations, a section for paint and possibly other procedures, and a section for the event semantics. The current xy position of the cursor is stored in the variables xPos and yPos. The length of the horizontal line that represents the cursor is stored in the variable lenCursor. The state of the hyperlink, i.e., if already visited or not, is stored in the variable visited. The state of the button, i.e., if currently being pressed or not, is stored in the variable isBeingPressed.

The next section contains the procedures. Execution starts at the main procedure. The painting of the user interface is performed by the paintUserInterface procedure. It calls the auxiliary procedures paintHyperlink and paintButton. If the hyperlink is not yet visited, it is painted with blue color, otherwise with red color. The background color of the button switches from green to red while being pressed by the user.

The last section defines the event semantics of the user interface components. The attributes of the latest occurring event are stored in the variables `deviceCode`, `eventCode` and `eventPars`. The `deviceCode` indicates the device where the event has occurred, e.g., `KEYBOARD`. The `eventCode` indicates the type of event, e.g., `PRESSED`, `RELEASED`. The array `eventPars` contains additional event parameters. For example, the key code of a pressed key is stored in `eventPars[0]`. Whenever a user event occurs, the CVM automatically first assigns the corresponding values to these variables and then executes the `eventTable` procedure.

In order to relieve the client from the task of performing layout computations, this user interface program explicitly contains the absolute xy coordinate positions of each user interface component. For example, the instruction `line 5, 57, 85, 57` draws a line between the points (5, 57) and (85, 57). The formatting and assignment of the xy coordinates is performed by the server. Thus, the client can draw immediately the elementary graphic shapes without large rendering efforts.

In contrast to an HTML document, which is in plain ASCII format, a CVM program is transmitted in a compact and executable binary format from the server to the client. This saves network bandwidth and relieves the client from assembling the CVM program into an executable form.

In general, the amount of CVM code that is required for a particular user interface component depends on how luxurious it is painted, e.g., with 3D look and feel, interactive highlighting effects, etc., and on its structural and functional complexity. Examples of complex user interface components are tables, frames, editable text fields, etc. Therefore, scalability — in terms of describing a user interface — can be achieved through the size and complexity of the corresponding CVM program.

2.2.2 Client Virtual Machine (CVM)

The main tasks of the CVM are the presentation of downloaded user interfaces and the communication with the server. The CVM should serve as a common subset of all possible client devices, i.e., small, restricted consumer and embedded devices as well as general purpose computers. Any client device should be able to run the CVM either with a software interpreter or as a hardware implementation without requiring a lot of system resources. Therefore, its architecture, instruction set, and runtime environment should be as simple as possible and restrict itself only to the most essential parts. Some concepts of related existing virtual machines, e.g., JVM [80], KVM [79], PostScript [4], DVI [41], etc., might be adopted. The JVM is an object-oriented virtual machine with automatic garbage collection. Because of its complexity, it is quite hard to implement the JVM together with the extensive Java APIs [75] purely in hardware. Therefore, shrunken versions of the JVM, e.g., the KVM, have been developed. The KVM, however, still shows a quite complex architecture because of its object-oriented design principles which are not considered in this thesis to be essential for a simple user interface machine. PostScript and DVI are not object oriented and they have instructions for drawing elementary graphic shapes. However, they are only designed for non-interactive documents. In addition, PostScript is a quite powerful, but also complex virtual machine. For example, it contains operators for coordinate system transformations, which are not considered to be essential for a simple user interface machine, either.

As the network enabled client devices may vary a lot in their characteristics and capabilities, the CVM must have a modular architecture which is illustrated in figure 2.3 (page 25). A

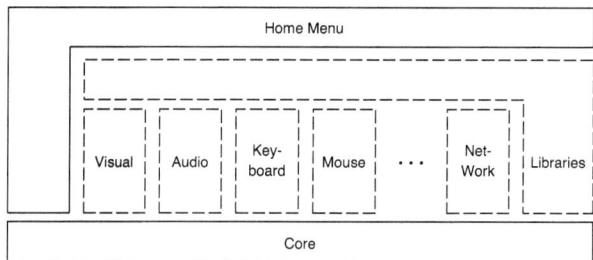

Figure 2.3: **Modular Architecture of the CVM**

particular device need not implement all components of the CVM, only those for which it has the corresponding hardware. The optional components are marked by dashed lines in figure 2.3 (page 25). The components of the CVM are specified in detail in section 3 (page 31). The component Core provides the fundamental runtime environment. User input is managed by the components Audio, Keyboard, Mouse, and possibly other, not yet specified components. User output is managed by the components Audio, Visual, and possibly other, not yet specified components. The module Home Menu represents the default menu system of the CVM. A mobile phone, for example, might contain the components Core, Network, Audio, Visual, Keyboard, and Home Menu.

The modular design enables a flexible handling of the capabilities of a device. For example, its capabilities might be enlarged by inserting a new plug-in card into the device that provides the required hardware and the implementation of the corresponding CVM module.

The description of the client characteristics and capabilities, called CVM profile, contains the configuration parameters of the existing CVM components, e.g., the memory size of the component Core, the resolution, available fonts and colors of the component Visual, etc.

The CVM is specified in detail in section 3 (page 31).

2.3 Server Side

Figure 2.4 (page 26) illustrates the proposed client-server architecture. The CVM packet server keeps a collection of abstract user interface descriptions for each offered interactive network service. For this purpose, an abstract user interface description language is required that contains language constructs to specify the user interface and the control logic of an interactive network service. The user interface consists of several user interface pages. Each user interface page in turn contains several "high-level" user interface components such as buttons, text fields, etc. as well as actions that are executed by the client, for

26   2. Proposed Client-Server Architecture — Overview

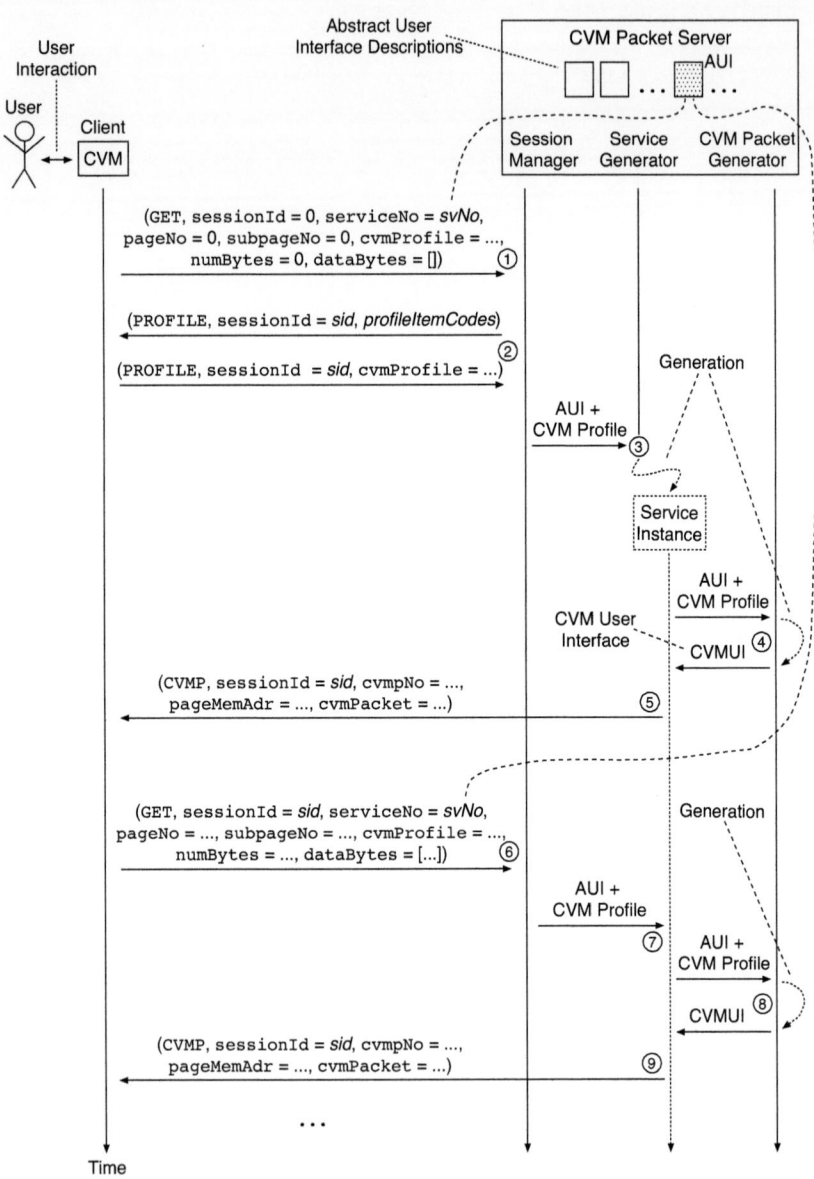

Figure 2.4: **Client-Server Session**

2.3. Server Side

example event handling procedures. The control logic of a network service contains actions that are executed on the server side. Each interactive network service is referenced by a well-defined service number. Let AUI be the abstract user interface description of the interactive network service with the service number $svNo$.

A new client-server session is initiated by a client request with a GET message from the CVM to the CVM packet server (step 1). Section 2.4 (page 29) gives an overview of the GET and other used protocol methods. The session manager module of the CVM packet server processes all client requests and stores the session-specific data. The CVM packet server first assigns a new identification value ($sid \neq 0$) to the new client-server session. A CVM packet server might serve more than one CVM at the same time and therefore needs this unique value to distinguish between them when it receives a message from a CVM. The value zero indicates the beginning of a new client-server session.

If the profile data of the CVM which is given by the message item cvmProfile in the GET message is incomplete, the CVM packet server responds with a PROFILE message to ask for the missing profile items (step 2). The CVM then sends a PROFILE message to the CVM packet server that contains these items. Note that the CVM packet server and the service instance can send a PROFILE message to the CVM at any time during the client-server session.

After all necessary profile data is available, the service generator module generates a client-specific service instance that meets the hardware and software capabilities as well as the user preferences of the client (step 3). It is generated from the abstract user interface description AUI and from the client description, the CVM profile. It mainly contains the state machine that implements the control logic of the network service that is specified in the AUI. The lifetime of the client-specific service instance is limited by the time span of the respective client-server session. Its limited lifetime is indicated by the dashed lines in the figure.

The CVM packet generator generates the CVM user interface CVMUI from the abstract user interface description AUI and the CVM profile (step 4). This CVM user interface is a CVM program that contains an adapted version of the requested AUI page. This version meets the client capabilities and user preferences. The CVM instructions of a CVM user interface mainly encode the appearance and event handling semantics of the user interface components at a low level of abstraction. Note that a CVM user interface may contain all user interface components of the respective AUI page or only a subset, depending on the client capabilities like memory, screen size, etc. The missing parts may be generated and delivered in subsequent client requests.

The generated CVMUI is then sent by the client-specific service instance to the requesting CVM in a binary format that is called the CVM packet format (step 5). The transmitted CVM packet is executed by the CVM.

The CVM packet may contain instructions that result in another GET request (step 6). Mostly, this is the case when the user interacts with a particular user interface component of the currently executed CVM packet, which causes the CVM to execute the respective event handling procedure that may contain such instructions. The GET request may also contain data that is encoded in the CVM packet or that results from client-side processings or user input. This data is sent in the message item dataBytes of the GET message. It is used by the state machine of the service instance as input for server-side processings.

Note that both the contents and format of this data are encoded in the instructions of the

CVM packet, whereas the CVM packet is generated by the CVM packet generator from the given AUI. Thus, the client-server communication and data transfer are mainly managed on the server side and the CVM does not need any "intelligence". It just executes the instructions in the received CVM packet.

In addition, the data in `dataBytes` might be needed by the CVM packet generator for the generation of subsequent CVM user interfaces. For example, this is the case when the user of the CVM receives a CVM packet that contains a summary of all data that the user has input in previous input forms. As a CVM user interface generally depends on user data that might dynamically change during the client-server session it needs to be generated each time again on demand. Therefore it is generally not possible to generate the CVM user interfaces of a given abstract user interface description in the beginning of the client-server session all at once.

Steps 6, 8, and 9 are equal to the steps 1, 4, and 5, respectively. Step 7 differs from step 3 in that the client-specific service instance already exists and need not be generated any more during this client-server session. The AUI description and the CVM profile are just passed by the session manager to this service instance.

In addition to the screen size of the CVM, its memory size is also a key factor in determining how a user interface needs to be customized for the CVM. If the CVM has enough memory, all parts of an AUI page can be sent in one CVM packet to it. Then, of course, a user interaction for navigating between the different parts need not cause any CVM requests. However, if the CVM does not have enough memory, the AUI page must be split into smaller subpages, where each CVM packet of a subpage must fit into the memory of the CVM. Then, the CVM packet server first sends to the CVM the CVM packet that contains the subpage with the starting user interface portion. Each subpage must provide user interface elements — or even simpler, just "invisible" event handling procedures — that serve as hyperlinks to the other subpages, in order to enable the user to navigate between them. The activation of such an hyperlink by the user results in a GET request for the demanded subpage. The CVM packet server then replies with the requested subpage. To reduce the amount of network transactions, the server should try to use the memory of the client as efficiently as possible when partitioning a user interface into smaller subpages. In general, smaller subpages might imply more client-server transactions. As a result, the partitioning of a user interface also leads to an optimization problem with respect to the memory size of the client and the number of network transactions.

Drawing an analogy to the field of document preparation systems, the user interface of an interactive network service corresponds to a document. The abstract description of the user interface corresponds to the description of the logical structure of the document, whereas the CVM packets correspond to the layout structure of the document. In addition, the CVM packet generator acts as a rendering engine, whereas the CVM profile represents a collection of formatting constraints.

The abstract specification of user interfaces for interactive network services requires a suitable language. The service providers on the server side can choose such a language freely. It is totally their concern how they specify their interactive network services and store their provided content. For example, the description languages XForms [24], UIML [86], BOSS [67], EmuGen [14] [15], WSDL [21], etc., might be used for specifying abstract user interfaces and Web services. It is also the service providers' business, how they generate appropriate and valid CVM packets. In addition to the client capabilities and user preferences, which are technical constraints, the service providers also have to consider layout- and ergonomic-related issues when generating user interfaces for client devices with limited input and output capabilities.

Compiler technology might be used for the generation of client-specific CVM user interfaces from abstract specifications. Depending on the specification language, the dynamic generation of client-specific service instances and CVM user interfaces from abstract user interface descriptions for interactive network services might be a quite complex task. Therefore, the CVM packet server might also keep "simpler" user interface descriptions such as HTML/XML documents that do not define complex workflows. Then, the CVM packet generator mainly resembles a compiler that translates HTML/XML documents into appropriate CVM user interfaces.

As a proof of concept, an exemplary language for abstract user interface descriptions, an exemplary structure for CVM user interfaces, and an exemplary server-side architecture for the generation of client-specific service instances and CVM packets are presented in this thesis. These components are specified in detail in the sections 5.1 (page 135), 5.5 (page 166), and 5 (page 135), respectively.

2.4 Communication Protocol

The protocol for the client-server communication should be as simple and universal as possible. On the one hand, any small and restricted client device should be able to implement it either in software or even in hardware without great use of system resources. On the other hand, this protocol should be suitable for all kinds of different interactive network services. Therefore, the application-specific protocol mechanisms must be separated from the elementary ones. The application-specific protocol mechanisms depend on the particular network service and might be shifted into the control logic of the network service. They might also be specified in the abstract description of the corresponding user interface. In effect, the communication protocol consists then mostly of the elementary protocol methods that are essential and always needed.

As a result, the proposed client-server architecture does not adopt the HTTP [10] protocol, which is used in the WWW for the client-server communication. Instead, a new communication protocol, called the *CVM packet transfer protocol* (CPTP) is proposed in this thesis. CPTP consists only of a few protocol methods. The protocol methods that occur in figure 2.4 (page 26) are described here briefly:

- CVMP: (CVMP, sessionId = sid, cvmpNo = ..., pageMemAdr = ..., cvmPacket = ...)
  This protocol method is used when the CVM packet server sends the CVM packet cvmPacket to the CVM. sessionId contains a value that identifies the current client-server session, because the CVM packet server might serve more than one client at the same time. cvmpNo contains the number of this CVM packet. pageMemAdr contains the absolute memory address of the CVM instruction, where the CVM should start execution, after it has loaded this CVM packet into its memory.

- GET: (GET, sessionId = 0, serviceNo = $svNo$, pageNo = ..., subpageNo = ..., cvmProfile = ..., numBytes = ..., dataBytes = [...])
  This protocol method is similar to the GET and POST methods of the HTTP [10] protocol. It is used by the CVM to send the data in the data array dataBytes to the

CVM packet server and then request from it the CVMUI page that is addressed by the page number **pageNo** and the subpage number **subpageNo**. **sessionId** contains a value that identifies the current client-server session, because the CVM packet server might serve more than one client at the same time. At the beginning of a new client-server session, the CVM packet server assigns a new value other than zero to the new session. **sessionId** has the value zero in the first **GET** message from the CVM to the CVM packet server. **serviceNo** contains a well-defined number ($svNo$) that refers to a particular interactive network service that is offered by the CVM packet server and requested by the CVM. **pageNo** and **subpageNo** each contain an unsigned integer number. They refer to a particular CVMUI page that belongs to the interactive network service with the number **serviceNo**. **cvmProfile** contains the profile data about the capabilities and user preferences of the requesting CVM. **numBytes** contains the number of bytes of the data array **dataBytes**. At the beginning of a client-server session, i.e., when **sessionId** is zero, **pageNo** and **numBytes** usually have the default value zero.

- PROFILE: (PROFILE, sessionId = sid, cvmProfile = ...) or
  (PROFILE, sessionId = sid, $profileItemCodes$)

This protocol method is used by the CVM and the CVM packet server for content negotiation. **sessionId** contains a value that identifies the current client-server session. **cvmProfile** contains the profile data about the capabilities and user preferences of the requesting CVM. $profileItemCodes$ lists the missing profile items whose values are needed by the CVM packet generator.

The CPTP protocol is specified in detail in section 4 (page 127).

Chapter 3

Client Virtual Machine (CVM)

The CVM is motivated and introduced in section 2.2 (page 13). The main task of the CVM is to display downloaded user interfaces for networked clients with different and restricted hardware capabilities. Therefore, the main design goal is a simple and modular architecture with a simple runtime environment to enable hardware implementations even on very "thin" and cheap clients. In addition, the CVM instructions should allow compact and also scalable encodings of user interfaces to make the CVM applicable to more powerful clients up to general purpose computers such as PCs or workstations as well. As there is no general and formal approach to "deduce" such a virtual machine, a lot of ideas have been examined, tried out, and also rejected mainly with the intuition of an engineer. As a result, the following proposal for the CVM is made without claiming that it is exclusively the best solution.

The proposed CVM architecture with its modules and functional units inside each module is illustrated in figure 3.1 (page 31). The optional modules and functional units inside a model are marked by dashed lines. However, at least one input module, e.g., Keyboard,

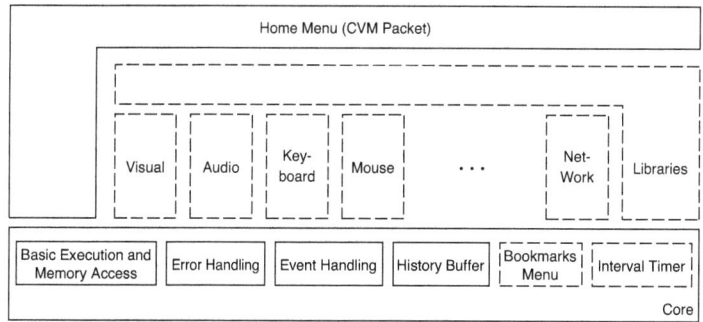

Figure 3.1: **CVM Modules and Functional Units**

Mouse, Audio, etc., and at least one output module, e.g., Visual, Audio, etc., should be available to enable user interaction. Other input and output modules may be defined in the future as well. Except for the Audio module, all the illustrated CVM modules and their functional units are going to be discussed in detail in the following sections. The description of the modules mainly focuses on their behavior and special characteristics. Everything else is left to the implementors' choice.

3.1 Core

The Core module provides the basic runtime environment. Its characteristic components are illustrated in figure 3.2 (page 32). The special registers of the CVM are reserved for

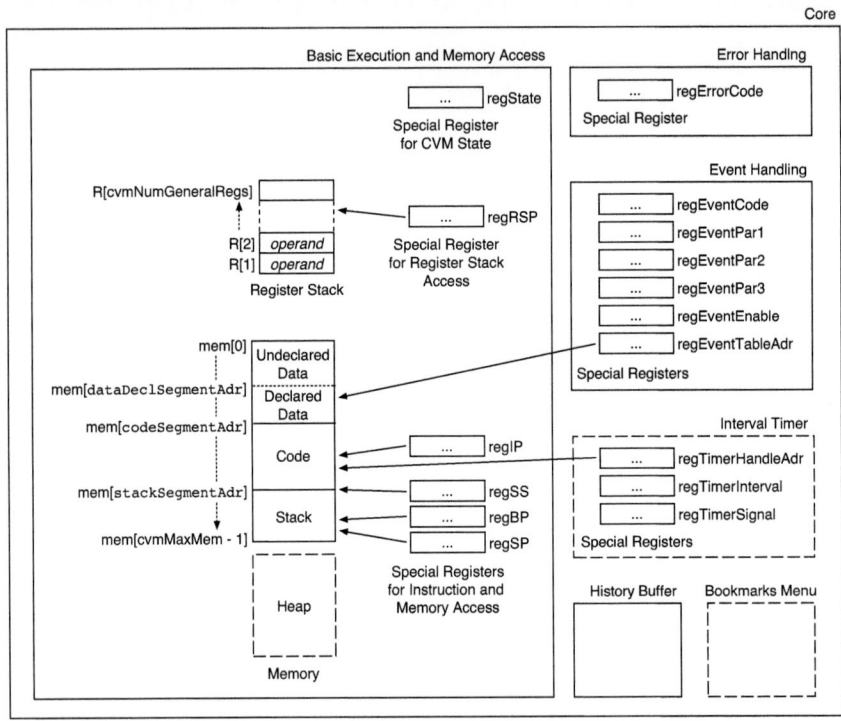

Figure 3.2: **CVM Core: Functional Units**

special purposes. Mainly, these registers store the current state of the CVM. Note that for the implementation of the CVM additional special registers might be required. However, as these internal special registers are not needed to specify the characteristic behavior of the CVM, they are not specified here and are left to the implementors' choice.

3.1.1 Data Types

The CVM operates on the data types Int, Nat, and String.

Int, Nat Int numbers are 1-, 2-, 3-, and 4-byte signed two's-complement integer numbers with values in the ranges of $[-2^7;\ 2^7 - 1]$ for 1-byte, $[-2^{15};\ 2^{15} - 1]$ for 2-byte, $[-2^{23};\ 2^{23} - 1]$ for 3-byte, and $[-2^{31};\ 2^{31} - 1]$ for 4-byte Int numbers. Nat numbers are 1-, 2-, 3-, and 4-byte unsigned one's-complement integer numbers with values in the ranges of $[0;\ 2^8 - 1]$ for 1-byte, $[0;\ 2^{16} - 1]$ for 2-byte, $[0;\ 2^{24} - 1]$ for 3-byte, and $[0;\ 2^{32} - 1]$ for 4-byte Nat numbers. Multibyte Int and Nat numbers are stored in big-endian order, i.e., the high bytes come first. In the following, the term Int1 (or Nat1) will be used as an abbreviation for "1-byte Int (or Nat)", the term Int2 (or Nat2) as an abbreviation for "2-byte Int (or Nat)", and so on. In addition, the term Int<1|...|4> and Nat<1|...|4> will be used to address all the Int and Nat types, respectively.

The distinction between signed (Int) and unsigned (Nat) integer numbers and the consideration of their required byte sizes mainly affects the CVM instructions with immediate operands and the declaration of integer numbers within the CVM packet. It reduces code size and thus saves network bandwidth and CVM memory usage, because for each integer value only the minimum number of required bytes is used in the CVM packet and corresponding CVM program. Refer to section 3.8 (page 93) for more information on CVM packets. The Nat type is useful, because unsigned integer numbers in the ranges of $[2^7;\ 2^8 - 1]$, $[2^{15};\ 2^{16} - 1]$, and $[2^{23};\ 2^{24} - 1]$ need 1, 2, and 3 bytes, when encoded as Nat numbers, but 2, 3, and 4 bytes, when encoded as Int numbers, respectively.

Larger integer numbers, from 5 bytes up to 8 bytes, and floating point numbers are not supported directly by the CVM, as they are scarcely needed for user interfaces — according to the author's point of view. When necessary, these numbers must be emulated by combining two or more directly supported integer numbers and providing appropriate procedures that implement their arithmetics. These procedures can be provided explicitly by the CVM programmer or packet generator, or implicitly by particular Core library functions. Refer to section 3.5 (page 83) for more information on library functions.

String Strings are character sequences. There are two binary string formats:

```
String   =    { Nat1  length;     // 0 < length ≤ 255
                Nat1[length]  bytes }
         or
              { Nat1  0;
                Nat2  length;     // 0 ≤ length ≤ 65535
                Nat1[length]  bytes }
```

The byte array `bytes` contains UTF-8 [89] string characters. Multibyte UTF-8 characters are stored in big-endian, i.e., high byte first, order. Note that the value of `length` represents the number of bytes in the byte array, but not the length of the resulting string. The second string representation is to enable longer strings, i.e., strings whose UTF-8 encodings require more than 255 bytes. However, the shorter binary string format should suffice in most cases. The binary representation of an empty string is { Nat1 0; Nat2 0 }.

3.1.2 Operation Modes

In order to address a broad range of client devices with different hardware complexities and system resources, the CVM can be implemented either as a 16- or 32-bit CVM. In the following, the term cvmIntLen is used to denote the byte length of an integer number on a given CVM implementation, depending on the operation mode (or equivalently called CVM mode). In addition, the CVM types Int and Nat often are also used in the following for Int<cvmIntLen> and Nat<cvmIntLen>, respectively, i.e., their byte lengths are cvmIntLen.

16-Bit CVM   On a 16-bit CVM, cvmIntLen is 2. A 16-bit CVM operates only on integer numbers with at most 16 bits. The general purpose registers of the register stack and the memory stack items are each 16 bit wide. The special registers are also 16 bits wide, except for some special registers like regRSP, regColorRed, etc., which might require less bits. All data items in memory including the memory stack items are 16-bit aligned. The memory size of a given 16-bit CVM implementation can be at most 2^{16}, i.e., cvmMemMaxAdr $\in$ [0; $2^{16} - 1$], with cvmMemMaxAdr referring to the highest memory address of a given CVM implementation. In addition, the memory load and store instructions loada, loadr, storea, and storer each access 16-bit signed integer numbers (Int2).

32-Bit CVM   On a 32-bit CVM, cvmIntLen is 4. A 32-bit CVM operates only on integer numbers with at most 32 bits. The general purpose registers of the register stack and the memory stack items are each 32 bit wide. The special registers are also 32 bits wide, except for some special registers like regRSP, regColorRed, etc., which might require less bits. All data items in memory including the memory stack items are 32-bit aligned. The memory size of a given 32-bit CVM implementation can be at most 2^{32}, i.e., cvmMemMaxAdr $\in$ [0; $2^{32} - 1$], with cvmMemMaxAdr referring to the highest memory address of a given CVM implementation. In addition, the memory load and store instructions loada, loadr, storea, and storer each access 32-bit signed integer numbers (Int4). In addition, the instructions aload4, astore4, loadc3, loadc4, loadcu2, loadcu3, setcolor32, setbgcolor32, and setfont32 are only supported by a 32-bit CVM.

3.1.3 Register Stack

The register stack is a set of 2- or 4-byte general purpose registers, dependent on the CVM mode. It serves as a quick operand stack for the CVM instructions. Except for a few instructions that have immediate operands, the instructions usually fetch their operands from the register stack. Immediate operands of an instruction appear in the CVM program right after the opcode. A possible result of an instruction is always pushed onto the top of the register stack. Therefore, the CVM code is a kind of stack machine or 0-address code and the register stack might be called operand stack, as well. Figure 3.2 (page 32) illustrates the register stack.

cvmNumGeneralRegs   The term cvmNumGeneralRegs is used for the total number of general purpose registers in the register stack of a given CVM implementation. The total number of general purpose registers can vary for each CVM implementation. However, there must be enough registers to store at least all the operands of each instruction and to enable further computation on the register stack. For example, the computation of the last operand of a given instruction with n operands by an addition of the two top-most register stack values causes a general stack depth of at least $n + 1$, which requires at least $n + 1$ registers. Approximately, 10 general purpose registers might be sufficient.

3.1. Core

regRSP The special register regRSP ("Register Stack Pointer") contains a Nat1 number that indexes the top-most general purpose register in the register stack. The top-most general purpose register — also called the top of the register stack — is the general purpose register that contains the most recently pushed value. The general purpose registers are indexed starting with 1. Therefore, the value of regRSP also corresponds to the number of available operands on the register stack. The term $R[i]$ ($1 \leq i \leq$ cvmNumGeneralRegs) represents the ith general purpose register or its value. The initial value of regRSP is zero, i.e., at the beginning of program execution the register stack is naturally empty. The value of regRSP is mainly affected and modified implicitly by the register stack behavior of the instructions. However, the instructions rdup, rempty, rskip, and rswap particularly aim at the management of the register stack.

Loading Values onto the Register Stack As already mentioned, values are pushed always onto the top of the register stack. The basic register stack loading instructions are loadc<1|...|4>, loadcu<1|...|3>, loadc_0, loadc_1, and loadc_m1. Other instructions, e.g., arithmetic operations, might produce new values onto the register stack as well. The loading process of a new value v consists of the following steps: First, the CVM checks if the value of the special register regRSP is below cvmNumGeneralRegs. If this is the case, the CVM increments the value of regRSP by 1 and then stores v into the register R[regRSP]. An error condition is reached, if the value of regRSP is not below cvmNumGeneralRegs before loading. Then, instead of loading, the CVM aborts execution of the current instruction and starts error handling with the error code RegisterStackOverflow. Refer to section 3.1.5 (page 41) for more information on error handling.

Retrieving Values from the Register Stack An operand consuming instruction fetches its register stack operands either from the current top of the register stack — which is referred to as *Dynamic Popping* — or from designated general purpose registers inside the register stack — which is referred to as *Static Popping*. The appropriate operand fetching method of each instruction is specified in the instruction reference in section 3.9.2 (page 100).

Dynamic Popping The process of Dynamic Popping for an instruction that needs n ($n > 0$) operands consists of the following steps: First, the CVM checks if the value of the special register regRSP is at least n. If this is the case, the n top-most values of the register stack, i.e., R[regRSP], ..., R[regRSP $- n + 1$], are popped and used as operands for the instruction. After all, regRSP is decremented by n. An error condition is reached, if the value of regRSP is below n before popping. Then, instead of popping, the CVM aborts execution of the current instruction and starts error handling with the error code RegisterStackUnderflow. Refer to section 3.1.5 (page 41) for more information on error handling.

The instructions that perform Dynamic Popping, e.g., arithmetic instructions, are called *in-between* instructions. Their main purpose is to compute the operands for the so called *final* instructions, which perform Static Popping.

Static Popping The process of Static Popping for an instruction that needs n ($n > 0$) operands consists of the following steps: First, the CVM checks if the value of the special register **regRSP** is equal to n. If this is the case, the values in the register stack, i.e., R[1], ..., R[n], are popped and used as operands for the instruction. Then, **regRSP** is set to its initial value zero. An error condition is reached, if the value of **regRSP** is not equal to n before popping. Then, instead of popping, the CVM aborts execution of the current instruction and starts error handling with the error code **RegisterStackUnderflow**, if **regRSP** is less than n, or with the error code **RegisterStackStaticOverflow**, if **regRSP** is greater than n. Refer to section 3.1.5 (page 41) for more information on error handling.

The instructions that perform Static Popping are called *final* instructions. The main purpose of Static Popping is to gain more runtime performance during operand fetching, because each operand is located in a designated register with a known index. For example, the drawing instructions of the CVM module Visual are final instructions.

3.1.4 Memory

The memory consists of an array of bytes that can be read and written during execution of a CVM program. The memory size depends on the given CVM implementation. Each byte in memory can be addressed by its array index, whereas counting starts with 0. The term **mem**[i] ($0 \leq i \leq$ **cvmMemMaxAdr**) represents the ith byte in memory or its value. The highest memory address of a given CVM implementation is referred to with the term **cvmMemMaxAdr**. Generally, all multibyte **Int** and **Nat** numbers and UTF-8 [89] characters are stored in big-endian, i.e., high byte first, order.

During execution of a CVM program, the memory is partitioned into four sections: the Data, Code, Stack, and the optional Heap section. Figure 3.2 (page 32) illustrates the partitioning of the memory.

Basically, every byte in any memory section can be read or written. Therefore, it is technically feasible that the CVM program overwrites its own instructions in the Code section during execution. Whether this is useful, is left to the responsibility of the CVM programmer or packet generator.

If during a memory access the resulting absolute memory address is not inside the range [0; **cvmMemMaxAdr**], the CVM aborts execution of the current instruction and starts error handling with the error code **IllegalMemoryAddress**. Refer to section 3.1.5 (page 41) for more information on error handling.

Absolute Memory Access An absolute memory address is always a **Nat** number. The instructions **loada**, **storea**, **aload**<1|2|4>, and **astore**<1|2|4> address the memory absolutely with their address operands. The address operands reside on the register stack and are absolute indices into the memory, respectively. The instruction **loada** reads a signed integer number in big-endian order from memory and pushes its value onto the register stack. The instruction **storea** pops a signed integer number from the register stack and writes its value into memory in big-endian order. The byte length of a signed and unsigned integer number depends on the CVM mode and is referred to with the term **cvmIntLen**. It is 2 on a 16-bit CVM and 4 on a 32-bit CVM. The instructions **aload**<1|2|4> and **astore**<1|2|4> read and write 1-, 2-, or 4-byte integer numbers from and into arrays in memory, respectively.

3.1. Core

Relative Memory Access A relative memory address is always an Int number, i.e., it can be positive as well as negative. The instructions loadr and storer address the memory relatively with their address operands. The address operands reside on the register stack and are relative indices into the memory segment that starts at the base address given by the special register regBP, respectively. The CVM computes the resulting absolute memory address by adding the relative address operand to the base address given by regBP. The resulting memory address can point to any byte in every memory section. The instruction loadr reads a signed integer number in big-endian order from the memory and pushes its value onto the register stack. The instruction storer pops a signed integer value from the register stack and writes its value into memory in big-endian order. Again, the byte length of a signed and unsigned integer number depends on the CVM mode and is referred to with the term cvmIntLen. It is 2 on a 16-bit CVM and 4 on a 32-bit CVM.

When not stated explicitly in this thesis that a memory address is relative, a memory address is always regarded as being absolute.

The main purpose of relative memory access instructions is to access procedure parameters and local variables that reside on the memory stack. For this topic, refer to section 3.1.4.2 (page 39).

regBP The special register regBP ("Base Pointer") contains an absolute memory address that marks the beginning of a memory segment anywhere in memory. It is used by the instructions loadr and storer as a base address for retrieving and storing values from and into memory. The value of regBP is modified by the instructions setbp, newstackframe, and oldstackframe. The initial value of this register is zero. The main purpose of regBP is to point to the current stack frame that contains the parameters and local variables of the currently executed procedure. For this topic, refer to section 3.1.4.2 (page 39).

The memory address in regBP is a Nat value and the byte length of this register depends on the given CVM implementation, but must be adequate to address the whole CVM memory. This rule also applies to the other special registers that store absolute memory addresses.

3.1.4.1 Data and Code

The Data section can be subdivided into the Undeclared and the Declared Data section, which contain undeclared and declared data, respectively. The Undeclared Data section starts at the memory address 0 and ends at dataDeclSegmentAdr − 1, whereas the Declared Data section starts at the memory address dataDeclSegmentAdr and ends at codeSegmentAdr − 1. The Code section starts at the memory address codeSegmentAdr and ends at stackSegmentAdr − 1. The Code section contains the instructions of the CVM program.

dataDeclSegmentAdr, codeSegmentAdr, and stackSegmentAdr are items of the CVM packet, which is transmitted from the CVM packet server to the CVM. Mainly, the CVM packet contains declared data with initial values and CVM instructions. Refer to section 3.8 (page 93) for more information on the structure of CVM packets and their items.

regIP The special register regIP ("Instruction Pointer") contains the absolute memory address of the opcode or of an immediate operand of the currently executed instruction.

The CVM increments regIP automatically during execution to fetch the next opcode or immediate operand unless the currently executed instruction sets regIP explicitly. Its value can be set or modified explicitly by the control flow instructions call, ret, jmp, je, jne, jl, jle, and page. If the CVM fetches the opcode or an immediate operand of an instruction while regIP has an address outside the interval [0; cvmMemMaxAdr], the CVM aborts execution of the current instruction and starts error handling with the error code IllegalMemoryAddress (page 43).

When loading the declared data items and instructions from a CVM packet into memory, the CVM sets regIP to the value of the CVM packet item codeSegmentAdr. Execution of the loaded CVM program starts at this memory address. Refer to section 3.8 (page 93) for more information on CVM packets and their items.

Note that during execution of a CVM program regIP can be loaded with any memory address that points to any byte in any memory section. Therefore, execution of CVM instructions outside the Code section in memory is technically feasible. Whether this is useful, is left to the responsibility of the CVM programmer or packet generator.

3.1.4.2 Stack

The Stack section starts at the memory address stackSegmentAdr and ends at cvmMemMaxAdr. stackSegmentAdr is an item of the CVM packet, which is transmitted from the CVM packet server to the CVM. Commonly, the stack is used for storing temporary and local variables, and for storing parameters and return addresses during procedure calls. Each stack item can hold a whole integer number. Therefore, the byte length of a stack item depends on the CVM mode and is referred to by the term cvmIntLen. It is 2 on a 16-bit CVM and 4 on a 32-bit CVM.

regSS The special register regSS ("Stack Segment") contains the absolute memory address of the beginning of the memory stack. The value of this register cannot be modified by the CVM instructions during execution of a CVM program. Its initial value is set to the value of the CVM packet item stackSegmentAdr when the CVM packet is loaded into memory. Refer to section 3.8 (page 93) for more information on CVM packets and their items.

regSP The special register regSP ("Stack Pointer") contains the memory address that marks the top of the memory stack, i.e., it contains the memory address of the next unused memory stack element. The value of this register is modified by the instructions addsp, decsp, incsp, push, pop, call, ret, newstackframe, and oldstackframe. The initial and minimum value of regSP is equal to the value of regSS. The maximum value of regSP is equal to the value of cvmMemMaxAdr.

Loading Values onto the Stack The instruction push pops an integer number from the register stack and pushes its value onto the memory stack. The loading process consists of the following steps: First, the CVM checks if the value of the special register regSP is less than or equal to cvmMemMaxAdr − cvmIntLen + 1. If this is the case, the CVM stores the value into the memory cells mem[regSP], mem[regSP + 1], ..., mem[regSP + cvmIntLen − 1] in big-endian order. Then, the CVM increments regSP by the value cvmIntLen. An error

3.1. Core

condition is reached, if the value of regSP is not less than or equal to cvmMemMaxAdr − cvmIntLen + 1 before loading. Then, instead of pushing, the CVM aborts execution of the current instruction and starts error handling with the error code StackOverflow. Refer to section 3.1.5 (page 41) for more information on error handling.

Retrieving Values from the Stack The instruction pop pops an integer number from the memory stack and pushes its value onto the register stack. The retrieving process consists of the following steps: First, the CVM checks if the value of the special register regSS is less than or equal to the value of regSP − cvmIntLen. If this is the case, the CVM loads the value that is stored in the memory cells mem[regSP − 1], ..., mem[regSP − cvmIntLen] in big-endian order onto the top of the register stack. Finally, the CVM decrements regSP by the value cvmIntLen. An error condition is reached, if the value of regSS is not less than or equal to regSP − cvmIntLen before retrieving. Then, instead of popping, the CVM aborts execution of the current instruction and starts error handling with the error code StackUnderflow. Refer to section 3.1.5 (page 41) for more information on error handling.

Procedure Parameters and Local Variables Figure 3.3 (page 40) illustrates the stack frame of a procedure proc with the return value *result*, the parameters par_1, ..., par_n, and the local variables loc_1, ..., loc_m at an arbitrary point of time during execution after it has been called by main. Let the return value, the parameters, and the local variables be integer numbers. The corresponding CVM assembler code fragment might be as follows:

```
main:
    incsp            // Reserve space for result on memory stack
    <Load value of par1 onto register stack>   push   // Load par1 onto memory stack
    ...
    <Load value of parn onto register stack>   push   // Load parn onto memory stack
    loadcr proc   call    // Call procedure proc
    loadc −n      addsp   // Discard procedure parameters on memory stack
    pop     // Load result from memory stack onto register stack
    ...
    halt

proc:
    loadc n + 1   newstackframe   // Adjust regBP to new stack frame
    loadc m       addsp           // Reserve space for local variables on memory stack
    ...
    loadc −m      addsp           // Discard local variables on memory stack
    oldstackframe    // Restore regBP to previous stack frame
    ret     // Return to caller main
```

Refer to sections B (page 216) and B.3 (page 224) for a description of the CVM assembler and the macros loadc and loadcr. Refer also to the instruction reference in section 3.9.2 (page 100) for a description of the used CVM instructions.

Then, the relative memory addresses of the result, the parameters par_i ($1 \leq i \leq n$), and the local variables loc_j ($1 \leq j \leq m$) are 0, $i * \text{cvmIntLen}$, and $(n + 2 + j) * \text{cvmIntLen}$, respectively.

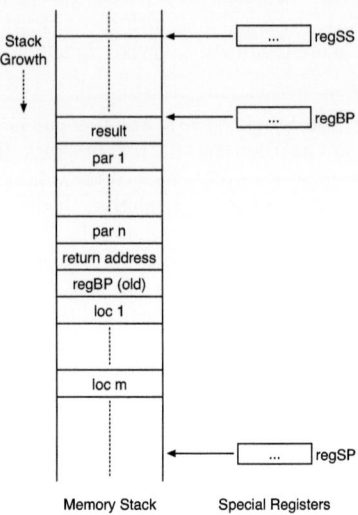

Figure 3.3: **Procedure Stack Frame**

An equivalent, but more convenient and readable version of the above CVM assembler code fragment by declaring the result, the parameters, and the local variables of the procedure, and by using the macro fcall is as follows:

```
main:
    incsp    // Reserve space for result on memory stack
    <Load value of par₁ onto register stack>    push   // Load par₁ onto memory stack
    ...
    <Load value of parₙ onto register stack>    push   // Load parₙ onto memory stack
    fcall proc    // Call procedure proc
    pop      // Load result from memory stack onto register stack
    ...
    halt

.fct proc (Int id(par₁), ..., Int id(parₙ)) Int {
    Int id(loc₁)
    ...
    Int id(locₘ)
    ...
    return }    // Return to caller main
```

The procedure (or equivalently called function) declaration and the macros are explained in the sections B.1 (page 220) and B.3 (page 224), respectively. $id(par_i)$ $(1 \leq i \leq n)$

3.1. Core

and $id(loc_j)$ ($1 \leq j \leq m$) represents the name of the ith parameter or jth local variable, respectively. A complete example that illustrates the access of procedure parameters and local variables within a procedure declaration is given in section B.6 (page 237).

3.1.4.3 Heap

The Heap section is used for storing all data that are created during runtime, i.e., dynamically during execution of a CVM program. The Heap section is optional and logically separated from the other memory sections Data, Code, and Stack, i.e., it does not need to belong to the same address space. In addition, the Heap section does not need to be explicitly and directly mapped by a given CVM implementation right after the Stack section. For example, the CVM might be emulated in software and the heap of the native computer architecture might be used for the Heap section.

In the following, the term "(CVM) memory" only refers to the Data, Code, and Stack section, whereas the Heap section is mentioned explicitly when referred to.

The Heap section cannot be accessed by the common memory load and store instructions loada, loadr, storea, storer, aload<1|2|4>, and astore<1|2|4>, but only with the special heap management instructions new, free, hload, and hstore to avoid ambiguities between equal memory addresses of different address spaces. A given CVM implementation only needs to support the heap management instructions if it possesses a Heap section.

The CVM profile item cvmLibraries reports to the CVM packet server whether the CVM possess a Heap section. Refer to section 3.7 (page 89) for more information on the CVM profile.

If a given CVM implementation does not have a Heap section but dynamic data is still needed in a particular application, the CVM programmer or packet generator can model the heap in the Data section and has to provide explicit procedures in the CVM code for its management. However, this is not going to be discussed here in more detail.

3.1.5 Error Handling

During loading a CVM packet and executing a CVM program errors might occur. For example, the format of the CVM packet might be malformed or the register stack might overflow during execution of a particular CVM instruction.

regErrorCode The special register regErrorCode stores the error code number of the recently occurred error. Refer to section 3.1.5.2 (page 42) for a complete list of all error types and their respective error codes. The value of this register cannot be modified by the CVM instructions, but is set automatically by the CVM each time an error occurs. Its initial value is zero.

3.1.5.1 Error Processing

If an error occurs, the CVM aborts its current activity, i.e., loading a CVM packet or executing a CVM program, and performs the following steps:

First, the CVM writes the respective error code number into the special register regError-Code and sets the special register regState to the state value Error, i.e., it moves to the state Error. Refer to section 3.1.10 (page 58) for more information on CVM states.

Then, the CVM deactivates the timer, if there is one and if it has been activated before. Refer to section 3.1.9 (page 57) for more information on interval timers.

Next, the CVM outputs an error message to the output device to inform the user. Depending on the type of the output device, i.e., a screen or speaker, the CVM outputs a written and/or an acoustic version of the error message. The written version of the error message has the following form: "CVM Error: *error name*". Section 3.1.5.2 (page 42) contains a list of all error names and their respective error code numbers. The CVM first clears the screen and then writes the error message on the blank screen. The background color of the screen, the foreground color and the font of the error message are not specified here and can be chosen freely by the CVM implementor. The acoustic version of the error message might be a particular signal tone or a voice that reads out the written version of the error message. If there is both a speaker and a screen existing, the CVM always outputs the written error message on the screen, whereas the acoustic error message is optional.

After the CVM has output the error message, it clears the event queue, i.e., it discards all buffered events that have not been processed yet, and waits until the user confirms the error message. If there is a keyboard available, the user can press the Enter key. If there is a microphone available, the user can reply by saying "OK". Alternatively, the user can as well raise one of the builtin events, e.g., menu_home. Refer to section 3.1.6.3 (page 49) for more information on builtin events. Refer also to the CVM state transitions in section 3.1.10 (page 58).

Finally, if the CVM program has been received from a CVM packet server, the CVM sends a notification message to the CVM packet server by using the protocol method ERROR. Refer to section 4.2 (page 129) for more information on the message format of this protocol method. The main purpose of the notification message is to provide additional information to enable bug fixes on the server side.

How the CVM proceeds after error processing depends on how the user has confirmed the error message. If the user has acknowledged with the Enter key or by speaking something like "OK" into the microphone, the CVM initializes itself and continues executing the current CVM packet. However, if the user has confirmed with one of the builtin events, the CVM performs the appropriate actions. Refer also to section 3.1.10 (page 58) for more information on the CVM's runtime behavior and particularly to the actions in the CVM state Error.

3.1.5.2 Error Codes

The instruction reference in section 3.9.2 (page 100) specifies for each instruction which errors might occur during its execution. In the following, the currently supported error codes are listed alphabetically and described using the following description format:

error_name = *error_code*
verbose_description

The *error_name* represents the mnemonic of the *error_code*. The *error_code* is a unique Nat1 number greater than zero identifying a particular error type.

3.1. Core

DivisionByZero $= 1$
This error occurs, if an (arithmetic) instruction tries to divide by zero.

IllegalMemoryAddress $= 2$
This error occurs with instructions that deal with memory addresses, e.g., with memory read and write instructions, if the involved memory address is out of the range [0; cvm-MemMaxAdr].

ImageLoadFailure $= 3$
This error occurs with instructions and library functions such as pixmap, etc., that load images from memory, if something goes wrong during the loading process, e.g., the image format is malformed.

InvalidScreenSection $= 4$
This error occurs only with the instructions mem2screen and screen2mem, if the specified rectangular area is not completely inside the visual drawing area of the CVM.

MalformedHomeMenu $= 5$
This error occurs, if the format of the HomeMenu CVM packet is malformed, when it is loaded into memory. Refer to sections 3.6 (page 86) and 3.8 (page 93) for more information on the HomeMenu and on the CVM packet format, respectively.

MalformedCPTPMessage $= 6$
This error occurs during a CPTP session, if the received CPTP message is malformed. Refer to section 4.1 (page 127) for more information on the CPTP message format and to section 4.2 (page 129) for more information on CPTP messages with the protocol method ERROR.

MalformedCVMPacket $= 7$
This error occurs, if the format of the CVM packet that is currently being loaded into memory is malformed. Refer to section 3.8 (page 93) for more information on the CVM packet format. The CVM packet has been received recently from a CVM packet server over the network.

MalformedCVMProfile $= 8$
This error occurs during a CPTP session, if the format of the CVM profile that the CVM has sent to a CVM packet server is malformed. Refer to section 3.7 (page 89) for more information on the CVM profile format and to section 4.2 (page 129) for more information on CPTP messages with the protocol method ERROR.

NetworkError $= 9$
This error occurs with the instructions rcv, send, and sendrcv, if the specified data cannot be received from or sent to the specified CVM packet server due to any network failure that might occur during the connection establishment or data transmission.

NoDNSLookup = 10
This error occurs with the instructions rcv, send, and sendrcv, if the specified host address is a DNS [45] name, but the given CVM implementation cannot perform automatic DNS lookup. Refer also to the profile item cvmDNSLookup (page 90).

RegisterStackOverflow = 11
This error occurs, if an instruction tries to push a value onto the register stack that already contains cvmNumGeneralRegs elements, i.e., regRSP = cvmNumGeneralRegs before pushing.

RegisterStackStaticOverflow = 12
This error occurs with a final instruction, i.e., an instruction that performs Static Popping, if the register stack before popping contains more elements than the instruction needs as operands.

RegisterStackUnderflow = 13
This error occurs with an instruction, if the register stack before popping contains less elements than the instruction needs as operands.

StackOverflow = 14
This error occurs, if during execution regSP reaches a value greater than cvmMemMaxAdr + 1. For example this is the case, if an instruction tries to push a new value onto a full memory stack, i.e., before the push operation the value of regSP is greater than cvmMemMaxAdr − cvmIntLen + 1. Refer to section 3.1.2 (page 33) for more information on cvmIntLen.

StackUnderflow = 15
This error occurs, if during execution regSP reaches a value less than regSS. For example this is the case, if an instruction tries to pop a value from an empty memory stack, i.e., before the pop operation the value of regSP − cvmIntLen is less than regSS. Refer to section 3.1.2 (page 33) for more information on cvmIntLen.

UnexpectedCPTPMethodCode = 16
This error occurs during a CPTP session, if the received CPTP message has an unexpected protocol method. Refer to section 4.2 (page 129) for more information on CPTP messages with the protocol method ERROR.

UnknownFont = 17
This error occurs with the instructions setfont, setfont32, setfontcode, and setfontsize, if the resulting font is not supported by the given CVM implementation. Refer to section 3.2.3 (page 79) for more information on fonts.

UnknownMouseFont = 18
This error occurs with the instruction setmousefont, if the specified mouse font code is not supported by the given CVM implementation. Refer to section 3.3 (page 81) for more information on the mouse.

3.1. Core   45

UnknownLibraryFunction = 19
This error occurs with the instruction lib, if the CVM encounters a library function code that it does not support. Refer to section 3.5 (page 83) for more information on the library functions.

UnknownOpcode = 20
This error occurs, if the CVM encounters an unknown instruction opcode during the execution.

Comments The error codes can also be grouped according to the CVM modules and their functional units they belong to, respectively:

- Core:
    - Execution: DivisionByZero, RegisterStackOverflow, RegisterStackStaticOverflow, RegisterStackUnderflow, StackOverflow, StackUnderflow, UnknownOpcode, MalformedCVMPacket
    - Memory Access: IllegalMemoryAddress
    - Error Handling: (So far, no error codes)
    - Event Handling: (So far, no error codes)
    - History Buffer: (So far, no error codes)
    - Bookmarks Menu: (So far, no error codes)
    - Interval Timer: (So far, no error codes)
- Visual: InvalidScreenSection, UnknownFont
- Audio: (Not covered in this thesis)
- Keyboard: (So far, no error codes)
- Mouse: UnknownMouseFont
- Network: MalformedCPTPMessage, MalformedCVMProfile, NetworkError, NoDNSLookup, UnexpectedCPTPMethodCode
- Libraries: UnknownLibraryFunction
- Home Menu: MalformedHomeMenu

3.1.6 Event Handling

Event handling enables user interaction. Here, an event is a notification of a user action on an input module of the client device. For example, the user might press a key on the keyboard, move the mouse, etc. The event data, i.e., the data describing the event, consists of the event code and possibly some event parameters. The event code is a positive integer number that identifies the action the user has performed on the input module, e.g., a key press. The event parameters depend on the event code and provide additional information on the event, e.g., the key code of a pressed key. Refer to section 3.1.6.4 (page 49) for a complete reference of the event code and the event parameters for each event type.

Events occur asynchronously during program execution and are buffered in an event queue in the FIFO (First In, First Out) manner. The length of the event queue is left to the implementors' choice. Naturally, it must be at least one. After the user has performed some action on an input device, e.g., pressed a key, the CVM inserts the corresponding event data, i.e., the event code number and the event parameters, into the event queue. However, if the event queue is already full, the new incoming event is discarded, instead.

The CVM regularly checks the event queue only in the states Error, EventProcessBuiltin, Execute, CptpGET, and Wait, i.e., regState = Error $\vee$ EventProcessBuiltin $\vee$ Execute $\vee$ CptpGET $\vee$ Wait.

In the following, the event handling of the CVM is described without going too much into details for reasons of readability. Refer to section 3.1.10 (page 58) for more details on event handling, CVM states, and the overall state behavior of the CVM.

3.1.6.1 Event Processing

Here it is described how the CVM behaves when it checks the event queue in the states Execute or Wait, i.e., regState = Execute $\vee$ Wait.

If there is an event in the event queue, the CVM removes the event from the event queue and writes the event code into the special event register regEventCode and the event parameters into the special event parameter registers regEventPar<1|2|...>. Next, the CVM sets the value of the special state register regState to the state value EventProcess.

In the state EventProcess the CVM first checks whether the event code matches the event code of a builtin event. If this is the case, it sets the value of the special state register regState to the state value EventProcessBuiltin and processes the builtin event. Refer to section 3.1.6.3 (page 49) for more information on builtin events.

However, if the event code does not match the event code of a builtin event, the CVM checks next in the state EventProcess whether the value of the special event register regEventEnable is zero. If this is the case, the event will not be further processed and is discarded. The user then has to wait until the value of that register is set to a non-zero value by the instruction enableevents within the CVM program and then repeat his/her input activity.

If regEventEnable is not zero, the CVM checks the event table from top to bottom, whether there is an entry with an event code that corresponds to the event code of the currently processed event. The event table is part of the CVM program and begins in memory at the absolute address given by the special register regEventTableAdr. Its binary data structure is described in section 3.1.6.2 (page 48). If there is an event table entry with an event code that corresponds to the event code of the currently processed event, the CVM first saves the current values of the special registers regIP, regRSP, regSP, regBP, the previous state — i.e., the state, when the CVM has detected the event in the event queue —, and the register stack values. It is left to the implementors' choice whether these values are saved into memory, e.g., onto the memory stack, or into some internal CVM structures. Then, the CVM loads the instruction pointer register regIP with the instruction address given by the found event table entry and sets the special registers regRSP and regBP to the value zero. Finally, it sets the special state register regState with the state value EventExecute

3.1. Core

and continues execution with the instruction at the address given by the new value of regIP. This instruction address marks the beginning of the respective event handling subroutine code for this type of event. As well as the event table, the event handling subroutine code is also specified by the CVM programmer or packet generator and thus it is a part of the CVM packet within the Code section. Event handling terminates when the CVM encounters the halt instruction in the event handling subroutine code. After event handling, the CVM reloads the previously saved values into the special registers regIP, regRSP, regSP, regBP, and regState, respectively. It also reloads the previously saved register stack values and resumes its previously interrupted activity.

If there is an event table entry with the event code 1, then the CVM aborts checking the current event table, jumps to the parent event table, and starts checking that event table in the same manner.

However, if there is no event table entry with an event code that corresponds to the event code of the currently processed event the CVM terminates event processing and resumes its previous activity.

Not checking the event queue in the states EventProcess and EventExecute ensures that an immediately following event cannot overwrite the current values of the regEventCode and regEventPar<1|2|...> registers while the current event is still being processed or its event handling subroutine is still being executed. As a result, successive events are processed completely one after another without mutual interference.

3.1.6.2 Event Registers

Several special registers are involved in the event handling process, called event registers.

regEventCode The special register regEventCode contains the event code, i.e., a Nat number, of the currently or recently processed event. Refer to section 3.1.6.4 (page 49) for a complete reference of all event codes. The value of this register is set automatically by the CVM during event processing and cannot be modified by the CVM instructions. Its initial value is zero.

regEventEnable The special register regEventEnable serves as a flag register. If its value is not zero, then all incoming events will be processed. Otherwise, all incoming events will be discarded — except for the builtin events. Refer to section 3.1.6.3 (page 49) for more information on builtin events. The value of this register is modified by the instructions enableevent and disableevent. Its initial value is zero.

regEventPar1, regEventPar2, regEventPar3 The special event parameter registers regEventPar<1|2|3> contain the event parameters of the currently processed event. The event parameters are integer (Int) values. Refer to section 3.1.6.4 (page 49) for a complete reference of the event parameters for each event type. The initial values of these registers are undefined. Note that the values of these registers are only defined, when an event is currently processed. Therefore, the access to these values should only take place in the provided event handling subroutines. Otherwise, the values of these registers are undefined. So far, only three event parameter registers are needed. Future releases of the CVM might have more, if necessary.

regEventTableAdr The special register regEventTableAdr contains the absolute memory address of the beginning of the event table in memory. The CVM only accepts an event for further processing if the value of this register is greater than zero. The value of this register is set by the instruction **seteventtableadr**. This instruction occurs in the CVM program usually after the user interface components have been placed onto the output module, e.g., drawn onto the screen. This instruction is also used to change the input focus of an graphical user interface component. The initial value of this register is zero, because user interaction generally starts after the user interface components have been placed onto the output module.

The event table is specified by the CVM programmer or packet generator and therefore it is a part of the CVM program. The binary data structure of an event table is as follows:

$EventTable$ = { $EventTableEntry[\,]$ $entries$;
  Int<cvmIntLen> 0 }

$EventTableEntry$ = { Int<cvmIntLen> eventCode;   // eventCode > 0
  Int<cvmIntLen> memAdr }

An event table is a (possibly empty) list of event table entries, whereas each entry consists of an event code (**eventCode**) and the absolute memory address (**memAdr**) of an instruction. However, if **eventCode** is 1, then **memAdr** contains the memory address of the parent event table. Refer to section 3.1.2 (page 33) for more information on **cvmIntLen**. The end of the list is indicated by the value 0 for the event code. During event processing, the CVM checks the event table from the beginning to the end. If the event code of an entry (**eventCode**) equals the event code of the currently processed event, the CVM loads the instruction pointer register **regIP** with the corresponding memory address and proceeds there with the execution. This memory address marks the beginning of the appropriate event handling subroutine which is specified by the CVM programmer or packet generator and thus is a part of the CVM program within the Code section. However, if **eventCode** is 1, the CVM jumps to the event table at the memory address **memAdr** and starts checking that event table. Note that it is left to the responsibility of the CVM programmer or packet generator to avoid infinite recursion. If **eventCode** is 0, the CVM terminates event processing and resumes its previous activity.

3.1.6.3 Special Events

In addition to the ordinary events there are also *special events*. They are grouped into *shortcut events* and *builtin events*.

Shortcut Events Shortcut events are very often needed in user interfaces and are therefore defined separately and directly. Generally, event subroutine code can be defined for their behavior in the event table the same way as it is defined for any other ordinary event. But under certain conditions, i.e., when the CVM is in a particular state, e.g., Error, particular shortcut events might also have a predefined meaning, which is specified by the CVM state transitions in section 3.1.10 (page 58).

So far, the following keyboard and mouse related shortcut events are defined: key_pressed_enter, key_released_enter, key_pressed_escape, key_released_escape, mouse_pressed_left, and

3.1. Core

mouse_released_left. Refer to section 3.1.6.4 (page 49) for more information on these event codes. If a given CVM implementation has a keyboard and/or mouse, all keyboard and/or mouse related shortcut events must be supported, respectively. Additional shortcut events may be defined in the future for the keyboard and mouse as well as for other input devices.

Builtin Events Builtin events differ from the ordinary events and the other special events, because no event handling subroutine code can be assigned for their behavior in the event table. Instead, their behavior is predefined. It is specified by the CVM state transitions in section 3.1.10 (page 58) in the CVM state EventProcessBuiltin. Refer also to section 3.1.6.4 (page 49).

In addition, builtin events are raised by very specific user actions, i.e., by reserved keys or buttons, if the CVM has a keyboard, or by reserved verbal commands, if the CVM has a microphone. The appearance of these keys and the wording of these commands is not specified here and can be chosen freely by the CVM implementor.

So far, the following builtin events are supported: cvm_quit, history_back, history_forward, history_reload, menu_bookmarks, menu_home, and input_hostAdr.

The handling of the builtin events cvm_quit, menu_home, history_back, history_forward, and history_reload is mandatory for all CVM implementations.

The builtin events history_back, history_forward, and history_reload refer to the history buffer. Refer to section 3.1.7 (page 52) for more information on the history buffer.

The builtin event menu_bookmarks may only occur and be handled, if the functional unit Bookmarks Menu in the Core module is implemented. Refer to section 3.1.8 (page 56) for more information on the bookmarks menu.

The builtin event input_hostAdr may only occur and be handled, if the CVM module Network is implemented.

Device Specific Builtin Events In addition to the builtin events that are specified here in the thesis, the CVM implementors are free to define further builtin events for their specific client devices. For example, they may define a builtin event that opens a menu for editing user preferences, or a builtin event that opens a help menu, etc. However, these device or vendor specific builtin events are not going to be discussed here in more detail.

3.1.6.4 Event Codes

In the following, the currently supported event codes are listed alphabetically and described using the following description format:

event_code_name = *event_code*: *event_parameters*
verbose_description

The *event_code_name* is the verbose name of the *event_code* and serves as a mnemonic. It can be used in a CVM assembler program. The *event_code_name* of an ordinary event consists of two parts: the name of the input module or one of its components and the name of the user action, e.g., key_pressed, mouse_pressed, etc. Mostly, the *event_code_name* is self-explanatory and need not be explained further.

The *event_code* is a unique Nat number and identifies a particular event type. In a CVM assembler program, however, the *event_code_name* should be used instead of its *event_code* to address a particular event type for reasons of readability. The CVM assembler then performs the mapping of the *event_code_name* to the corresponding *event_code* number.

The *event_parameters* depend on each event, but a particular event may also have none. The order of the event parameters from left to right reflects in which event parameter register each event parameter is stored, i.e., the first event parameter is stored into the regEventPar1 register, the second into the regEventPar2 register, and so on. Each event parameter is shown in the form *ident$_{type}$*. *ident* can be any identifier to characterize the use of the parameter. *type* denotes the type of the operand and must be one of the CVM types Int or Nat. For example, x_{Nat} might be used to identify an x coordinate of the type Nat. If not otherwise stated, the byte length of Int and Nat is given by cvmIntLen. Refer to section 3.1.2 (page 33) for more information on cvmIntLen. An empty parameter list is marked by "−".

cvm_quit = 2: −
Terminate CVM execution and turn off the CVM.

history_back = 3: −
"Load previous page from history buffer".
If the history buffer contains a preceding entry relative to the current history buffer position, the CVM sets the current history buffer position to the preceding entry and starts loading the respective CVMUI page. If this CVMUI page is not inside the currently processed CVM packet, the CVM requests that page from the respective CVM packet server. If the history buffer position does not contain a preceding entry, do nothing. Refer also to section 3.1.7 (page 52) for more information on the history buffer and to the CVM state EventProcessBuiltin in the CVM state transitions in section 3.1.10 (page 58).

history_forward = 4: −
"Load next page from history buffer".
Same functionality as history_back. However, the next entry in the history buffer is concerned instead of the previous one.

history_reload = 5: −
"Reload current page".
The CVM starts reloading the currently processed CVMUI page. If this CVMUI page is not a part of the HomeMenu, the CVM requests that page from the respective CVM packet server. Refer also to the CVM state EventProcessBuiltin in the CVM state transitions in section 3.1.10 (page 58).

input_hostAdr = 6: −
"Input host address and load page".
The CVM opens a dialog mask that asks the user of the client device to input an address of a network host, which acts as a CVM packet server, and the number of one of its offered network services. Then, the CVM loads the CVMUI page that is provided by that host

3.1. Core

and belongs to the offered network service. The output methods for presenting the dialog mask and the input methods for editing the network address depend on the modules that are available on the given CVM implementation. If the CVM has a screen and a keyboard, the dialog mask appears on the screen and the network address can be typed in by the user. If the CVM has only a speaker and a microphone, the dialog box is output acoustically by the CVM through the speaker and the URL is spoken by the user into the microphone. Whether the dialog mask accepts IP [62] addresses and/or DNS [45] names depends on the implementors' choice. Refer to the profile item **cvmDNSLookup** (page 90). Refer also to the CVM state **EventProcessBuiltin** in the CVM state transitions in section 3.1.10 (page 58).

key_pressed = 7: $keyCode_{Int}$
$keyCode$ reflects the key that was pressed by the user. Refer to section 3.3 (page 81) for a list of all key codes. If the user holds the key pressed, the CVM generates a sequence of key_pressed and key_released events as long as the key is being pressed. This is to enable smooth cursor movements while pressing one of the arrow keys. The number of generated events within the sequence depends on the given CVM implementation. Note that this event is not raised, if it matches one of the respective shortcut events. Then, only the respective shortcut event is raised.

key_pressed_enter = 8: −
This event is raised, if the user presses the Enter key.

key_pressed_escape = 9: −
This event is raised, if the user presses the Escape key.

key_released = 10: $keyCode_{Int}$
$keyCode$ reflects the key that was released by the user. Refer to section 3.3 (page 81) for a list of all key codes. Note that this event is not raised, if it matches one of the respective shortcut events. Then, only the respective shortcut event is raised.

key_released_enter = 11: −
This event is raised, if the user releases the Enter key.

key_released_escape = 12: −
This event is raised, if the user releases the Escape key.

menu_bookmarks = 13: −
"Open bookmarks menu".
Refer also to section 3.1.8 (page 56) for more information on the bookmarks menu and to the CVM state **EventProcessBuiltin** in the CVM state transitions in section 3.1.10 (page 58).

menu_home = 14: –
"Load HomeMenu".
The CVM starts loading the HomeMenu. Refer to section 3.6 (page 86) for more information on the HomeMenu and refer also to the CVM state **EventProcessBuiltin** in the CVM state transitions in section 3.1.10 (page 58).

mouse_moved = 15: x_{Int} y_{Int} $button_{\text{Int}}$
This event occurs when the mouse is moved while at the same time one or none of its mouse buttons is being pressed. mouse_moved events will continue to be delivered until the mouse is not moved anymore. x and y reflect the new xy coordinate position of the mouse pointer. *button* indicates which mouse button is being held down. Refer to section 3.3 (page 81) for the code numbers of the mouse buttons.

mouse_pressed = 16: x_{Int} y_{Int} $button_{\text{Int}}$
x and y reflect the xy coordinate position of the mouse pointer. *button* indicates which mouse button was pushed down. Refer to section 3.3 (page 81) for the code numbers of the mouse buttons. Note that this event is not raised, if it matches one of the respective shortcut events. Then, only the respective shortcut event is raised.

If the user rotates the mouse wheel up (or down), a mouse_pressed (or mouse_released) event is generated with the *button* value being **wheelUp** (or **wheelDown**).

In addition, another event code such as mouse_doubleClicked could be defined as well in this section to reflect immediate double clicks on one of the mouse buttons by the user. Right now, however, the CVM programmer or packet generator has to provide additional CVM code in the event handling subroutines that detects mouse double clicks.

mouse_pressed_left = 17: x_{Int} y_{Int}
This event is raised, if the user presses the left button. x and y reflect the xy coordinate position of the mouse pointer.

mouse_released = 18: x_{Int} y_{Int} $button_{\text{Int}}$
x and y reflect the xy coordinate position of the mouse pointer, respectively. *button* indicates which mouse button was let up. Refer to section 3.3 (page 81) for the code numbers of the mouse buttons. Note that this event is not raised, if it matches one of the respective shortcut events. Then, only the respective shortcut event is raised.

mouse_released_left = 19: x_{Int} y_{Int}
This event is raised, if the user releases the left button. x and y reflect the xy coordinate position of the mouse pointer.

3.1.7   History Buffer

The history buffer is mandatory for a given CVM implementation. Similar to the common browsers, the CVM automatically saves the addresses of the recently loaded CVMUI pages into an internal buffer. The size of the internal buffer, i.e., the maximum number of entries

3.1. Core

it can store, is implementation dependent but must be at least one. In addition, it is also left to the implementors' choice whether the history buffer is cleared each time the user switches the CVM off.

The term *current history buffer position* is used here to refer to the position of the entry within the history buffer that is currently active, i.e., the entry at the current history buffer position references the CVMUI page that has been loaded most recently and is currently processed by the CVM.

History Buffer Entry A history buffer entry addresses a particular CVMUI page. Generally, a CVM user interface contains several CVMUI pages that are grouped into CVM packets. The internal structure of a history buffer entry is left to the implementors' choice, but must contain at least the following items:

```
{ Nat1[] hostAdr;
  Nat1[4] sessionId;
  Nat serviceNo, pageNo, subpageNo, cvmpNo, pageMemAdr }
```

`hostAdr` represents the address of the network host where the respective CVM packet comes from. Whether it is an IP [62] address or a DNS [45] name is left to implementors' choice. Refer also to the profile item `cvmDNSLookup` (page 90). If the respective CVM packet is the `HomeMenu`, then `hostAdr` refers to the host name "_home_". Otherwise, `hostAdr` refers to the network address of a particular CVM packet server. The array type `Nat1[]` is used for a byte stream of any data.

`sessionId` identifies the respective client-server session. Refer to `regSessionId` in section 3.4 (page 82) and to `sessionId` in section 4.1 (page 128) for more information on session identifiers.

`serviceNo` represents the number of an interactive network service that is offered by the CVM packet server with the host address `hostAdr`. The addressed CVMUI page is part of the CVM user interface that belongs to the interactive network service with the number `serviceNo`. The data type Nat is used as a shortcut for the data type Nat<cvmIntLen>. Refer to section 3.1.2 (page 33) for more information on `cvmIntLen`.

`pageNo` represents the number of the abstract user interface (AUI) page. An AUI description consists of several AUI pages that are numbered starting with zero. During the customization process one or more CVM user interface (CVMUI) pages are generated from the requested AUI page. Each CVMUI page represents a subpage of the respective AUI page. An AUI subpage contains all or a smaller subset of the user interface components in the respective AUI page, depending on the client capabilities. Subpages are also numbered starting with zero. Refer to sections 5.1 (page 135), 5.5 (page 166), and 5.4 (page 163) for more information on AUI descriptions, CVMUIs, and the generation process.

`subpageNo` represents the number of the AUI subpage.

`cvmpNo` represents the number of the CVM packet that contains the respective CVMUI page. CVM packets are numbered starting with zero.

`pageMemAdr` represents an absolute memory address of an instruction where the respective CVMUI page starts in memory after the respective CVM packet has been loaded into memory.

In the future, additional history buffer entries that save the state of a CVMUI page when it was last visited may be defined. For example, common browsers save the most recent x and y positions of the cursor or viewport area within the respective CVMUI page and reload them automatically at the beginning of the next page access.

History Buffer Events The following builtin events apply to the history buffer: history_back, history_forward, history_reload. With the builtin events history_back and history_forward the user can move in the history buffer backward and forward and — if there is such an entry — reload the referenced CVMUI page. The current history buffer position then is moved one position backward or forward, too. The builtin event history_reload reloads the currently processed CVMUI page from the respective CVM packet server, if it does not belong to the HomeMenu. Refer also to section 3.1.6.4 (page 50) and to the CVM state EventProcessBuiltin in the CVM state transitions in section 3.1.10 (page 58) for more information on these builtin events and the CVM's predefined behavior on these events.

Example The behavior of the history buffer is illustrated by an example. Figure 3.4 (page 55) shows an example of a client-server session. Figure 3.5 (page 56) shows the corresponding dynamic behavior of the history buffer during that CVM session. The short and dashed horizontal arrows in figure 3.5 mark the current history buffer position.

At the beginning, the CVM first starts with the 0th page of the HomeMenu.

When the CVM encounters the instruction "page 3, $memAdr3$" (step 1), it loads the third subpage of the HomeMenu. Refer to the instruction reference in section 3.9.2 (page 108) for more information on the instruction page. $memAdr3$ represents the memory address of the instruction, where the code block of the third subpage starts in CVM memory. The service number, the AUI page number, and the CVM packet number of the HomeMenu are always zero by definition. How the CVM comes to encounter the instruction "page 3, $memAdr3$" is not important here. Normally, this instruction might occur in some event handling subroutine code and be executed after the user has raised an event.

When the CVM encounters the instruction "rcv $remoteHostAdr1$, 7, 0" (step 2), it contacts the CVM packet server with the network address $remoteHostAdr1$ and requests the 0th subpage of the 0th AUI page of the user interface that belongs to the interactive network service with the service number 7 — provided that the value of the special register regSessionId is zero. Refer to the instruction reference in section 3.9.2 (page 108) for more information on the instruction rcv and to section 3.4 (page 82) for more information on the special register regSessionId. The specified CVM packet server then sends the CVM packet $cvmpR10$ which contains the CVMUI pages with the numbers 0, 1, and 2. After the CVM has loaded this CVM packet into its memory, it starts execution at the memory address pageMemAdr$_{CVMP}$, where the code block of the 0th subpage starts. Refer to section 4.2 (page 129) for more information on the protocol message item pageMemAdr of the CPTP protocol method CVMP.

When the CVM encounters the instruction "page 2, $memAdr2$" (step 3), it loads the second subpage of the CVM packet $cvmpR10$. As the second page is part of the currently processed CVM packet, the CVM only has to jump to the code block of the second page and execute its instructions.

When the CVM encounters the instruction "rcv $remoteHostAdr1$, 9, 4" (step 4), it contacts the CVM packet server with the network address $remoteHostAdr1$ again to request the 4th

3.1. Core

subpage of the 9th page of the user interface. The specified CVM packet server then sends the CVM packet *cvmpR14* which contains the CVMUI pages with the numbers 0, 1, 2, 3, and 4. After the CVM has loaded this CVM packet into its memory, it starts execution at the memory address **pageMemAdr**$_{\text{CVMP}}$, where the code block of the 4th subpage starts. The CVM packets *cvmpR10* and *cvmpR14* belong to the user interface of the same network service.

When the CVM encounters the instructions "sidzero" and "rcv *remoteHostAdr2*, 5, 0" (step 5), it first sets the value of the special register **regSessionId** to zero and then contacts the CVM packet server with the network address *remoteHostAdr2* to request the 0th subpage of the 0th page that belongs to the interactive network service with the service number 5.

In the steps 6 to 9 the user raises the builtin events history_back and history_forward. The current history buffer position then moves one position backward or forward each time and the CVM reloads the respective CVMUI page. Note that in the steps 6 and 7 the CVM has to contact the respective CVM packet server to load the requested CVMUI page, because it is not part of the currently processed CVM packet.

Step 10 is analogous to step 4. Note that the CVM additionally deletes all history buffer entries behind the current history buffer position.

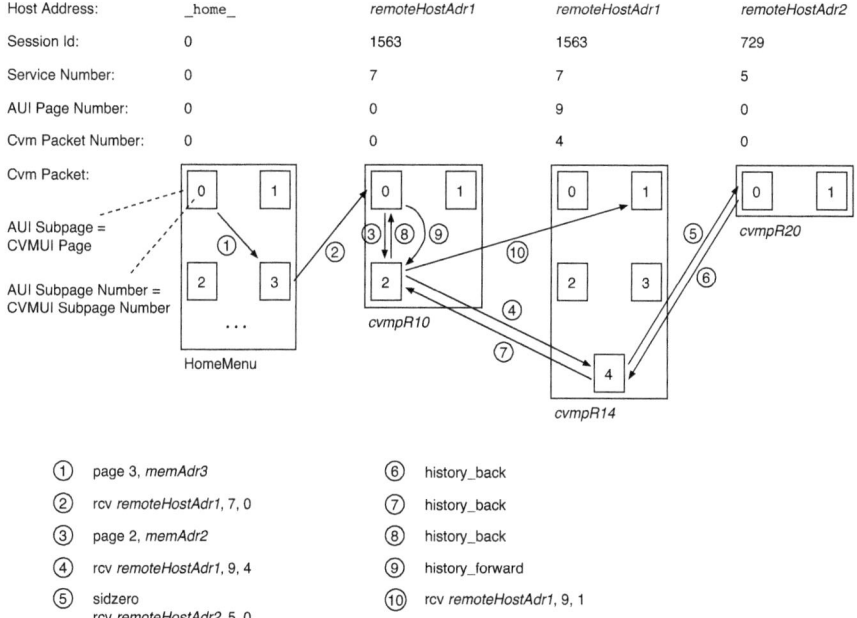

Figure 3.4: **Example of a Client-Server Session**

3. Client Virtual Machine (CVM)

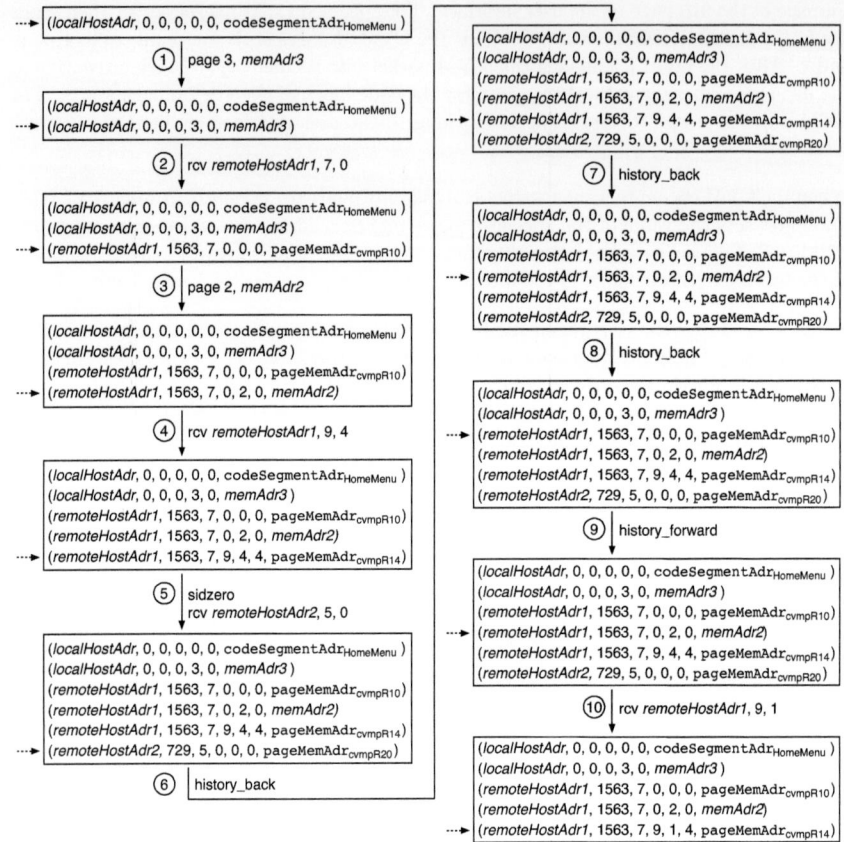

Figure 3.5: **History Buffer Behavior of an Exemplary Client-Server Session**

3.1.8 Bookmarks Menu

The bookmarks menu is optional for a given CVM implementation. Similar to common browsers, the user can store in it the addresses of frequently visited CVMUI pages in order to retrieve them later conveniently. Naturally, the bookmark entries are not cleared after the user switches the CVM off. The maximum number of bookmark entries as well as the user interface of the bookmarks menu itself is left to the implementors' choice. The internal structure of a bookmarks entry is left to the implementors' choice, too, but must contain at least the following items:

{ Nat1[] hostAdr; Nat serviceNo, pageNo }

`hostAdr` represents the address of the network host where the respective CVM packet comes from. Whether it is an IP [62] address or a DNS [45] name is left to implementors'

3.1. Core

choice. Refer also to the profile item cvmDNSLookup (page 90). If the respective CVM packet is the HomeMenu, then hostAdr refers to the host name "_home_". Otherwise, hostAdr refers to the network address of a particular CVM packet server. The array type Nat1[] is used for a byte stream of any data.

serviceNo represents the number of an interactive network service that is offered by the CVM packet server with the host address hostAdr. The addressed CVMUI page is part of the user interface that belongs to the interactive network service with the number serviceNo. The data type Nat is used as a shortcut for the data type Nat<cvmIntLen>. Refer to section 3.1.2 (page 33) for more information on cvmIntLen.

pageNo represents the number of the AUI page.

The builtin event menu_bookmarks opens the bookmarks menu. Refer to section 3.1.6.4 (page 51) and to the CVM state EventProcessBuiltin in the CVM state transitions in section 3.1.10 (page 58) for more information on this event.

3.1.9 Interval Timer

The interval timer component is optional for the CVM. Its purpose is to provide an interrupt mechanism that is controlled periodically. The interval timer provides millisecond accuracy. When active, it runs over and over again, sending a signal each time it expires. For example, the interval timer might be used to manage several execution threads that are part of the same CVM program and run concurrently. In the following, the special interval timer registers are described. Refer also to section 3.1.10 (page 58) for more details on the interval timer concept, CVM states, and the overall state behavior of the CVM.

regTimerSignal The special register regTimerSignal contains a flag bit with the possible values 0 ("unset") and 1 ("set"). Whenever the time period that is given by the special register regTimerInterval expires, the timer sets the value of this register to 1. On the other hand, the CVM automatically unsets this register each time it checks its value. The CVM checks the value of this register in the states Execute, EventExecute, and Wait, i.e., regState = Execute ∨ EventExecute ∨ Wait. This register cannot be modified by the CVM instructions. The initial value of this register is zero.

regTimerHandleAdr The special register regTimerHandleAdr stores the absolute memory address, a Nat value, of the first instruction of the timer handle code block in memory. The timer handle code block is a part of the loaded CVM program (and packet). Each time the CVM notices that the interval timer has expired, the CVM interrupts its current activity and jumps to that code block to continue execution there. The instruction settimerhandleadr sets the value of this register. The initial value of this register is zero.

regTimerInterval The special register regTimerInterval stores a Nat value that defines the time period in milliseconds. If the value is zero, the timer function is deactivated, otherwise activated. The instruction settimerinterval sets the value of this register. The initial value of this register is zero.

Note that it is left to the responsibility of the CVM programmer or packet generator to ensure that the interval timer is not activated before the memory address of the timer handle code block has been declared by the instruction **settimerhandleadr**.

3.1.10 Runtime Behavior

The runtime behavior of the CVM can be modelled as a state machine. Note that the state machine that is presented in this section only specifies the functional runtime behavior of the CVM, but does not provide a concrete implementation for it.

regState The special register **regState** ("State Register") stores the current state of the CVM, which is a Nat number. There are the following CVM states: CptpGET = 1, Error = 2, EventExecute = 3, EventProcess = 4, EventProcessBuiltin = 5, Execute = 6, Init = 7, LoadCvmPacket = 8, TimerExecute = 9, and Wait = 10. The value of this register cannot be modified by the CVM instructions. Its initial value is **LoadCvmPacket**.

State Transitions The actions the CVM performs in each state, and the conditions under which the CVM performs a particular state transition are specified by the following pseudo-code in a generally understandable notation. Note that this pseudo-code only *specifies* the runtime behavior of the CVM but does not represent a concrete implementation. Whenever possible, particular parts are described informally and as general as possible to leave CVM implementors most freedom. Italic font is used for auxiliary variables. Informal descriptions appear as internal procedure calls and are presented in italics as well. These procedures have meaningful names and are not specified in more detail. Instead, they are described informally afterwards in the alphabetically sorted list.

```
#IF CVM module Visual available
regMeasure := ...;   // Refer to section 3.2.1 (page 77).
#ENDIF   // (CVM module Visual available)
#IF CVM module Network available
regSessionId := 0;
regServiceNo := 0;
#ENDIF   // (CVM module Network available)
```
$cvmPacket := $ HomeMenu;
$historyEntry := addHistoryEntry(\text{"\_home\_"}, 0, 0, 0, 0, 0, 0)$;
regState := LoadCvmPacket;   // CVM always starts with the state LoadCvmPacket.
repeat forever {
  switch (regState) {
```
#IF CVM module Network available
```
    CptpGET:
      /* $cptpMethod = $ GET */
      $cvmPacketIsLoaded = $ false;
      $cptpTransactionStart()$;
      while (regState = CptpGET) {
        if (regErrorCode $\neq$ 0) {
          $newError := $ true;
          regState := Error;

3.1. Core

        } else if ($cptpTransactionFinished() = $ true) {
           $cvmPacket :=$ cvmPacket$_{\text{CVMP}}$;
           regSessionId := sessionId$_{\text{CVMP}}$;
           sessionId$_{historyEntry}$:= sessionId$_{\text{CVMP}}$;
           cvmpNo$_{historyEntry}$:= cvmpNo$_{\text{CVMP}}$;
           pageMemAdr$_{historyEntry}$:= pageMemAdr$_{\text{CVMP}}$;
           regState := LoadCvmPacket;
        } else if ($checkEventQueue() = $ true $\land$ $isEscapeEvent() = $ true) {
```
#IF Interval timer available
```
           regTimerInterval $= 0;$ // Deactivate timer, if currently active
```
#ENDIF  // (Interval timer available)
```
           regEventEnable := 0;
           regState := Wait;
        } else {
           $cptpTransactionContinue()$;
        }
    }
```
#ENDIF  // (CVM module Network available)
```
    Error: // Refer also to section 3.1.5.1 (page 41).
```
#IF Interval timer available
```
        regTimerInterval $= 0;$ // Deactivate timer, if currently active
```
#ENDIF  // (Interval timer available)
```
    $outputErrorMessage()$;
    $clearEventQueue()$;
    repeat {
      while ($checkEventQueue() = $ false) { $sleepOrSkip()$; }
    } until ($isBuiltinEvent() = $ true);   // Other events are discarded.
```
#IF CVM module Network available
```
      if ($newError = $ true $\land$ hostAdr$_{historyEntry} \neq$ "_home_" $\land$
        regErrorCode $\neq$ NetworkError) {
        $cptpMethod :=$ ERROR;
        $cptpTransactionStart()$;
        while ($cptpTransactionFinished() = $ false) {
          $cptpTransactionContinue()$;
        }
      }
```
#ENDIF  // (CVM module Network available)
```
    $newError :=$ false;
    $nextState :=$ Error;
    regState := EventProcessBuiltin;
  EventExecute:
```
#IF Interval timer available
```
      if (regTimerSignal $= 1$) {
        regTimerSignal := 0;
        $save$(regIP, regRSP, regBP, regState, R[ ]);
        regIP := regTimerHandleAdr;
        regRSP := 0;
        regBP := 0;

```
            regState := TimerExecute;
            break;
        }
#ENDIF   // (Interval timer available)
        checkInstruction();
        if (regErrorCode ≠ 0) /* Error code depends on each instruction. */ {
            newError := true;
            regState := Error;
            break;
        }
        if ($opcode_{instruction}$ = halt) {
            restore(regIP, regRSP, regBP, regState, R[ ]);
            /* regState ∈ {Execute, Wait} */
        } else if ($opcode_{instruction}$ = page) {
            historyEntry := addHistoryEntry(hostAdr$_{historyEntry}$, sessionId$_{historyEntry}$,
                                serviceNo$_{historyEntry}$, pageNo$_{historyEntry}$, $subpageNo_{page}$,
                                cvmpNo$_{historyEntry}$, regIP + $pageMemAdrRel_{page}$);
            regState := Init;
        }
#IF CVM module Network available
        else if ($opcode_{instruction}$ = rcv ∨ $opcode_{instruction}$ = sendrcv) {
            readHostAdrFromMemAt(hostAdrMemAdr$_{<rcv\,|\,sendrcv>}$, cptpHostAdr);
            if (regErrorCode ≠ 0) {
                // regErrorCode ∈ {IllegalMemoryAddress, NoDNSLookup}
                newError := true;
                regState := Error;
                break;
            }
            cptpMethod := GET;
            if (regSessionId = 0) {
                regServiceNo := pageOrServiceNo$_{<rcv|sendrcv>}$;
                cptpPageNo := 0;
                cptpSubpageNo := 0;
            } else {
                cptpPageNo := pageOrServiceNo$_{<rcv|sendrcv>}$;
                cptpSubpageNo := subpageNo$_{<rcv|sendrcv>}$;
            }
            if ($opcode_{instruction}$ = rcv) {
                cptpNumBytes := 0;
                cptpDataBytesMemAdr := 0;
            } else {
                cptpNumBytes := numBytes$_{sendrcv}$;
                cptpDataBytesMemAdr := dataBytesMemAdr$_{sendrcv}$;
            }
            historyEntry := addHistoryEntry(cptpHostAdr, regSessionId, regServiceNo,
                                            cptpPageNo, cptpSubpageNo, 0, 0);
            regState := CptpGET;
        }
```

3.1. Core   61

```
#ENDIF   // (CVM module Network available)
    else {
        executeInstruction();
    }
    EventProcess:    // Refer also to section 3.1.6.1 (page 46).
```
  // $nextState \in \{\text{Execute}, \text{Wait}\}$
  if ($isBuiltinEvent()$ = true) {
      regState := EventProcessBuiltin;
  } else if (regEventEnable = 0) {
      regState := $nextState$;   // Discard event.
      $nextState$:= $\bot$;
  } else {
      $memAdr$:= regEventTableAdr;
      repeat {   // Search event table:
          if ($readIntFromMemAt(memAdr, eventCode)$ = false) {
              $nextState$:= $\bot$;
              $newError$:= true;
              regErrorCode := IllegalMemoryAddress;
              regState := Error;
          } else if ($eventCode$ = 0) {
              regState := $nextState$;
              $nextState$:= $\bot$;
          } else if ($eventCode$ = 1) {   // Jump to parent event table.
              if ($readIntFromMemAt(memAdr + \text{cvmIntLen}, memAdr)$ = false) {
                  $nextState$:= $\bot$;
                  $newError$:= true;
                  regErrorCode := IllegalMemoryAddress;
                  regState := Error;
              }
          } else if ($eventCode$ = regEventCode) {
              $save$(regIP, regRSP, regBP, $nextState$, R[ ]);
              $nextState$:= $\bot$;
              if ($readIntFromMemAt(memAdr + \text{cvmIntLen}, \text{regIP})$ = false) {
                  $newError$:= true;
                  regErrorCode := IllegalMemoryAddress;
                  regState := Error;
              } else {
                  regRSP := 0;
                  regBP := 0;
                  regState := EventExecute;
              }
          } else {
              $memAdr$:= $memAdr + 2 *$ cvmIntLen;
          }
      } until (regState = Error $\vee$ $eventCode$ = 0 $\vee$ $eventCode$ = regEventCode);
  }
  EventProcessBuiltin:
      /∗ $nextState \in \{\text{Error}, \text{Execute}, \text{Wait}\}$ ∗/

```
        if (regEventCode = cvm_quit) {
            turnOffCVM();
        } else if (regEventCode = history_back ∨
                   regEventCode = history_forward) {
            historyEntryTmp := historyEntry;
            if (setHistoryPosition(historyEntry) = true) {
                nextState := ⊥;
                regErrorCode := 0;
                if (hostAdr_{historyEntry} = "_home_") {
                    if (hostAdr_{historyEntryTmp} = "_home_" ∧
                        cvmPacketIsLoaded = true) {
                        regState := Init;
                    } else {
                        cvmPacket := HomeMenu;
                        regSessionId := sessionId_{historyEntry};
                        regServiceNo := serviceNo_{historyEntry};
                        regState := LoadCvmPacket;
                    }
                }
#IF CVM module Network available
                else if (hostAdr_{historyEntry} = hostAdr_{historyEntryTmp} ∧
                         sessionId_{historyEntry} = sessionId_{historyEntryTmp} ∧
                         pageNo_{historyEntry} = pageNo_{historyEntryTmp} ∧
                         cvmpNo_{historyEntry} = cvmpNo_{historyEntryTmp} ∧
                         cvmPacketIsLoaded = true) {
                    regState := Init;
                } else {
                    regSessionId := sessionId_{historyEntry};
                    regServiceNo := serviceNo_{historyEntry};
                    cptpMethod := GET;
                    cptpHostAdr := hostAdr_{historyEntry};
                    cptpPageNo := pageNo_{historyEntry};
                    cptpSubpageNo := subpageNo_{historyEntry};
                    cptpNumBytes := 0;
                    cptpDataBytesMemAdr := 0;
                    regState := CptpGET;
                }
#ENDIF       // (CVM module Network available)
            } else {
                regState := nextState;
                nextState := ⊥;
            }
        } else if (regEventCode = history_reload) {
            nextState := ⊥;
            regErrorCode := 0;
#IF CVM module Network available
            if (hostAdr_{historyEntry} ≠ "_home_") {
                cptpMethod := GET;
```

3.1. Core   63

```
            cptpHostAdr := hostAdr_{historyEntry};
            cptpPageNo := pageNo_{historyEntry};
            cptpSubpageNo := subpageNo_{historyEntry};
            cptpNumBytes := 0;
            cptpDataBytesMemAdr := 0;
            regState := CptpGET;
          } else {
#ENDIF   // (CVM module Network available)
            regState := LoadCvmPacket;
          }
#IF CVM module Network available
        }
#ENDIF   // (CVM module Network available)
#IF CVM module Network available
        else if (regEventCode = input_hostAdr) {
          openInputHostAdrAndServiceNoUI();
          repeat {
            while (checkEventQueue() = false) { sleepOrSkip(); }
            if (isInputHostAdrAndServiceNoEvent() = true) {
              doInputHostAdrAndServiceNoAction();
            }
          } until (isAcknowledgeEvent() = true  ∨  isEscapeEvent() = true)
          closeInputHostAdrAndServiceNoUI();
          if (isEscapeEvent() = true) {
            regState := nextState;
            nextState := ⊥;
          } else {    // isAcknowledgeEvent() = true
            nextState := ⊥;
            regErrorCode := 0;
            regSessionId := 0;
            regServiceNo := inputServiceNo;
            historyEntry := addHistoryEntry(inputHostAdr, regSessionId, regServiceNo,
                                            0, 0, 0, 0);
            if (inputHostAdr = "_home_") {       // regServiceNo = 0
              cvmPacket := HomeMenu;
              regState := LoadCvmPacket;
            } else {
              cptpMethod := GET;
              cptpHostAdr := hostAdr_{historyEntry};
              cptpPageNo := pageNo_{historyEntry};
              cptpSubpageNo := subpageNo_{historyEntry};
              cptpNumBytes := 0;
              cptpDataBytesMemAdr := 0;
              regState := CptpGET;
            }
          }
        }
#ENDIF   // (CVM module Network available)
```

```
#IF Bookmarks available
      else if (regEventCode = menu_bookmarks) {
         openBookmarksMenu();
         repeat {
            while (checkEventQueue() = false) { sleepOrSkip(); }
            if (isBookmarksEvent() = true) { doBookmarksAction(); }
         } until (isBookmarksEventFinished() = true);
         closeBookmarksMenu();
         if (bookmarkEntryHasBeenSelected() = false) {
            regState := nextState;
            nextState := ⊥;
         } else {
            nextState := ⊥;
            regErrorCode := 0;
#IF CVM module Network available
            regSessionId := 0;
            regServiceNo := serviceNo_{bookmarksEntry};
#ENDIF  // (CVM module Network available)
            historyEntry := addHistoryEntry(hostAdr_{bookmarksEntry}, regSessionId,
                                            regServiceNo, pageNo_{bookmarksEntry}, 0, 0, 0);
#IF CVM module Network available
            if (hostAdr_{historyEntry} = "_home_") {
#ENDIF  // (CVM module Network available)
               cvmPacket := HomeMenu;
               regState := LoadCvmPacket;
            }
#IF CVM module Network available
            else {
               cptpMethod := GET;
               cptpHostAdr := hostAdr_{historyEntry};
               cptpPageNo := pageNo_{historyEntry};
               cptpSubpageNo := 0;
               cptpNumBytes := 0;
               cptpDataBytesMemAdr := 0;
               regState := CptpGET;
            }
         }
#ENDIF  // (CVM module Network available)
      }
#ENDIF  // (Bookmarks available)
      else if (regEventCode = menu_home) {
         cvmPacket := HomeMenu;
         nextState := ⊥;
         regErrorCode := 0;
#IF CVM module Network available
         regSessionId := 0;
         regServiceNo := 0;
#ENDIF  // (CVM module Network available)
```

3.1. Core   65

    $historyEntry := addHistoryEntry("\_home\_", \text{regSessionId}, \text{regServiceNo},$
                                                  $0, 0, 0, 0);$
    regState := LoadCvmPacket;
  } else {
    $processDeviceSpecificBuiltinEvent();$
  }
  Execute:
#IF Interval timer available
    if (regTimerSignal = 1) {
      regTimerSignal := 0;
      $save(\text{regIP}, \text{regRSP}, \text{regBP}, \text{regState}, R[\ ]);$
      regIP := regTimerHandleAdr;
      regRSP := 0;
      regBP := 0;
      regState := TimerExecute;
      break;
    }
#ENDIF // (Interval timer available)
    if $(checkEventQueue() = \text{true})$ {
      $nextState := \text{Execute};$
      regState := EventProcess;
      break;
    }
    $checkInstruction();$
    if (regErrorCode $\neq 0$) /* Error code depends on each instruction. */ {
      $newError := \text{true};$
      regState := Error;
      break;
    }
    if ($opcode_{instruction}$ = halt) {
      regState := Wait;
    } else if ($opcode_{instruction}$ = page) {
      $historyEntry := addHistoryEntry(\text{hostAdr}_{historyEntry}, \text{sessionId}_{historyEntry},$
                              $\text{serviceNo}_{historyEntry}, \text{pageNo}_{historyEntry}, \text{subpageNo}_{page},$
                              $\text{cvmpNo}_{historyEntry}, \text{regIP} + pageMemAdrRel_{page});$
      regState := Init;
    }
#IF CVM module Network available
    else if ($opcode_{instruction}$ = rcv $\vee$ $opcode_{instruction}$ = sendrcv) {
      $readHostAdrFromMemAt(hostAdrMemAdr_{<\text{rcv}\,|\,\text{sendrcv}>}, cptpHostAdr);$
      if (regErrorCode $\neq 0$) {
        // regErrorCode $\in$ {IllegalMemoryAddress, NoDNSLookup}
        $newError := \text{true};$
        regState := Error;
        break;
      }
      $cptpMethod := \text{GET};$
      if (regSessionId = 0) {

regServiceNo := $pageOrServiceNo_{<\text{rcv}|\text{sendrcv}>}$;
cptpPageNo := 0;
cptpSubpageNo := 0;
} else {
    cptpPageNo := $pageOrServiceNo_{<\text{rcv}|\text{sendrcv}>}$;
    cptpSubpageNo := $subpageNo_{<\text{rcv}|\text{sendrcv}>}$;
}
if ($opcode_{instruction}$ = rcv) {
    cptpNumBytes := 0;
    cptpDataBytesMemAdr := 0;
} else {
    cptpNumBytes := $numBytes_{\text{sendrcv}}$;
    cptpDataBytesMemAdr := $dataBytesMemAdr_{\text{sendrcv}}$;
}
historyEntry := addHistoryEntry(cptpHostAdr, regSessionId, regServiceNo,
                                 cptpPageNo, cptpSubpageNo, 0, 0);
regState := CptpGET;
}
#ENDIF // (CVM module Network available)
    else {
        executeInstruction();
    }

Init:
regIP := $pageMemAdr_{historyEntry}$;
regRSP := 0;
regSS := $stackSegmentAdr_{cvmPacket}$;
regSP := regSS;
regBP := 0;
regErrorCode := 0;
regEventEnable := 0;
regEventCode := 0;
regEventTableAdr := 0;
#IF Interval timer available
    regTimerHandleAdr := 0;
    regTimerInterval := 0;
    regTimerSignal := 0;
#ENDIF // (Interval timer available)
#IF CVM module Visual available
    regClipX := 0; regClipY := 0;
#IF regMeasure = 0
    regClipWidth := cvmScreenWidth;
    regClipHeight := cvmScreenHeight;
    regLineWidth := 1;
#ELSE // (regMeasure = 0)
    regClipWidth := cvmScreenWidthMM;
    regClipHeight := cvmScreenHeightMM;
    regLineWidth := ...;   // $\approx 1pt$
#ENDIF // (regMeasure = 0)

3.1. Core   67

```
        regColorRed := 0; regColorGreen := 0; regColorBlue := 0;
        regBgColorRed := 255; regBgColorGreen := 255; regBgColorBlue := 255;
        regFontCode := fontFixedStandard; regFontSize := 13;
        regHTextLine := 0; regXTextLine := 0;
```
        $clearScreen()$;
```
#ENDIF  // (CVM module Visual available)
#IF CVM module Mouse available
```
        regMouseFont = XC_top_left_arrow;
```
#ENDIF  // (CVM module Mouse available)
```
        $clearEventQueue()$;
        regState := Execute;
    LoadCvmPacket:
        if ($loadCvmPacketIntoMem() = $ true) {
            $cvmPacketIsLoaded := $ true;
            if ($\text{hostAdr}_{historyEntry} = \text{"\_home\_"} \land$
                $\text{pageNo}_{historyEntry} = 0 \land \text{subpageNo}_{historyEntry} = 0$) {
                $\text{pageMemAdr}_{historyEntry} := \text{codeSegmentAdr}_{cvmPacket}$;
            }
            regState := Init;
        } else {
            $cvmPacketIsLoaded := $ false;
            $newError := $ true;
            if ($\text{hostAdr}_{historyEntry} = \text{"\_home\_"}$) {
                regErrorCode := MalformedHomeMenu;
            } else {
                regErrorCode := MalformedCVMPacket;
            }
            regState := Error;
        }
```
#IF Interval timer available
```
    TimerExecute:
        $checkInstruction()$;
        if (regErrorCode $\neq$ 0) /∗ Error code depends on each instruction. ∗/ {
            $newError := $ true;
            regState := Error;
            break;
        }
        if ($opcode_{instruction} = $ halt) {
            $restore$(regIP, regRSP, regBP, regState, R[ ]);
            /∗ regState $\in$ {EventExecute, Execute, Wait} ∗/
        } else if ($opcode_{instruction} = $ page) {
            $historyEntry := addHistoryEntry(\text{hostAdr}_{historyEntry}, \text{sessionId}_{historyEntry},$
                      $\text{serviceNo}_{historyEntry}, \text{pageNo}_{historyEntry}, subpageNo_{\text{page}},$
                      $\text{cvmpNo}_{historyEntry}, \text{regIP} + pageMemAdrRel_{\text{page}})$;
            regState := Init;
        }
```
#IF CVM module Network available
```
        else if ($opcode_{instruction} = $ rcv $\lor$ $opcode_{instruction} = $ sendrcv) {

$readHostAdrFromMemAt(hostAdrMemAdr_{\text{<rcv | sendrcv>}}, cptpHostAdr);$
if (regErrorCode $\neq$ 0) {
   // regErrorCode $\in$ {IllegalMemoryAddress, NoDNSLookup}
   $newError :=$ true;
   regState := Error;
   break;
}
$cptpMethod :=$ GET;
if (regSessionId = 0) {
   regServiceNo := $pageOrServiceNo_{\text{<rcv|sendrcv>}}$;
   $cptpPageNo := 0;$
   $cptpSubpageNo := 0;$
} else {
   $cptpPageNo := pageOrServiceNo_{\text{<rcv|sendrcv>}};$
   $cptpSubpageNo := subpageNo_{\text{<rcv|sendrcv>}};$
}
if ($opcode_{instruction}$ = rcv) {
   $cptpNumBytes := 0;$
   $cptpDataBytesMemAdr := 0;$
} else {
   $cptpNumBytes := numBytes_{\text{sendrcv}};$
   $cptpDataBytesMemAdr := dataBytesMemAdr_{\text{sendrcv}};$
}
$historyEntry := addHistoryEntry(cptpHostAdr,$ regSessionId, regServiceNo,
                                   $cptpPageNo, cptpSubpageNo, 0, 0);$
   regState := CptpGET;
}
#ENDIF // (CVM module Network available)
   else {
     $executeInstruction();$
   }
#ENDIF // (Interval timer available)
Wait:
#IF Interval timer available
   if (regTimerSignal = 1) {
     regTimerSignal := 0;
     $save($regIP, regRSP, regBP, regState, R[ ]$);$
     regIP := regTimerHandleAdr;
     regRSP := 0;
     regBP := 0;
     regState := TimerExecute;
     break;
   }
#ENDIF // (Interval timer available)
   if ($checkEventQueue()$ = true) {
     $nextState :=$ Wait;
     regState := EventProcess;
     break;

3.1. Core

}
$sleepOrSkip()$;

} // End of switch block
} // End of repeat block

Comments:

- #IF *condition*
  pseudo-code$_1$
  #ELSE
  pseudo-code$_2$
  #ENDIF
  groups conditional parts of the pseudo-code. The *condition* is expressed informally. If the *condition* is true, then the *pseudo-code*$_1$ is inserted at this place, otherwise the *pseudo-code*$_2$. The #ELSE part is optional and is omitted, if *pseudo-code*$_2$ is empty.

- *addHistoryEntry(hostAdr, sessionId, serviceNo, pageNo, subpageNo, cvmpNo, pageMemAdr)* creates a new entry in the history buffer and returns it. The components of the entry are given by the parameters *hostAdr, sessionId, serviceNo, pageNo, subpageNo, cvmpNo,* and *pageMemAdr*. The new history entry is always inserted behind the current history position and the current history position is then set to the new entry. The other entries behind the new entry are deleted, if available. If the history buffer is already full, then the first entry is deleted before the new entry is inserted behind the current history position. If the maximum size of the history buffer is only one, then the old entry is simply replaced by the new one. If the history entry of the current history position has the same *hostAdr, sessionId, pageNo,* and *subpageNo,* then no new history entry is created and the current history entry is returned. Refer to section 3.1.7 (page 52) for more information on the history buffer.

- *bookmarkEntryHasBeenSelected()* returns true, if the user has previously selected a bookmark entry to be accessed, otherwise false.

- *checkEventQueue()* returns true, if the event queue is not empty, otherwise false. If the event queue is not empty, it removes the first event from the event queue and sets the event registers **regEventCode** and **regEventPar**<1|2|3> with the appropriate values of that event. As already said, events are buffered in an event queue in the FIFO (First In, First Out) manner. Note that a new event can occur and be appended into the event queue at any time in any state. However, the CVM checks the event queue only in the states **Error, EventProcessBuiltin, Execute, CptpGET,** and **Wait.** In addition, the CVM checks here in the state **Execute** every time for a new event. However, this frequency is not necessary in a given implementation provided that ergonomic event handling is ensured for the user.

- *checkInstruction()* checks whether the execution of the current instruction might cause an error. The memory address of the current instruction is given by the instruction pointer register **regIP**. If an error might occur, the special error register **regErrorCode** is automatically set to the appropriate error code value that depends on the instruction. Refer to section 3.1.5.2 (page 42) for a list of all error codes. The instruction reference in section 3.9.2 (page 100) describes for each instruction which errors might occur.

- *clearEventQueue*() removes all events from the event queue and discards them.

- *clearScreen*() fills the whole visual drawing area with the default background color, which is white. Refer also to section 3.2.1 (page 76).

- *closeBookmarksMenu*() closes the bookmarks menu that has previously been opened by *openBookmarksMenu*(). If the bookmarks menu has been displayed on the screen, the screen sections that have been obscured by the bookmarks menu are restored with their original contents.

- *closeInputHostAdrAndServiceNoUI*() closes the *input host address user interface* that has previously been opened by *openInputHostAdrAndServiceNoUI*(). If this user interface has been displayed on the screen, the screen sections that have been obscured by that user interface, are restored with their original contents.

- *cptpMethod*, *cptpHostAdr*, *cptpPageNo*, *cptpSubpageNo*, *cptpNumBytes*, *cptpDataBytesMemAdr* are variables for building up CPTP transactions. In general, these variables are set before the CVM enters the state stateCptpGET. Refer to section 4 (page 127) for more information on the CPTP protocol. It depends on the protocol method (*cptpMethod*) which of these variables are needed for a CPTP transaction, whereas *cptpMethod* and *cptpHostAdr* are always needed. If the protocol method is GET, the variables *cptpPageNo*, *cptpSubpageNo*, *cptpNumBytes*, and *cptpDataBytesMemAdr* are needed as well. Refer also to the instructions rcv (page 108) and sendrcv (page 110).

- *cptpTransactionStart*() starts a CPTP transaction with a CVM packet server. The CPTP protocol method is given by the variable *cptpMethod*. The host address of the CVM packet server is given by the variable *cptpHostAdr*. If the value of *cptpMethod* is ERROR, then *cptpHostAdr* refers to the CVM packet server from which the currently processed or executed CVM packet comes from. Refer also to the comments on the variables *cptpMethod*, *cptpHostAdr*, etc., in this section and to the CPTP protocol methods ERROR and GET in section 4.2 (page 129).

  Note that the amount of data that the CVM sends to and/or receives from the CVM packet server at a time is left to the implementors' choice. However, the user should be able to interrupt and stop the transaction with an escape event. If an error occurs during the transaction, the special error register regErrorCode is set automatically with the appropriate error code. However, if the protocol method is ERROR, then an error during the transaction, e.g., NetworkError (page 43), can be ignored silently by the CVM.

  It is left to the implementors' choice whether a mechanism for local caching of CVMUI pages is implemented or not. If yes, then *cptpTransactionStart*() first checks the local cache, if it already contains the requested CVMUI page. It only starts a CPTP transaction with a CVM packet server, if the CVM does not have a valid copy in its local cache.

- *cptpTransactionContinue*() resumes the previously started and still ongoing CPTP transaction. As already said, the amount of data that the CVM sends to and/or

3.1. Core

receives from the CVM packet server at a time is left to the implementors' choice. In addition, each time, the CVM receives a CPTP message from a CVM packet server, it stores the value of the received message item sessionId into its special register regSessionId. Refer to sections 3.4 (page 82) and 4.1 (page 128) for more information on regSessionId and sessionId, respectively.

- *cptpTransmissionFinished*() returns true, if the previously started CPTP transaction is finished, i.e., all the relevant data have been sent and/or received by the CVM over the network. Otherwise, *cptpTransmissionFinished*() returns false.

- *cvmPacket* is a variable that refers to the currently processed CVM packet. At the beginning, it refers to the HomeMenu. The binary format of a CVM packet is specified in section 3.8 (page 93).

- *cvmPacketIsLoaded* is a variable that indicates whether the CVM memory contains a loaded and valid CVM packet that conforms to the current history entry.

- *doBookmarksAction*() performs the respective actions according to the currently processed bookmarks event. Among other things, these actions might include the selection, creation, and deletion of a bookmark entry. These actions are implementation dependent and need not be specified here in more detail.

- *doInputHostAdrAndServiceNoAction*() performs the respective actions according to the currently processed event that applies to the *input host address dialog mask*. These actions are implementation dependent and need not be specified here in more detail. Mainly, these actions might include the input, presentation, and editing of a character string that represents the address of a network host and a service number. Whether the address is an IP [62] address and/or a DNS [45] name is left to the implementors' choice. Refer also to the profile item cvmDNSLookup (page 90).

- *executeInstruction*() executes the instruction at the memory address given by the instruction pointer register regIP and afterwards automatically sets regIP to the memory address of the next instruction. Refer to the instruction reference in section 3.9.2 (page 100) for a description of each instruction.

- *eventCode* is a variable that stores an event code for temporary use. Refer also to the comments on *readIntFromMemAt*(*memAdr*, *eventCode*).

- *historyEntry* is a variable that refers to the history entry at the current history position.

- *historyEntryTmp* is a variable that refers to a history entry for temporary use.

- HomeMenu refers to the home menu of the CVM. Refer to section 3.6 (page 86) for more information on the home menu.

- codeSegmentAdr$_{cvmPacket}$ and stackSegmentAdr$_{cvmPacket}$ refer to the CVM packet items codeSegmentAdr and stackSegmentAdr of the CVM packet *cvmPacket*. Refer to section 3.8 (page 93) for more information on these packet items.

- $<hostAdrMemAdr \mid subpageNo \mid pageOrServiceNo \mid pageMemAdrRel \mid numBytes \mid dataBytesMemAdr>_{<page \mid rcv \mid sendrcv>}$ each refer to the parameters $hostAdrMemAdr$, $subpageNo$, $pageOrServiceNo$, $pageMemAdrRel$, $numBytes$, and $dataBytesMemAdr$ of the CVM instructions page, rcv, and sendrcv, respectively.

- $<$hostAdr $\mid$ sessionId $\mid$ serviceNo $\mid$ pageNo $\mid$ subpageNo $\mid$ cvmpNo $\mid$ pageMemAdr$>_{<historyEntry \mid historyEntryTmp>}$ each refer to the hostAdr, sessionId, serviceNo, pageNo, subpageNo, cvmpNo, and pageMemAdr item of an history entry structure, respectively. The variables $historyEntry$ and $historyEntryTmp$ refer to an history entry structure. Refer also to section 3.1.7 (page 52) for more information on the history buffer.

- $<$hostAdr $\mid$ serviceNo $\mid$ pageNo$>_{<bookmarksEntry>}$ each refer to the hostAdr, serviceNo, and pageNo item of a bookmarks entry structure, respectively. The variable $bookmarksEntry$ refers to a bookmarks entry structure. Refer also to section 3.1.8 (page 56) for more information on the bookmarks menu.

- $inputHostAdr$ is a variable that refers to the IP [62] address or the DNS [45] name of a network host. It stems from $openInputHostAdrAndServiceNoUI()$.

- $inputServiceNo$ is a variable that refers to the number of an interactive network service. It stems from $openInputHostAdrAndServiceNoUI()$.

- $isAcknowledgeEvent()$ returns true, if the values of the special event registers regEventCode and regEventPar<1|2|3> indicate an acknowledgment by the user. For example, this is the case if the CVM has a keyboard and if the value of regEventCode is key_pressed_enter. However, if the CVM has a microphone instead, the user might as well speak something like "Yes" into it. Otherwise, $isAcknowledgeEvent()$ returns false. It is left to the implementors' choice which user actions cause an acknowledge event. However, for reasons of usability they should be self-evident.

- $isBookmarksEvent()$ returns true, if the value of the special event register regEventCode matches an event code that applies to the bookmarks menu. These event codes can be chosen freely by the CVM implementor and need not be specified here in more detail. In addition to the standard event codes, the CVM implementor might also add vendor-specific bookmark event codes. However, these must not interfere with the standard CVM event codes, which are listed in section 3.1.6.4 (page 49). Otherwise, $isBookmarksEvent()$ returns false.

- $isBookmarksEventFinished()$ returns true, if the value of the special event register regEventCode matches an event code that applies to the bookmarks menu, i.e., $isBookmarksEvent()$ = true, and if that event code indicates that the user wants to finish the bookmarks menu. These event codes can be chosen freely by the CVM implementor, e.g., key_pressed_enter (page 51), key_pressed_escape (page 51), etc. Otherwise, $isBookmarksEventFinished()$ returns false.

- $isBuiltinEvent()$ returns true, if the value of the special event register regEventCode matches the event code of a builtin event. Refer to section 3.1.6.3 (page 49) for more information on builtin events.

3.1. Core

- *isEscapeEvent()* returns true, if the value of the special event registers regEventCode and regEventPar<1|2|3> indicate an escape or abort by the user. For example, this is the case if the CVM has a keyboard and if the value of regEventCode is key_pressed_escape. However, if the CVM has a microphone instead, the user might as well speak something like "Stop", "Escape", or "Abort" into it. It is left to the implementors' choice which user actions cause an escape-event. However, for reasons of usability they should be self-evident.

- *isInputHostAdrAndServiceNoEvent()* returns true, if the value of the special event register regEventCode matches an event code that applies to the *input host address dialog mask*. The set of these events can be chosen freely by the CVM implementor and need not be specified here in more detail. Besides the standard events like key_pressed, other, i.e., non-standard, event codes are also possible. The non-standard event codes are also implementation dependent and need not be specified here in more detail. However, they must not interfere with the standard event codes. The standard event codes are listed in section 3.1.6.4 (page 49).

- *loadCvmPacketIntoMem()* loads the data and code of the current CVM packet (*cvmPacket*) into memory. Refer to section 3.8 (page 93) for more information on the CVM packet format. The current CVM packet might be the HomeMenu or it might have been received over the network from a CVM packet server. If the format of the CVM packet is malformed, *loadCvmPacketIntoMem()* returns false, otherwise true.

  Note that the CVM does not clear its memory before it loads a new CVM packet into memory. This enables incremental download of additional data and code and selective overwriting of specific data and code of the recently executed CVM program. For example, the user might decide during execution of a CVM program, whether optional images should be downloaded and embedded into the current CVM program to be displayed.

- *memAdr* is a variable that stores a memory address for temporary use.

- *nextState* is a variable that refers to a CVM state. The purpose of this variable is to save a default state into which the CVM might fall back in the further processing.

- *newError* is a variable that indicates whether the current error has already been processed in the state Error. If not, then it's value is true, otherwise false.

- *opcode$_{instruction}$* refers to the operation code of the currently executed instruction. Refer to the instruction reference in section 3.9.2 (page 100) for a complete list of all operation codes.

- *openBookmarksMenu()* presents the bookmarks menu on the output device of the CVM. If the CVM has a screen, it displays a GUI that contains the bookmark entries. If the CVM has no screen, but a speaker, an acoustic version of the bookmarks menu is presented. The appearance of the user interface for the bookmarks menu can be chosen freely by the CVM implementor and need not be specified here in more detail.

- *openInputHostAdrAndServiceNoUI()* presents a user interface on the output device of the CVM in which the user can input the address of a network host (*inputHostAdr*) and the number (*inputServiceNo*) of one of its provided interactive network services.

The appearance of this user interface can be chosen freely by the CVM implementor and need not be specified here in more detail. In the following, this user interface is referred to with the term *input host address dialog mask*.

- *outputErrorMessage*() outputs an error message on the output device to inform the user. Refer also to section 3.1.5.1 (page 41).

- *processDeviceSpecificBuiltinEvent*() is implementation dependent and therefore not specified here in more detail. Refer to section 3.1.6.3 (page 49) for more information on device specific builtin events.

- *readHostAdrFromMemAt* (*hostAdrMemAdr*$_{<rcv\,|\,sendrcv>}$, *cptpHostAdr*) reads a host address from CVM memory which starts at the memory address *hostAdrMemAdr* and assigns it to the variable *cptpHostAdr*. The host address might be a DNS [45] name or an IP address [62] in standard dot notation. It is not checked whether the host address is valid or not. If the memory is not accessed inside its bounds, which is given by the interval [0; cvmMemMaxAdr], the special error register regErrorCode is set to the error code value IllegalMemoryAddress (page 43). If the host address is a DNS name, but the CVM does not support automatic DNS lookup, the special error register regErrorCode is set to the error code value NoDNSLookup (page 44). Refer also to the profile item cvmDNSLookup (page 90).

- *readIntFromMemAt*(*memAdr*, *eventCode*) reads an integer (Int<cvmIntLen>) value from the memory at the address *memAdr* and assigns it to the variable *eventCode*. If the memory is not accessed inside its bounds, which is given by the interval [0; cvmMemMaxAdr], the return value is false, otherwise true.

- *readIntFromMemAt*(*memAdr* + cvmIntLen, *memAdr*) reads an integer (Int<cvmInt-Len>) value from the memory at the address *memAdr* + cvmIntLen and assigns it to the variable *memAdr*. If the memory is not accessed inside its bounds, which is given by the interval [0; cvmMemMaxAdr], the return value is false, otherwise true.

- *readIntFromMemAt*(*memAdr*, regIP) reads an integer (Int<cvmIntLen>) value from the memory at the address *memAdr* and stores it into the special register regIP. If the memory is not accessed inside its bounds, which is given by the interval [0; cvmMemMaxAdr], the return value is false, otherwise true.

- *restore*(...) writes the values back into the respective special and general registers that have been saved previously with *save*(...).

- *save*(...) saves the current execution context that is given by the parameters in (...) onto the memory stack or into an internal structure inside the CVM which is not specified here in more detail, but left to the implementors' choice.

    Note that in the state EventProcess the state *nextState* is saved instead of the current state which is given by the special state register regState. After the CVM finishes event handling in the state EventExecute and restores the saved execution context with *restore*(...), it loads the previously saved state *nextState* into regState, i.e., it resumes with the state *nextState*, which is Execute or Wait.

- <sessionId | cvmpNo | pageMemAdr | cvmPacket>$_{CVMP}$ each refer to the protocol message items sessionId, cvmpNo, pageMemAdr, and cvmPacket of the CPTP message with the protocol method CVMP. Refer to sections 4 (page 127) and 4.2 (page 129) for more information on the CPTP protocol and on the protocol method CVMP.

- *setHistoryPosition(historyEntry)* moves the current history buffer position to the previous or next history entry, if the value of the special event register regEventCode matches the event code history_back or history_forward, respectively. Next, it assigns the variable *historyEntry* the history entry that is referred to by the new current history buffer position and returns true. However, if there is no previous or next history entry, respectively, the current history buffer position is not changed and the variable *historyEntry* remains unchanged. The return value then is false. Refer also to the builtin events history_back (page 50) and history_forward (page 50) and to section 3.1.7 (page 52) for more information on the history buffer.

- *sleepOrSkip()* is implementation dependent. The following actions are possible: The CVM may wait until an event or a timer signal occurs. Or the CVM might sleep for a fixed amount of time. This time period then should be small enough to enable smooth event and timer interrupt handling. However, the CVM may as well not wait or sleep at all. Then, if *sleepOrSkip()* appears with *checkEventQueue()* in a loop, the CVM performs a kind of waiting that is generally known as "busy waiting".

- *turnOffCVM()* turns the CVM off.

- XC_top_left_arrow refers to an X11 [52] cursor font name. Refer also to section 3.3 (page 82).

- Note that a timer signal can occur in any CVM state. As already said, a timer signal sets the value of the special timer register regTimerSignal to 1. However, the CVM checks for the value of regTimerSignal only in the states EventExecute, Execute, and Wait, i.e., interval timer interrupt handling is performed only in these states. To ensure real-time conformity as much as possible, the CVM code that is executed in the state TimerExecute should not consume too much time, i.e., its execution time should not exceed the time period of the interval timer. Therefore, instructions like rcv and sendrcv should be omitted in that CVM state, because in the state CptpGET no interval timer interrupt is handled.

3.2 Visual

The CVM module Visual controls the visual output on the client device's visual drawing area of the screen. Mainly, this module covers the basic graphic operations such as drawing elementary graphic shapes, text, and pixel maps, because these tasks occur most often in graphical user interfaces. The more complicated tasks such as scrolling, affine transformations, and animations as well as the more complex drawing operations such as drawing cubic curves or handling diverse image and multimedia formats like GIF [29], JPEG [39], MPEG [47], etc. are not supported directly by this module. These tasks can be achieved either explicitly by providing appropriate procedures in the CVM program or by calling appropriate library functions. Refer to section 3.5 (page 83) for more information on the library functions.

3.2.1 Graphics State

The graphics state includes the current foreground and background colors, the text font, etc. These informations are used by the graphics primitives, i.e., the CVM drawing instructions, implicitly. As a result, they need not be provided as operands for each graphics primitive, which reduces network traffic between the CVM packet server and the client. The graphics state is stored in the following special registers:

regColorRed, regColorGreen, regColorBlue The special registers regColorRed, regColorGreen, and regColorBlue store with their Nat1 values the red, green, and blue components of the current foreground color — according to the 24-bit RGB [70] color model. The foreground color for drawing shapes and writing text onto the screen is defined by these three registers and used by all graphics primitives implicitly. The foreground color represents the drawing color. Most drawing instructions only draw with the foreground color in the foreground and leave the background untouched. The initial value of each register is zero, which corresponds to the black color. The values of these registers are modified by the instructions setred, setgreen, setblue, setcolor, and setcolor32.

Note that a given CVM implementation need not be able to display 24-bit RGB colors. How the CVM approximates these colors and whether it uses internal colormaps is left to the implementors' choice.

regBgColorRed, regBgColorGreen, regBgColorBlue The special registers regBgColorRed, regBgColorGreen, and regBgColorBlue store with their Nat1 values the red, green, and blue components of the current background color — according to the 24-bit RGB [70] color model. The background color is only used by the drawing instructions bitmapbg, textbg, textbgl, textbglm, textbgm. These instructions draw their graphic shapes with the foreground color and fill the background area of the bounding box of the respective shape with the background color, respectively. The initial value of each register is 255, which corresponds to the white color. The values of these registers are modified by the instructions setbgred, setbggreen, setbgblue, setbgcolor, and setbgcolor32.

regClipX, regClipY, regClipWidth, regClipHeight The special registers regClipX, regClipY, regClipWidth, and regClipHeight store with their integer values the xy coordinate position, width, and height of the current rectangular clip area within the screen's visual drawing area. Only the pixels inside this clip area are affected in a drawing operation. The measuring unit of the xy coordinate system is defined by the special register regMeasure. The initial values of these registers are 0, 0, cvmScreenWidth (or cvmScreenWidthMM) and cvmScreenHeight (or cvmScreenHeightMM), respectively. If the value of regMeasure is zero, cvmScreenWidth and cvmScreenHeight are used, otherwise cvmScreenWidthMM and cvmScreenHeightMM. That is, the initial clip area is the entire visual drawing area of the screen. Refer to section 3.7 (page 92) for more information on cvmScreenWidth(MM) and cvmScreenHeight(MM). The values of these registers are modified by the instruction setclip (page 112).

regFontCode The special register regFontCode stores with its Nat value the code number of the current font that is used by all text-drawing graphics primitives. The respective font

3.2. Visual

size is given by the special register regFontSize. Refer to section 3.2.3 (page 79) for a list of all font codes. The initial value of this register is fcFixedStandard. The value of this register can be modified by the instructions setfontcode, setfont, and setfont32.

regFontSize The special register regFontSize stores with its Nat value the size of the current font. The size is given in pixels, if the value of the special register regMeasure is zero, otherwise in tenths of a Point (pt). The initial value of this register is 13. The value of this register can be modified by the instructions setfontsize, setfont, and setfont32.

regLineWidth The special register regLineWidth stores with its Nat value the line width that is used by the drawing instructions for drawing the borders of the elementary graphic shapes such as lines, rectangles, circles, etc. The measuring unit of the line width is defined by the special register regMeasure. If the value of regMeasure is zero, the initial value of regLineWidth is one, which corresponds to one pixel point. Otherwise, the initial value of regLineWidth can be chosen freely by the CVM implementor. However, it should be then approximately one pt or less, with $1\,pt = 1/72\,inch \approx 0.3528\,mm$. pt refers to the *Big Point* (or shortly *Point*) and is widely used as the typographic unit in computer industry. The value of this register can be modified by the instruction setlinewidth.

regMeasure The special register regMeasure defines with its Nat2 value the measuring unit of the xy coordinate system in the visual drawing area. All Visual instructions refer to this measuring unit. If its value is zero, a pixel point of the visual drawing area serves as one unit of measure. The measuring unit is then device specific. If the value of regMeasure is greater than zero, one unit of measure is defined by the expression $pt/regMeasure$, with $pt = 1/72\,inch \approx 0.3528\,mm$. pt refers to the *Big Point* (or shortly *Point*) and is widely used as the typographic unit in computer industry. For example, if the value of regMeasure is 1000, the length of the measuring unit is $1/1000\,pt$. The measuring unit is then absolute and platform independent and the client has to perform the rasterization. Whether the client applies anti-aliasing during rasterization is left to the implementors' choice.

The coordinates of the upper left corner are $(0, 0)$. Going right or down increases the x or y coordinate, respectively.

The value of regMeasure depends on the CVM implementation and cannot be modified at all. For restricted client devices it will typically be zero. The value is sent by the client to the server within the CVM profile during a client request. Refer to section 3.7 (page 89) for more information on the CVM profile.

regHTextLine, regXTextLine The special registers regHTextLine and regXTextLine store a Nat and Int value that represents the height of a text line and the x coordinate of the beginning of a text line, respectively. These values are used by the text drawing instructions textp, textpm, textpbg, and textpmbg for drawing a text paragraph, which consists of one or several lines of text, onto the visual drawing area. The measuring unit of the xy coordinate system is defined by the special register regMeasure. The initial values of both registers are zero. The values of these register can be modified by the instructions sethtextline and setxtextline, respectively.

3.2.2 Graphics Primitives

The CVM instructions that perform drawing operations are called *graphics primitives*. However, a graphics primitive only specifies the general shape, i.e., a line, rectangle, circle, text, etc., of a graphic object, whereas the graphics state provides additional information on the appearance of the graphic object. Therefore, the operands of a graphics primitive mainly concentrate on specifying the shape of the graphic object that is to be drawn.

Note that if a graphics primitive tries to draw beyond the current clip area of the screen, the CVM only draws that part which is inside this clip area. Everything else is clipped automatically without producing an error.

Elementary Graphic Shapes Elementary graphic shapes for constructing graphical user interfaces are horizontal and vertical lines, rectangles, and circles. As already said, these shapes are essential for most graphical user interfaces. In the following, the CVM instructions for these elementary graphic shapes are introduced. Refer to section 3.9.2 (page 100) for a complete reference. The drawing of other graphic shapes like arbitrary lines, quadratic or cubic curves, etc., requires appropriate CVM library functions. Refer to section 3.5 (page 83) for more information on the CVM library functions.

Horizontal and Vertical Lines The instructions linehoriz and linevert draw horizontal and vertical lines on the screen in the current color, respectively. Horizontal lines are often needed for underlining text. In addition, both horizontal and vertical lines might be used for drawing tables and for the visual separation of the drawing area into logical parts.

Rectangles The instructions rect and rectfill draw and fill rectangles in the current color, respectively. Rectangles are often needed for buttons in user interfaces. rect and rectfill can also be used to draw single pixel points. Then, the width and height values of the rectangle must both be set to one.

Circles The instructions circle and circlefill draw and fill circles in the current color, respectively. Circles are often needed for round buttons in user interfaces and for tickmarks in enumeration lists.

Text The instructions text, textm, textp, textpm, textbg, textmbg, textpbg, and textpmbg write text on the visual drawing area in the current font and color. The instructions textp, textpm, textpbg, and textpmbg are useful for writing a whole text paragraph, i.e., several successive lines of text.

Bitmaps The instructions bitmap and bitmapbg draw bitmap images. The image data is located in memory. The format of the bitmap image complies to the X BitMap format XBM [96]. Bitmaps are often needed for icons. For the rendering of images in the XPM [38], GIF [29], JPEG [39], or other formats and of multimedia content in MPEG [47] format, etc., appropriate CVM library functions are required. Refer to section 3.5 (page 83) for more information on the CVM library functions.

3.2. Visual

Screen Buffering Sometimes a particular screen section needs to be buffered in memory and later restored again because it is obscured temporarily by another graphic shape, e.g., a moving text cursor or a pop-up window. The instruction screen2mem performs the buffering from screen into memory, whereas the instruction mem2screen restores the screen section by drawing the buffered screen section from memory onto the screen. The format of the buffered screen section in memory is internal for the given CVM implementation. However, each pixel value may take at most three bytes. This predefined upper boundary is necessary, because the CVM programmer or packet generator must reserve enough bytes for it in the Data section of the CVM memory.

3.2.3 Fonts

There are a lot of different fonts from different font providers like Adobe [3], TrueType [85], etc., available. Unfortunately, there is neither a well-defined and universally accepted taxonomy for classifying all different kinds of fonts nor a standardized unique code number for each type of font. The font capabilities of the client devices may vary and naturally a restricted client device cannot be assumed to cope with all existing fonts. As a proof of concept, the code numbers of some commonly used pixel-based fonts in X11 [51] are defined here. The definition of additional fonts and of specific fonts for devices with restricted display capabilities is left as an open issue in this thesis. Besides, CVM library functions for managing more complex fonts may be defined in the future and are left as an open issue as well.

In the following, the currently supported font codes are listed using the following description format:

font_code_name = *font_code*: *pixel_sizes*; *tenth_point_sizes*
X11_font_descriptor_name

The *font_code_name* represents the mnemonic of the *font_code* and can be used in a CVM assembler program. The *font_code* is a unique **Nat** number greater than zero identifying a particular font type. *pixel_sizes* is a comma separated list of positive integer numbers that contains the legal sizes of the respective font in pixels. *tenth_point_sizes* is a comma separated list of positive integer numbers that contains the legal sizes of the respective font in tenths of a Point (*pt*). If the special register **regFontCode** of a given CVM contains a particular *font_code* value, the special register **regFontSize** can only contain one of the respective values. Whether the font size is given in pixels or tenths of a point, depends on the value of the special register **regMeasure**. The unit is assumed to be a pixel, if the value of **regMeasure** is zero, otherwise a tenth of a Point. The *X11_font_descriptor_name* specifies the font by using the X11 terminology XLFD [50, 51].

- fcFixedStandard = 1: 13; 120
  -misc-fixed-medium-r-semicondensed--*-*-75-75-c-60-iso8859-*

- fcFixedStandardBold = 2: 13; 120
  -misc-fixed-bold-r-semicondensed--*-*-75-75-c-60-iso8859-*

- fcFixedStandardItalic = 3: 13; 120
  -misc-fixed-medium-o-semicondensed--*-*-75-75-c-60-iso8859-*

- fcFixed = 4:   6, 8, 10, 13, 15, 20;   60, 80, 100, 120, 140, 200
  -misc-fixed-medium-r-normal--*-*-75-75-c-*-iso8859-*

- fcFixedBold = 5:   13, 15;   120, 140
  -misc-fixed-bold-r-normal--*-*-75-75-c-*-iso8859-*

- fcFixedItalic = 6:   13;   120
  -misc-fixed-medium-o-normal--13-120-75-75-c-70-iso8859-*

- fcCourier = 7:   8, 10, 12, 14, 18, 24;   80, 100, 120, 140, 180, 240
  -adobe-courier-medium-r-normal--*-*-75-75-m-*-iso8859-*

- fcCourierBold = 8:   8, 10, 12, 14, 18, 24;   80, 100, 120, 140, 180, 240
  -adobe-courier-bold-r-normal--*-*-75-75-m-*-iso8859-*

- fcCourierItalic = 9:   8, 10, 12, 14, 18, 24;   80, 100, 120, 140, 180, 240
  -adobe-courier-medium-o-normal--*-*-75-75-m-*-iso8859-*

- fcCourierBoldItalic = 10:   8, 10, 12, 14, 18, 24;   80, 100, 120, 140, 180, 240
  -adobe-courier-bold-o-normal--*-*-75-75-m-*-iso8859-*

- fcHelvetica = 11:   8, 10, 12, 14, 18, 24;   80, 100, 120, 140, 180, 240
  -adobe-helvetica-medium-r-normal--*-*-75-75-p-*-iso8859-*

- fcHelveticaBold = 12:   8, 10, 12, 14, 18, 24;   8, 10, 12, 14, 24
  -adobe-helvetica-bold-r-normal--*-*-75-75-p-*-iso8859-*

- fcHelveticaItalic = 13:   8, 10, 12, 14, 18, 24
  -adobe-helvetica-medium-o-normal--*-*-75-75-p-*-iso8859-*

- fcHelveticaBoldItalic = 14:   8, 10, 12, 14, 18, 24
  -adobe-helvetica-bold-o-normal--*-*-75-75-p-*-iso8859-*

- fcNewCenturySchoolbook = 15:   8, 10, 12, 14, 18, 24;   80, 100, 120, 140, 180, 240
  -adobe-new century schoolbook-medium-r-normal--*-*-75-75-p-*-iso8859-*

- fcNewCenturySchoolbookBold = 16:
  8, 10, 12, 14, 18, 24;   80, 100, 120, 140, 180, 240
  -adobe-new century schoolbook-bold-r-normal--*-*-75-75-p-*-iso8859-*

- fcNewCenturySchoolbookItalic = 17:
  8, 10, 12, 14, 18, 24;   80, 100, 120, 140, 180, 240
  -adobe-new century schoolbook-medium-i-normal--*-*-75-75-p-*-iso8859-*

- fcNewCenturySchoolbookBoldItalic = 18:
  8, 10, 12, 14, 18, 24;   80, 100, 120, 140, 180, 240
  -adobe-new century schoolbook-bold-i-normal--*-*-75-75-p-*-iso8859-*

- fcTimes = 19:   8, 10, 12, 14, 18, 24;   80, 100, 120, 140, 180, 240
  -adobe-times-medium-r-normal--*-*-75-75-p-*-iso8859-*

- fcTimesBold = 20:   8, 10, 12, 14, 18, 24;   80, 100, 120, 140, 180, 240
  -adobe-times-bold-r-normal--*-*-75-75-p-*-iso8859-*

- fcTimesItalic = 21:   8, 10, 12, 14, 18, 24;   80, 100, 120, 140, 180, 240
  `-adobe-times-medium-i-normal--*-*-75-75-p-*-iso8859-*`
- fcTimesBoldItalic = 22:   8, 10, 12, 14, 18, 24;   80, 100, 120, 140, 180, 240
  `-adobe-times-bold-i-normal--*-*-75-75-p-*-iso8859-*`
- fcSymbol = 23:   8, 10, 12, 14, 18, 24;   80, 100, 120, 140, 180, 240
  `-adobe-symbol-medium-r-normal--*-*-75-75-p-*-adobe-fontspecific`

The font code fcFixedStandard is supported by every CVM implementation, whereas all other font codes are optional. Refer also to cvmFonts in section 3.7 (page 90).

3.3 Keyboard, Mouse

The CVM modules Keyboard and Mouse are optional in a given CVM implementation.

Keyboard The keyboard may differ from device to device. Smaller devices often have less keys than customary keyboards for PCs or workstations. In addition, restricted devices often have special keys that are not available on customary keyboards, e.g., a button on the mobile phone to open the address book immediately. Unfortunately, the character codes for these special buttons have not been standardized yet. The definition of keyboard (or keypad) layouts and character sets especially suited for restricted client devices is not addressed in this thesis. Therefore, as a proof of concept, the virtual key code values of the X11 type KeySym [50, 51, 52] are used to address the individual keys of the client device's keyboard. The virtual key codes and their names are defined in the X11 system file <X11/keysymdef.h>. Of course, a given CVM implementation does not need to support all of them. As far as needed, the special keys are emulated by particular key combinations. The keyboard events are key_pressed, key_pressed_enter, key_pressed_released, key_released, key_released_enter, and key_released_escape. Refer to section 3.1.6.4 (page 51) for more information on these events.

Mouse The positive Nat numbers 1, 2, 3, 4, 5 reflect the left (leftButton), middle (middleButton), right (rightButton), wheel up (wheelUp), and wheel down (wheelDown) mouse buttons, respectively. The names enclosed within the parentheses serve as mnemonics and might be used in a CVM assembler program. Note that the wheel up and wheel down buttons are physically the same wheel button. However, the wheel up button signifies that the mouse wheel was rotated up, i.e., away from the user, whereas the wheel down button signifies that the mouse wheel was rotated down, i.e., towards the user.

The mouse events are mouse_moved, mouse_pressed, mouse_pressed_left, mouse_released, and mouse_released_left. Refer to section 3.1.6.4 (page 52) for more information on these events.

In an application, the mouse may have different graphic shapes on the screen, depending on its position. For example, if the mouse points into a text box, it often looks like a vertical line to symbolize a cursor. However, if it points at a hyperlink, it often looks like a pointing hand. Here, as a proof of concept, the X11 [52] cursor fonts are used for the different mouse shapes. The names and integer code numbers of the X11 cursor fonts are defined in the X11 system file <X11/cursorfont.h>. The X11 cursor font names can be used in the CVM assembler programs. Refer to section B (page 216) for a description of the CVM assembler.

Note that the screen section that is obscured by the mouse shape at its current screen position is restored automatically by the CVM, when the mouse moves to another screen position.

regMouseFont The special register regMouseFont stores with its Nat value the code number of the current mouse font (or shape). The initial value of this register is 132, which corresponds to the X11 cursor font name XC_top_left_arrow. The value of this register can be modified by the instruction setmousefont.

3.4 Network

For the data transmission over the network a reliable network transport service, like TCP/IP [69] in the Internet, is assumed. How such a transport service is established in mobile, wireless and ad-hoc [61] networks is not addressed in this thesis. Generally, the CVM communicates over the network with a CVM packet server. The used application protocol is CPTP. It runs on top of the transport layer and is a very "thin" counterpart to the HTTP [10] application protocol in the World Wide Web. Refer to section 4 (page 127) for more information on CPTP.

The instruction rcv initiates a request for a particular CVMUI page. Then, the addressed CVM packet server sends a CVM packet that contains the requested CVMUI page to the CVM. The instruction sendrcv is similar to the instruction rcv. However, it first sends data to the specified CVM packet server before it requests a particular CVMUI page from that CVM packet server.

Refer also to the CVM state transitions in section 3.1.10 (page 58), especially to states EventExecute, EventProcessBuiltin, Execute, CptpGET, and TimerExecute.

Note that if the CVM has not implemented the Network module, it can only execute its Home Menu. In particular cases this may be sufficient, for example for home devices with only "local" tasks such as washing machines. However, in the normal case, the Network module is available for a given CVM implementation.

regSessionId The special register regSessionId contains a Nat1[4] value that identifies the current client-server session with a particular CVM packet server. Each time, when the CVM receives a CPTP message from a CVM packet server, it stores the value of the CPTP message item sessionId into its special register regSessionId. Each time, when the CVM sends a CPTP message to a CVM packet server, it writes the current value of regSessionId into this message item. Refer to section 4.1 (page 128) for more information on the CPTP protocol and on sessionId.

The value of this register is modified by the instruction sidzero and by any received CPTP message from a CVM packet server. Otherwise, its value is modified internally by the CVM. Refer to the CVM state transitions in section 3.1.10 (page 58), especially to the states EventExecute, EventProcessBuiltin, Execute, CptpGET, and TimerExecute. The initial value of this register is zero. The value zero indicates that currently no session with any CVM packet server is running.

regServiceNo The special register regServiceNo contains an integer value that refers to the service number of the most recently requested and possibly currently still ongoing interactive network service which is offered by a particular CVM packet server. The value of this special register is used each time the CVM sends a GET message to the CVM packet server. If the CVM packet server has "forgotten" the client during a client-server session, it can still resume that session from the informations provided by the GET message. This may happen, if the CVM sends a GET message to the CVM packet server after a long time of idleness, so that the CVM packet server has in the meantime assumed that this session is not alive anymore and therefore has deleted this client from its maintenance table.

Under certain conditions, the value of this register is modified by the instruction rcv. Otherwise, its value is modified internally by the CVM. Refer to the CVM state transitions in section 3.1.10 (page 58), especially to the states EventExecute, EventProcessBuiltin, Execute, and TimerExecute. The initial value of this register is zero.

3.5 Libraries

The CVM instruction set covers only the most essential operations that are needed for a client device to display user interfaces. In addition, CVM libraries might be provided for more complex tasks that occur frequently. For example, a math library might enable additional mathematical operations and even floating point arithmetics. A POSIX thread [18] library might be used for concurrent tasks. A graphics library might provide additional drawing operations such as drawing arbitrary lines, quadratic or cubic curves, etc. A GUI library that is intended for more powerful client devices might provide whole user interface components such as buttons, selection lists, etc. Then, these user interface components need not be programmed manually with the simple CVM instructions.

For some operations, however, it is difficult to determine clearly whether they should be specified as CVM instructions or library functions. For example, the CVM instructions bitmap and bitmapbg might as well be specified as library functions, instead. Or the library function line might be specified as an CVM instruction, instead.

It is left to the implementors' choice which libraries are supported and how they are implemented in a given CVM.

A library contains a set of library functions. Each library is identified by a unique integer number, called the libCode, and each library function is as well identified by a unique integer number, called the libFctCode. Note that two different library functions must always have different libFctCodes, even if they belong to different libraries. However, libCodes and libFctCodes need not be different. The libCode is used in the CVM profile by the profile item cvmLibraries. If a given CVM implementation supports a particular library, it must implement all its library functions. For reasons of flexibility, a CVM library might be provided through an interchangeable plug-in card.

The CVM instruction lib calls the library function whose libFctCode resides on the register stack. The definition of CVM libraries is left as an open issue in this thesis. Here, as a proof of concept, only the libraries that have been needed so far are defined and described. Of course, these libraries should be considered more prototypical than final. In the future, additional libraries for file operations, e.g., managing cookies files, etc., may be defined.

In the following, these libraries are defined using the following description format:

library_name = libCode:
verbose_description_overview

- *library_function_name* = libFctCode:
  register_stack_behavior
  verbose_description_of_semantics

- ...

Refer to section 3.9.2 (page 100) for *register_stack_behavior*. The rest of this description format should be self-explanatory.

CoreMisc = 1
The CoreMisc library contains utility routines for the Core module.

- getDate = 1:
  ... $\rightarrow$ ..., $year_{Nat}$, $month_{Nat}$, day_{Nat}
  Get the current date, with $year \geq 1900$, $1 \leq month \leq 12$, and $1 \leq day \leq 31$.

- setDate = 2:
  ..., $year_{Nat}$, $month_{Nat}$, day_{Nat} $\rightarrow$ ...
  Set the current date. However, if the specified *year*, *month*, and *day* are not inside the legal bounds, do nothing.

- getTime = 3:
  ... $\rightarrow$ ..., $hour_{Nat}$, $minute_{Nat}$, $second_{Nat}$
  Get the current time, with $0 \leq hour \leq 23$, $0 \leq minute \leq 59$, and $0 \leq second \leq 59$.

- setTime = 4:
  ..., $hour_{Nat}$, $minute_{Nat}$, $second_{Nat}$ $\rightarrow$ ...
  Set the current time. However, if the specified *hour*, *minute*, and *second* are not inside the legal bounds, do nothing.

VisualMisc = 2
The VisualMisc library contains utility routines for drawing graphical shapes or displaying data, e.g., numbers, on the visual drawing area of the screen.

- line = 5:
  x_{Int}, y_{Int}, dx_{Int}, dy_{Int} $\rightarrow \varepsilon$
  Draw line from start point (x, y) to end point $(x + dx, y + dy)$. Note, for drawing horizontal or vertical lines use the CVM instructions linehoriz (page 105) or linevert (page 105) instead.

- printInt = 6:
  num_{Int}, x_{Int}, y_{Int} $\rightarrow \varepsilon$
  Write the integer number *num* onto the visual drawing area at the xy coordinate position (x, y) with the current foreground color.

3.5. Libraries

- printIntBg = 7:

  $num_{\mathsf{Int}}, x_{\mathsf{Int}}, y_{\mathsf{Int}} \to \varepsilon$

  Write the integer number num onto the visual drawing area at the xy coordinate position (x, y) with the current foreground color. At the same time, fill the rest of the bounding rectangle with the current background color.

- printKeyName = 8:

  $keyCode_{\mathsf{Int}}, x_{\mathsf{Int}}, y_{\mathsf{Int}} \to \varepsilon$

  Write the key name of the key with the X11 [51] key code $keyCode$ onto the visual drawing area at the xy coordinate position (x, y). The mapping of the key code to its key name corresponds to the mapping method of the Xlib [52] function XKeysymToString().

- rectRound, rectRoundFill = 9, 10:

  $x_{\mathsf{Int}}, y_{\mathsf{Int}}, width_{\mathsf{Nat}}, height_{\mathsf{Nat}}, ewidth_{\mathsf{Nat}}, eheight_{\mathsf{Nat}} \to \varepsilon$

  If $width > 0$ and $height > 0$, draw or fill rectangle with rounded corners. Otherwise, do nothing. The upper-left and the lower-right corners of the rectangle are at the xy coordinate positions (x, y) and $(x + width - 1, y + height - 1)$, respectively. The width and height of the rectangle are given by $width$ and $height$. $ewidth$ and $eheight$ are the width and height of the bounding box that the rounded corners are drawn inside of. However, if $ewidth$ or $eheight$ are zero or more than half of $width$ or $height$, respectively, no rounded corners are drawn. These library functions correspond to the Xmu Library [52] functions XmuDrawRoundedRectangle() and XmuFillRoundedRectangle().

- triangle, trianglefill = 11, 12:

  $x_{\mathsf{Int}}, y_{\mathsf{Int}}, dx1_{\mathsf{Int}}, dy1_{\mathsf{Int}}, dx2_{\mathsf{Int}}, dy2_{\mathsf{Int}} \to \varepsilon$

  Draw, fill triangle with the corners (x, y), $(x + dx1, y + dy1)$, and $(x + dx2, y + dy2)$.

VisualImage = 3

The VisualImage library contains utility routines for rendering and displaying images in various formats on the visual drawing area of the screen. So far, only the X PixMap format XPM [38] is supported.

- pixmap = 13:

  $x_{\mathsf{Int}}, y_{\mathsf{Int}}, width_{\mathsf{Nat}}, height_{\mathsf{Nat}}, memAdrAbs_{\mathsf{Nat}} \to \varepsilon$

  Draw pixmap image. The image data is located in memory and starts at the address $memAdrAbs$. The rectangular area of the screen given by the corners (x, y) and $(x + width - 1, y + height - 1)$ is tiled with the pixmap image. The image data is an ASCII character string that represents an exact copy of an X PixMap (XPM) [38] file in memory. Note that the terminating null character is not mandatory. Pixmaps are useful for small icons and background patterns. Refer also to the error code ImageLoadFailure (page 43).

- pixmapgz = 14:

  $x_{\mathsf{Int}}, y_{\mathsf{Int}}, width_{\mathsf{Nat}}, height_{\mathsf{Nat}}, memAdrAbs_{\mathsf{Nat}} \to \varepsilon$

  Same functionality as pixmap. However, the image data is additionally compressed with gzip [35].

- png = 15:
  x_{Int}, y_{Int}, $width_{\mathsf{Nat}}$, $height_{\mathsf{Nat}}$, $memAdrAbs_{\mathsf{Nat}} \to \varepsilon$
  Draw PNG image. The image data is located in memory and starts at the address $memAdrAbs$. The rectangular area of the screen given by the corners (x, y) and $(x + width - 1, y + height - 1)$ is tiled with the image. The format of the image data complies to the Portable Network Graphics (PNG) [1] image format. Refer also to the error code ImageLoadFailure (page 43).

3.6 Home Menu

The home menu (HomeMenu) is the default menu system of the CVM. The CVM starts execution with the home menu as soon as it is switched on. Therefore, the home menu is an essential part of the CVM and is not requested over the network from a CVM packet server. Its format complies with the CVM packet format. Refer to section 3.8 (page 93) for more information on the CVM packet format.

Note that the contents and complexity of the home menu is implementation dependent and can be chosen freely by the vendor. For example, home menus might be provided that are similar to the menu systems of the mobile and embedded devices in the common market nowadays. To gain more flexibility, the home menu need not be fixed but can be realized through an interchangeable card or it might be obtained from the vendor by software download, which is quite useful for installing updates.

In the following, a very simple home menu is presented as a CVM assembler program. Refer to section B (page 216) for a description of the CVM assembler. Figures 3.6 (page 86) and 3.7 (page 87) contain exemplary screen shots.

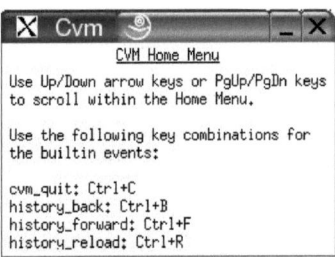

Figure 3.6: **CVM Screen Shot 1:** homeMenu.cvm

```
.16Bit                              // Misc
// or .16BitEmu, .32Bit, .32BitEmu  ///////

.code                               .const
  loadcr page_main                    _cvmScreenWidth   250
  jmp                                 _cvmScreenHeight  150

///////                              ///////
```

3.6. Home Menu

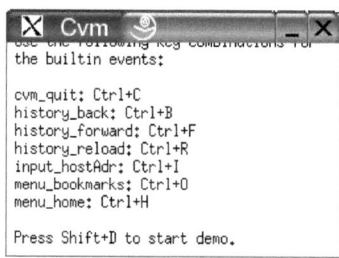

Figure 3.7: **CVM Screen Shot 2:** homeMenu.cvm

```
// Page
///////
.const
page_x    5

.data
Int  page_y   0

.const
page_dy    6
page_w     MAX (caption_w, par_w)
page_h     caption_h + par_h

// Foreground Color
page_fgr    0    // Red
page_fgg    0    // Green
page_fgb    0    // Blue

// Background Color
page_bgr    255    // Red
page_bgg    255    // Green
page_bgb    255    // Blue

// Font
page_fc    fcFixedStandard   // Font Code
page_fs    13   // Font Size
page_fh    fontHeight (page_fc, page_fs)

.code
page_main:
  loadc page_fc  loadc page_fs  setfont
  loadc page_x   setxtextline
  fcall page_draw
  loadc page_et  seteventtableadr
  enableevents
  halt
.code
.fct page_draw ()
{
  Int yCaption
  Int yPar
  loadc page_bgr  loadc page_bgg
    loadc page_bgb  setcolor
  loadc 0   loadc 0
    loadc _cvmScreenWidth
    loadc _cvmScreenHeight
    rectfill
  loadc page_fgr  loadc page_fgg
    loadc page_fgb  setcolor
  load page_y   loadc caption_fh  add
    store yCaption
  loadc caption_x   load yCaption
    text caption_str
  loadc caption_x   load yCaption  inc
    loadc caption_w   linehoriz
  load yCaption   loadc caption_h   add
    store yPar
  load yPar   textp par_str
  return
}

.fct page_mv (Int dy)
{
  load dy  loadc 0  loadcr page_mv_dn
    jl
page_mv_up:
  loadc 0   load page_y  loadcr page_mv_
    je
  loadcr page_mv_1   jmp
page_mv_dn:
  load page_y
```

```
    loadc 2*caption_fd + page_h  add       loadep1  loadc XK_D
    loadc _cvmScreenHeight                   loadcr page_page_kp_  jne
      loadcr page_mv_  je                  loadc cvmps_hostAdr
page_mv_1:                                 loadc cvmps_serviceNo
  load page_y  load dy  add                loadc 0  rcv
  rdup  loadc 0  loadcr page_mv_2  jl      halt
  rskip loadc 0  loadcr page_mv_3  jmp   page_page_kp_:
page_mv_2:                                 halt
  rdup  loadc _cvmScreenHeight -
          page_h - 2*caption_fd          //////////
    rswap loadcr page_mv_3  jle          // Caption
    rskip loadc _cvmScreenHeight -       //////////
          page_h - 2*caption_fd
page_mv_3:                               .const
    store page_y                         caption_str  "CVM Home Menu"
    fcall page_draw                      caption_x    page_x + (par_w - caption_w)
page_mv_:                                                   / 2
  return                                 caption_w    textWidth (caption_str,
}                                                            page_fc, page_fs)
                                         caption_h    textHeight (caption_str,
.data                                                        page_fc, page_fs, 0) + 6
EventTable  page_et   [                  caption_fh   fontHeight (page_fc,
  key_pressed, page_kp                                        page_fs)
]                                        caption_fd   fontDescent (page_fc,
                                                              page_fs)
.code
page_kp:                                 ////////////
page_kp_down:                            // Paragraph
  loadep1  loadc XK_Down                 ////////////
    loadcr page_kp_up  jne
  loadc page_dy  neg  push               par_str   textBreakLines (
    fcall page_mv                          "Use Up/Down arrow keys or "
  halt                                   + "PgUp/PgDn keys to scroll within "
page_kp_up:                              + "the Home Menu.\n\n"
  loadep1  loadc XK_Up                   + "Use the following key "
    loadcr page_kp_pgDn  jne             + "combinations for the builtin "
  loadc page_dy  push  fcall page_mv     + "events:\n\n"
  halt                                   + "cvm_quit: Ctrl+C\n"
page_kp_pgDn:                            + "history_back: Ctrl+B\n"
  loadep1  loadc XK_Next                 + "history_forward: Ctrl+F\n"
    loadcr page_kp_pgUp  jne             + "history_reload: Ctrl+R\n"
  loadc _cvmScreenHeight  neg  push      + "input_hostAdr: Ctrl+I\n"
    fcall page_mv                        + "menu_bookmarks: Ctrl+O\n"
  halt                                   + "menu_home: Ctrl+H\n\n"
page_kp_pgUp:                            + "Press Shift+D "
  loadep1  loadc XK_Prior                + "to start demo.",
    loadcr page_kp_shiftD  jne             page_fc, page_fs,
  loadc _cvmScreenHeight  push             _cvmScreenWidth - 2 * page_x)
    fcall page_mv                        par_w    textWidth (par_str, page_fc,
  halt                                                      page_fs)
page_kp_shiftD:                          par_h    textHeight (par_str, page_fc,
```

```
                page_fs, 0)         .data
/////////////////////               String  cvmps_hostAdr   "127.0.0.1"
// CVM Packet Server
/////////////////////               .const
                                    cvmps_serviceNo  1
```

Examples of home menus can be found in the subdirectory Implementation/Cvm/Home-Menu/.

3.7 CVM Profile

At the beginning of a request, the CVM sends its CVM profile to the CVM packet server to report its capabilities and user preferences. The CVM packet generator then uses these informations to generate the client-specific CVM packets. The format of the CVM profile is presented here as a tuple data structure by using the generally understandable notation from section A.3 (page 208). Successive components within a tuple or array structure are stored in the CVM profile sequentially, without padding or alignment. Multibyte values are stored in big-endian order. Refer to section 3.1.1 (page 32) for more information on the CVM data types Nat<1|...|4>. The array type Nat1[] is used for byte streams of any data. The format of the CVM profile is as follows:

CVMProfile = { Nat1 cvmMode;
                    Nat4 profileId;
                    ProfileItem[] *profileItems*;
                    Nat1 0 }

ProfileItem = { Nat1 profileItemCode;
                    Nat1[] *profileItemValue* }

cvmMode This item reports to the server the mode of the CVM implementation on the client device. Refer to section 3.1.2 (page 33) for more information on CVM modes. There are the following values for cvmMode: 16Bit = 0, 16BitEmu = 1, 32Bit = 2, and 32BitEmu = 3. On a 16-bit CVM, cvmMode must be 16Bit or 16BitEmu. On a 32-bit CVM, cvmMode must be 32Bit or 32BitEmu.

The emulation modes 16BitEmu and 32BitEmu indicate that the CVM is implemented efficiently in software, i.e., some properties in the data and code block of the CVM program are evaluated only once at the beginning of execution and then reused all the time during execution. Therefore, the received CVM packet must meet some restrictions to be executed correctly. These restrictions are listed in section 3.8 (page 98).

profileId The profiles of the common client devices on the market might be stored by the CVM packet server or any other server. Then, each of these profiles might be referenced by a unique integer number (profileId) and a client device with a well-known profile has to transmit only its profile identification number to the CVM packet server. In addition, subsequent profile items (*profileItems*) in the CVM profile are optional and only to change the values of that profile items which differ from those in the referenced profile.

However, if `profileId` has the value zero, no profile is referenced and all the characteristics of the client device are listed in the subsequent list (or array) of profile items.

The definition of profiles and `profileIds` for common client devices on the market is left as an open issue in this thesis.

profileItems   *profileItems* is a possibly empty list of profile items (*ProfileItem*). The order of the profile items is not important. Each profile item consists of a profile item code (`profileItemCode`) that identifies a particular component of the CVM, and of its value (*profileItemValue*). Each profile item code is greater than zero. In the following, the currently supported profile items are listed alphabetically and described using the following description format:

profile_item_name   = `profileItemCode`:   *profileItemValue*
verbose_description

The *profile_item_name* is the verbose name of the `profileItemCode`. *profileItemValue* is shown as a data structure. Again, subsequent items within a tuple structure are stored without padding or alignment.

Additional profile items, for example for the Audio module, as it is not covered in this thesis, may be defined in the future. In addition, new profile items especially for reporting user preferences may be defined in the future as well. For example, the user of the client device might wish to enable or disable explicitly the reception of images, sound files, or other multimedia content to save network bandwidth and thus speed up download time.

cvmAudioAvailable   = 1:   -
This profile item reports to the CVM packet server, whether the CVM module Audio is implemented on the CVM. If this profile item is not specified, no Audio module is available. Otherwise, it is available. This profile item does not have a *profileItemValue*. The specification of the Audio module is not covered in this thesis but left for future work. Therefore, if new profile items for the description of the Audio module are defined later, this profile item must not be needed anymore in this specification, because the presence of these Audio related profile items already indicates, whether there is an Audio module available or not.

cvmDNSLookup   = 2:   -
This profile item reports to the CVM packet server, whether the CVM can perform automatic DNS [45] lookup. If this profile item is specified, the CVM can perform automatic DNS lookup. Otherwise, it cannot. If the CVM supports automatic DNS lookup, the instructions `rcv`, `send`, and `sendrcv` can each use DNS names to address a network host — besides IP [62] addresses in standard dot notation. This profile item does not have a *profileItemValue*.

cvmFonts   = 3:   { Nat2 maxFontCode } | { Nat2 0; Nat2[] fontCodes; Nat2 0 }
This profile item reports to the CVM packet server the fonts that are supported by the CVM. `maxFontCode` represents the maximal font code that is supported by the CVM, i.e., the CVM supports all fonts with font codes less or equal than `maxFontCode`. If

3.7. CVM Profile

maxFontCode is zero, then each supported font code is listed in the following zero terminated byte array fontCodes. Each font code is greater than zero. If this profile item is not specified, the maximal supported font code is fcSymbol. This profile item must not be specified, if the CVM has no Visual module. Refer also to section 3.2.3 (page 79) for more information on CVM fonts.

cvmHeapAvailable = 4: -
This profile item reports to the CVM packet server, whether the CVM has a Heap section. If this profile item is not specified, no Heap section is available. Otherwise, it is available. This profile item does not have a *profileItemValue*. Refer to section 3.1.4.3 (page 41) for more information on the Heap section.

cvmKeyCodeSet = 5: { Nat2 keyCodeSetId }
This profile item reports to the CVM packet server the key codes that are supported by the keyboard of the CVM. Therefore, standardized key code sets with unique identification numbers (keyCodeSetId) especially for restricted client devices are required. However, if keyCodeSetId has the value zero, all the characters (or key codes) of a customary keyboard are supported by the CVM. If this profile item is not specified, no keyboard is available on the CVM. Refer also to section 3.3 (page 81) for more information on the CVM module Keyboard.

cvmLibraries = 6: { Nat1 byteLen; Nat<byteLen>[] libCode; Nat<byteLen> 0 }
This profile item reports to the CVM packet server the libraries that are supported by the CVM. byteLen must be in the range of 1 to 4. The following zero terminated array of numbers with the byte length byteLen contains the libCodes of the supported libraries. Each libCode is greater than zero. If this profile item is not specified in the profile, then no libraries are supported by the CVM. Refer also to section 3.5 (page 83) for more information on CVM libraries.

cvmMeasure = 7: { Nat2 regMeasure }
This profile item reports to the CVM packet server the measuring unit of the visual drawing area of the CVM. regMeasure equals the value of the special register regMeasure. If this profile item is not specified, the default value zero is assumed. If a given CVM implementation has no Visual module, then this profile item must not be specified. Refer also to section 3.2.1 (page 77) for more information on the special register regMeasure.

cvmMemMaxAdr = 8: { Nat<cvmIntLen> cvmMemMaxAdr }
This profile item reports to the CVM packet server the size of the CVM memory. cvmMemMaxAdr refers to the highest memory address of the given CVM implementation. If this profile item is not specified, the memory of the CVM is "unlimited". This is the case, if the CVM runs as an emulation on a general purpose computer with sufficient system resources. Refer also to the sections 3.1.2 (page 33) and 3.1.4 (page 36) for more information on the CVM modes and the CVM memory, respectively.

cvmMouseButtons = 9:   { Nat1 numButtons }
This profile item reports to the CVM packet server the number of mouse buttons of the CVM, i.e., the CVM module Mouse has the mouse buttons with the numbers from 1 to numButtons, with $1 \leq$ numButtons ≤ 5. If the CVM has implemented the CVM module Mouse, this profile item must be specified. Otherwise, not. Refer to section 3.3 (page 81) for more information on the Mouse module.

cvmNumGeneralRegs = 10:   { Nat1 cvmNumGeneralRegs }
This profile item reports to the CVM packet server the number of general purpose registers in the register stack of the CVM. If this profile item is not specified, the default value 10 is assumed. However, the value zero indicates that an "unlimited" number of general purpose registers are available. This is the case, if the CVM runs as an emulation on a general purpose computer with sufficient system resources such as a PC or workstation. Refer also to section 3.1.3 (page 34) for more information on the register stack.

cvmOutputCharSet = 11:   { Nat1[] charBlockNames; Nat1 0 }
This profile item reports to the CVM packet server the Unicode [88] character blocks that are supported by the CVM's output device(s) to display. `charBlockNames` consists only of printable ASCII characters from the US-ASCII charset and contains a comma separated list of Unicode character block names. For example, the value of `charBlockNames` might be "`Basic Latin,Latin-1 Supplement,Miscellaneous Symbols,Supplemental Mathematical Operators`". However, if this profile item is not specified, then the default Unicode character blocks "`Basic Latin,Latin-1 Supplement`" are assumed.

cvmUPLanguage = 12:   { Nat2 num }
This profile item reports to the CVM packet server the preferred language of the textual content that is presented on the CVM. *num* is a unique number greater than zero identifying a particular natural language. The definition of unique numbers for all kinds of existing languages is left as an open issue in this thesis. Here, as a proof of concept, the numbers 1 and 2 are defined for the languages English-US and German, respectively. Note that this user preference is just a *hint* but not a *must* for the CVM packet server. It can still send the textual content in another language. If this profile item is not specified, then the CVM packet server can choose the language.

cvmScreenHeight = 13:   { Nat2 num }
This profile item reports to the CVM packet server the height of the client device's visual drawing area in pixels. If the CVM has a screen and the module Visual is implemented, this profile item must always be specified; there is no default value for it. If this profile item is not specified, then the CVM has no Visual module.

cvmScreenHeightMM = 14:   { Nat2 num }
This profile item reports to the CVM packet server the height of the client device's visual drawing area in tenths of a millimeter. If the CVM has the module Visual implemented and if the value of the special register `regMeasure` is not zero, this profile item must always be specified; there is no default value for it.

cvmScreenWidth = 15: { Nat2 num }
This profile item reports to the CVM packet server the width of the client device's visual drawing area in pixels. If the CVM has a screen and the module Visual is implemented, this profile item must always be specified; there is no default value for it. If this profile item is not specified, then the CVM has no Visual module.

cvmScreenWidthMM = 16: { Nat2 num }
This profile item reports to the CVM packet server the width of the client device's visual drawing area in tenths of a millimeter. If the CVM has implemented the module Visual and if the value of the special register regMeasure is not zero, this profile item must always be specified; there is no default value for it.

cvmTimerAvailable = 17: -
This profile item reports to the CVM packet server, whether the CVM has an interval timer. If this profile item is not specified, no interval timer is available. Otherwise, it is available. This profile item does not have a *profileItemValue*. Refer to section 3.1.9 (page 57) for more information on the interval timer.

Comments The profile items can also be grouped according to the CVM module they belong to, respectively. Profile items that refer to the user preferences are listed at the end.

- Core: cvmHeapAvailable, cvmMemMaxAdr, cvmNumGeneralRegs, cvmTimerAvailable

- Visual: cvmFonts, cvmMeasure, cvmOutputCharSet, cvmScreenWidth, cvmScreenWidthMM, cvmScreenHeight, cvmScreenHeightMM

- Audio: cvmAudioAvailable, cvmOutputCharSet

- Keyboard: cvmKeyCodeSet

- Mouse: cvmMouseButtons

- Network: cvmDNSLookup

- Libraries: cvmLibraries

- User Preferences: cvmUPLanguage

3.8 CVM Packet

A CVM packet is transmitted from the CVM packet server to the client and represents the binary executable for the CVM. The term CVM program, however, is used to refer to the data and code of the CVM packet after it has been loaded into memory by the CVM. A CVM packet is a stream of 8-bit bytes. Its format is presented here as a tuple data structure by using the generally understandable notation from section A.3 (page 208). Successive components within a tuple or array structure are stored in the CVM packet sequentially, without padding or alignment. Multibyte values are stored in big-endian order. Refer to section 3.1.1 (page 32) for more information on the CVM data types Int<1|...|4> and Nat<1|...|4>. The array type Nat1[] is used for byte streams of any data. The general CVM packet format is as follows:

```
CVMPacket   = { Nat4  magic;
                Nat1  attributes;
                Nat<cvmpAdrLen>  dataDeclSegmentAdr,
                                 codeSegmentAdr,
                                 stackSegmentAdr,
                                 lenDataDecl,
                                 lenInstructions;
                Declaration[]  data;
                Instruction[]  instructions }

Declaration = { Nat1  declCode;
                Nat1[]  dataBytes }

Instruction = { Nat1  opcode;
                Nat1[]  immOperands }
```

magic The value of the `magic` item identifies the format of the byte stream and must be 0x63766D70, which corresponds to the ASCII sequence 'CVMP'.

attributes This packet item contains the operation mode of the CVM, for which this CVM packet is destined to, and the byte length of the memory addresses that are hardcoded in the CVM packet. Hardcoded memory addresses are the next three following packet items and the memory addresses in the event table structure. Refer to the data declaration code `eventtable` in section 3.8 (page 96) for more information on the event table structure in the CVM packet. The operation mode is referred to with the term `cvmMode`, the byte length of the hardcoded memory addresses is referred to with the term `cvmpAdrLen`. `cvmMode` must be equal to the CVM profile item `cvmMode` which has been sent by the CVM previously to the CVM packet server during the client request. The values of `cvmMode` and `cvmpAdrLen` are extracted from `attributes` as follows:

`cvmMode = attributes & 0x03`. So far, `cvmMode` may only have the value 0, 1, 2, or 3, which corresponds to the CVM mode 16Bit, 16BitEmu, 32Bit, or 32BitEmu, respectively. As already said in section 3.1.2 (page 33), the value of `cvmIntLen` is 2, if `cvmMode` is 16Bit or 16BitEmu, and 4, if `cvmMode` is 32Bit or 32BitEmu.

`cvmpAdrLen = ((attributes >> 4) & 0x03) + 1`. If the value of `cvmMode` is 16Bit or 16BitEmu, then `cvmpAdrLen` may only have the value 1 or 2. If the value of `cvmMode` is 32Bit or 32BitEmu, then `cvmpAdrLen` may only have the value 1, 2, 3, or 4. To save packet size and thus network bandwidth, `cvmpAdrLen` is set by the CVM packet generator to the minimum number of bytes that is required by the largest hardcoded memory address which appears in this CVM packet.

dataDeclSegmentAdr This packet item contains the starting memory address of the data that is declared in this packet. The declared data is listed in the *data* section of the CVM

3.8. CVM Packet

packet and copied into CVM memory beginning at the address `dataDeclSegmentAdr`. The Declared Data section extends to the beginning of the Code section which starts at the memory address `codeSegmentAdr`. Refer to section 3.1.4.1 (page 37) for more information on the Data section. The byte length of this packet item depends on the value of `cvmpAdrLen`.

Depending on the CVM mode, the first byte of the declared data in CVM memory is aligned on a 2- or 4-byte boundary. That is, on a 16-bit CVM, `dataDeclSegmentAdr` is a multiple of 2, and on a 32-bit CVM, `dataDeclSegmentAdr` is a multiple of 4.

If the CVM mode is not an emulation mode, i.e., if the CVM mode is not `16BitEmu` or `32BitEmu`, then only data with essential initial values are declared in the CVM packet. The event table data items are declared by the declaration code `eventtable`. All other data items are grouped together and declared by using one of the appropriate declaration codes `bytesz<1|...|4>` and `bytes<1|...|4>`, respectively, to save packet size and thus network bandwidth.

If the CVM mode is an emulation mode, then every single data item is declared separately with at least the "dummy" initial value zero.

`dataDeclSegmentAdr` must be an unsigned integer number less than or equal to `cvmMemMaxAdr`.

`codeSegmentAdr` This packet item contains the starting memory address of the Code section in CVM memory. The transmitted CVM instructions inside the *instructions* array are copied into this memory section starting at the address `codeSegmentAdr`. The Code section extends to the beginning of the Stack section. Refer to section 3.1.4.1 (page 37) for more information on the Code section.

After loading the CVM packet into CVM memory, the CVM starts execution with the instruction at the memory address `codeSegmentAdr`. However, if the CVM packet has been received from a CVM packet server within a CPTP message using the protocol method `CVMP`, the CVM starts execution at the memory address that is given by the protocol message item `pageMemAdr`. Refer to sections 4 (page 127) and 4.2 (page 129) for more information on the CPTP protocol and on the protocol method `CVMP`.

Depending on the CVM mode, the first byte of the code array in CVM memory is aligned on a 2- or 4-byte boundary. That is, on a 16-bit CVM, `codeSegmentAdr` is a multiple of 2, and on a 32-bit CVM, `codeSegmentAdr` is a multiple of 4.

`codeSegmentAdr` must be an unsigned integer number greater than or equal to `dataDeclSegmentAdr + lenDataDecl`, but less than or equal to `stackSegmentAdr`.

`stackSegmentAdr` This packet item contains the starting memory address of the Stack section in CVM memory. The Stack section extends to the end of the CVM memory. Refer to section 3.1.4.2 (page 38) for more information on the Stack section.

Depending on the CVM mode, the first byte of the Stack section in CVM memory is aligned on a 2- or 4-byte boundary. That is, on a 16-bit CVM, `stackSegmentAdr` is a multiple of 2, and on a 32-bit CVM, `stackSegmentAdr` is a multiple of 4.

`stackSegmentAdr` must be an unsigned integer number greater than or equal to `codeSegmentAdr + lenInstructions`, but less than or equal to `cvmMemMaxAdr`.

lenDataDecl This packet item contains the total byte length of all data declarations within the *data* section of the CVM packet. **lenDataDecl** must be an unsigned integer number less than or equal to **cvmMemMaxAdr**.

lenInstructions This packet item contains the total byte length of all instructions within the *instructions* section of the CVM packet. **lenInstructions** must be an unsigned integer number less than or equal to **cvmMemMaxAdr**.

data *data* is a sequence (or array) of data declarations and their initial values. Each declaration consists of its declaration code (**declCode**) and the data bytes (**dataBytes**) that contain the initial value. During loading a CVM packet, the CVM copies the initial values into the Declared Data section in memory starting at the address **dataDeclSegmentAdr** in the same order as they appear in the CVM packet. Note that depending on the CVM mode, all initial values are aligned on a 2- or 4-byte boundary. That is, the CVM places the first byte of each initial value in memory at an address that is a multiple of 2 on a 16-bit CVM, or a multiple of 4 on a 32-bit CVM. In the following, the currently supported declaration codes are listed alphabetically and described using the following description format:

declaration_code_name = declCode: dataBytes
verbose_description

The *declaration_code_name* is the verbose name of the **declCode**. **dataBytes** is specified as a tuple structure. Dependent on the declaration code, however, it may also be empty.

bytes$<i>$ ($1 \leq i \leq 4$) $= 1 + i - 1$: { Nat$<i>$ numBytes; Nat1[numBytes] val }
Declaration of a sequence of bytes with **numBytes** representing its byte length and **val** representing the initial byte values. Note that only the first byte of the byte array **val** is aligned on a 2- or 4- byte boundary on a 16-bit or 32-bit CVM, respectively. For performance reasons, integer numbers that occur inside this byte array should be aligned properly in the CVM packet by padding zero bytes. Note that the declaration codes **bytes3** and **bytes4** are only supported by a 32-bit CVM.

bytesz$<i>$ ($1 \leq i \leq 4$) $= 5 + i - 1$: { Nat$<i>$ numBytes }
Declaration of a sequence of zero bytes with **numBytes** representing its byte length. The initial zero bytes are not transmitted over the network to save bandwidth. The CVM automatically fills the memory cells mem[j], ..., mem[j + numBytes $- 1$] with zero bytes, with j representing the next following absolute memory address that is a multiple of 2 or 4 on a 16-bit or 32-bit CVM, respectively. For performance reasons, integer numbers that occur inside this byte array should be aligned properly in the CVM packet by padding zero bytes. Note that the declaration codes **bytesz3** and **bytesz4** are only supported by a 32-bit CVM.

eventtable = 9: *EventTable*
The binary packet format of *EventTable* is as follows:

3.8. CVM Packet   97

$EventTable$ =   { $EventTableEntry$[] $entries;$
                         Nat1 0 }

$EventTableEntry$ =   { Nat1 eventCode,   // eventCode > 0
                         Nat<cvmpAdrLen> memAdr }

An event table is a (possibly empty) list of event table entries, whereas each entry consists
of an event code (eventCode) and the absolute memory address (memAdr) of an instruction.
cvmpAdrLen is a part of the CVM packet item attributes and specifies the byte length
of each memory address. The end of the list is indicated by the value 0 for the event code.
Refer also to section 3.1.6.2 (48) for the binary format of the event table in CVM memory,
after it has been loaded by the CVM.

On a 16- or 32-bit CVM, each memAdr must be an unsigned integer number less than 2^{16}
or 2^{31}, respectively.

int<i>   ($1 \leq i \leq 4$) $= 10 + i - 1$:   { Int<i> val }
Declaration of an i-byte signed integer number (Int<i>) with the initial value val. On a
16-bit CVM, only the declaration codes int1 and int2 are supported and val is copied as
an Int2 value into memory. On a 32-bit CVM, val is copied as an Int4 value into memory.
These declaration codes are only supported, if the CVM is emulated in software, i.e., if the
CVM mode is 16BitEmu or 32BitEmu. Otherwise, all data items with initial values unequal
to zero must be combined by using the bytes<i> ($1 \leq i \leq 4$) declaration code.

intz   = 14:   -
Declaration of a signed integer number (Int<cvmIntLen>) with the initial value zero. The
CVM automatically fills the memory cells mem[j], ..., mem[j + cvmIntLen − 1] with zero
bytes, with j representing the next following absolute memory address which is a multiple
of 2 or 4 on a 16-bit or 32-bit CVM, respectively. This declaration code is only supported,
if the CVM is emulated in software, i.e., if the CVM mode is 16BitEmu or 32BitEmu.
Otherwise, all data items with initial values equal to zero must be grouped together by
using the bytesz declaration code.

nat<i>   ($1 \leq i \leq 3$) $= 15 + i - 1$:   { Nat<i> val }
Declaration of an i-byte unsigned integer number (Nat<i>) with the initial value val.
On a 16-bit CVM, only the declaration code nat1 is supported and val is then copied
as an Int2 value into memory. On a 32-bit CVM, val is copied as an Int4 value into
memory. An arithmetic overflow is not checked by the CVM. These declaration codes are
only supported, if the CVM is emulated in software, i.e., if the CVM mode is 16BitEmu or
32BitEmu. Otherwise, all data items with initial values unequal to zero must be combined
by using the bytes<i> ($1 \leq i \leq 4$) declaration code.

string   = 18:   (String val)
Declaration of the string val. This declaration code is only supported, if the CVM is
emulated in software, i.e., if the CVM mode is 16BitEmu or 32BitEmu. In addition, the
string val must not be modified, but must be treated as a constant during execution of
the CVM program.

instructions *instructions* is a sequence of CVM instructions. Each instruction consists of its operation code (`opcode`) and possibly some immediate operands (`immOperands`). The opcode and — if existent — the immediate operands of each instruction are copied into memory starting at the memory address `codeSegmentAdr` without alignment, except for the opcode of the first instruction. Forgoing alignment makes CVM code in memory more compact; however, possibly at the cost of a performance penalty in particular CVM implementations. Refer to section 3.9.2 (page 100) for a complete reference of all CVM instructions.

CVM Packet Verifier During loading of a CVM packet into memory the CVM packet verifier checks the constraints that are mentioned in the description of the CVM packet format. This prevents the CVM from executing malformed CVM packets. As a result, a simple kind of low-level security is achieved.

Restrictions for an Emulated CVM If the CVM is emulated, i.e., `cvmMode` is 16Bit-Emu or 32BitEmu, the data and code part of the CVM packet has to meet the following conditions:

- During runtime, the instructions are not overwritten and no new instruction is created to be executed.

- All jump target addresses of the control flow instructions `call`, `jmp`, ..., are known before runtime and do not change during runtime.

- Every data item is declared in the CVM packet and properly accessed by the CVM instructions according to the type of its declaration. Refer to section 3.8 (page 96) for more information on data declarations within the CVM packet.

- Declared strings (`string`) remain constant in memory, i.e., they are not modified during runtime.

As a result, the CVM can be implemented more efficiently in software, because certain properties, e.g., the memory addresses of the data items and the jump targets, can be evaluated once at the beginning of program execution and then reused all the time during execution. In addition, similar to the Java HotSpot Virtual Machine [76], Just-In-Time compilation techniques may be applied as well. Note that the implementation of such optimizations is not mandatory and left to the implementors' choice. Therefore, these optimizations are not going to be discussed here in more detail.

3.9 Instruction Set

In order to keep the CVM architecture as simple as possible, the CVM instruction set contains only the most essential operations that are needed for networked clients. In addition to instructions for common processing, it covers mainly instructions for displaying user interfaces. So far, there are 111 instructions altogether for the CVM modules Core, Visual, Keyboard, Mouse, Network, and Libraries.

3.9. Instruction Set   99

However, a given CVM implementation does not need to support any instructions that belong to a nonexistent module or functional unit. The modules Visual, Audio, Keyboard, Mouse, and Libraries as well as the functional units for the management of the optional Heap section and the optional interval timer within the Core module are optional.

Note that the instructions aload4, astore4, loadc3, loadc4, loadcu2, loadcu3, setcolor32, setbgcolor32, and setfont32 are only supported by a 32-bit CVM, but not by a 16-bit CVM. Therefore, a very "thin" 16-bit CVM implementation with a screen and keyboard, but without a Heap section, an interval timer, a mouse, and without any libraries has to support only 94 instructions.

3.9.1 Overview

This section summarizes all CVM instructions and groups them according to the CVM modules they belong to, and within a CVM module according to their purposes. Most instructions are motivated and introduced in the respective CVM module descriptions in the previous sections. A comprehensive description of each instruction is given in the following reference section.

Core

- Load immediate integer value onto register stack: loadc<1|...|4>, loadcu<1|...|3>, loadc_0, loadc_1, loadc_m1

- Load integer value from memory onto register stack: loada, loadr

- Write integer value from register stack into memory: storea, storer

- Load integer value from array in memory onto register stack: aload<1|2|4>

- Write integer value from register stack into array in memory: astore<1|2|4>

- Load integer value from memory stack onto register stack and vice versa: pop, push

- Heap management: new, free, hload, hstore
  Note that the Heap section is optional for a given CVM implementation.

- Bit test and set operations: testsetbits, unsetbits

- Register stack management: rdup, rempty, rskip, rswap

- Base Pointer (regBP): newstackframe, oldstackframe, getbp, setbp

- Stack Pointer (regSP): addsp, decsp, incsp

- Binary arithmetic operations: add, sub, mul, div, rem, and, or, xor, shl, shr, shrs

- Unary arithmetic operations: dec, inc, neg, not

- Control flow: halt, call, ret, jmp, je, jne, jl, jle, page

- Event handling: enableevents, disableevents, loadep<1|2|3>, seteventtableadr

- Interval timer: settimerinterval, settimerhandleadr
  Note that the interval timer is optional for a given CVM implementation.

Visual

- Graphics state: setbgcolor, setbgcolor32, setbgred, setbggreen, setbgblue, setcolor, setcolor32, setred, setgreen, setblue, setfont, setfont32, setfontcode, setfontsize, sethtextline, setxtextline, setclip, setlinewidth
- Lines: linehoriz, linevert
- Rectangles: rect, rectfill
- Circles: circle, circlefill
- Text: text, textm, textp, textpm, textbg, textmbg, textpbg, textpmbg
- Bitmaps: bitmap, bitmapbg
- Screen buffering: mem2screen, screen2mem,

Audio (Not covered in this thesis)

Keyboard (So far, no instructions)

Mouse, Network, Libraries

- Set mouse shape: setmousefont
- Receive and send data over network: rcv, sendrcv
- Set regSessionId to zero: sid
- Call library function: lib
  Note that the lib instruction is always implemented, even if no libraries are available. Then, a library call always results in the error UnknownLibraryFunction.

3.9.2 Reference

This section serves as a reference and describes all instructions. They are listed alphabetically using the following description format:

mnemonic = *opcode*: *immediate_operands*
register_stack_behavior
verbose_description_of_semantics

opcode is the positive integer number that identifies the instruction in the binary code.

immediate_operands represents a (possibly empty) list of immediate operands. Immediate operands of an instruction appear in the binary code right after the instruction opcode. Each immediate operand is shown in the form $ident_{type}$. *ident* can be any identifier and is usually chosen to characterize the use of the operand. *type* denotes the type of the operand and may be one of the CVM data types Int, Nat, or String. For example, x_{Nat} might be

3.9. Instruction Set

used to identify an x coordinate value of the type Nat. If the instruction does not have any immediate operands, *immediate_operands* is omitted in the description of that instruction. Only a few instructions have immediate operands.

register_stack_behavior illustrates how the instruction affects the register stack. It is shown in the form $preRegStack \rightarrow postRegStack$. $preRegStack$ represents the register stack right before the execution of the instruction. It has the form "..., $value_1$, $value_2$, ..., $value_n$" with $value_i = \text{R}[\text{regRSP} - n + i]$ ($0 < i \leq n \leq$ cvmNumGeneralRegs). $postRegStack$ represents the register stack right after the execution of the instruction. It has the form "..., $result_1$, $result_2$, ..., $result_m$" with $result_j = \text{R}[\text{regRSP} - m + j]$ ($0 < j \leq m \leq$ cvmNumGeneralRegs). An instruction pops the values $value_1$, ..., $value_n$ ($0 \leq n \leq$ cvmNumGeneralRegs) as operands from the register stack and pushes the results $result_1$, ..., $result_m$ ($0 \leq m \leq$ cvmNumGeneralRegs) onto it. The values of the numbers n and m depend on the particular instruction. $value_i$ ($0 < i \leq n$) and $result_j$ ($0 < j \leq m$) are shown in the form $ident_{type}$ as well. Accordingly, if no underflow or overflow occurs, the Register Stack Pointer regRSP is adjusted automatically during the execution of the instruction, i.e., $\text{regRSP}_{postRegStack} = \text{regRSP}_{preRegStack} - n + m$. Refer also to the error codes RegisterStackOverflow, RegisterStackStaticOverflow, and RegisterStackUnderflow.

The remainder of the register stack, i.e., the initial "..." in $preRegStack$ and $postRegStack$, remains unaffected by the instruction. Note that if the instruction is a final one, the remainder is supposed to be empty and therefore omitted in the instruction description. Then it holds: $value_i = \text{R}[i]$ ($0 < i \leq n \leq$ cvmNumGeneralRegs) in $preRegStack$ and $result_j = \text{R}[j]$ ($0 < j \leq m \leq$ cvmNumGeneralRegs) in $postRegStack$. An empty register stack is indicated by the symbol ε. If the instruction does not affect the register stack at all, *register_stack_behavior* is omitted in the instruction description.

verbose_description_of_semantics provides a verbose description of the instruction semantics.

The byte lengths of Int and Nat are given by cvmIntLen. Note that if cvmIntLen is 4, the biggest Nat number is $2^{31} - 1$, but not $2^{32} - 1$.

Note that all CVM instructions are atomic, i.e., no instruction may be interrupted during its execution. Interrupt handling may only take place between two subsequent instructions.

add = 1:
..., $num1_{\text{Int}}$, $num2_{\text{Int}} \rightarrow$ ..., $result_{\text{Int}}$
Add the numbers *num1* and *num2*. On a 16-bit CVM, $result = (num1 + num2)$ & 0xFFFF. On a 32-bit CVM, $result = (num1 + num2)$ & 0xFFFFFFFF.

addsp = 2:
..., $numStackCells_{\text{Int}} \rightarrow$ ...
Increment/Decrement stack pointer register regSP. On a 16-bit CVM, regSP := (regSP + ((*numStackCells* * 2) & 0xFFFF)) & 0xFFFF. On a 32-bit CVM, regSP := (regSP + ((*numStackCells* * 4) & 0xFFFFFFFF)) & 0xFFFFFFFF. If the new value of regSP is less than regSS or greater than cvmMemMaxAdr + 1, start error handling with the error code StackUnderflow (page 44) or StackOverflow (page 44), respectively.

aload1 = 3:
..., $arrayAdr_{Nat}$, $index_{Int}$ → ..., $arrayElem_{Nat}$
Load Nat1 number from byte array in memory onto register stack with zero extension. The number is an array element. On a 16-bit CVM, it starts in memory at the address ($arrayAdr + index$) & 0xFFFF. On a 32-bit CVM, its memory address is ($arrayAdr + index$) & 0xFFFFFFFF. Refer also to the error code IllegalMemoryAddress (page 43).

aload<2|4> = 4, 5:
..., $arrayAdr_{Nat}$, $index_{Int}$ → ..., $arrayElem_{Int}$
Load Int<2|4> number from integer array in memory onto register stack with sign extension, respectively. The (big-endian) number is an array element. On a 16-bit CVM, it starts in memory at the address ($arrayAdr + ((index * 2)$ & 0xFFFF)) & 0xFFFF. On a 32-bit CVM, its memory address is ($arrayAdr + ((index * i)$ & 0xFFFFFFFF)) & 0xFFFFFFFF, with $i = 2$ or 4, respectively. aload4 is only supported by a 32-bit CVM. Refer also to the error code IllegalMemoryAddress (page 43).

and = 6:
..., $num1_{Int}$, $num2_{Int}$ → ..., $result_{Int}$
Bitwise AND conjunction with $result = num1$ & $num2$.

astore1 = 7:
..., $value_{Int}$, $arrayAdr_{Nat}$, $index_{Int}$ → ...
Store the least significant byte of $value$, i.e., $value$ & 0xFF, into the byte array in memory at the address $targetAdr$. On a 16-bit CVM, $targetAdr = (arrayAdr + index)$ & 0xFFFF. On a 32-bit CVM, $targetAdr = (arrayAdr + index)$ & 0xFFFFFFFF. Refer also to the error code IllegalMemoryAddress (page 43).

astore<2|4> = 8, 9:
..., $value_{Int}$, $arrayAdr_{Nat}$, $index_{Int}$ → ...
Store the least 2 or 4 significant bytes of $value$, i.e., $value$ & 0xFFFF or $value$ & 0xFFFFFFFF, into the integer array in memory at the address $targetAdr$ in big-endian order. On a 16-bit CVM, $targetAdr = (arrayAdr + ((index * 2)$ & 0xFFFF)) & 0xFFFF. On a 32-bit CVM, $targetAdr = (arrayAdr + ((index * i)$ & 0xFFFFFFFF)) & 0xFFFFFFFF, with $i = 2$ or 4, respectively. astore4 is only supported by a 32-bit CVM. Refer also to the error code IllegalMemoryAddress (page 43).

bitmap, bitmapbg = 10, 11:
x_{Int}, y_{Int}, $width_{Nat}$, $height_{Nat}$, $memAdrAbs_{Nat}$ → ε
Draw bitmap image. The image data is located in memory and starts at the address $memAdrAbs$. The rectangular area of the screen given by the corners (x, y) and $(x + width - 1, y + height - 1)$ is tiled with the bitmap image. The pixels that are set in the bitmap image are drawn with the foreground color. The only difference between bitmap and bitmapbg is that bitmap leaves the unset pixels untouched, whereas bitmapbg additionally draws the unset pixels with the background color. The binary format of the image data in memory, shown as a tuple structure, is as follows:
(Nat bitmapWidth, Nat bitmapHeight, Nat1[bitmapWidth*bitmapHeight] dataBytes)

3.9. Instruction Set

On a 16-bit CVM, the byte length of Nat is 2. On a 32-bit CVM, it is 4. bitmapHeight and bitmapWidth specify the width and height of the bitmap, respectively. The binary format of dataBytes complies to the X BitMap format XBM [96]. Refer to the section 3.2.1 (page 76) for more information on foreground and background colors. Refer also to the error code ImageLoadFailure (page 43).

call = 12:
..., $memAdrRel_{Int}$ → ...
Procedure call. Push the memory address of the immediately following instruction onto the memory stack, i.e., store that memory address onto the top of the memory stack and increment regSP by cvmIntLen. Then jump to the instruction at the relative memory address $memAdrRel$ and continue execution there, i.e., regIP := regIP + $memAdrRel$. Note that the value of regIP on the right side equals the absolute memory address of the instruction opcode. After execution of the procedure is finished, i.e., the instruction ret within that procedure is encountered, resume execution with the immediately following instruction from before. Refer also to the error codes StackOverflow (page 44) and IllegalMemoryAddress (page 43), to the instruction ret (page 109), to the procedure stack frame (page 40), and to section 3.1.2 (page 33) for more information on cvmIntLen.

circle, circlefill = 13, 14:
x_{Int}, y_{Int}, $width_{Nat}$ → ε
If $width > 0$, draw or fill circle that is delimited by the bounding square, respectively. Otherwise, do nothing. The coordinates of the upper left corner and the width of the bounding square are given by x, y, and $width$.

dec = 15:
..., num_{Int} → ..., $result_{Int}$
Decrement num. On a 16-bit CVM, $result = (num - 1)$ & 0xFFFF. On a 32-bit CVM, $result = (num - 1)$ & 0xFFFFFFFF.

decsp = 16:
Decrement stack pointer register regSP. On a 16-bit CVM, regSP := (regSP − cvmIntLen) & 0xFFFF. On a 32-bit CVM, regSP := (regSP − cvmIntLen) & 0xFFFFFFFF. If the new value of regSP is less than regSS or greater than cvmMaxMemAdr + 1, start error handling with the error code StackUnderflow (page 44) or StackOverflow (page 44), respectively. Refer to section 3.1.2 (page 33) for more information on cvmIntLen.

disableevents = 17:
Disable event handling, i.e., regEventEnable := 0. From now on, all events except for the builtin events will be discarded until the instruction enableevents occurs.

div = 18:
..., $num1_{Int}$, $num2_{Int}$ → ..., $result_{Int}$
Integer division. If $num2 \neq 0$, $result = num1 \;/\; num2$. Otherwise, start error handling with error code DivisionByZero (page 43).

enableevents = 19:
Enable event handling, i.e., regEventEnable := 1. From now on, all events will be processed until the instruction disableevents occurs.

free = 20:
..., $heapAdr_{Nat}$ → ...
Free the memory region in the Heap section that starts at the heap address $heapAdr$. Note that this memory region must have been reserved before with the library function new. The byte length of the memory region is known, because it is an operand of new. If the specified memory region has not been reserved before or if it has already been freed before, undefined behavior occurs. Refer to section 3.1.4.3 (page 41) for more information on the Heap section.

getbp = 21:
... → ..., $memAdrAbs_{Nat}$
Load the value of the base pointer register onto the register stack, i.e., $memAdrAbs$:= regBP.

halt = 0:
... → ε
Stop execution and wait.

hload = 22:
..., $heapAdr_{Nat}$ → ..., $value_{Int}$
Load integer number from the Heap section onto the register stack. The number resides in the Heap section at the address $heapAdr$. The byte length of the integer number depends on the CVM mode and is given by cvmIntLen. If the heap address $heapAdr$ is not valid, the CVM aborts execution and starts error handling with the error code IllegalMemoryAddress. Refer to the sections 3.1.2 (page 33) and 3.1.4.3 (page 41) for more information on CVM modes and cvmIntLen and on the Heap section, respectively.

hstore = 23:
..., $value_{Int}$, $heapAdr_{Nat}$ → ...
Store integer number $value$ from register stack into the Heap section at the address $heapAdr$. The byte length of the integer number depends on the CVM mode and is given by cvmIntLen. If the heap address $heapAdr$ is not valid, the CVM aborts execution and starts error handling with the error code IllegalMemoryAddress. Refer to the sections 3.1.2 (page 33) and 3.1.4.3 (page 41) for more information on CVM modes and cvmIntLen and on the Heap section, respectively.

inc = 24:
..., num_{Int} → ..., $result_{Int}$
Increment num. On a 16-bit CVM, $result = (num + 1)$ & 0xFFFF. On a 32-bit CVM, $result = (num + 1)$ & 0xFFFFFFFF.

3.9. Instruction Set

incsp $= 25$:
Increment stack pointer register regSP. On a 16-bit CVM, regSP := (regSP + cvmIntLen) & 0xFFFF. On a 32-bit CVM, regSP := (regSP + cvmIntLen) & 0xFFFFFFFF. If the new value of regSP is less than regSS or greater than cvmMaxMemAdr + 1, start error handling with the error code StackUnderflow (page 44) or StackOverflow (page 44), respectively. Refer to section 3.1.2 (page 33) for more information on cvmIntLen.

jmp $= 26$:
..., $memAdrRel_{\mathsf{Int}} \to$ ...
Unconditional jump to the instruction at the relative memory address $memAdrRel$. Proceed execution there, i.e., regIP := regIP + $memAdrRel$. Note that the value of regIP on the right side equals the absolute memory address of the instruction opcode. Refer also to the error code IllegalMemoryAddress (page 43).

j<e | ne | l | le> $= 27, 28, 29, 30$:
..., $num1_{\mathsf{Int}}$, $num2_{\mathsf{Int}}$, $memAdrRel_{\mathsf{Int}} \to$ ...
Conditional jump. If the condition is true, jump to the instruction at the relative memory address $memAdrRel$ and proceed execution there, i.e., regIP := regIP + $memAdrRel$. Note that the value of regIP on the right side equals the absolute memory address of the instruction opcode. The conditions are defined by: "e" $\equiv$ "$num1 = num2$", "ne" $\equiv$ "$num1 \neq num2$", "l" $\equiv$ "$num1 < num2$", "le" $\equiv$ "$num1 \leq num2$". Refer also to the error code IllegalMemoryAddress (page 43).

lib $= 31$:
..., $par1_{\mathsf{Int}}$, ..., $parN_{\mathsf{Int}}$, $fctCode_{\mathsf{Nat}} \to$ ...
Call library function with the libFctCode $fctCode$. $par1, ..., parN$ ($N \geq 0$) are the parameters of the library function. Refer to section 3.5 (page 83) for a list of all currently available library functions. Refer also to the error code UnknownLibraryFunction (page 45).

linehoriz $= 32$:
x_{Int}, y_{Int}, $len_{\mathsf{Nat}} \to \varepsilon$
If $len > 0$, draw horizontal line from start point (x, y) to end point $(x + len - 1, y)$. Otherwise, do nothing.

linevert $= 33$:
x_{Int}, y_{Int}, $len_{\mathsf{Nat}} \to \varepsilon$
If $len > 0$, draw vertical line from start point (x, y) to end point $(x, y+len-1)$. Otherwise, do nothing.

loada $= 34$:
..., $memAdrAbs_{\mathsf{Nat}} \to$ ..., num_{Int}
Load integer number from memory onto register stack. The number resides in memory at the address $memAdrAbs$ in big-endian order. The byte length of the integer number depends on the CVM mode and is given by cvmIntLen. Refer to section 3.1.2 (page 33) for more information on CVM modes and cvmIntLen. Refer also to the error code IllegalMemoryAddress (page 43).

loadc_0, loadc_1, loadc_m1   = 35, 36, 37:
... → ..., num_Int
Load the integer constants 0, 1, −1 onto the register stack, respectively.

loadc$<i>$ ($1 \leq i \leq 4$)   = 38, 39, 40, 41: $num_{\text{Int}<i>}$
... → ..., num_Int
Load the i-byte signed integer constant num in big-endian order onto the register stack (with sign extension). loadc3 and loadc4 are only supported by a 32-bit CVM.

loadcu$<i>$ ($1 \leq i \leq 3$)   = 42, 43, 44: $num_{\text{Nat}<i>}$
... → ..., num_Nat
Load the i-byte unsigned integer constant num in big-endian order onto the register stack (without sign extension). loadcu2 and loadcu3 are only supported by a 32-bit CVM.

loadep$<i>$ ($1 \leq i \leq 3$)   = 45, 46, 47:
... → ..., val_Int
Load the value of the special event parameter register regEventPar$<i>$ onto the register stack, with $val = $ regEventPar$<i>$.

loadr   = 48:
..., $memAdrRel_\text{Int}$ → ..., num_Int
Load integer number from memory onto register stack. The number resides in memory at the address $memAdrAbs$ in big-endian order. On a 16-bit CVM, $memAdrAbs = $ (regBP + $memAdrRel$) & 0xFFFF. On a 32-bit CVM, $memAdrAbs = $ (regBP + $memAdrRel$) & 0xFFFFFFFF. The byte length of the integer number depends on the CVM mode and is given by cvmIntLen. Refer to section 3.1.2 (page 33) for more information on CVM modes and cvmIntLen. Refer also to the error code IllegalMemoryAddress (page 43).

mem2screen   = 49:
x_Int, y_Int, $width_\text{Nat}$, $height_\text{Nat}$, $memAdrAbs_\text{Nat}$ → ε
Draw buffered screen section. The data of the buffered screen section resides in memory and starts at the memory address $memAdrAbs$. The upper-left corner, the width, and the height of the buffered screen section within the visual drawing area are given by (x, y), $width$, and $height$, respectively. x, y, $width$, and $height$ are always measured in pixels — nevertheless of the value of the special register regMeasure. The format of the image data in memory is internal for the CVM and thus implementation dependent. The use of colormaps for storing the pixel values is also left to the implementors' choice. However, each pixel value may take at most 3 bytes. If the rectangle specified by the corners (x, y) and ($x + width - 1$, $y + height - 1$) is not completely inside the visual drawing area of the CVM, which is given by the rectangle with the corners (0, 0) and (cvmScreenWidth − 1, cvmScreenHeight − 1), start error handling with the error code InvalidScreenSection (page 43). Refer to section 3.7 (page 92) for more information on cvmScreenHeight and cvmScreenWidth. Refer also to the error code IllegalMemoryAddress (page 43) and to the instruction screen2mem (page 110).

3.9. Instruction Set

mul $= 50$:
..., $num1_{\text{Int}}$, $num2_{\text{Int}}$ → ..., $result_{\text{Int}}$
Multiply the numbers $num1$ and $num2$. On a 16-bit CVM, $result = (num1 * num2)$ & 0xFFFF. On a 32-bit CVM, $result = (num1 * num2)$ & 0xFFFFFFFF.

neg $= 51$:
..., num_{Int} → ..., $result_{\text{Int}}$
Negate integer number num, i.e., $result = -num$.

new $= 52$:
..., $numBytes_{\text{Nat}}$ → ..., $memAdrHeap_{\text{Nat}}$
Allocate and reserve an unused block of $numBytes$ bytes in the Heap section. If successful, $memAdrHeap$ is the starting heap address greater than zero of the found block in the Heap section, otherwise zero. Refer to section 3.1.4.3 (page 41) for more information on the Heap section.

newstackframe $= 53$:
..., $numStackCells_{\text{Nat}}$ → ...
First, push the value of the base pointer register **regBP** onto the memory stack, i.e., store **regBP** onto the top of the memory stack and increment **regSP** by **cvmIntLen**. Then, store the value (**regSP** $- ((\text{cvmIntLen} * ((2 + numStackCells)$ & $bitMask))$ & $bitMask))$ & $bitMask$ into the special register **regBP**, with $bitMask = $ 0xFFFF on a 16-bit CVM and 0xFFFFFFFF on a 32-bit CVM, respectively. This instruction usually occurs at the beginning of a procedure that has parameters and/or local variables. It adjusts the new stack frame and thus enables convenient access to the parameters and/or local variables with the **loadr** and **storer** instructions. Refer also to the error code **StackOverflow** (page 44), to the instruction **oldstackframe**, to the procedure stack frame (page 40), and to section 3.1.2 (page 33) for more information on **cvmIntLen**.

not $= 54$:
..., num_{Int} → ..., $result_{\text{Int}}$
$result$ is the bitwise complement of num.

oldstackframe $= 55$:
Pop the value, which is a memory address, from the top of the memory stack and store it into the base pointer register **regBP**. If the memory address is not inside the address interval [0; **cvmMemMaxAdr**], start error handling with the error code **IllegalMemoryAddress**. This instruction usually occurs at the end of a procedure before returning to the caller to restore the previous stack frame, i.e., the stack frame of the caller. Refer also to the error code **StackUnderflow** (page 44), to the instruction **newstackframe**, and to the procedure stack frame (page 40).

or $= 56$:
..., $num1_{\text{Int}}$, $num2_{\text{Int}}$ → ..., $result_{\text{Int}}$
Bitwise OR disjunction with $result = num1 \mid num2$.

page = 57:
..., $subpageNo_{Nat}$, $pageMemAdrRel_{Int}$ → ...
Display CVMUI page with the page number *subpageNo*. A CVMUI page represents an AUI subpage. *pageMemAdrRel* is the relative memory address where the instruction block of the respective CVMUI page starts in CVM memory. The CVM jumps to that address and continues execution there, i.e., regIP := regIP + *pageMemAdrRel*. Note that the value of regIP on the right side equals the absolute memory address of the instruction opcode. Refer also to the error code IllegalMemoryAddress (page 43). This instruction also creates a new history buffer entry with the appropriate **subpageNo** and **pageMemAdr** fields. The **hostAdr**, **sessionId**, **serviceNo**, **pageNo**, and **cvmpNo** fields of the new history buffer entry are copied from the current history buffer entry.

Refer also to the CVM state transitions in section 3.1.10 (page 58), especially to the CVM states Execute, EventExecute, and TimerExecute. For more information on the history buffer, refer to section 3.1.7 (page 52). For more information on AUI and CVMUI pages, refer to the sections 2.3 (page 27), 5.1 (page 135), and 5.5 (page 166).

Note that the CVM does not check whether the instruction block of the respective CVMUI page really starts at the relative memory address *pageMemAdrRel*. This is left to the responsibility of the CVM programmer or packet generator.

pop = 58:
... → ..., num_{Int}
Pop the value — a signed integer number — from the top of the memory stack and push it onto the register stack. The byte length of the integer number on the memory stack is given by cvmIntLen. Refer to section 3.1.2 (page 33) for more information on cvmIntLen. Refer also to the sections 3.1.4.2 (page 39) and 3.1.3 (page 35), and to the error code StackUnderflow (page 44).

push = 59:
..., num_{Int} → ...
Pop the value — a signed integer number — from the top of the register stack and push it onto the top of the memory stack. The byte length of the integer number on the memory stack is given by cvmIntLen. Refer to section 3.1.2 (page 33) for more information on cvmIntLen. Refer also to the sections 3.1.3 (page 35) and 3.1.4.2 (page 38), and to the error code StackOverflow (page 44).

rcv = 60:
..., $hostAdrMemAdr_{Nat}$, $pageOrServiceNo_{Nat}$, $subpageNo_{Nat}$ → ...
Contact CVM packet server and request CVMUI page. A CVMUI page represents an AUI subpage. *hostAdrMemAdr* contains the memory address where the host address of the CVM packet server starts in CVM memory. The host address is a string (String) and might be either an IP [62] address in standard dot notation or a DNS [45] name. Note that if the host address is a DNS name, but the given CVM implementation does not support automatic DNS lookup, the CVM aborts execution and starts error handling with the error code NoDNSLookup (page 44). Refer also to the profile item cvmDNSLookup (page 90) and to the error code IllegalMemoryAddress (page 43).

3.9. Instruction Set

If the value of the special register regSessionId is not zero, *pageOrServiceNo* contains the AUI page number of the requested CVMUI page. Otherwise, *pageOrServiceNo* contains the number of the interactive network service. Then, the AUI page number is zero by definition and the CVM starts a new session with the respective CVM packet server. *subpageNo* contains the number of the requested AUI subpage. Refer to section 3.4 (page 82) for more information on the special register regSessionId. If no error occurs, the CVM packet server finally sends a CVM packet, which contains the requested CVMUI page, to the CVM.

The communication with the CVM packet server is based on the application protocol CPTP. The used protocol method for starting the request is GET. Refer to section 4 (page 127) for more information on the CPTP protocol and on the GET method (page 130). Refer also to the error codes MalformedCPTPMessage (page 43), MalformedCVMProfile, NetworkError, and UnexpectedCPTPMethodCode.

This instruction blocks until the respective CVM packet has been received completely or until the user aborts the data transmission by raising an appropriate event, e.g., key_pressed_escape. Refer to the CVM state transitions in section 3.1.10 (page 58), especially to the CVM states Execute, EventExecute, TimerExecute, and CptpGET.

This instruction also creates a new history buffer entry with the appropriate hostAdr, serviceNo, pageNo, and subpageNo fields. Refer to section 3.1.7 (page 52) for more information on the history buffer.

For more information on AUI and CVMUI pages and CVM packets, refer to the sections 2.3 (page 27), 5.1 (page 135), and 5.5 (page 166), and 3.8 (page 93).

Note that the instructions that immediately succeed this instruction will never be executed unless they are accessed from other parts of the CVM program with appropriate jump instructions.

rdup = 61:
..., $value_{\mathsf{Int}}$ → ..., $value_{\mathsf{Int}}$, $value_{\mathsf{Int}}$
Duplicate the top register stack value. Refer also to the error code RegisterStackOverflow (page 44).

rect, rectfill = 62, 63:
x_{Int}, y_{Int}, $width_{\mathsf{Nat}}$, $height_{\mathsf{Nat}}$ → ε
If $width > 0$ and $height > 0$, draw or fill rectangle with the upper-left corner at (x, y) and the lower-right corner at $(x + width - 1, y + height - 1)$, respectively. Otherwise, do nothing.

rem = 64:
..., $num1_{\mathsf{Int}}$, $num2_{\mathsf{Int}}$ → ..., $result_{\mathsf{Int}}$
Remainder integer division. If $num2 \neq 0$, $result = num1 - (num1\ /\ num2) * num2$. Otherwise, refer to the error code DivisionByZero (page 43).

ret = 65:
Return from procedure call. Pop the memory address from the top of the memory stack

and store it into the instruction pointer register regIP. Execution continues there. If the popped memory address is not inside the address interval [0; cvmMemMaxAdr], start error handling with the error code IllegalMemoryAddress (page 43). Refer also to section 3.1.4.2 (39), to the error code StackUnderflow (page 44), to the instruction call (page 103), to the procedure stack frame (page 40), and to section 3.1.2 (page 33) for more information on cvmIntLen.

rempty = 66:
$... \rightarrow \varepsilon$
Pop all values from the register stack and discard them.

rskip = 67:
$..., dummy_{\text{Int}} \rightarrow ...$
Pop the top register stack value and discard it. Refer also to the error code RegisterStackUnderflow (page 44).

rswap = 68:
$..., value1_{\text{Int}}, value2_{\text{Int}} \rightarrow ..., value2_{\text{Int}}, value1_{\text{Int}}$
Swap the top two register stack values. Refer also to the error code RegisterStackUnderflow (page 44).

screen2mem = 69:
$x_{\text{Int}}, y_{\text{Int}}, width_{\text{Nat}}, height_{\text{Nat}}, memAdrAbs_{\text{Nat}} \rightarrow \varepsilon$
Store specified screen section into memory at the address $memAdrAbs$. The screen section is defined by the rectangle with the upper-left corner at (x, y) and the given $width$ and $height$. x, y, $width$, and $height$ are always measured in pixels — nevertheless the value of the special register regMeasure. The format of the image data in memory is internal for the CVM and therefore implementation dependent. However, each pixel value may take at most 3 bytes. If the rectangle specified by the corners (x, y) and $(x + width - 1, y + height - 1)$ is not completely inside the visual drawing area of the CVM which is given by the rectangle with the corners $(0, 0)$ and (cvmScreenWidth $- 1$, cvmScreenHeight $- 1$), start error handling with the error code InvalidScreenSection (page 43). Refer to section 3.7 (page 92) for more information on cvmScreenHeight and cvmScreenWidth. Refer also to the error code IllegalMemoryAddress (page 43) and to the instruction mem2screen (page 106).

sendrcv = 70:
$..., hostAdrMemAdr_{\text{Nat}}, pageOrServiceNo_{\text{Nat}}, subpageNo_{\text{Nat}},$
$numBytes_{\text{Nat}}, dataBytesMemAdr_{\text{Nat}}$
$\rightarrow ...$
Contact CVM packet server, send data to it, and request CVMUI page. A CVMUI page represents an AUI subpage. $hostAdrMemAdr$ contains the memory address where the host address of the CVM packet server starts in CVM memory. The host address is a string (String) and might be either an IP [62] address in standard dot notation or a DNS [45] name. Note that if the host address is a DNS name, but the given CVM implementation does not support automatic DNS lookup, the CVM aborts execution and starts error handling with

3.9. Instruction Set

the error code NoDNSLookup (page 44). Refer also to the profile item cvmDNSLookup (page 90) and to the error code IllegalMemoryAddress (page 43). $dataBytesMemAdr$ contains the memory address where the data bytes start in CVM memory. $numBytes$ contains the number of bytes. Therefore, the data bytes reside in a byte array that is limited by the address interval $[dataBytesMemAdr;\ dataBytesMemAdr + numBytes - 1]$.

If the value of the special register regSessionId is not zero, $pageOrServiceNo$ contains the AUI page number of the requested CVMUI page. Otherwise, $pageOrServiceNo$ contains the number of the interactive network service. Then, the AUI page number is zero by definition and the CVM starts a new session with the respective CVM packet server. $subpageNo$ contains the number of the requested AUI subpage. Refer to section 3.4 (page 82) for more information on the special register regSessionId. If no error occurs, the CVM packet server finally sends a CVM packet, which contains the requested CVMUI page, to the CVM.

The communication with the CVM packet server is based on the application protocol CPTP. The used protocol method for starting the data transmission and request is GET. Refer to section 4 (page 127) for more information on the CPTP protocol and on the GET method (page 130). Refer also to the error codes MalformedCPTPMessage (page 43), MalformedCVMProfile, NetworkError, and UnexpectedCPTPMethodCode.

This instruction blocks until all the data bytes have been sent and the requested CVMUI page has been received or until the user aborts the data transmission by raising an appropriate event, e.g., key_pressed_escape. Refer to the CVM state transitions in section 3.1.10 (page 58), especially to the CVM states Execute, EventExecute, TimerExecute, and CptpGET.

This instruction also creates a new history buffer entry with the appropriate hostAdr, serviceNo, pageNo, and subpageNo fields. Refer to section 3.1.7 (page 52) for more information on the history buffer.

For more information on AUI and CVMUI pages and CVM packets, refer to the sections 2.3 (page 27), 5.1 (page 135), and 5.5 (page 166), and 3.8 (page 93).

Note that the instructions that immediately succeed this instruction will never be executed unless they are accessed from other parts of the CVM program with appropriate jump instructions.

setbgblue = 71:
..., $blue_{\text{Nat}} \rightarrow$ ...
Store the color component $blue$ into the special background color register regBgColorBlue, i.e., regBgColorBlue := $blue$ & 0xFF.

setbgcolor = 72:
..., red_{Nat}, $green_{\text{Nat}}$, $blue_{\text{Nat}}$, $\rightarrow$ ...
Store the red, $green$, and $blue$ color components into the special background color registers, respectively, i.e., regBgColorRed := red & 0xFF, regBgColorGreen := $green$ & 0xFF, regBgColorBlue := $blue$ & 0xFF.

setbgcolor32 = 73:
..., $color_{\text{Nat}} \rightarrow$ ...

Store *color* into the special background color registers, i.e., regBgColorRed := (*color* ≫ 16) & 0xFF, regBgColorGreen := (*color* ≫ 8) & 0xFF, regBgColorBlue := *color* & 0xFF. This instruction is only supported by a 32-bit CVM.

setbggreen = 74:
..., *green*_{Nat} → ...
Store the color component *green* into the special background color register regBgColorGreen, i.e., regBgColorGreen := *green* & 0xFF.

setbgred = 75:
..., *red*_{Nat} → ...
Store the color component *red* into the special background color register regBgColorRed, i.e., regBgColorRed := *red* & 0xFF.

setblue = 76:
..., *blue*_{Nat} → ...
Store the color component *blue* into the special foreground color register regColorBlue, i.e., regColorBlue := *blue* & 0xFF.

setbp = 77:
..., *memAdrAbs*_{Nat} → ...
Store the memory address *memAdrAbs* into the base pointer register, i.e., regBP := *memAdrAbs*. If the new value of regBP is not inside the address interval [0; cvmMemMaxAdr], start error handling with the error code IllegalMemoryAddress (page 43).

setclip = 78:
..., x_{Int}, y_{Int}, *width*_{Nat}, *height*_{Nat} → ...
Store x, y, *width*, and *height* into the special registers regClipX, regClipY, regClipWidth, and regClipHeight, respectively. Then set the clip-mask to the rectangle with the upper-left corner at (x, y) and the lower-right corner at $(x + width - 1, y + height - 1)$, respectively. Usually, this instruction is used to limit the effect of future graphic drawing operation to a particular rectangular area inside the visual drawing area of the screen. This technique is called *clipping*.

setcolor = 79:
..., *red*_{Nat}, *green*_{Nat}, *blue*_{Nat}, → ...
Store the *red, green*, and *blue* color components into the special foreground color registers, respectively, i.e., regColorRed := *red* & 0xFF, regColorGreen := *green* & 0xFF, regColorBlue := *blue* & 0xFF.

setcolor32 = 80:
..., *color*_{Int} → ...
Store *color* into the special foreground color registers, i.e., regColorRed := (*color* ≫ 16) & 0xFF, regColorGreen := (*color* ≫ 8) & 0xFF, regColorBlue := *color* & 0xFF. This instruction is only supported by a 32-bit CVM.

3.9. Instruction Set

seteventtableadr = 81:
..., $memAdrAbs_{\mathsf{Nat}} \rightarrow$ ...
Store the memory address $memAdrAbs$ into the special register regEventTableAdr, i.e.,
regEventTableAdr := $memAdrAbs$. Refer also to section 3.1.6 (page 45) for more information
on event handling. Refer also to the error code IllegalMemoryAddress (page 43).

setfont = 82:
..., $fontcode_{\mathsf{Nat}}, fontsize_{\mathsf{Nat}} \rightarrow$ ...
Store $fontcode$ and $fontsize$ into the special font registers regFontCode and regFontSize, i.e.,
regFontCode := $fontcode$ & 0xFFFF, regFontSize := $fontsize$ & 0xFFFF. Refer also to the
error code UnknownFont (page 44).

setfont32 = 83:
..., $font_{\mathsf{Int}} \rightarrow$ ...
Store $font$ into the special font registers regFontCode and regFontSize, i.e., regFontCode :=
$font$ & 0xFFFF, regFontSize := ($font \gg 16$) & 0xFFFF. This instruction is only supported
by a 32-bit CVM. Refer also to the error code UnknownFont (page 44).

setfontcode = 84:
..., $fontcode_{\mathsf{Nat}} \rightarrow$ ...
Store $fontcode$ into the special font register regFontCode, i.e., regFontCode := $fontcode$ &
0xFFFF. Refer also to the error code UnknownFont (page 44).

setfontsize = 85:
..., $size_{\mathsf{Nat}} \rightarrow$ ...
Store $size$ into the special font register regFontSize, i.e., regFontSize := $size$ & 0xFFFF.
Refer also to the error code UnknownFont (page 44).

setgreen = 86:
..., $green_{\mathsf{Nat}} \rightarrow$ ...
Store the color component $green$ into the special foreground color register regColorGreen,
i.e., regColorGreen := $green$ & 0xFF.

sethtextline = 87:
..., $height_{\mathsf{Nat}} \rightarrow$ ...
Store $height$ into the special register regHTextLine, i.e., regHTextLine := $height$.

setlinewidth = 88:
..., $width_{\mathsf{Nat}} \rightarrow$ ...
If $width > 0$, store $width$ into the special register regLineWidth, i.e., regLineWidth := $width$.
Otherwise, do nothing.

setmousefont = 89:
..., $mouseFontCode_{Nat}$ → ...
Store the mouse font code *mouseFontCode* into the special register regMouseFont, i.e., regMouseFont := *mouseFontCode* & 0xFF. Refer also to the error code UnknownMouseFont (page 44).

setred = 90:
..., red_{Nat} → ...
Store the color component *red* into the special foreground color register regColorRed, i.e., regColorRed := *red* & 0xFF.

settimerhandleadr = 91:
..., $memAdrAbs_{Nat}$ → ...
Store the memory address *memAdrAbs* into the special register regTimerHandleAdr, i.e., regTimerHandleAdr := *memAdrAbs*. The timer handle code block starts at this memory address. Refer also to section 3.1.9 (page 57) for more information on the interval timer and to the error code IllegalMemoryAddress (page 43).

settimerinterval = 92:
..., $timerInterval_{Nat}$ → ...
First store *timerInterval* into the special register regTimerInterval, i.e., regTimerInterval := *timerInterval*. *timerInterval* specifies the interval time period in milliseconds. Then activate the interval timer. Note that it is left to the responsibility of the CVM programmer or packet generator to ensure that the interval timer is not activated before the memory address of the timer handle code block has been declared by the instruction settimerhandleadr. Refer also to the section 3.1.9 (page 57) for more information on the interval timer.

setxtextline = 93:
..., x_{Int} → ...
Store *x* into the special register regXTextLine, i.e., regXTextLine := *x*.

shl = 94:
..., $num1_{Int}$, $num2_{Nat}$ → ..., $result_{Int}$
Bitwise shift left operation, i.e., *result* = (*num1* ≪ (*num2* & 0x0F)) & 0xFFFF on a 16-bit CVM and *result* = (*num1* ≪ (*num2* & 0x1F)) & 0xFFFFFFFF on a 32-bit CVM, respectively.

shr = 95:
..., $num1_{Int}$, $num2_{Nat}$ → ..., $result_{Int}$
Bitwise logical shift right operation with zero extension, i.e., *result* = *num1* ⋙ (*num2* & 0x0F) on a 16-bit CVM and *result* = *num1* ⋙ (*num2* & 0x1F) on a 32-bit CVM, respectively.

3.9. Instruction Set

shrs $= 96$:
..., $num1_{\text{Int}}$, $num2_{\text{Nat}} \rightarrow$ ..., $result_{\text{Int}}$
Bitwise arithmetic shift right operation with sign extension. i.e., $result = num1 \gg (num2$ & 0x0F$)$ on a 16-bit CVM and $result = num1 \gg (num2$ & 0x1F$)$ on a 32-bit CVM, respectively.

sidzero $= 97$:
... $\rightarrow$ ...
Set the value of the special register **regSessionId** to zero, i.e., **regSessionId** := 0. Usually, this instruction is used right before a **rcv** instruction to start a new session with a particular CVM packet server.

storea $= 98$:
..., $value_{\text{Int}}$, $memAdrAbs_{\text{Nat}} \rightarrow$ ...
Store $value$ into memory in big-endian order at the starting absolute memory address $memAdrAbs$. The byte length of the integer number depends on the CVM mode and is given by **cvmIntLen**. Refer also to the error code **IllegalMemoryAddress** (page 43) and to section 3.1.2 (page 33) for more information on CVM modes and **cvmIntLen**.

storer $= 99$:
..., $value_{\text{Int}}$, $memAdrRel_{\text{Int}} \rightarrow$ ...
Store $value$ into memory in big-endian order at the starting absolute memory address $memAdrAbs$. On a 16-bit CVM, $memAdrAbs = ($**regBP** $+ memAdrRel)$ & 0xFFFF. On a 32-bit CVM, $memAdrAbs = ($**regBP** $+ memAdrRel)$ & 0xFFFFFFFF. The byte length of the integer number depends on the CVM mode and is given by **cvmIntLen**. Refer also to the error code **IllegalMemoryAddress** (page 43) and to section 3.1.2 (page 33) for more information on CVM modes and **cvmIntLen**.

sub $= 100$:
..., $num1_{\text{Int}}$, $num2_{\text{Int}} \rightarrow$ ..., $result_{\text{Int}}$
Subtract the numbers $num1$ and $num2$. If no overflow occurs, $result = num1 - num2$. Otherwise, $result = (num1 - num2)$ & 0xFFFF on a 16-bit CVM, and $(num1 - num2)$ & 0xFFFFFFFF on a 32-bit CVM.

testsetbits $= 101$:
..., $memAdrAbs_{\text{Nat}}$, $bitMask_{\text{Int}} \rightarrow$ ..., val_{Int}
Test and set the bits of the integer value val that resides in memory at the address $memAdrAbs$. At first, val is loaded unchanged onto the register stack. Then, the new value $val \mid bitMask$ is stored into memory at the address $memAdrAbs$. Refer also to the error code **IllegalMemoryAddress** (page 43). This instruction is used for access synchronization of memory variables that are shared by different threads running concurrently. Particularly, this instruction locks a mutex.

text, textbg $= 102, 103$: $text_{\text{String}}$
x_{Int}, $y_{\text{Int}} \rightarrow \varepsilon$

Draw the glyphs of *text* in the current font and foreground color beginning at the coordinate position (x, y). y refers to the baseline of *text*. The instruction **textbg** additionally fills the background area of the bounding box of *text* with the current background color. Refer to the section 3.2.1 (page 76) for more information on foreground and background colors.

textp, textpbg = 104, 105: $\ textParagraph_{String}$
$y_{Int} \to \varepsilon$
Draw the glyphs of *textParagraph* in the current font and foreground color beginning at the position (**regXTextLine**, y). y refers to the baseline of the first line of *textParagraph*. *textParagraph* consists of several lines of text which are separated by the '\n' character. The '\n' character is not drawn with a particular glyph. Instead, after each '\n' character, the CVM continues drawing the glyphs of the following characters in the next line. The y position of the next line is the y position of the previous line plus *height*. If the value of the special register **regHTextLine** is greater than zero, then *height* equals the value of **regHTextLine**. Otherwise, *height* equals the height of the current font. The height of a font is the sum of its ascent and descent. The x position of each text line is given by the special register **regXTextLine**. The instruction **textpbg** additionally fills the background area of the bounding box of each text line with the current background color. Refer to the section 3.2.1 (page 76) for more information on foreground and background colors.

textpm, textpmbg = 106, 107:
$y_{Int}, memAdrAbs_{Nat} \to \varepsilon$
Same functionality as **textp** and **textpbg**. However, the string *textParagraph* is not given as an immediate operand. Instead, it resides in memory and starts at the address *memAdrAbs*. Refer also to the error code **IllegalMemoryAddress** (page 43).

textm, textmbg = 108, 109:
$x_{Int}, y_{Int}, memAdrAbs_{Nat} \to \varepsilon$
Same functionality as **text** and **textbg**. However, the text string is not given as an immediate operand. Instead, it resides in memory and starts at the address *memAdrAbs*. Refer also to the error code **IllegalMemoryAddress** (page 43).

unsetbits = 110:
..., $memAdrAbs_{Nat}, bitMask_{Int} \to $ ...
Unset the bits of the integer value *num* that resides in memory at the starting address *memAdrAbs*. The new value *num* & *bitMask* is stored into memory at the same address. Refer also to the error code **IllegalMemoryAddress** (page 43). This instruction is used for access synchronization of memory variables that are shared by different threads running concurrently. Particularly, this instruction releases a mutex.

xor = 111:
..., $num1_{Int}, num2_{Int} \to$ ..., $result_{Int}$
Bitwise XOR operation with *result* = $num1 \oplus num2$.

3.10 Implementation Notes

The CVM has been implemented in software with the C [20] programming language under the Linux [43] operating system. The used C compiler is `gcc` [32] with the optimization level `-O1`. The CVM implementation covers the modules Core, Visual, Keyboard, Mouse, Network, and the so far specified Libraries.

Source Files The C source files for the CVM interpreter are in the subdirectories `Implementation/Cvm/Src/` and `Implementation/RghLib/Src/`. The latter subdirectory contains only source files whose names start with the prefix "`rgh`".

- `Core/`: The source files in this subdirectory implement the CVM module Core.

- `Visual/`: The source files in this subdirectory implement the CVM module Mouse. Note that the basic graphic output with X11 is handled in the source files `rghX11.{h,c}`.

- `Keyboard/`: The source files in this subdirectory implement the CVM module Keyboard. So far, this subdirectory is empty, because no CVM specific source files are needed here. The basic control of the keyboard with X11 is handled in the source files `rghX11.{h,c}`.

- `Mouse/`: The source files in this subdirectory implement the CVM module Mouse. Note that the basic control of the mouse with X11 is handled in the source files `rghX11.{h,c}`.

- `Network/`: The source files in this subdirectory implement the CVM module Network.

- `Libraries/`: The source files in this subdirectory implement the CVM module Libraries, as far as currently specified. Each implemented library starts with the prefix "`lib`".

- `Profiles/`: This subdirectory contains a collection of different CVM profiles. Each CVM profile specifies the capabilities of the respective CVM to be generated and is a C header file that starts with the prefix "`cvm`". So far, the following CVM profiles have been defined: `cvm16.h`, `cvm16Emu.h`, `cvm16Thin.h`, `cvm32.h`, `cvm32Emu.h`, and `cvm32Thin.h`. Additional CVM profiles may be defined in the future.

    The file `_profile.h` is a link to one of these CVM profiles. During the compilation, it is included by the other source files to build an appropriate CVM executable that fits to the capabilities which are specified in the currently active CVM profile.

- `cvmMain.c`: This source file contains the `main()` function.

- `RghLib/Src/`: These source files contain general utility functions and definitions for managing the heap and input/output on streams, for debugging, and for managing strings, TCP/IP [69] network connections, and the graphic input/output with X11 [51], respectively.

    For the implementation of the graphic input/output in X11 the Xlib [51, 52] programming library has been used. Xlib is the low-level programming library of the X11 [51] system.

For the implementation of the TCP/IP [69] network communication the Linux socket interface, which is compatible to the BSD [17] socket interface, has been used. However, this implementation supports only IPv4, but not IPv6.

Not Implemented Parts Except for the following restrictions, the CVM has been implemented completely:

- Module Core:

    - The UTF-8 [89] characters in strings (String) may contain only printable ASCII [7] characters, including the space character (" ").
    - 16BitEmu, 32BitEmu: These CVM modes have been implemented as well but without specific optimizations that increase runtime performance for CVMs with these emulation modes. Refer also to the sections 3.7 (page 89) and 3.8 (page 98) for more information on this topic. Note that the implementation of such optimizations is not mandatory and left to the implementors' choice.

- Module Visual: The measuring unit is always a pixel point and must not be a fraction of a pt, i.e., the value of the special register regMeasure is always zero.

- Module Libraries:

    - The library functions new, free, hload, and hstore are only implemented for a 32-bit CVM. If these functions are called on a 16-bit CVM, the CVM aborts execution and starts error handling with the error code UnknownLibraryFunction.
    - The library functions pixmapgz and png are not implemented so far.

As these parts are not necessarily needed for the demonstration purpose of this implementation, they can be added later.

Building The Makefile [34], which is in the subdirectory Implementation/Cvm/, manages the compilation of the source files to build the executable CVM interpreter which is located in the subdirectory Implementation/Cvm/Bin/. In the same subdirectory where Makefile is located, the make [34] command must be invoked in a shell [31] with the following options to start compilation:

```
make [TARGET] [CFLAGS="[-DDEBUG]"]
```

Optional parts are enclosed with [...].

The CFLAGS option -DDEBUG directs the CVM interpreter to produce debugging messages onto the standard output. For example, the name of each called and executed C function is printed each time at the beginning of its execution.

TARGET might be either empty or cvm, cvm16, cvm16Emu, cvm16Thin, cvm32, cvm32Emu, cvm32Thin, cvmi16, cvmi16Emu, cvmi16Thin, cvmi32, cvmi32Emu, cvmi32Thin, or allCvms. It specifies which CVM profile should be used to build the CVM. The respective CVM profiles cvm16.h, cvm16Emu.h, cvm16Thin.h, cvm32.h, cvm32Emu.h, and cvm32Thin.h are located in the subdirectory Implementation/Cvm/Src/Profiles/.

3.10. Implementation Notes

If `TARGET` is not `allCvms`, the name of the executable file is `TARGET`. However, if `TARGET` is `allCvms`, then all the listed CVMs from `cvm16` to `cvmi32Thin` are built.

The CVM executables starting with the prefix "`cvmi`" are based on the same CVM profile as the respective "`cvm...`". However, they additionally print informative messages about the CVM activities during runtime to the standard output. These messages mainly consist of the opcode and operands of the currently executed instruction, the current contents of the special registers, the register stack, the history buffer, and the bookmarks list. In addition, these messages also report the CVM state transitions and the exchanged CPTP packets with the contacted CVM packet server over the network. All these messages are useful for demonstration purposes and for debugging.

If `TARGET` is empty or `cvm`, then the recently used CVM profile is used again for the compilation and the name of the executable CVM interpreter is `cvm`.

Invocation   The invocation syntax of the CVM interpreter `cvm...` is as follows:

$$\text{cvm... } fileName$$

At the beginning, `cvm...` first reads the CVM packet with the name *fileName* and then executes it. This CVM packet represents the `HomeMenu`. Examples of HomeMenu CVM packets (`*.cvmp`) can be found in the subdirectory `Implementation/Cvm/HomeMenu/`.

Interval Timer   Due to the Linux operating system, the precision of the interval timer currently is not smaller than 10 ms. In a CVM program, therefore, it doesn't make sense, to set the value of the special timer register `regTimerInterval` to a smaller value.

Builtin Events   As specified in section 3.1.6.3 (page 49), the type of user actions that cause builtin events are implementation dependent. In this implementation, the builtin events are raised by the following control (Ctrl) key combinations:

- cvm_quit: Ctrl+C
- history_back: Ctrl+B
- history_forward: Ctrl+F
- history_reload: Ctrl+R
- input_hostAdr: Ctrl+I
- menu_bookmarks: Ctrl+O
- menu_home: Ctrl+H

Bookmarks Menu (menu_bookmarks) The size of the bookmarks list is specified in the CVM profile. The bookmarks menu can be controlled by the user with the following events:

- Exit bookmarks menu:
  - key_pressed_escape or
  - mouse_pressed with regEventPar3 = 3 (rightButton)
- Mark unmarked bookmark entry:
  - Previous: key_pressed with regEventPar1 = XK_Up
  - Next: key_pressed with regEventPar1 = XK_Down
  - At mouse position: mouse_pressed_left
- Select already marked bookmark entry:
  - key_pressed_enter
  - At mouse position: mouse_pressed_left
- Scroll up bookmarks menu: mouse_pressed with regEventPar3 = 4 (wheelUp)
- Scroll down bookmarks menu: mouse_pressed with regEventPar3 = 5 (wheelDown)
- Delete marked bookmark entry:
  - key_pressed with regEventPar1 = XK_d
  - At mouse position: mouse_pressed with regEventPar3 = 2 (middleButton)
- Add new bookmark entry that refers to the current CVMUI page: Mark and then select first bookmark entry, which is labeled with "Add"

The bookmarks are stored in the file `Implementation/Cvm/Src/bookmarks.dat`.

Input Host Address (input_hostAdr) The input syntax for the host address and service number is as follows:

$$host\_address\,[\,'\!:\!'\,[serviceNo]\,]$$

Optional parts are enclosed with [...].

host_address might be either an IP [62] address in standard dot notation or a DNS [45] name.

serviceNo is a Nat2 number. If no *serviceNo* is given, the default value zero is assumed.

Examples are "`131.159.58.35:132`", "`131.159.58.35`", "`rayhalle.in.tum.de:132`", or "`rayhalle.in.tum.de`".

History Buffer The size of the history buffer is specified in the CVM profile.

3.10. Implementation Notes

Byte Sizes of Different CVMs To give an idea about the complexity of different CVM implementations, the byte sizes of the executable CVM interpreters that are created in the `Makefile` are listed in the following:

cvm16:	74295 Bytes
cvm16Emu:	74295 Bytes
cvm16Thin:	64036 Bytes
cvm32:	72970 Bytes
cvm32Emu:	73418 Bytes
cvm32Thin:	62660 Bytes

Here, the executable files of a CVM interpreter requires only approximately 64 to 74 Kbytes[†]. The corresponding CVM profile `cvm16.h` is as follows:

```
#define cvmProfileId 0
#define cvmMode 0
#define cvmNumGeneralRegs 10
#define cvmMemMaxAdr 0xFFFF
#define cvmTimerAvailable
#define cvmBookmarksSize 30
#define cvmHistorySize 10
#define cvmMeasure 0
#define cvmFontsMaxFontCode 23
#define cvmScreenHeight 150
#define cvmScreenWidth 250
#define cvmKeyCodeSet 0
#define cvmMouseButtons 3
#define cvmNetworkAvailable
#define cvmDNSLookup
#define cvmLibrariesCoreMisc
#define cvmLibrariesVisualImage
#define cvmLibrariesVisualMisc
```

The corresponding CVM profile `cvm16Thin.h` is as follows:

```
#define cvmProfileId 0
#define cvmMode 0
#define cvmNumGeneralRegs 10
#define cvmMemMaxAdr 0x27FF    // 10 Kbytes - 1
#define cvmBookmarksSize 10
#define cvmHistorySize 10
#define cvmMeasure 0
#define cvmFontsMaxFontCode 14
#define cvmScreenHeight 150
#define cvmScreenWidth 250
#define cvmKeyCodeSet 0
#define cvmNetworkAvailable
```

[†]Note that here the executables of the 16-bit CVMs are larger than the corresponding 32-bit CVMs, because on a 32-bit platform it's more laborious to implement an interpreter for a 16-bit CVM.

The corresponding CVM profile cvm32.h is similar to cvm16.h. However, the values of cvmMode and cvmMemMaxAdr are 2 and 0xFFFFFF, respectively.

The corresponding CVM profile cvm32Thin.h is similar to cvm16Thin.h. However, the value of cvmMode is 2.

Example To demonstrate the CVM behavior especially during the state transitions between the CVM states Execute, EventExecute, and TimerExecute, the CVM assembler program fibTimer in section B.6 (page 237) is executed by the CVM interpreter cvmi32. Figure 3.8 (page 122) contains an exemplary screen shot. In the following, appropriate

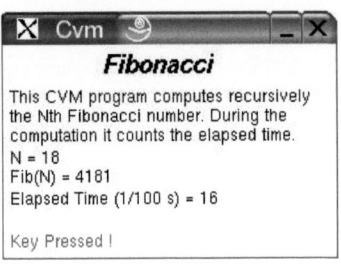

Figure 3.8: **CVM Screen Shot:** fibTimer.cvm

extracts of the output that is produced by the interpreter cvmi32 during runtime are shown:

```
...

regIP = 447, regRSP = 0, regSS = 476,
    regSP = 700, regBP = 672
R[] = _

regState = Execute

/* 447*/    loadc1 -36    // -36
/* 449*/    call          // _
/* 413*/    loadcu1 2     // 2
/* 415*/    newstackframe // _
/* 416*/    loadc_1       // 1

...

/* 437*/    loadc_m1      // -1
/* 438*/    addsp         // _
/* 439*/    incsp         // _
/* 440*/    loadcu1 4     // 4
/* 442*/    loadr         // 6

regEventCode = 10 (key_released)
```

```
regEventPar1 = 32 (key code = space)
regEventPar2 = 0 (unused)
regEventPar3 = 0 (unused)

regState = EventProcess

regIP = 120, regRSP = 0, regSS = 476,
    regSP = 644, regBP = 0
R[] = _

regState = EventExecute

/* 120*/    loadcu1 255   // 255
/* 122*/    loadcu1 255   // 255 255
/* 124*/    loadcu1 255   // 255 255 255
/* 126*/    setcolor

regTimerSignal = 1

// _

regTimerSignal = 0
```

```
regIP = 459, regRSP = 0, regSS = 476,
    regSP = 644, regBP = 0
R[] = _

regState = TimerExecute

/* 459*/    loadc_0   // 0
/* 460*/    loada     // 207
/* 461*/    inc       // 208
/* 462*/    loadc_0   // 208 0
/* 463*/    storea    // _
/* 464*/    loadc_0   // 0
/* 465*/    loada     // 208
/* 466*/    loadcu1 148  // 208 148
/* 468*/    loadcu1 116  // 208 148 116
/* 470*/    loadcu1 7    // 208 148 116 7
/* 472*/    lib /*printIntBg*/  // _
/* 473*/    halt      // _

regIP = 127, regRSP = 0, regSS = 476,
    regSP = 644, regBP = 0
R[] = _

regState = EventExecute

/* 127*/    loadcu1 4    // 4
/* 129*/    loadcu1 147  // 4 147
/* 131*/    textbg "Key Pressed !"  //
                                     _
/* 146*/    loadc_0   // 0
/* 147*/    loadc_0   // 0 0
/* 148*/    loadc_0   // 0 0 0
/* 149*/    setcolor  // _
/* 150*/    halt      // _

regIP = 443, regRSP = 1, regSS = 476,
    regSP = 644, regBP = 620
R[] = 6

regState = Execute

/* 443*/    loadcu1 2  // 6 2
/* 445*/    sub        // 4
/* 446*/    push       // _
/* 447*/    loadc1 -36 // -36
/* 449*/    call       // _

...
```

Note the state transitions ... → Execute → EventProcess → EventExecute → TimerExecute → EventExecute → Execute → ... in the output. They occur when a timer signal interrupts execution of an event handling subroutine, whereas the corresponding event in turn has previously interrupted normal execution of the CVM.

3.11 Related Work

JVM The main analogies and differences between the JVM [80] from Sun Microsystems and the CVM are listed in the following table:

JVM	CVM
Main Architecture:	
object oriented	not object oriented
only core functionality; anything else via Java APIs	Core module provides core functionality; additional modules for Visual, Audio, Network, etc., each with appropriate CVM instructions, e.g., basic drawing instructions of the Visual module; module Library contains CVM libraries for more complex tasks.
Data Types:	
byte	Int1

short	Int2
int	Int4
boolean	Nat1
char	Nat2
–	Int3, Nat3, Nat4
long, float, double	–
returnAddress	Nat
reference	–

Arithmetics:

integer and floating point	only integer; for floating point arithmetic additional CVM code or libraries are needed

Stack:

JVM stack	memory stack

General Purpose Registers:

–	register stack

Note, the JVM loads the instruction operands onto the JVM stack, whereas the CVM loads the instructions operands onto the register stack.

Heap:

always present	optional

Garbage Collection:

supported automatically	only via additional CVM code or CVM libraries

Exception Handling:

can be defined by programmer	–

Error Handling:

can be defined by programmer	predefined by functional unit in the Core module, cannot be changed by programmer

Event Handling:

only via Java APIs	supported directly by functional unit in the Core module

History Buffer:

–	supported directly by functional unit in the Core module

Bookmarks Menu:

–	supported directly by functional unit in the Core module, however optional

Interval Timer:

only via Java APIs	supported directly by functional unit in the Core module, however optional

Synchronization:

3.11. Related Work

via monitors	via test and set instructions (testsetbits, unsetbits)

Binary Executable Format:

Java Class File	CVM Packet; much simpler format
complex verification process	simple verification process, checks mainly whether a CVM packet complies to the CVM packet format and to the system properties given by the CVM profile.
constant pool	*data* section
Note, in addition to the numeric and string constants known at compile time, the constant pool also contains method and field references that must be resolved at run time by the JVM (*dynamic linking*). The constant pool is similar to a symbol table for a conventional programming language.	

Table 3.1: **Comparison:** JVM ↔ CVM

J2ME: CLDC, MIDP A J2ME [74] enabled, mobile low-end device has to implement at least both CLDC [73] and MIDP [78]. The proposed CVM represents an alternative to the CLDC/MIDP platform. The main differences of CLDC/MIDP and the CVM are listed in the following:

The KVM executable from the CLDC Reference Implementation Version 1.1 for a Linux platform requires about 280 Kbytes, whereas the CVM executable from this implementation requires only about 70 Kbytes.

The memory requirements of CLDC/MIDP are much higher than of the CVM. For example, at least 128 Kbytes volatile memory for the Java runtime (e.g., Java heap) are required. However, the CVM can work properly with even less than 1 Kbyte of volatile memory as long as the CVM packet server generates such small CVM packets that do not need too much additional memory for storing runtime data.

CLDC/MIDP is not as flexible as the CVM, because it can not be modularized like the CVM. A CLDC/MIDP enabled device has to implement all parts of it. Besides, the system requirements of CLDC/MIDP are higher than that of the CVM. The CVM, however has a modular architecture with optional components and reports its system properties and capabilities to the CVM packet server within a CVM profile.

WAP: WML, WMLScript, UAProf The client user interface language WML [56] is descriptive and therefore more difficult to interpret than CVM code which is operational. Therefore, WML has to include WMLScript [58] for dynamic tasks, which additionally requires a WMLScript interpreter that runs on the client device. The CVM code format does not need any other client languages. It enables more scalability than WML/WMLScript when desribing user interfaces. As it provides at least equal functionality, WML/WMLScript documents might be translated with a given CVM profile completely into appropriate CVM packets.

UAProf [59] is the WAP counterpart of the CVM profile. Both formats are binary. UAProf provides a rich vocabulary set to describe the client capabilities from the hardware level up to the application level, whereas the CVM profile focuses mainly on the configuration and special characteristics of the CVM and on the user preferences. The UAProf component "HardwarePlatform" contains some attributes that are identical or similar to some profile items in the CVM profile, e.g., `Keyboard` and `ScreenSize`. However, it does not have attributes that describe the memory size and supported fonts of the client device as precisely as the CVM profile item codes `cvmMemMaxAdr` and `cvmFonts`. All in all, the CVM profile describes the hardware capabilities of the client device a little more detailed and at a slightly lower level.

Nevertheless, some UAProf attributes might be adopted for the CVM profile in the future, if required.

W3C: XHTML Basic, XML, CSS, XSL, XForms, CC/PP As XHTML Basic [8] is a subset of HTML [65], it is still declarative with high-level markup elements and therefore lacks of the same disadvantages as HTML in terms of scalability and functionality. These disadvantages are discussed in detail in section 2.2 (page 13).

CSS [12] and XSL [2] are very powerful languages to describe the layout structure of an XML [16] document. However, they are too complex to be interpreted by a resource-constrained client device. CSS Mobile Profile [95] contains some simplifications, but still the client device needs to perform the formatting task on its own by a rendering engine that runs on the client device.

XForms [24] is a powerful language to describe user interfaces. However, as XForms is a declarative and a quite high-level language, the task of interpreting and rendering an XForms document might be too complex for a resource-constrained client device. Alleviations for restricted client devices have not been defined, so far.

As the CC/PP Profile is based on XML [16] and RDF [44], it is more complex than the CVM profile that is proposed in this thesis. The CC/PP Exchange Protocol [53] assumes an underlying application protocol such as HTTP [10], whereas the proposed CPTP protocol runs directly on top of the transport service. In addition, the CC/PP framework does not define a new virtual machine that acts as the user agent. As the CC/PP attribute vocabulary is similar to UAProf for the WAP Forum, refer also to the comments on UAProf in section 3.11 (page 126).

To sum up, all the XML-based technologies such as XHTML Basic, XML, CSS, XSL, and XForms provide less scalability when describing user interfaces and impose more system requirements for the client device than the proposed CVM approach. However, they might be used as user-friendly front ends to specify documents and user interfaces on the server side. With a given CVM profile, the CVM packet generator might transform these front-end specifications into appropriate CVM packets.

Chapter 4
CVM Packet Transfer Protocol (CPTP)

The CVM packet transfer protocol (CPTP) is an application protocol that manages the communication between the CVM and the CVM packet server. It runs on top of the transport layer and is a very "thin" counterpart to the HTTP [10] application protocol in the World Wide Web (WWW). HTTP was developed especially for the WWW and has a lot of advanced and complex protocol aspects for caching, authorization, handling of server response codes and error conditions, etc., which are quite hard to implement on a resource limited client. With the request headers Accept, Accept-Charset, Accept-Encoding, and Accept-Language, HTTP also covers some aspects of content negotiation — however at a high level of abstraction, i.e., no detailed description of the hardware capabilities of the client device, but a few directives on the preferred document formats, character sets, content encodings, and language. The HTTP equivalent of the WAP protocol stack is the Wireless Session Protocol [57] (WSP). However, this protocol provides full HTTP 1.1 functionality and additionally incorporates some other features.

In contrast, CPTP provides only a few basic protocol methods for requesting and delivering CVM packets, for sending CVM profile data that is used for content negotiation, for sending arbitrary data that is processed on the server side, and for reporting error messages. The advanced and complex protocol aspects like the handling of all kinds of server response codes and error conditions are not specified by the CPTP protocol. Instead, the CVM packet server might send in such a situation an appropriate CVM packet to the CVM that contains a user interface which informs the user and also provides a list of actions how the user can react to that server response. As a result, these application-specific protocol aspects are dealt with on the server side by the control logic of the network service. The CVM is not required to interpret such server responses on its own, i.e., generate appropriate user interfaces and perform appropriate actions on its own, as it is the case with the HTTP protocol. An example of an error condition might be when the CVM requests a nonexistent user interface page from a CVM packet server.

4.1 Message Format

Each CPTP message consists of a protocol method and possibly some operands, called *message items*. Its binary format is presented here as a tuple data structure by using the generally understandable notation from section A.3 (page 208). Successive components within a tuple or array structure are stored in a CPTP message sequentially, without padding or alignment. Multibyte values are stored in big-endian order. Refer to section 3.1.1 (page 32) for more information on the CVM data types Nat<1|...|4>. The array type Nat1[] is used for byte streams of any data. The general binary format of a CPTP message is as follows:

CptpMessage = { Nat1 methodCode;
                  Nat1[4] sessionId;
                  Nat1 cvmIntLen;
                  Nat1[] *messageItems* }

methodCode is a unique integer number that identifies the protocol method and thus the desired CPTP operation. In contrast to the HTTP [10] protocol, all CPTP protocol methods are encoded as binary values, but not as a sequence of ASCII characters.

sessionId identifies the current client-server session. A CVM packet server might serve more than one CVM at the same time and therefore needs this value to distinguish between them when it receives a CPTP message from a CVM. (Note that the IP [62] address of the CVM is not sufficient, because — as the case may be — several CVM processes may run on the same client host, each having a session with the same CVM packet server.) Each time, the CVM sends a CPTP message to a CVM packet server, it writes the current value of regSessionId into this message item. Each time, the CVM receives a CPTP message from a CVM packet server, it stores the value of sessionId into its special register regSessionId. Refer to section 3.4 (page 82) for more information on regSessionId. At the beginning of a new client-server session, the value of sessionId is zero in the GET message from a CVM to the CVM packet server. The CVM packet server then assigns a value other than zero to the new session and uses this value for the message item sessionId in its response message. As a result, the CVM packet server can determine which CPTP message belongs to which client-server session.

With a 4-byte value each CVM packet server can serve $2^{32} - 1$ clients at same time. However, if necessary, a 6- or 8-byte value might be used in the future.

cvmIntLen reports to the CVM packet server the value of cvmIntLen, which depends on the CVM mode of the CVM. Refer to section 3.1.2 (page 33) for more information on cvmIntLen and on CVM modes.

messageItems is a possibly empty array of data values which depend on the protocol method.

All protocol methods and their message items are listed in the next section.

4.2 Protocol Methods

In the following, the currently specified CPTP protocol methods are listed alphabetically and described using the following description format:

method_name = methodCode: *messageItems*

method_name is the verbose name of the methodCode. *messageItems* is specified as a tuple

4.2. Protocol Methods

structure. Depending on the method code, however, it may also be empty.
The data type Nat is used as a shortcut for the data type Nat<cvmIntLen>.
Additional protocol methods may be defined in the future. A client-server session always starts with a GET message which is sent from the CVM to a CVM packet server.

CVMP = 1: { Nat cvmpNo, pageMemAdr; *CVMPacket* cvmPacket }
This protocol method is used by the CVM packet server when it sends the CVM packet cvmPacket to the CVM. Refer to section 3.8 (page 93) for more information on the CVM packet format. cvmpNo contains the number of this CVM packet. A CVM packet contains one or more CVMUI pages. Refer to sections 2.3 (page 27) and 5.5 (page 166) for more information on CVM user interfaces. pageMemAdr contains the absolute memory address of the CVM instruction, where the CVM should start execution, after it has loaded this CVM packet into its memory. Generally, this memory address represents the beginning of the instruction block of a particular CVMUI page. The CVM does not respond to a received CVMP message.

ERROR = 2: { Nat1 errorCode; Nat memAdr } |
{ Nat1 errorCode }
This protocol method is used by the CVM and the CVM packet server to report errors. If the CVM or the CVM packet server receives an ERROR message, it does not respond to it. Two tuple structures for the message items are possible:

The first tuple structure is used only by the CVM. If the CVM encounters an error while processing and executing a received CVM packet, it sends an ERROR message to the CVM packet server from which the CVM packet comes from. Refer also to section 3.1.5.1 (page 41) and to the CVM state transitions in section 3.1.10 (page 58), especially to the state Error. The message items errorCode and memAdr refer to the current values of the special registers regErrorCode and regIP, respectively. They report which error has occurred and where in the CVM program. However, if the value of the message item errorCode is MalformedCPTPMessage or UnexpectedCPTPMethodCode, the value of the message item memAdr is not relevant. Refer also to section 3.1.5.2 (page 43) for more information on the error codes MalformedCPTPMessage and UnexpectedCPTPMethodCode. The CVM packet server might collect the received ERROR messages to enable bug-fixes by the server administrators, afterwards.

The second tuple structure is used only by the CVM packet server. Then, the message item errorCode might only have the value MalformedCPTPMessage, MalformedCVMProfile, or UnexpectedCPTPMethodCode:

It has the value MalformedCPTPMessage, if the CVM packet server receives a malformed CPTP message from the CVM. Refer also to section 3.1.5.2 (page 43) for more information on the error code MalformedCPTPMessage.

It has the value MalformedCVMProfile, when the CVM packet server receives a malformed CVM profile from the CVM. Refer to section 3.7 (page 89) for more information on the CVM profile format. Note that a CVM profile may be malformed, even if the entire CPTP message is well-formed. For example, the given profile item values might not fit together. Refer also to section 3.1.5.2 (page 43) for more information on the error code MalformedCVMProfile.

It has the value UnexpectedCPTPMethodCode, if the CVM packet server receives a CPTP message with an unexpected protocol method (methodCode). For example, if the CVM packet does not receive a GET message from the CVM at the beginning of a client-server session. Refer also to section 3.1.5.2 (page 44) for more information on the error code UnexpectedCPTPMethodCode.

GET = 3: { Nat serviceNo, pageNo, subpageNo; *CVMProfile* cvmProfile;
            Nat numBytes; Nat1[numBytes] dataBytes }
This protocol method is similar to the GET and POST methods of the HTTP [10] protocol. It is used by the CVM to send the data in the data array dataBytes to the CVM packet server and then request from it the CVMUI page that is addressed by the page number pageNo and the subpage number subpageNo. serviceNo refers to the current value of the special register regServiceNo. It contains the number of the interactive network service that is requested by the CVM. pageNo and subpageNo each contain an unsigned integer number. They refer to a particular CVMUI page that belongs to the interactive network service with the number serviceNo. Refer to sections 2.3 (page 27) and 5.5 (page 166) for more information on CVM user interfaces. cvmProfile reports to the CVM packet server the capabilities of the CVM and also the currently active user preferences. The CVM packet server then passes these informations to the CVM packet generator which creates appropriate CVM packets for the CVM. Refer to section 3.7 (page 89) for more information on the CVM profile format.

The CVM only sends a GET message to the CVM packet server, when it encounters the rcv or sendrcv instruction, or when the user of the client device has successfully raised a builtin event such as history_back, history_forward, history_reload, menu_bookmarks, or input_hostAdr. However, numBytes is always zero unless the CVM has encountered the sendrcv instruction. Refer also to the CVM state transitions in section 3.1.10 (page 58), especially to the states EventExecute, Execute, TimerExecute, EventProcessBuiltin, and CptpGET.

Depending on the situation, the CVM packet server might respond with a CVMP, PROFILE, or an ERROR message: If everything goes well with CVM packet generation, it responds with a CVMP message to send the CVM packet that contains the requested CVMUI page to the CVM. If the CVM profile is not complete and the CVM packet generator needs more information on the client capabilities and user preferences, the CVM packet server responds with a PROFILE message that lists the required profile item values. After successful content negotiation, the CVM packet server finally sends to the CVM a CVMP message that contains the requested CVMUI page. However, if the CVM profile cvmProfile is malformed, the CVM packet server responds with an ERROR message with the errorCode MalformedCVMProfile.

Note that it is left to the implementors' choice whether the CVM always sends a complete CVM profile which contains all profile item values within the GET message. For example, the CVM could instead send in the GET message only its cvmMode and profileId. If the CVM packet server needs more information, it can ask the CVM for particular profile item values by sending a PROFILE message to the CVM where it lists all the needed profile item values. The CVM then responds with a PROFILE message that contains all requested profile item values.

4.3. Implementation Notes 131

PROFILE = 4: { *CVMProfile* cvmProfile } |
              { Nat1[] profileItemCodes; Nat1 0 }
This protocol method is used by the CVM and the CVM packet server for content negotiation. Two tuple structures for the message items are possible: The first one is used only by the CVM whereas the second one is used only by CVM packet server. If during a request, which is initiated by the CVM with a GET message, the CVM packet server needs some particular profile item values of the CVM, it sends a PROFILE message to the CVM and lists all desired profile item codes in the data array profileItemCodes. Refer to section 3.7 (page 90) for a list of all currently defined profile item codes. As all profile item codes are greater than zero, the end of the list is marked by the value zero. If the CVM packet server needs all profile item values, then profileItemCodes is empty. The CVM then responds with a PROFILE message and sends a *CVMProfile* structure that contains the values for all desired profile item codes. Refer to section 3.7 (page 89) for more information on the CVM profile format.

Note that PROFILE messages are only sent during a request, i.e., between a GET message from the CVM to the CVM packet server and a CVMP message from the CVM packet server to the CVM, and only when it is necessary. In addition, the CVM only sends a PROFILE message to the CVM packet server, after it has received a PROFILE message from the CVM packet server.

4.3 Implementation Notes

The CPTP application protocol has been implemented on top of the TCP/IP [69] protocol stack. The reserved port number is 60507.

The client part of the CPTP protocol belongs to the CVM module Network. The corresponding source files cptpClient.{h,c} are located in the subdirectory Implementation/Cvm/Src/Network/. Refer to section 3.10 (page 117) for more information on the entire CVM implementation.

The server part of the CPTP protocol is implemented by the source files cptp.h and cptpServer.{h,c} which are located in the subdirectory Implementation/CvmPacket-Server/Src/. Refer to section 5.6 (page 198) for more information on the entire CVM packet server implementation.

For the implementation of the TCP/IP [69] network communication the Linux socket interface, which is compatible to the BSD [17] socket interface, has been used. However, this implementation supports only IPv4, but not IPv6.

4.4 Example

The use of the protocol methods will be demonstrated by an example session that is illustrated in figure 4.1 (page 132). Let there be a CVM client with the CVM profile

{ cvmMode = 16Bit;
  profileId = 483721;
  cvmNumGeneralRegs = 10;

4. CVM Packet Transfer Protocol (CPTP)

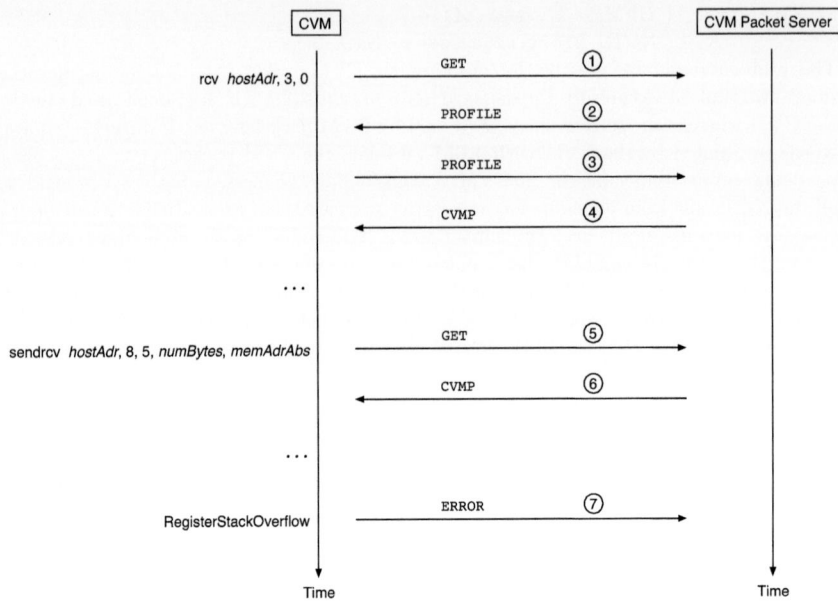

Figure 4.1: **CPTP Example Session**

cvmMemMaxAdr = 2 Kbytes - 1;
cvmScreenWidth = 150;
cvmScreenWidthMM = 600;
cvmScreenHeight = 100;
cvmScreenHeightMM = 400;
cvmFonts = 14;
cvmKeyCodeSet = 173;
0 }

and a CVM packet server with the host address *hostAdr*.

Let's assume that the value of the special register regSessionId is zero. When the CVM encounters the instruction "rcv *hostAdr*, 3, 0", it sends a GET message to the CVM packet server with the following contents (step 1):

{ methodCode = GET;
  sessionId = 0;
  cvmIntLen = 2;
  serviceNo = 3;
  pageNo = 0;
  subpageNo = 0;
  cvmProfile = { cvmMode = 16Bit;
                 profileId = 483721;

4.4. Example

```
                   0 };
  numBytes = 0;
  dataBytes = [] }
```

As there is a new client request, which is indicated by the value of `sessionId = 0`, the CVM packet server first assigns a new value to this session. Let the value be in this example 42. In addition, the CVM at first has not sent a complete CVM profile to the CVM packet server where all profile item values are listed. However, here the CVM packet server does not have the profile item values for a CVM with the `profileId = 483721` available in its database. Therefore, the CVM packet server has to ask the CVM for a detailed CVM profile by sending a `PROFILE` message to it with the following contents (step 2):

```
{ methodCode = PROFILE;
  sessionId = 42;
  cvmIntLen = 2;
  0 }
```

The CVM then responds with the following `PROFILE` message (step 3):

```
{ methodCode = PROFILE;
  sessionId = 42;
  cvmIntLen = 2;
  cvmProfile = { cvmMode = 16Bit;
                 profileId = 483721;
                 cvmNumGeneralRegs = 10;
                 cvmMemMaxAdr = 2 Kbytes - 1;
                 cvmScreenWidth = 150;
                 cvmScreenWidthMM = 600;
                 cvmScreenHeight = 100;
                 cvmScreenHeightMM = 400;
                 cvmFonts = 14;
                 cvmKeyCodeSet = 173;
                 0 }}
```

After the CVM packet generator has generated the CVM packets, the CVM packet server sends to the CVM the following `CVMP` message which contains the CVM packet with the requested CVMUI page (step 4).

```
{ methodCode = CVMP;
  sessionId = 42;
  cvmIntLen = 2;
  cvmpNo = 0;
  pageMemAdr = 2370;
  cvmPacket = ... }
```

When the CVM encounters the instruction "sendrcv $hostAdr$, 8, 5, $numBytes$, $memAdrAbs$", it sends a `GET` message to the CVM packet server with the following contents (step 5):

```
{ methodCode = GET;
  sessionId = 42;
  cvmIntLen = 2;
  serviceNo = 3;
  pageNo = 8;
  subpageNo = 5;
  cvmProfile = { cvmMode = 16Bit;
                 profileId = 483721;
                 0 };
  numBytes = numBytes;
  dataBytes = [...] }
```

The CVM packet server first processes the received data in the data array **dataBytes**. Then it sends to the CVM the following **CVMP** message which contains the CVM packet with the requested CVMUI page (step 7).

```
{ methodCode = CVMP;
  sessionId = 42;
  cvmIntLen = 2;
  cvmpNo = 5;
  pageMemAdr = 832;
  cvmPacket = ... }
```

At the end, the error **RegisterStackOverflow** occurs during the CVM executes the recently loaded CVM packet. The CVM then sends an **ERROR** message to the CVM packet server to notify the CVM packet server. The **ERROR** message has the following contents (step 8):

```
{ methodCode = ERROR;
  sessionId = 42;
  cvmIntLen = 2;
  errorCode = regErrorCode;
  memAdr = regIP }
```

Note that in the normal case the CVM packet generator creates valid CVM packets, so that no runtime errors should occur when the CVM executes the CVM packets.

Chapter 5
CVM Packet Server (CVMPS)

The CVM packet server processes the client requests and generates session instances and CVM packets that are optimized for the individual client capabilities. The client-server communication is determined by the CPTP protocol, which is specified in section 4 (page 127). The client capabilities are described in the CVM profile. The CVM packet format and the CVM profile format are specified in the sections 3.8 (page 93) and 3.7 (page 89), respectively.

Note that the service providers can freely choose the design and implementation of their server-side architecture as far as it conforms to the specified CVM packet format, the CVM profile format, and the CPTP communication protocol. As a proof of concept, a CVM packet server has been developed and implemented in this thesis as well. Its main components are as follows:

- Abstract User Interface Description (AUI): The abstract user interface description language is used to specify interactive network services on the application layer.

- Session Manager: The session manager processes all incoming client messages and stores the data that are involved during the client-server sessions.

- Service Generator: The service generator generates the client-specific service instance from a given AUI description and CVM profile.

- CVM Packet Generator: The CVM packet generator generates customized CVM packets from a given AUI description and CVM profile. These CVM packets are called CVM user interfaces.

- CVM User Interface (CVMUI): A CVM user interface is a CVM packet that is generated by the CVM packet generator from a given AUI description. It may contain all parts of a given AUI page or only a smaller subset. Here an exemplary structure of a CVMUI is specified.

5.1 Abstract User Interface Description (AUI)

In this thesis an exemplary abstract user interface description language, called AUI, has been developed and implemented. It is used to specify interactive network services on the application layer which consist of user interfaces for the CVM and state-dependent actions that are executed on the client and server side. A given AUI description is used both by the service generator and by the CVM packet generator when they generate the client-specific service instance and the client-specific CVM packets, respectively.

An AUI description contains several pages that are displayed by the CVM, whereas each page consists of several user interface components. AUI contains language constructs to specify the structure and appearance of the pages and their user interface components. However, AUI does not contain language constructs to specify directly the server-side and client-side actions, which make up the operational semantics of the network service and are state dependent. AUI rather provides language constructs where the service programmer can embed client-side and server-side code. Client-side actions are specified in CVM assembler whereas server-side actions are specified in a common programming language.

The idea that a description language provides language constructs only for a special purpose and leaves everything else, in particular state-dependent actions that make up the operational semantics, to a native programming language can also be found in the generation tools flex[†] [33] and bison[‡] [30]. While flex and bison focus on the specification of regular expressions and context free grammars, respectively, AUI focuses on the structure and appearance of user interfaces for interactive network services.

So far, AUI offers only a few and elementary types of user interfaces components. Additional and more complex user interface components may be defined in the future.

5.1.1 Concrete Syntax

AUIs are case sensitive. The grammar for the concrete syntax of the AUI is presented in a generally understandable notation. Refer to section A.2 (page 207) for a short description of the used notation. The grammar of the AUI can be split into a syntactic and a lexical part. First, the grammar is listed, then additional explanations and context conditions are provided for particular syntactic constructs in alphabetical order.

Syntactic Grammar The syntactic part of the grammar with the root *Aui* is as follows:

Aui	::=	*ServiceNo* ',' *ServiceId*
		'%%' *ServiceVar*∗
		'%%' *Page*+
		'%%' *ServerLng ServerActionCmd*∗
		'%%' *ServerActionPage*+
		('%%' *ServerCodeMisc*)?
ServiceNo	::=	*NatLiteral*
ServiceId	::=	*Identifier*
ServiceVar	::=	*VarType Identifier* ('=' *Expr*)?
Page	::=	*PageId* '{' *Attr*∗ (*GuiCmpt* | *CvmAs*)∗ '}'
PageId	::=	*Identifier*

[†]Successor of lex
[‡]Successor of yacc

5.1. Abstract User Interface Description (AUI)

Attr	::=	*AttrName* '=' *Expr* ';'
GuiCmpt	::=	*GuiCmptType Identifier* '{' *Attr*∗ *Event*∗ '}'
Event	::=	*EventType* '{' *CvmAsEntity*∗ '}'
CvmAsEntity	::=	... // refer to section B.1 (page 216), "*CvmAsEntity*"
CvmAs	::=	'`CvmAs`' '{' *CvmAsEntity*∗ '}'
ServerActionCmd	::=	*ServiceCmdId* ':' '{' *ServerCode* '}'
ServiceCmdId	::=	*Identifier*
ServerCode	::=	...
ServerActionPage	::=	(*StatePageId* ',')? *StatePageId* ':' '{' *ServerCode* '}'
StatePageId	::=	*PageId* | '∗' | '^'
ServerCodeMisc	::=	*ServerCode*
Expr	::=	*MulExpr* | *Expr* ('+' | '-') *MulExpr*
MulExpr	::=	*Factor* | *MulExpr* ('∗' | '/' | '%') *Factor*
Factor	::=	'(' *Expr* ')' | '-' *Factor* | *NatLiteral* | *StringLiteral* |
		FontCode | *ImgStyle* | *BuiltinFct* '(' (*Expr* (',' *Expr*)∗)? ')' |
		AttrName | '.' *AttrName* | *Identifier* '.' *AttrName* |
		Identifier

Lexical Grammar The lexical part of the grammar is as follows:

GuiCmptType	::=	'`Btn`' | '`Hlk`' | '`Ixt`' | '`Txp`' | '`Txt`'
EventType	::=	'`evDwn`' | '`evUp`'
AttrName	::=	'`x`' | '`y`' | '`w`' | '`h`' | '`fg`' | '`bg`' | '`fc`' | '`fs`' | '`str`' | '`yStr`' |
		'`strLenMax`' | '`hostAdr`' | '`serviceNo`' | '`img`' | '`imgStyle`' |
		'`svIdx`'
ImgStyle	::=	'`imgTile`' | '`imgScale`'
VarType	::=	'`Int`' | '`String`'
ServerLng	::=	'`C`' | '`C++`' | '`C#`' | '`Java`' | ...
BuiltinFct	::=	... // refer to section 5.1.3 (page 148), "*builtin_function_name*"
FontCode	::=	... // refer to section 3.2.3 (page 79), "*font_code_name*"
Identifier	::=	*Alpha* (*Alpha* | *Digit*)∗
NatLiteral	::=	*Digit*+
StringLiteral	::=	'"' (ASCII \ '"')∗ ('\\' (ASCII \ '"')∗)∗ '"'
Alpha	::=	'`a`'..'`z`' | '`A`'..'`Z`' | '`_`'
Digit	::=	'`0`'..'`9`'
WhiteSpace	::=	'` `' | '`\f`' | '`\n`' | '`\r`' | '`\t`'

Comment ::= '/*' ASCII* \ (ASCII* '*/' ASCII*) '*/' |
              '//' ASCII* \ (ASCII* '\n' ASCII*) '\n'

To resolve ambiguities within the lexical part of the grammar, the longest possible character sequence of the AUI that matches one of the productions in the lexical grammar is selected. For example, the character sequence 'abc12' is recognized as one *Identifier*, and not as the *Identifier* 'abc' followed by the *NatLiteral* '12'. If the longest possible character sequence matches more than one production, the production listed first is chosen.

White space characters (*WhiteSpace*) and comments (*Comment*) are discarded at lexical level. They may appear at any place in the AUI between the syntactic units listed in the syntactic part of the grammar.

Attr   An attribute definition consists of an attribute name (*AttrName*) and an integer or a string value that is specified by an expression (*Expr*).

- **x, y, w, h:** *Expr* must evaluate to an integer value that specifies the x, y coordinate position or the width, height of a user interface component (*GuiCmpt*) in pixels, respectively. **x** and **y** define the coordinate position of the upper left corner of the user interface component within the page (*Page*). The origin of the coordinate system lies in the upper left corner of the page.

- **fg, bg:** *Expr* must evaluate to an integer value that specifies the foreground (**fg**) or background (**bg**) color of the page (*Page*) or user interface component (*GuiCmpt*). Refer also to the builtin function **rgb** in section 5.1.3 (page 149). Note that a user interface component inherits the **fg** or **bg** value from the respective page (*Page*), if it does not specify its own **fg** or **bg** value, i.e., **fg** or **bg** does not appear in the attribute list (*Attr**) of the user interface component (*GuiCmpt*).

- **fc, fs:** *Expr* must evaluate to an integer value that specifies the font code (**fc**) or font size (**fs**) of the text **str** which is displayed by the user interface component (*GuiCmpt*). Refer also to the font names in section 3.2.3 (page 79). Note that a user interface component inherits the **fc** or **fs** value from the respective page (*Page*), if it does not specify its own **fc** or **bg** value.

- **str:** *Expr* must evaluate to a string value that is displayed by the user interface component (*GuiCmpt*). If **strLenMax** is also specified, then the string value may only contain at most **strLenMax** characters. If **str** is not specified, then its default value is an empty string ("").

- **yStr:** *Expr* must evaluate to an integer value that defines the y coordinate position of the base line of the text **str**. Note that **yStr** may only be specified, if **str** is specified in the attribute list (*Attr**) as well. In addition, if **yStr** is specified, **y** must not be specified at the same time, because its value is then derived from **yStr**, i.e., **yStr** = **y** + **fontAscent(fc, fs)** $- 1 + dy$. **fontAscent** is equivalent to the CVMA builtin function in section B.4 (page 229) of the same name and dy is an integer number ($dy \geq 0$) that can be freely chosen by the CVM packet generator.

- **strLenMax:** *Expr* must evaluate to an integer value that specifies the maximum number of characters in the text **str**. This attribute must only be specified, if the

5.1. Abstract User Interface Description (AUI) 139

user interface component (*GuiCmpt*) gets text input from the user, e.g., `Ixt`. If `strLenMax` is specified, `str` must be specified in the attribute list (*Attr*∗) as well.

- `hostAdr`: *Expr* must evaluate to a string value that refers to the host address of a CVM packet server. The host address might be a DNS [45] name or an IP address [62] in standard dot notation.

- `serviceNo`: *Expr* must evaluate to an integer value that addresses the number of a service that is offered by a particular CVM packet server. Refer also to *ServiceNo* (page 145).

- `img`: *Expr* must evaluate to a string value that contains the path of an image file, i.e., `"Img/imgOK32x32.gif"`, or an empty string (`""`). If the string value is not an empty string, then the addressed image is rendered into the background area of the page (*Page*) or user interface component (*GuiCmpt*). Otherwise, no image is drawn. If `img` is not specified, then its default value is `""`.

- `imgStyle`: *Expr* must evaluate to an integer value that specifies how the image `img` is rendered into the background area of the respective page (*Page*) or user interface component (*GuiCmpt*). So far, only the following values are valid:

  - 0: The image is tiled. The constant `imgTile` might be used as an alias.
  - 1: The image is scaled. The constant `imgScale` might be used as an alias.
  - 2: The image is displayed in its original size. The upper left corner of the image lies in the upper left corner of the background area. That part of the image that does not fit inside the background area is clipped. That part of the background area that is not covered by the image remains empty with the background color of the area, which is specified by the attribute `bg`. The constant `imgOrig` might be used as an alias.

  If `imgStyle` is not specified, then its default value is `imgTile`.

- `svIdx`: *Expr* must be an identifier (*Identifier*) that refers to a service variable (*ServiceVar*). This attribute applies only to interactive user interface components (*GuiCmpt*) that contain user data, e.g., `Ixt`. `svIdx` associates the user data of an interactive user interface component with a service variable. Different user interface components of a page (*Page*) must not associate their user data with the same service variable, i.e., their `svIdx` attribute values must be different. Refer also to *GuiCmpt* (page 141) and *ServiceVar* (page 145).

  The value of `svIdx` is the index number of the referenced service variable. If `svIdx` is not specified, it must not be referenced in an expression (*Expr*). There is no default value for it.

For each page (*Page*) and user interface component (*GuiCmpt*) an attribute with a particular name (*AttrName*) may be defined at least once. In addition, cyclic attribute definitions are not allowed. Refer also to *Page* and *GuiCmpt* for attribute information that is specific for *Page* and the different user interface components (*GuiCmpt*).

CvmAs CvmAs specifies CVM assembler code that is executed by the CVM. Usually, it contains additional data declarations and CVM instructions that are needed when the CVM executes the instructions (*CvmAsEntity*∗) specified in *Event*. Refer to section B (page 216) for more information on the CVM assembler.

Event Event specifies the behavior of a user interface component after an event of a particular type (*EventType*) has occurred. Usually, an event occurs after the user of the CVM has performed some action, e.g., pressed a key or clicked a mouse button, etc. *CvmAsEntity*∗ contains CVM instructions that are executed then by the CVM.

Note that the AUI event types are not identical to the CVM event types. One or a combination of single CVM events may be mapped to a particular AUI event. It is left to the CVM packet generator to determine which CVM events make up an AUI event. Refer to section 3.1.6 (pages 45) for more information on CVM events.

So far, the AUI event types evDwn and evUp are defined. These events apply to the user interface component Btn. The evDwn/evUp event occurs when the user presses/releases a button with a mouse click or with a particular key stroke, e.g., the Blank or Return key, if the button currently has mouse or keyboard focus, i.e.,

evDwn ≡ mouse_pressed_left ∨
key_pressed_enter ∨
key_pressed ∧ $keyCode$ = XK_space
evUp ≡ mouse_released_left ∨
key_released_enter ∨
key_released ∧ $keyCode$ = XK_space

Note that several CVM events are already processed implicitly by the AUI components. For example the user interface component Hlk automatically starts a new request for the network service that is specified by the attribute values hostAdr and serviceNo after an evDwn event occurs. In addition, the user interface component Ixt processes all the key and mouse events for text input and text editing implicitly. Moreover, the user might release or change the focus of the current user interface component and navigate to another one with the following events:

"Focus Next": key_pressed ∧ $keyCode$ = XK_Tab
"Focus Previous": key_pressed ∧ $keyCode$ = XK_ISO_Left_Tab // Shift+Tab
"Focus Release": key_pressed_escape ∧ $keyCode$ = XK_ISO_Left_Tab // Shift+Tab

The CVM code for the implicit event processing is provided by the CVM packet generator and also defined in the CVMUI libraries. Refer to section C (page 249) for more information on CVMUI libraries. During event handling first the CVM instructions are executed that are specified explicitly in the AUI description for a given user interface component and for a given event. If no explicit event behavior is specified, then the the implicit actions — if available — are processed. For each user interface component (*GuiCmpt*) an event with a particular type (*EventType*) may be defined at least once.

Additional event types for any user interface component types (*GuiCmptType*) may be defined in the future.

5.1. Abstract User Interface Description (AUI) 141

Expr The value of an expression (*Expr*) might be an integer number or a string and is evaluated by the CVM packet generator during generation of CVMUIs.

If its value is a string, then the expression consists of a single string literal (*StringLiteral*), or of a single builtin function call (*BuiltinFct*) that returns a string, or of a single attribute reference (*AttrName* | '.' *AttrName* | *Identifier* '.' *AttrName*) that refers to a string value, or of a single identifier (*Identifier*) that refers to a service variable with a string value, or of a concatenation of two string expressions with the '+' operator.

AttrName refers to the attribute (*Attr*) which has the same name *AttrName* and is specified in the attribute list (*Attr**) of the page (*Page*) or user interface component (*GuiCmpt*) where this expression (*Expr*) occurs.

The syntactic construct '.' *AttrName* refers to the attribute (*Attr*) which has the same name *AttrName* and is specified in the attribute list (*Attr**) of the page (*Page*).

The syntactic construct *Identifier* '.' *AttrName* refers to the attribute (*Attr*) which has the same name *AttrName* and is specified in the attribute list (*Attr**) of the user interface component (*GuiCmpt*) with the identifier *Identifier*.

A single identifier (*Identifier*) refers to a service variable (*ServiceVar*).

The values of *BuiltinFct* and *FontCode* are specified in the sections that are referred to in the comments of the respective productions in the lexical grammar specification.

All arithmetic operations with integer numbers are based on integer but not floating point arithmetic.

GuiCmpt *GuiCmpt* defines a user interface component. It consists of its type (*GuiCmpt-Type*), identifier (*Identifier*), attributes (*Attr**), and event behavior (*Event**).

So far, there are the following different user interface component types:

- Txt: A Txt user interface component is used to display single-line text. The following attributes apply to it: x, y, w, h, fg, bg, fc, fs, str, yStr.

  Only the attributes that apply to the user interface component can be specified, i.e., can appear in the attribute list (*Attr**). In addition, the following restrictions must be met:

  – The attributes x, str, and either y or yStr must be specified, i.e., must appear in the attribute list (*Attr**).

  – The attributes w and h must not be specified, because their values are derived from str, fc, and fs.

- Txp: A Txp user interface component is used to display a text paragraph which usually consists of several lines. The following attributes apply to it: x, y, w, h, fg, bg, fc, fs, str, yStr.

  Only the attributes that apply to the user interface component can be specified, i.e., can appear in the attribute list (*Attr**). In addition, the following restrictions must be met:

  – The attributes x, w, str, and either y or yStr must be specified, i.e., must appear in the attribute list (*Attr**). The attribute w specifies the width of the text paragraph. The text is aligned and broken into several lines automatically.

– The attribute h must not be specified, because its value is derived from str, fc, fs, and the number of the lines in the text paragraph.

- **Hlk**: A Hlk user interface component is used to display a hyperlink that is similar to a hyperlink in HTML [65]. The following attributes apply to it: x, y, w, h, fg, bg, fc, fs, str, yStr, hostAdr, serviceNo.

  Only the attributes that apply to the user interface component can be specified, i.e., can appear in the attribute list (*Attr*∗). In addition, the following restrictions must be met:

  – The attributes x, str, hostAdr, serviceNo, and either y or yStr must be specified, i.e., must appear in the attribute list (*Attr*∗).

  – The attributes w and h must not be specified, because their values are derived from str, fc, and fs.

- **Ixt**: An Ixt user interface component is used to display a text box where the user can input some text. The following attributes apply to it: x, y, w, h, fg, bg, fc, fs, str, yStr, strLenMax, svIdx.

  Only the attributes that apply to the user interface component can be specified. In addition, the following restrictions must be met:

  – The attributes x, w, str, strLenMax, and either y or yStr must be specified.

  – The attribute h must not be specified, because its value is derived from fc and fs.

  – The attribute svIdx is optional. If it is specified, the data type of the referenced service variable (*ServiceVar*) must be **String**. Refer to section 3.1.1 (page 33) for more information on the CVM data type **String**.

  The text that the user types in is stored into the attribute str and displayed immediately. At most strLenMax characters are stored, further characters are ignored. As in any common text box the width of the text may be longer then w. The attribute w defines the width of the text box and thus the clip area of the text that is visible all at once.

  svIdx associates the user data of this user interface component, which is stored in the attribute str, with the given service variable. If svIdx is not specified, then the user data of this user interface component is not associated with a service variable. So far, Ixt is the only interactive user interface component type that contains user data. Additional interactive user interface component types with user data may be defined in the future.

- **Btn**: A Btn user interface component is used to display a button. The button must contain text (str) or a background image (img) or both. The following attributes apply to it: x, y, w, h, fg, bg, fc, fs, str, yStr, img, imgStyle.

  Only the attributes that apply to the user interface component can be specified. In addition, the following restrictions must be met:

  – The attribute x must be specified always.

5.1. Abstract User Interface Description (AUI)

- If the button contains text, then the attributes str and either y or yStr must be specified as well. However, the attributes w and h must not be specified then, because their values are derived from str, fc, and fs.
- If the button does not contain text, i.e., the attribute str is not specified, then the attributes y, w, and h must be specified as well.
- If the button contains an image, then the attributes img and imgStyle must be specified as well.

Refer also to *Attr* for more information on attributes. Note that user interface components of the type Btn, Hlk, or Ixt are interactive, as they receive user input. Refer also to *Event* for more information on user interaction and event behavior of the user interface components.

In the future, additional (non-)interactive user interface component types may be defined, e.g., check boxes, combo boxes, list boxes, tables, etc.

Identifier Lexically, an identifier (*Identifier*) must not match *GuiCmptType*, *EventType*, *AttrName*, *ImgStyle*, *VarType*, *ServerLng*, *BuiltinFct*, *FontCode*, and 'CvmAs'. An identifier is used to name the service (*ServiceId*), the service variables (*ServiceVar*), pages (*PageId*), and user interface component (*GuiCmpt*) when they are declared. The service identifiers must be unique only for a particular CVM packet server. An identifier of a service variable or page must be unique only within the identifiers of the other declared service variables or pages, respectively. An identifier of a user interface component must be unique only within the identifiers of the other declared user interface components within the same page.

NatLiteral If the positive integer number specified by *NatLiteral* exceeds the maximum value $2^{31} - 1$, it is truncated automatically to that limit by the CVM packet generator.

Page *Page* defines a complete AUI page. *PageId* is a unique page identifier and is used within the AUI to refer to a particular page. Note that the CVM packet generator assigns to each page identifier a unique number greater than or equal to zero. This number is then used by the CVM to address a particular page during a request. Refer also to the CVM instructions rcv and sendrcv.

Attr contains an attribute definition. The following attributes apply to a page: x, y, w, h, fg, bg, fc, fs, img, imgStyle.

Only the attributes that apply to a page can be specified, i.e., can appear in the attribute list (*Attr*∗). However, the attributes x, y, w, and h must not be specified. Their values cannot be changed and are by default always 0, 0, cvmScreenWidth, and cvmScreenHeight, respectively.

If the attributes fg, bg, fc, fs, img, and imgStyle are not specified, they are provided with default values. These are rgb(0, 0, 0), rgb(255, 255, 255), fcFixedStandard, 13, "", and imgTile, respectively.

GuiCmpt contains a graphical user interface component. *CvmAs* contains CVM assembler instructions that are executed by the CVM.

ServerActionCmd *ServerActionCmd* ("Server Action Command") specifies actions that are executed on the server side, when the CVM requests a page. The CVM requests a page with the instructions `rcv` and `sendrcv`. A *ServerActionCmd* is identified by its unique *ServiceCmdId*. The service generator assigns to each *ServiceCmdId* a unique index number greater than or equal to zero. During a client request the CVM packet server first checks the `dataBytes` section of the `GET` request. The binary format of the `dataBytes` section is specified in *ServiceVar* (page 146). When it encounters the index number (`svcCmdIdx`) of a *ServiceCmdId*, it executes the actions (*ServerCode*) of the respective *ServerActionCmd* right after the `dataBytes` section of the `GET` request has been processed completely.

Refer also to the example in section 5.1.4 (page 149), to *processDataBytes* in section 5.2.2 (page 157), and to _svcInst_actionsCmd in the sections 5.3.1 (page 160) and 5.3.2 (page 161).

ServerActionPage *ServerActionPage* also specifies actions that are executed on the server side, when the CVM requests a page. However, these actions are always executed after the actions of a possibly referenced *ServerActionCmd*. The server-side actions of *ServerActionPage* are depending on the state of the client-server session which is given by the following values:

- The number of the page that is currently executed by the CVM. This page is referenced by the first *StatePageId*. If the CVM starts requesting a page in the beginning of a client-server session, i.e., the CVM is currently not executing a page that belongs to this network service, then the first *StatePageId* is omitted or given as '*'.

- The number of the page that is requested by the CVM. This page is referenced by the second *StatePageId*.

The CVM packet server always stores for each CVM it serves the number of the page that the CVM is currently executing, i.e., the number of the previously sent page during the client-server session. When the CVM requests a new page, the CVM packet server checks the server actions (*ServerActionPage+*) from top to bottom to find the first rule whose first *StatePageId* corresponds to the number of the page that the CVM is currently executing. If there is such a rule, the CVM packet server executes the actions within *ServerCode* and sends a new page to the CVM. Note that the number of the new page may be changed within *ServerCode* and therefore may be different than the number of the requested page, which is referred to by the second *StatePageId*.

In the very beginning of a client-server session, i.e., when the CVM makes a first request, the CVM packet server looks for the first rule where the first *StatePageId* is omitted or given as '*' which is a placeholder for any or no page. If *StatePageId* is specified by a *PageId*, then a page with the same name (*PageId*) must be defined in *Page+*.

Within *ServerCode* the following variable identifiers have special meanings:

- `pageNow` refers to the number of the previously sent page during the client-server session. If there is no such page, which is the case in the beginning of a client-server session, the value of `pageNow` is -1.

- `pageReq` refers to the number of the requested page.

5.1. Abstract User Interface Description (AUI) 145

- `pageNext` refers to the number of the page that is sent by the CVM packet server to the client after the server-side actions have been processed. In the beginning of the server-side actions the value of `pageNext` is initialized each time with the value of `pageReq`. Note that within *ServerCode* the value of `pageNext` may be changed. In the end of the server-side actions the value of `pageNext` is always checked. If its value refers to a non-existing page number then its value is set to −1 and the CVM packet server does not send any page to the client.

The number of an existing page with the identifier *PageId* is referred to by the term _svcInst_*PageId*.

Refer also to the example in section 5.1.4 (page 149), and to _svcInst_actionsPage in the sections 5.3.1 (page 160) and 5.3.2 (page 161).

ServerCode *ServerCode* contains the instructions that are executed by the CVM packet server. The used programming language for the server code is indicated by *ServerLng*.

ServerCodeMisc *ServerCodeMisc* contains additional declarations and definitions of constants, variables, and functions that are referenced in the instructions (*ServerCode*) of the server-side actions (*ServerActionCmd*, *ServerActionPage*). The used programming language is indicated by *ServerLng* and is the same as the programming language that is used in *ServerActionCmd* and *ServerActionPage*.

ServerLng *ServerLng* indicates the programming language that is used to specify the server-side actions (*ServerCode*). Note that the service providers can choose the programming language freely.

ServiceNo, ServiceId A CVM packet server might offer several network services. Each service is addressed by a number (*ServiceNo*) that is unique for a particular CVM packet server. The *ServiceId* is just an descriptive alias name for the respective *ServiceNo*.

Note that for every CVM packet server the service number zero is always reserved for the service that lists and describes all available services that are offered by the CVM packet server. The user interface of this service also contains a menu for the user to select and start a particular service.

ServiceVar *ServiceVar* declares a variable that stores a value during the client-server session. In the following, these variables are called *service variables*. The service variables are mainly used to store the values of the user interface components that take input from the user of the CVM, e.g., the input string of a text box control. *Expr* defines an initial value for a service variable. If *VarType* is `Int` then *Expr* might only consist of a single integer number. If *VarType* is `String` then *Expr* might only consist of a single string literal. If no initial value is specified explicitly, then the default value of a service variable is either 0 or "".

The CVM packet generator assigns to each service variable a unique index number greater than zero and allocates for each service variable enough memory to store two values: its *current* and *saved* value. In the beginning of a client-server session both values are equal.

The dataBytes section of a GET request overwrites only the current value of a service variable. Refer to section 4.2 (page 130) for more information on the CPTP protocol method GET. The binary format of the dataBytes section in the GET request is:

({ Nat<*svIdxLen*> svIdx;   *VarType* svVal } |
  { Nat<*svIdxLen*> 0;   Nat2 svcCmdIdx })∗

svIdx contains the index number of a particular service variable. *svIdxLen* is determined by the CVM packet generator and may have the value 1, 2, or 4. Depending on the total number of service variables the smallest byte size, i.e., the smallest possible value for *svIdxLen*, is used to specify the index numbers. If *VarType* is Int, then svVal represents an integer number and its binary format complies to a CVM integer number (Int) with the byte length cvmIntLen. If *VarType* is String, then svVal represents a string and its format complies to a CVM string (String). Refer to section 3.1.1 (page 32) for more information on the CVM data types.

svcCmdIdx contains the index number of a *ServiceCmdId*. Refer to page 144 for more information on *ServiceCmdId* and *ServerActionCmd*.

The values of the service variables can be accessed on the server side within the *ServerCode* of the server actions (*ServerActionCmd*, *ServerActionPage*) for further processing. Note that the precise syntax for accessing the service variables within the server actions need not be specified here. This depends on the programming language (*ServerLng*) that is used for the server actions and is therefore left to the service providers. In the current implementation the service variables are accessed as follows:

- svcVarInt_get(svcVarId) returns the current integer (Int) value of the service variable with the *Identifier* svcVarId.

- svcVarInt_set(svcVarId, val) assigns the current integer value val to the service variable svcVarId, e.g., svcVarInt_set(var1, 18).

- svcVarStr_get(svcVarId) returns the current string (String) value of the service variable svcVarId.

- svcVarStr_set(svcVarId, val) assigns the current string value val to the service variable svcVarId, e.g., svcVarStr_set(var2, "hello world!").

- svcVar_reset() resets the current values of all service variables with their saved values.

- svcVar_save() saves the current values of all service variables, i.e., overwrites the (old) saved values with their current values.

Refer to the example in section 5.1.4 (page 149) for a demonstration of these server-side functions.

The current and the saved value for each service variable is needed because of the following reason: When the user navigates through the AUI subpages, the values of the user interface components that store user input are only saved as current values on the server-side. Then the user has the ability to reset all values of these controls to the latest saved values. The current values are only saved when the function svcVar_save() is called on the server side in *ServerCode*.

5.1. Abstract User Interface Description (AUI) 147

StatePageId   *StatePageId* refers to a page. If it matches *PageId*, then it refers to a particular page (*Page*) with the same identifier. If it matches '*', then it refers to any page regardless of whether it has been defined in the AUI description. If it matches '^', then it refers to any page that has not been defined in the AUI description.

StringLiteral   Refer to "***StringLiteral***" in section B.1 (page 222).

5.1.2 Abstract Syntax

The abstract syntax of the AUI grammar is specified as a data type definition with the root *Aui*. Refer to section A.3 (page 208) for a description of the used notation. The abstract syntax is used in the following sections that describe the structure of the generated CVM code from a given AUI description.

Aui	=	{ *Int* *serviceNo*;
		  String *serviceId*;
		  ServiceVar∗ *serviceVars*;
		  Page+ *pages*;
		  Int *serverLng*;
		  ServerActionCmd∗ *serverActionsCmd*;
		  ServerActionPage+ *serverActionsPage*;
		  String *serverCodeMisc* }

ServiceVar	=	{ *String* *id*;
		  Int *varType*;
		  (*Int* | *String*) *valInit* }

Page	=	{ *String* *id*;
		  Int *pageNo*, *subpageNo*;
		  PageItem∗ *pageItems* }

PageItem	=	*Attr* | *GuiCmpt* | *CvmAs*
ServerActionCmd	=	{ *String* *idServiceCmd*, *serverCode* }
ServerActionPage	=	{ *String* *idPageCurrent*, *idPageNext*, *serverCode* }

GuiCmpt	=	{ *String* *id*;
		  Int *guiCmptType*;
		  GuiCmptItem∗ *guiCmptItems* }

GuiCmptItem	=	*Attr* | *Event*
Attr	=	{ *Int* *attrName*; *Expr* *expr* }
Event	=	{ *Int* *eventType*; *String* *cvmAs* }

CvmAs	=	{ String *cvmAs* }
Expr	=	*Add* | *Sub* | *Mul* | *Div* | *Rem* | *UnMinus* |
		AttrRefLocal | *AttrRefGuiCmpt* | *AttrRefPage* |
		Id |
		BuiltinFct |
		IntLit | *StrLit*
Add	=	{ *Expr* *expr1*, *expr2* }
Sub	=	{ *Expr* *expr1*, *expr2* }
Mul	=	{ *Expr* *expr1*, *expr2* }
Div	=	{ *Expr* *expr1*, *expr2* }
Rem	=	{ *Expr* *expr1*, *expr2* }
UnMinus	=	{ *Expr* *expr* }
BuiltinFct	=	{ Int *fctCode*;
		Expr∗ *pars* }
AttrRefGuiCmpt	=	{ Int *attrName*;
		String *idGuiCmpt* }
AttrRefLocal	=	{ Int *attrName* }
AttrRefPage	=	{ Int *attrName* }
Id	=	{ String *id* }
IntLit	=	{ Int *val* }
StrLit	=	{ String *val* }

Note that if *aui* represents the abstract syntax tree after a given AUI description has been parsed, then $aui.pages[q].pageNo := q \land aui.pages[q].subpageNo := 0$ ($q \geq 0$). The tuple item *subpageNo* is needed later for the numbering of the generated subpages of a given AUI page, because the data type *Page* is also used to formally refer to an AUI subpage. Refer to section 5.2 (pages 154 ff.) for more information on AUI subpages.

5.1.3 Builtin Functions

For reasons of convenience, the AUI also provides some builtin functions to simplify specifying user interfaces with AUI. The CVM packet generator processes a builtin function during it generates the corresponding CVMUI. In the following, the builtin functions are listed alphabetically and described using the following description format:

builtin_function_name (*parameters*) : *return_type*
verbose_description

builtin_function_name serves as a one-word description of the purpose of the function. *parameters* is a (comma separated and possibly empty) list of function parameters. Each parameter is shown in the form $ident_{type}$. *ident* can be any identifier and is usually chosen to characterize the meaning of the parameter. *type* determines the syntactic type of the parameter according to the grammar specification in section 5.1.1 (page 136). The parameter must match the production for *type*. For example, val_{Expr} might be used to specify a value that matches the production for *Expr*. *return_type* specifies the data type of the result and is one of the CVM data types Int, Nat, String, or a tuple structure. Afterwards, a verbose description of the builtin function is given.

5.1. Abstract User Interface Description (AUI)

So far, the following builtin functions are defined. Additional builtin functions may be defined in the future:

rgb (red_{Expr}, $green_{Expr}$, $blue_{Expr}$) : Int4
The builtin function **rgb** encodes the given red, green, and blue color components into an appropriate Int4 number according to the following format: $(red \ll 16) \mid (green \ll 8) \mid blue$. The values of the expressions red, $green$, and $blue$ must be unsigned integer numbers in the range of $[0; 255]$.

5.1.4 Example

The following description of a simple network service demonstrates the use of AUI. This example can be found in the subdirectory `Implementation/CvmPacketServer/Aui/`.

registration.aui This service consists of two pages which are illustrated by the figures 5.1 (page 149) and 5.2 (page 150). The first page (`p0`) reads the name and email address from the user. The user can navigate through the user interface components with the Tab and Shift+Tab keys. When the user presses the "Reset" button, the contents of the two text boxes are reset to their initial values. When the user presses the "Submit" button, the contents of the two text boxes are send to the CVM packet server and saved. The CVM packet server then sends the second page (`p1`) which confirms the data the user has input in the previous page.

Figure 5.1: **CVM Screen Shot:** AUI Page p0 from `registration.aui`

Concrete Syntax The concrete syntax of `registration.aui` is as follows:

```
1, registration

%%

String name  = "your name"
String email = "your email"

%%
```

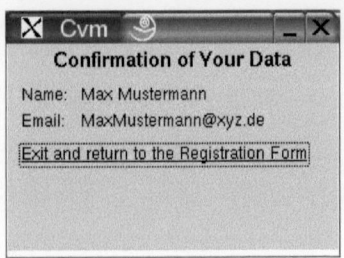

Figure 5.2: **CVM Screen Shot:** AUI Page p1 from `registration.aui`

```
p0 {
  fg = rgb(0, 0, 0); bg = rgb(222, 218, 210);
  fc = fcHelvetica; fs = 12;

  Txt txtTitle {
    x = (.w - w) / 2; y = 5;
    fc = fcHelveticaBold; fs = 14;
    str = "Registration";
  }

  Txp txpIntro {
    x = 10; y = txtTitle.y + txtTitle.h + 5; w = .w - 2 * x;
    str = "Welcome to the registration form. " +
          "Please enter your name and email address:";
  }

  Txt txtName {
    x = 10; yStr = ixtName.yStr; str = "Name";
  }

  Ixt ixtName {
    x = txtName.x + txtName.w + 10; y = txpIntro.y + txpIntro.h + 5; w = 150;
    bg = rgb(255, 255, 255);
    fc = fcCourier; str = name; strLenMax = 80;
    svIdx = name;
  }

  Txt txtEmail {
    x = txtName.x; yStr = ixtEmail.yStr; str = "Email";
  }

  Ixt ixtEmail {
    x = ixtName.x; y = ixtName.y + ixtName.h + 5; w = 150;
    bg = rgb(255, 255, 255);
    fc = fcCourier; str = email; strLenMax = 80;
    svIdx = email;
  }
```

5.1. Abstract User Interface Description (AUI)

```
  Btn btnReset {
    x = txtName.x; y = ixtEmail.y + ixtEmail.h + 10;
    fg = rgb(51, 51, 51); bg = rgb(210, 218, 230);
    str = "Reset";

    evDwn {
      fcall _svBufIdx_reset
      fcall_I _svBuf_svcCmd_write, svcCmd_Reset
      sendrcvpage_a _pageNo, _subpageNo
    }
  }

  Btn btnSubmit {
    x = btnReset.x + btnReset.w + 5; y = btnReset.y;
    fg = btnReset.fg; bg = btnReset.bg;
    str = "Submit";

    evDwn {
      fcall _svBuf_write
      fcall_I _svBuf_svcCmd_write, svcCmd_Submit
      sendrcvpage _p1, 0
    }
  }
}

p1 {
  fg = rgb(0, 0, 0); bg = rgb(222, 218, 210);
  fc = fcHelvetica; fs = 12;

  Txt txtTitle {
    x = (.w - w) / 2; y = 5;
    fc = fcHelveticaBold; fs = 14;
    str = "Confirmation of Your Data";
  }

  Txt txtName {
    x = 10; y = txtTitle.y + txtTitle.h + 10;
    str = "Name:";
  }

  Txt txtNameVal {
    x = txtName.x + txtName.w + 10; y = txtName.y;
    str = name;
  }

  Txt txtEmail {
    x = txtName.x; y = txtName.y + txtName.h + 5;
    str = "Email:";
  }

  Txt txtEmailVal {
```

```
    x = txtNameVal.x; y = txtEmail.y;
    str = email;
  }

  Hlk hlkService {
    x = txtEmail.x; y = txtEmail.y + txtEmail.h + 10;
    str = "Exit and return to the Registration Form";
    hostAdr = "127.0.0.1";
    serviceNo = 1;
  }
}

pNotExist {
  fg = rgb(0, 0, 0); bg = rgb(222, 218, 210);

  Txt txtErrMsg {
    x = (.w - w) / 2; y = 5;
    str = "Requested page does not exist";
  }
}

pIllegal {
  fg = rgb(0, 0, 0); bg = rgb(222, 218, 210);

  Txt txtErrMsg {
    x = (.w - w) / 2; y = 5;
    str = "Illegal page request";
  }
}

%% C

svcCmd_Reset:
  {
  printf("svcCmd_Reset\n");
  svcVar_reset();
  printf("name = \"%s\", email = \"%s\"\n",
         svcVarStr_get("name"), svcVarStr_get("email"));
  }


svcCmd_Submit:
  {
  printf ("svcCmd_Submit\n");
  svcVar_save();
  printf("name = \"%s\", email = \"%s\"\n",
         svcVarStr_get("name"), svcVarStr_get("email"));
  }

%%
```

5.1. Abstract User Interface Description (AUI)   153

```
p0:              { printf("-> p0\n"); }
p0, p1:          { printf("p0 -> p1\n"); }
*, ^:            { pageNext = _svcInst_pNotExist; }
*, pNotExist:    { pageNext = _svcInst_pIllegal; }
*, *:            {}
```

Refer to section 5.5 (pages 166 ff.) for more information on _svbufIdx_reset, _svBuf_svc-Cmd_write, svcCmd_Reset, _pageNo, _subpageNo, _svBuf_write, svcCmd_Submit, and _p1.

Abstract Syntax In the following, the data structure of its abstract syntax is presented in a generally understandable notation. For better readability, some tuple structures are decorated with their type names. For example,

$$\{ \text{val} = \texttt{fcHelvetica} \}_{IntLit}$$

denotes that the type of the specified tuple structure is *IntLit*.

$aui = \{$
  $serviceNo = 1;$
  $serviceId =$ "registration";
  $serviceVars = serviceVars[\,];$
  $pages = pages[\,];$
  $serverLng = \texttt{C};$
  $serverActionsCmd = serverActionsCmd[\,];$
  $serverActionsPage = serverActionsPage[\,];$
  $serverCodeMisc =$ "" $\}$

$serviceVars[0] = \{ id =$ "name"; $varType = \texttt{String}; valInit =$ "your name" $\}$
$serviceVars[1] = \{ id =$ "email"; $varType = \texttt{String}; valInit =$ "your email" $\}$

$pages[0] = \{ id =$ "p0";
  $pageNo = 0; \quad subpageNo = 0;$
  $pageItems = pages[0]\_pageItems[\,] \}$

$pages[0]\_pageItems[0] = \{$
  $attrName = \texttt{fg}; \quad expr = \{ val = (0 \ll 16) + (0 \ll 8) + 0 \}_{IntLit} \}_{Attr}$
$pages[0]\_pageItems[1] = \{$
  $attrName = \texttt{bg}; \quad expr = \{ val = (217 \ll 16) + (218 \ll 8) + 202 \}_{IntLit} \}_{Attr}$
$pages[0]\_pageItems[2] = \{$
  $attrName = \texttt{fc}; \quad expr = \{ val = \texttt{fcHelvetica} \}_{IntLit} \}_{Attr}$
$pages[0]\_pageItems[3] = \{$
  $attrName = \texttt{fs}; \quad expr = \{ val = 12 \}_{IntLit} \}_{Attr}$
$pages[0]\_pageItems[4] = \{$
  $id =$ "txtTitle"; $\quad guiCmptType = \texttt{Txt};$
  $guiCmptItems = pages[0]\_pageItems[4]\_guiCmptItems[\,] \}_{GuiCmpt}$

$pages[0]\_pageItems[4]\_guiCmptItems[0] = \{$

$attrName = \text{x};$
$expr = \{\ expr1 = \{\ expr1 = \{\ attrName = \text{w}\ \}_{AttrRefPage};$
$\qquad\qquad\qquad\qquad expr2 = \{\ attrName = \text{w}\ \}_{AttrRefLocal}\ \}_{Sub};$
$\qquad\qquad expr2 = \{\ val = 2\ \}_{IntLit}\ \}_{Div}$
$\}_{Attr}$
$pages[0]\_pageItems[4]\_guiCmptItems[1] = \{$
$\quad attrName = \text{y};\quad expr = \{\ val = 5\ \}_{IntLit}\ \}_{Attr}$
$pages[0]\_pageItems[4]\_guiCmptItems[2] = \{$
$\quad attrName = \text{fc};\quad expr = \{\ val = \text{fcHelveticaBold}\ \}_{IntLit}\ \}_{Attr}$
$pages[0]\_pageItems[4]\_guiCmptItems[3] = \{$
$\quad attrName = \text{fs};\quad expr = \{\ val = 14\ \}_{IntLit}\ \}_{Attr}$
$pages[0]\_pageItems[4]\_guiCmptItems[4] = \{$
$\quad attrName = \text{str};\quad expr = \{\ val = \text{"Registration"}\ \}_{StrLit}\ \}_{Attr}$
...
$pages[0]\_pageItems[11]\_guiCmptItems[3] = \{$
$\quad attrName = \text{bg};$
$\quad expr = \{\ attrName = \text{bg};\quad idGuiCmpt = \text{"btnReset"}\ \}_{AttrRefGuiCmpt}\ \}_{Attr}$
...
$pages[0]\_pageItems[11]\_guiCmptItems[5] = \{$
$\quad eventType = \text{evDwn};$
$\quad cvmAs = \text{``fcall \_svBuf\_write}$
$\qquad\qquad\quad\text{fcall\_I \_svBuf\_svcCmd\_write, svcCmd\_Submit}$
$\qquad\qquad\quad\text{sendrcvpage \_p1, 0''}\ \}_{Event}$

$pages[1] = \ldots\ \text{// etc.}$

...

$serverActionsCmd[0] = \{$
$\quad idServiceCmd = \text{"svcCmd\_Reset"};$
$\quad serverCode = \text{"printf("svcCmd\_Reset}\backslash\text{n");}$
$\qquad\qquad\qquad\quad\text{svcVar\_reset();}$
$\qquad\qquad\qquad\quad\text{printf("name = }\backslash\text{"\%s}\backslash\text{", email = }\backslash\text{"\%s}\backslash\text{"}\backslash\text{n",}$
$\qquad\qquad\qquad\quad\text{svcVarStr\_get("name"), svcVarStr\_get("email"));"}\ \}$

...

$serverActionsPage[1] = \{$
$\quad idPageCurrent = \text{"p0"};$
$\quad idPageNext = \text{"p1"};$
$\quad serverCode = \text{"printf("p0 -> p1}\backslash\text{n");"}\ \}$

5.2 Session Manager

The session manager processes all incoming client messages and stores the session data. The abstract AUI syntax trees of the offered network services are stored in a list structure and referred to by the variable *auiDescrs*:

5.2. Session Manager

Aui∗   auiDescrs
The abstract AUI syntax tree of the network service with the service number *serviceNo* is referred to by the expression *auiDescrs*[*serviceNo*], i.e., *auiDescrs*[*serviceNo*].*serviceNo* = *serviceNo*.

5.2.1 Session Data

The data that is involved in a client-server session is stored in a separate data structure of the type *CVMSession*. All sessions are stored in a list structure and referred to by the variable *sessions*:

CVMSession∗   sessions

CVMSession = { Nat1[4]   *sessionId*;
                    Int   *serviceNo, timestamp*;
                    String   *cvmHostAdr*;
                    CVMProfile   cvmProfile;
                    Aui[$num_{CvmPackets}$]   *genAuis*;
                    Int   *pageNo, pageNoGen, pageNoReq, subpageNoReq*;
                    ServiceVar[$num_{SvcVars}$]   *serviceVars, serviceVarsSaved*;
                    Int   *svcCmdIdx* }

ServiceVar = { Int   *idx*;
                   String   *id*;
                   Int   *type*;
                   (Int | String)   *val* }

Comments

- *sessionId* identifies the current client-server session. For each new client-server session the CVM packet server assigns a unique value for *sessionId*. A client-server session usually consists of several CPTP transactions whereas the time between two `GET` messages depends on the user of the CVM and therefore may vary. All CPTP messages that belong to the same client-server session share the same unique value for the message item `sessionId`. Refer also to `sessionId` in section 4.1 (page 128).

- *serviceNo* contains the number of the service that is processed during the respective client-server session. Refer also to `serviceNo` in section 4.2 (page 130) and to *ServiceNo* in section 5.1.1 (page 145).

- *timestamp* contains the time when the CVM packet server has received the most recent message from the CVM. The session manager regularly checks the *timestamp* values of all sessions in *sessions*. Those sessions whose *timestamp* value exceed a predefined value will be treated as terminated. They will be removed from *sessions* and their system resources will be cleaned up.

- *cvmHostAdr* contains the host address of the CVM. The host address might be a DNS [45] name or an IP address [62] in standard dot notation.

- *cvmProfile* contains the CVM profile of the requesting CVM. Refer also to *CvmProfile* in section 3.7 (page 89) and to `cvmProfile` in section 4.2 (page 130).

- *genAuis* is generated by the CVM packet generator and serves as an intermediate presentation of the generated CVM packets that belong to the currently requested AUI page. The CVM packet generator generates from a given AUI page one or more AUI subpages which are grouped into CVM packets. $num_{CvmPackets}$ refers to the number of generated CVM packets. $genAuis[i]$ ($0 \leq i < num_{CvmPackets}$) refers to the intermediate presentation of the ith CVM packet. It contains the AUI subpages of the ith CVM packet. Refer to section 5.4 (page 163) for more information on the generation process and the structure of *genAuis*.

  The translation of $genAuis[i]$ into a CVM packet is specified in section 5.5 (page 166). During the translation, each AUI subpage is translated into a CVMUI page. Thus, a CVMUI page is addressed by the respective AUI page and subpage number.

- *pageNo* contains the AUI page number of the CVMUI page that has been sent by the CVM packet server to the CVM most recently. In the beginning of a client-server session *pageNo* contains a predefined negative integer number to indicate that no CVMUI page has been sent to the CVM so far during the session. Here such a value is expressed with the term *pageNoNull*. The value of *pageNoNull*, e.g., -1, is left to the implementors' choice.

- *pageNoGen* contains the AUI page number of the AUI page that has been customized by the CVM packet generator most recently.

- *pageNoReq* and *subpageNoReq* contain the AUI page and subpage number of the requested CVMUI page, respectively.

- *serviceVars* and *serviceVarsSaved* contain the values of the service variables that belong to the network service that is processed during the client-server session. *serviceVars* contains the *current* values, *serviceVarsSaved* contains the *saved* values. Refer to *ServiceVar* in section 5.1.1 (page 145) and to the procedure *processDataBytes* in section 5.2.2 (page 157).

- $num_{SvcVars} = \#(auiDescrs[serviceNo].serviceVars)$, with $\#(...)$ refers to the number of elements in the given list structure.

- *svcCmdIdx* contains the index of a service command, if available. Refer to *ServerActionCmd* in section 5.1.1 (page 144), to *ServiceVar* in section 5.1.1 (page 145), and to the procedure *processDataBytes* in section 5.2.2 (page 157).

- *idx*, *id*, *type*, and *val* contain the index number, the name, the type, and the current value of a service variable, respectively. Refer also to *ServiceVar* in section 5.1.1 (page 145).

5.2.2 Main Loop

The behavior of the session manager is described in a generally understandable pseudo-code notation and mainly consists of the following loop:

5.2. Session Manager

repeat forever {
  $CptpMessage\ cptpMsg := waitForClientMessage()$;
  switch ($cptpMsg$.methodCode) {
    ERROR:
      $processErrorMsg(sessions, cptpMsg$.sessionId$, cptpMsg$.errorCode$, cptpMsg$.memAdr$)$;
    PROFILE:
      if ($\exists k \geq 0 : sessions[k].sessionId = cptpMsg$.sessionId)
        { $sessions[k].cvmProfile := cptpMsg$.cvmProfile; }
    GET:
      if ($\nexists auiDescrs[cptpMsg$.serviceNo])
        { $processRequestForUnknownService(cptpMsg$.serviceNo$)$; }
      else
        if ($\nexists k \geq 0 : sessions[k].sessionId = cptpMsg$.sessionId) {
          $k := \#(sessions)$;
          $sessions[k].sessionId := newSessionId()$;
          $sessions[k].serviceNo := cptpMsg$.serviceNo;
          $sessions[k].pageNo := pageNoNull$;
          $sessions[k].pageNoGen := pageNoNull$;
          $sessions[k].cvmHostAdr := cvmHostAdr()$;
          for (Int $j := 0;\ j < \#(auiDescrs[sessions[k].serviceNo].serviceVars);\ j$++) {
            $sessions[k].serviceVars[j].idx := j + 1$;
            $sessions[k].serviceVars[j].id :=$
              $auiDescrs[cptpMsg$.serviceNo$].serviceVars[j].id$;
            $sessions[k].serviceVars[j].type :=$
              $auiDescrs[cptpMsg$.serviceNo$].serviceVars[j].varType$;
            $sessions[k].serviceVars[j].val :=$
              $auiDescrs[cptpMsg$.serviceNo$].serviceVars[j].valInit$;
          }
          $sessions[k].serviceVarsSaved := sessions[k].serviceVars$;
        }
        // $\exists k \geq 0 : sessions[k].sessionId = cptpMsg$.sessionId $\wedge$
        // $sessions[k].serviceNo = cptpMsg$.serviceNo
        $sessions[k].pageNoReq := cptpMsg$.pageNo;
        $sessions[k].subpageNoReq := cptpMsg$.subpageNo;
        $sessions[k].timestamp := timestampNow()$;
        $processDataBytes()$;
        $checkSndRcvCVMProfile(sessions[k].cvmProfile,$
                            $cptpMsg$.serviceNo$, cptpMsg$.pageNo$, cptpMsg$.cvmProfile$)$;
        if ($\neg existServiceInstance()$) {
          $generateServiceInstance(auiDescrs[sessions[k].serviceNo], sessions[k].cvmProfile)$;
        }
        $execServiceInstance(sessions[k])$;
      }
  }
}

The procedure $processDataBytes()$ is defined as follows:

$processDataBytes()$ {
  $sessions[k].svcCmdIdx := -1$;
  for (Int $i := 0;\ i < cptpMsg$.numBytes$;\ i$++) {

$\text{Int } svcVarIdx := \text{Nat}^{i,svIdxLen}_{cptpMsg.\texttt{dataBytes}};$
$i := i + svIdxLen;$
if $(svcVarIdx = 0)$ {
    $sessions[k].svcCmdIdx := \text{Nat}^{i,2}_{cptpMsg.\texttt{dataBytes}};$
    $i := i + 2;$
}
else {
    switch $(sessions[k].serviceVars_{svcVarIdx}.type)$ {
        Int: $sessions[k].serviceVars_{svcVarIdx}.val := \text{Int}^{i,cvmIntLen}_{cptpMsg.\texttt{dataBytes}};$
                $i := i + cvmIntLen;$
        String: $sessions[k].serviceVars_{svcVarIdx}.val := \text{String}^{i}_{cptpMsg.\texttt{dataBytes}};$
                $i := i + byteLen(\text{String}^{i}_{cptpMsg.\texttt{dataBytes}});$
        }
    }
}
}

Comments

- *CptpMessage*: Refer to section 4.1 (page 128) for more information on this data type.

- *waitForClientMessage*() makes the session manager wait until it receives a message from a CVM. When it receives a message, *waitForClientMessage*() stores the incoming message into a data structure of the type *CptpMessage*. Refer to section 4.1 (page 128) for more information on the data type *CptpMessage*.

- *processErrorMsg*(...): The server implementors can decide on their own how they handle incoming error messages. Usually, error messages might be collected for debugging purposes, particularly when they result from malformed CVM packets.

- $\exists auiDescrs[cptpMsg.\texttt{serviceNo}] \Leftrightarrow$
  $\exists i \geq 0 : auiDescrs[i].serviceNo = cptpMsg.\texttt{serviceNo}$

- *processRequestForUnknownService*(*cptpMsg*.serviceNo): The server implementors can decide on their own how they handle incoming requests for network services that are not offered by this CVM packet server.

- #(...) refers to the number of elements in the given list structure.

- *newSessionId*() returns a unique 4-byte number not equal to zero that is not already used by another session in the session list as a *sessionId*, i.e., $\forall k \geq 0 :$ $session[k].sessionId \neq newSessionId().$

- *cvmHostAdr* refers to the host address of the CVM. The host address might be a DNS [45] name or an IP address [62] in standard dot notation.

- *timestampNow*() returns an integer value that contains the current date and time.

- *checkSndRcvCVMProfile*(...) checks whether the CVM profile *session*.cvmProfile contains all the essential CVM profile data that are needed for the generation of the

5.3. Service Generator   159

client-specific service instance and the CVM packets. If some profile items are missing the session manager sends a CPTP message to the CVM to request the missing items. Refer also to the CPTP protocol method `PROFILE` in section 4.2 (page 130).

- *existServiceInstance*() returns true, if the executable file of the client-specific service instance has already been generated previously during this client-server session. Otherwise, it returns false. Here, the service instance is generated for each client-server session only once and in the beginning of the session, i.e., when the first client request with the CPTP method `GET` is being processed by the session manager.

- *generateServiceInstance*(...) generates from a given AUI description and a given CVM profile an executable file that represents the client-specific service instance. Refer to the sections 5.3.1 (page 160) and 5.3 (page 159) for more information on the service instance and its generation.

- *execServiceInstance*(...) executes the previously generated service instance file. Whether a separate and concurrent process is started for the service instance is left to the implementors' choice.

- $\text{Nat}^{i,svIdxLen}_{cptpMsg.\text{dataBytes}}$ refers to the $\text{Nat}<svIdxLen>$ number that starts in the byte array $cptpMsg.\text{dataBytes}$ at the index position i.

  $\text{Int}^{i,cvmIntLen}_{cptpMsg.\text{dataBytes}}$ refers to the $\text{Int}<cvmIntLen>$ number that starts in the byte array $cptpMsg.\text{dataBytes}$ at the index position i.

  $\text{String}^{i}_{cptpMsg.\text{dataBytes}}$ refers to the CVM String that starts in the byte array $cptpMsg.\text{dataBytes}$ at the index position i.

  $byteLen(\text{String}^{i}_{cptpMsg.\text{dataBytes}})$ refers to the byte length of the whole given CVM String structure.

  Refer to section 3.1.1 (page 32) for more information on the CVM data types. Refer to section 5.1.1 (page 145) for more information on service variables.

- $session.serviceVars_{svcVarIdx}$ refers to the service variable that meets the following conditions:
  $\exists j \geq 0 : (session.serviceVars[j] = session.serviceVars_{svcVarIdx} \land$
  $session.serviceVars[j].idx = svcVarIdx)$

- Note that the pseudo-code that decides which sessions in the session list are considered as terminated — according to their *timestamp* values — and that regularly cleans up the session list is not shown here. This is left to the implementors' choice as well.

5.3 Service Generator

The service generator creates from the given *Aui* and *CVMProfile* data structures an executable file that represents the service instance. The *Aui* and the *CVMProfile* data types are specified in the sections 5.1.2 (page 147) and 3.7 (page 89), respectively. The service instance consists of a fixed and a generated part. The fixed part of the service instance does not depend on the given AUI description and CVM profile and therefore is the same in every client-server session. The generated part, however, does depend on the given AUI description and CVM profile and therefore might vary for each client-server session.

5.3.1 Fixed Part of the Service Instance

The fixed part of the service instance contains the main procedure of the service instance and is described in a generally understandable pseudo-code notation:

$execServiceInstance\,(sessions[k])$ {
 Int $pageNoNew$;
 $\_svcInst\_actionsCmd(sessions[k].svcCmdIdx)$;
 $pageNoNew := \_svcInst\_actionsPage(sessions[k].pageNo, sessions[k].pageNoReq)$;
 if $(pageNoNew \neq pageNoNull)$ {
   if $(sessions[k].pageNoReq \neq pageNoNew)$ {
     $sessions[k].pageNoReq := pageNoNew$;
     $sessions[k].subpageNoReq := 0$;
   }
   if $(sessions[k].pageNoReq \neq sessions[k].pageNoGen)$ {
     $sessions[k].genAuis := generateAuis(auiDescrs[sessions[k].serviceNo],$
                                    $sessions[k].pageNoReq, sessions[k].cvmProfile,$
                                    $sessions[k].serviceVars)$;
     $sessions[k].pageNoGen := sessions[k].pageNoReq$;
   }
   $CVMPacket\ \ cvmp := aui2cvmui(sessions[k].genAuis[cvmpNo_{sessions[k].genAuis}^{sessions[k].subpageNoReq}],$
                             $sessions[k].cvmProfile,$
                             $sessions[k].pageNoReq, sessions[k].subpageNoReq,$
                             $sessions[k].serviceVars)$;
   if $(sndCvmp(cvmp))$ {
     $sessions[k].pageNo := sessions[k].pageNoReq$;
   }
 }
}

Comments

- $\_svcInst\_actionsCmd(...)$ and $\_svcInst\_actionsPage(...)$ are generated functions. Refer to section 5.3.2 (page 161) for more information on the generated part of a service instance.

- $generateAuis(...)$ generates the intermediate presentations of the customized CVM packets that belong to the currently processed AUI page. This generation is performed by the CVM packet generator in the first step. Refer to the section 5.4 (page 163) for more information on the CVM packet generator.

- $aui2cvmui(...)$ translates the given Aui structure into a CVM packet that contains CVMUI pages. This translation is performed by the CVM packet generator in the second step. Refer to section 5.5 (page 166) for the structure of a CVMUI.

5.3. Service Generator   161

- $0 \le cvmpNo_{sessions[k].genAuis}^{sessions[k].subpageNoReq} < num_{CvmPackets}$
  $\wedge$
  $\exists_1 u, v \ge 0 : sessions[k].genAuis[u].pages[v].pageNo =$
  $\qquad sessions[k].pageNoReq \wedge$
  $\qquad sessions[k].genAuis[u].pages[v].subpageNo =$
  $\qquad sessions[k].subpageNoReq$
  $\wedge$
  $u = cvmpNo_{sessions[k].genAuis}^{sessions[k].subpageNoReq}$

- $sndCvmp(...)$ sends the generated CVM packet to the client-side CVM by using the CPTP protocol method `CVMP`. If no error occurs, $sndCvmp(...)$ returns true, otherwise false. Refer to section 4.2 (page 129) for more information on `CVMP`.

5.3.2 Generated Part of the Service Instance

The generated output is a C [20] program that contains the declarations and initializations of the service variables (*ServiceVar**), the server actions (*ServerActionCmd*, *ServerActionPage*), and, if available, additional server-side code (*ServerCodeMisc*). For easier readability the following definition is used:

$Aui \quad aui := auiDescrs[sessions[k].serviceNo]$

The following code template specifies the generated output:

```
#include "_svcInst.h"

///////////////
// Page Numbers
///////////////

enum {
   <∀page ∈ aui.pages>
     _svcInst_<page.id> <if : isLastListElem(page)> , <end>
   <end>
};

////////////////
// ServerCodeMisc
////////////////

<aui.serverCodeMisc>

//////////////////
// ServerActionsCmd
//////////////////

<∀i : 0 ≤ i < #(aui.serverActionsCmd)>
   #define _svcInst_<aui.serverActionsCmd[i].idServiceCmd>  <i>
<end>
```

```
int _svcInst_actionsCmd (int svcCmdIdx)
 { dprint {
 <if : #(aui.serverActionsCmd) > 0>
   switch (svcCmdIdx)
     {
     <∀serverActionCmd ∈ aui.serverActionsCmd>
       case _svcInst_<serverActionCmd.idServiceCmd>:
         {
         <serverActionsCmd.serverCode>
         }
         break;
     <end>
     }
 <end>
 }}


///////////////////
// ServerActionsPage
///////////////////

int _svcInst_actionsPage (int pageNow, int pageReq)
 { dprint {
 int pageNext = pageReq;
 <∀serverActionPage ∈ aui.serverActionsPage>
   <if : isFirstListElem(serverActionPage)>
     if (
   <else>
     else if (
   <end>
         <call : statePageId2boolExpr( pageNow, serverActionPage.idPageCurrent )>
         &&
         <call : statePageId2boolExpr( pageReq, serverActionPage.idPageNext )>)
         {
         <serverActionPage.serverCode>
         }
 <end>
 if (pageNext < _svcInst_<aui.pages[0].id> ||
     pageNext > _svcInst_<lastListElem(aui.pages).id>)
   { pageNext = _svcInst_pageNoNull; }
 return pageNext;
 }}

<fct : statePageId2boolExpr( String pageId, String statePageId )>
  <if : statePageId = "">
    <pageId> == _svcInst_pageNoNull
  <elseif : statePageId = "*">
    true
  <elseif : statePageId = "^">
    <pageId> < _svcInst_<aui.pages[0].id> ||
    <pageId> > _svcInst_<lastListElem(aui.pages).id>
  <else>
```

⟨pageId⟩ == _svcInst_⟨statePageId⟩
⟨end⟩

Comments

- $isLastListElem(page) = true \Leftrightarrow$
  $page$ is the last element in the list structure $aui.pages$

- $isFirstListElem(serverActionPage) = true \Leftrightarrow$
  $serverAction$ is the first element in the list structure $aui.serverActions$

- $lastListElem(aui.pages)$ refers to the page that is the last element in the list structure $aui.pages$.

- `_svcInst_pageNoNull` equals to $pageNoNull$. Refer to section 5.2.1 (page 155) for more information on $pageNoNull$.

- Note that this (simple) code template does not depend on $sessions[k].cvmProfile$, because its main purpose is only to demonstrate the proposed concepts. As already mentioned, the service providers can freely choose the complexity of their server-side architectures.

5.4 CVM Packet Generator

The CVM packet generator generates from a given AUI page one or more AUI subpages which are grouped into CVM packets. Here the generation of the CVM packets takes place in two steps:

First a tree transformation is performed where the input tree represents the AUI description of the currently processed network service and the output tree contains the intermediate presentations of the customized CVM packets. Note that for the intermediate presentation of a generated CVM packet the data type Aui is used as well. In addition, an AUI subpage is represented by the data type $Page$. These data types are defined in section 5.1.2 (page 147).

In the second step, the intermediate presentation of a customized CVM packet that contains the requested AUI subpage is translated into a binary and executable CVM packet. During the translation, each AUI subpage is translated into a CVMUI page. Thus, a CVMUI page is addressed by the respective AUI page and subpage number. The structure of a CVMUI is specified in section 5.5 (page 166).

The tree transformation ($generateAuis$) in the first step is described as follows:

$$generateAuis : \quad Aui \; \times \; Nat \; \times \; CVMProfile \; \times \; ServiceVar* \; \longmapsto \; Aui*$$

$generateAuis$ must meet particular conditions. For the specification of these conditions, first some definitions are made with respect to the previous sections:

Aui $aui := auiDescrs[sessions[k].serviceNo]$
Nat $num_{Pages} := \#(aui.pages)$, with $\#(...)$ refers to the number of elements in the given list structure.
Without loss of generality: $\forall q\ (0 \leq q < num_{Pages}) : aui.pages[q].pageNo = q \wedge$
$\qquad\qquad\qquad\qquad\qquad\qquad\qquad aui.pages[q].subpageNo = 0$
Nat $pageNoReq := sessions[k].pageNoReq$
CVMProfile $cvmProfile := sessions[k].cvmProfile$
ServiceVar $serviceVars := sessions[k].serviceVars$
$Aui[num_{CvmPackets}]$ $genAuis := generateAuis(aui, pageNoReq, cvmProfile,$
$\qquad\qquad\qquad\qquad\qquad\qquad serviceVars)$

Then, *genAuis* must meet the following conditions:

(1) $num_{CvmPackets} > 0$

(2) $\forall p\ (0 \leq p < num_{CvmPackets}) :$
$\quad genAuis[p].serviceNo = aui.serviceNo \wedge$
$\quad genAuis[p].serviceId = aui.serviceId \wedge$
$\quad genAuis[p].serviceVars = aui.serviceVars \wedge$
$\quad genAuis[p].serverLng = aui.serverLng \wedge$
$\quad genAuis[p].serverActionsCmd = aui.serverActionsCmd \wedge$
$\quad genAuis[p].serverActionsPage = aui.serverActionsPage \wedge$
$\quad genAuis[p].serverCodeMisc = aui.serverCodeMisc \wedge$

(3) $\exists num_{Subpages} > 0 \wedge \exists num^p_{Subpages} > 0\ (0 \leq p < num_{CvmPackets}) :$
$\quad \forall p\ (0 \leq p < num_{CvmPackets}) :$
$\quad \sum_p num^p_{Subpages} = num_{Subpages} \wedge$
$\quad \#(genAuis[p].pages) = num_{Pages} + num^p_{Subpages} - 1$

(4) $\forall p\ (0 \leq p < num_{CvmPackets}) \wedge \forall q\ (0 \leq q < num_{Pages}) :$
$\quad q < pageNoReq \Rightarrow genAuis[p].pages[q] = aui.pages[q] \wedge$
$\quad q > pageNoReq \Rightarrow genAuis[p].pages[q + num^p_{Subpages} - 1] = aui.pages[q]$

(5) $\forall p\ (0 \leq p < num_{CvmPackets}) \wedge \forall r\ (0 \leq r < num^p_{Subpages}) :$
$\quad genAuis[p].pages[pageNoReq + r].id = aui.pages[pageNoReq].id \wedge$
$\quad genAuis[p].pages[pageNoReq + r].pageNo = aui.pages[pageNoReq].pageNo \wedge$
$\quad 0 \leq genAuis[p].pages[pageNoReq + r].subpageNo < num_{Subpages}$

(6) $\forall j\ (0 \leq j < num_{Subpages}) :$
$\quad \exists_1 p\ (0 \leq p < num_{CvmPackets}) \wedge \exists_1 q\ (0 \leq q < \#(genAuis[p].pages)) :$
$\quad genAuis[p].pages[q].pageNo = pageNoReq \wedge$
$\quad genAuis[p].pages[q].subpageNo = j$

(7) $\forall p\ (0 \leq p < num_{CvmPackets}) \wedge \forall r\ (0 \leq r < num^p_{Subpages}) :$
$\quad checkCvmPacket(aui2cvmui(genAuis[p], cvmProfile,$
$\qquad\qquad\qquad\qquad\qquad genAuis[p].pages[pageNoReq + r].pageNo,$
$\qquad\qquad\qquad\qquad\qquad genAuis[p].pages[pageNoReq + r].subpageNo,$
$\qquad\qquad\qquad\qquad\qquad serviceVars),$
$\qquad\qquad cvmProfile) = true$

5.4. CVM Packet Generator

Figure 5.3 (page 165) illustrates the structure of the output tree $genAuis$. In this figure $subpage_r^p$ ($0 \leq r < num_{Subpages}^p$) refers to $genAuis[p].pages[pageNoReq + r]$.

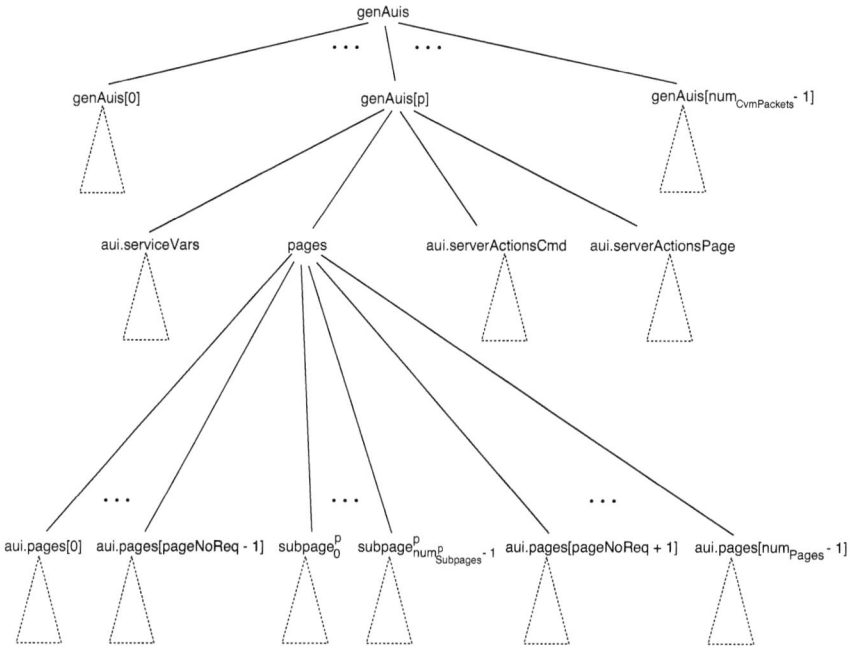

Figure 5.3: **generateAuis:** Structure of the output tree $genAuis$

$checkCvmPacket(...)$ verifies a customized CVM packet and returns true if the capabilities and restrictions of the requesting client device that are listed in the given CVM profile are completely respected by the CVM packet. For example, the CVM packet must neither exceed the memory size of the CVM nor use font codes or library functions that are not supported by the CVM. Refer to section 3.7 (page 89) for more information on the CVM profile.

$aui2cvmui(Aui\ genAui,\ CVMProfile\ cvmProfile,\ Nat\ pageNoReq,\ Nat\ subpageNoReq,\ ServiceVar*\ serviceVars)$ translates the given Aui tree $genAui$ into a binary and executable CVM packet, called CVMUI. $genAui$ represents the intermediate presentation of a customized CVM packet. Refer to section 5.5 (page 166) for more information on CVMUIs.

Note that the page items ($pageItems$) of the AUI subpages $genAuis[p].pages[pageNoReq + r]$ ($0 \leq p < num_{CvmPackets}, 0 \leq r < num_{Subpages}^p$) are not further specified. By designing the contents of the AUI subpages layout-related and ergonomic decisions have to be made which are left completely to the service providers. As far as the generated CVM packet conforms to the constraints listed in the CVM profile no further restrictions are dictated by the proposed client-server architecture. As a proof of concept, a very simple customization algorithm has been implemented and is demonstrated in the example in section D.2.2 (page 295). The investigation of more complex customization algorithms is left for future work.

5.5 CVM User Interface (CVMUI)

A CVMUI is a CVMA program that contains a whole AUI page or only parts of it. This section describes the structure of a CVMUI. The proposed structure particularly takes into account the GUI functionality, because a CVMUI mostly contains graphical user interface components. The abstraction level of such an operational user interface description apparently is quite low, because a CVMUI consists of CVM instructions. The CVM assembler translates a generated CVMUI into an executable CVM packet. Note that the CVMUI structure that is presented in this thesis is only one exemplary structure of many other possible structures to demonstrate the proposed concepts.

In this section, the structure of the CVMA program for a generated Aui tree is presented. The following input values are used:

Aui $genAui$
$CVMProfile$ $cvmProfile$
Int $pageNoReq, subpageNoReq$
$ServiceVar*$ $serviceVars$

$genAui$ represents the generated Aui tree for a customized CVM packet. $cvmProfile$ refers to the transmitted CVM profile. $pageNoReq$ and $subpageNoReq$ contain the AUI page and subpage number of the requested CVMUI page, respectively. $serviceVars$ contains the current values of the service variables.

Refer to section A.4 (page 212) for a description of the used notation for the following CVMA code templates. For easier readability, the additional definitions are used in the following code templates:

Int $num_{SvcVars} := \#(genAui.serviceVars)$,
$\quad num_{Pages} := genAui.pages[\#(genAui.pages) - 1].pageNo + 1$

num_{Pages} refers to the number of AUI pages of the original Aui tree from which $genAui$ is generated.

5.5.1 Global Structure

CVMA Code Template The CVMA code template for the global structure of a CVM-UI is as follows:

```
.<cvmProfile.cvmMode>Bit

.code
  loadcr <page_{pageNoReq,subpageNoReq}.id>_<subpageNoReq>_main
  jmp

//////////
// Misc
//////////
```

5.5. CVM User Interface (CVMUI)

```
.const
_cil           <cvmIntLen>
_cvmScreenWidth    <cvmProfile.cvmScreenWidth>
_cvmScreenHeight   <cvmProfile.cvmScreenHeight>

.data
String  _hostAdrSrv    "<hostAdrCvmPacketServer>"
```

////////////////////////
// Page Numbers
////////////////////////

```
.const
_pageNo    <pageNoReq>
```

$<\forall i : 0 \leq i < pageNoReq>$
  $\_<page_{i,0}.id>$ $<i>$
$<end>$

$\_<page_{pageNoReq, subpageNoReq}.id>$ $<pageNoReq>$

$<\forall i : pageNoReq < i < num_{Pages}>$
  $\_<page_{i,0}.id>$ $<i>$
$<end>$

```
.data
Int    _subpageNo
```

////////////////////////////
// Service Commands
////////////////////////////

```
.const
```
$<\forall v : 0 \leq v < \#(genAui.serverActionsCmd)>$
  $<genAui.serverActionsCmd[v].idServiceCmd>$ $<v>$
$<end>$

////////////////////////////
// Service Variables
////////////////////////////

```
.const
_svIdxLen    <svIdxLen>
```
$<\forall v : 0 \leq v < num_{SvcVars}>$
  $\_svIdx\_<genAui.serviceVars[v].id>$ $<v+1>$
$<end>$

```
.data
Int    _svBufIdx    0
Bytes  _svBuf
```

$<\forall guiCmpt \in guiCmptsSvIdx_{pageNoReq,j}, j \geq 0>$
  svIdxLen + $<page_{pageNoReq,j}.id>$ $<j>$_$<guiCmpt.id>$_svBufLen +
$<end>$
_svIdxLen + 2

$<if$: Function _svBufIdx_reset() is referenced within this CVMUI$>$
  .fct _svBufIdx_reset()
  {
  // _svBufIdx := 0
  loadc_0
  store _svBufIdx
  return
  }
$<end>$

$<if$: Function _svBuf_svcCmd_write is referenced within this CVMUI$>$
  .fct _svBuf_svcCmd_write (Int svcCmdIdx)
  {
  // _svBuf [_svBufIdx] := 0#svIdxLen
  loadc_0
  loadc _svBuf
  load _svBufIdx
  astore$<svIdxLen>$
  // _svBufIdx += _svIdxLen
  load _svBufIdx
  loadc _svIdxLen
  add
  store _svBufIdx
  // _svBuf [_svBufIdx] := svcCmdIdx#2
  load svcCmdIdx
  loadc _svBuf
  load _svBufIdx
  astore2
  // _svBufIdx += 2
  load _svBufIdx
  loadc 2
  add
  store _svBufIdx
  return
  }
$<end>$

$<if$: Function _svBuf_write() is referenced within this CVMUI$>$
  .fct _svBuf_write()
  {
  fcall _svBufIdx_reset
  $<\forall j \geq 0 : guiCmptsSvIdx_{pageNoReq,j} \neq \emptyset>$
    fcall $<page_{pageNoReq,j}.id>$_$<j>$_svBuf_write
  $<end>$
  return
  }

5.5. CVM User Interface (CVMUI)

$<end>$

////////////////////////
// CVMUI Pages
////////////////////////

$<\forall j \geq 0 : \exists page_{pageNoReq,j}>$
  $<import$: CVMUI code for $page_{pageNoReq,j}>$ // Refer to section 5.5.2 (page 170)
$<end>$

////////////////////////
// CVMUI Lib
////////////////////////

$<import$: CVMUI code for all referenced CVMUI Lib items$>$
  // Refer to section C (page 249)

Comments

- $page_{i,j}$ with $i, j \geq 0$ refers to an AUI subpage that meets the following conditions:
  $\exists q \geq 0 : (genAui.pages[q] = page_{i,j} \wedge$
  $\quad genAui.pages[q].pageNo = i \wedge$
  $\quad genAui.pages[q].subpageNo = j)$

- *cvmIntLen* depends on *cvmProfile.cvmMode* and refers to the byte length of an integer number the client CVM operates on. Refer to section 3.1.2 (page 33) for more information on *cvmIntLen*.

- $cvmProfile.cvmScreenWidth \equiv$
  $cvmProfile.profileItems[j]$.`num`, with $j \geq 0$ and $cvmProfile.profileItems[j]$.`profileItemCode` = `cvmScreenWidth`
  The access to the other CVM profile item values is likewise.

- *hostAdrCvmPacketServer* refers to the IP [62] address or DNS [45] name of the CVM packet server that serves the client.

- $guiCmptsSvIdx_{pageNoReq,j} :=$
  $\{guiCmpt \in page_{pageNoReq,j}.pageItems : svIdx \in guiCmpt.guiCmptItems\}$

- $guiCmpt \in page_{i,j}.pageItems \Leftrightarrow$
  $\exists k \geq 0 : page_{i,j}.pageItems[k]_{GuiCmpt} \wedge page_{i,j}.pageItems[k] = guiCmpt$,
  with $page_{i,j}.pageItems[k]_{GuiCmpt} \equiv$
  The data type of $page_{i,j}.pageItems[k]$ is $GuiCmpt$.

- $svIdx \in guiCmpt.guiCmptItems \Leftrightarrow$
  $\exists l \geq 0 : guiCmpt.guiCmptItems[l]_{Attr} \wedge$
  $\quad guiCmpt.guiCmptItems[l].attrName = svIdx$,
  with $guiCmpt.guiCmptItems[l]_{Attr} \equiv$
  The data type of $guiCmpt.guiCmptItems[l]$ is $Attr$.

- *svIdxLen*: Refer to *ServiceVar* in section 5.1.1 (page 146).

5.5.2 Page

CVMA Code Template The CVMA code template for the CVMUI page that represents the AUI subpage $page_{pageNoReq,j}$ ($j \geq 0$) is as follows:

```
/////////////////
// Attributes
/////////////////

.const
```
$<page_{pageNoReq,j}.id>$_$<j>$_x   0
$<page_{pageNoReq,j}.id>$_$<j>$_y   0
$<page_{pageNoReq,j}.id>$_$<j>$_w   _cvmScreenWidth
$<page_{pageNoReq,j}.id>$_$<j>$_h   _cvmScreenHeight

$<if : fg \in page_{pageNoReq,j}.pageItems>$
  $<page_{pageNoReq,j}.id>$_$<j>$_fgr $<(attr(page_{pageNoReq,j}, fg) \gg 16)$ & $0xFF>$
  $<page_{pageNoReq,j}.id>$_$<j>$_fgg $<(attr(page_{pageNoReq,j}, fg) \gg 8)$ & $0xFF>$
  $<page_{pageNoReq,j}.id>$_$<j>$_fgb $<attr(page_{pageNoReq,j}, fg)$ & $0xFF>$
$<else>$
  $<page_{pageNoReq,j}.id>$_$<j>$_fgr   0
  $<page_{pageNoReq,j}.id>$_$<j>$_fgg   0
  $<page_{pageNoReq,j}.id>$_$<j>$_fgb   0
$<end>$

$<if : bg \in page_{pageNoReq,j}.pageItems>$
  $<page_{pageNoReq,j}.id>$_$<j>$_bgr $<(attr(page_{pageNoReq,j}, bg) \gg 16)$ & $0xFF>$
  $<page_{pageNoReq,j}.id>$_$<j>$_bgg $<(attr(page_{pageNoReq,j}, bg) \gg 8)$ & $0xFF>$
  $<page_{pageNoReq,j}.id>$_$<j>$_bgb $<attr(page_{pageNoReq,j}, bg)$ & $0xFF>$
$<else>$
  $<page_{pageNoReq,j}.id>$_$<j>$_bgr   255
  $<page_{pageNoReq,j}.id>$_$<j>$_bgg   255
  $<page_{pageNoReq,j}.id>$_$<j>$_bgb   255
$<end>$

$<page_{pageNoReq,j}.id>$_$<j>$_fc $<if : fc \in page_{pageNoReq,j}.pageItems>$
                                   $<attr(page_{pageNoReq,j}, fc)>$
                                   $<else>$
                                   fcFixedStandard
                                   $<end>$

$<page_{pageNoReq,j}.id>$_$<j>$_fs $<if : fs \in page_{pageNoReq,j}.pageItems>$
                                   $<attr(page_{pageNoReq,j}, fs)>$
                                   $<else>$
                                   13
                                   $<end>$

$<page_{pageNoReq,j}.id>$_$<j>$_img $<if : img \in page_{pageNoReq,j}.pageItems>$
                                   $<attr(page_{pageNoReq,j}, img)>$
                                   $<else>$
                                   ""
                                   $<end>$

5.5. CVM User Interface (CVMUI) 171

$<page_{pageNoReq.j}.id>\_<j>\_$imgStyle $<if : imgStyle \in page_{pageNoReq.j}.pageItems>$
                                          $<attr(page_{pageNoReq.j}, imgStyle)>$
                                          $<else>$
                                          0 // imgTile
                                          $<end>$

.data
Bytes $<page_{pageNoReq.j}.id>\_<j>\_$prp   [$<page_{pageNoReq.j}.id>\_<j>\_$et]
Int $<page_{pageNoReq.j}.id>\_<j>\_$bInit   0

//////////
// Misc
//////////

.code
.fct $<page_{pageNoReq.j}.id>\_<j>\_$main()
{
loadc $<j>$
store _subpageNo
fcall $<page_{pageNoReq.j}.id>\_<j>\_$init
fcall $<page_{pageNoReq.j}.id>\_<j>\_$drw
$<if : idxGuiCmptsInteractive_{pageNoReq.j} \neq \emptyset>$
   loadc $<page_{pageNoReq.j}.id>\_<j>\_<guiCmpt^{a0}.id>\_$prp   push
   loadc libGui$<libGuiAbbr(guiCmpt^{a0}.guiCmptType)><libGuiStyle>\_$drwFcs   push
$<else>$
   loadc $<page_{pageNoReq.j}.id>\_<j>\_$prp   push
   loadc libMisc_emptyProc   push
$<end>$
fcall libGui_setFcs
enableevents
halt
}

.fct $<page_{pageNoReq.j}.id>\_<j>\_$init()
{
load $<page_{pageNoReq.j}.id>\_<j>\_$bInit
loadc_0
loadcr $<page_{pageNoReq.j}.id>\_<j>\_$init_$<lblCntr_1>$
jne
$<\forall guiCmpt \in page_{pageNoReq.j}.pageItems>$
   $<if : guiCmpt.guiCmptType = Ixt>$
      fcall $<page_{pageNoReq.j}.id>\_<j>\_<guiCmpt.id>\_$init
   $<end>$
$<end>$
loadc_1
store $<page_{pageNoReq.j}>\_<j>\_$bInit
$<page_{pageNoReq.j}>\_<j>\_$init_$<lblCntr_1>$:
return
}

.fct $<page_{pageNoReq.j}.id>\_<j>\_$drw()

```
{
loadc  <page_{pageNoReq,j}.id>_<j>_bgr
loadc  <page_{pageNoReq,j}.id>_<j>_bgg
loadc  <page_{pageNoReq,j}.id>_<j>_bgb
setcolor
loadc  <page_{pageNoReq,j}.id>_<j>_x
loadc  <page_{pageNoReq,j}.id>_<j>_y
loadc  <page_{pageNoReq,j}.id>_<j>_w
loadc  <page_{pageNoReq,j}.id>_<j>_h
rectfill
<∀guiCmpt ∈ page_{pageNoReq,j}.pageItems>
   <if : guiCmpt.guiCmptType = Txt ∨ guiCmpt.guiCmptType = Txp>
      fcall  <page_{pageNoReq,j}.id>_<j>_<guiCmpt.id>_drw
   <elseif : guiCmpt.guiCmptType = Btn ∨ guiCmpt.guiCmptType = Hlk ∨
             guiCmpt.guiCmptType = Ixt>
      loadc  <page_{pageNoReq,j}.id>_<j>_<guiCmpt.id>_prp  push
      fcall libGui<libGuiAbbr(guiCmpt.guiCmptType)><libGuiStyle>_drw
   <end>
<end>
return
}
```

$<if : \exists page_{p,pageNoReq,j-1}>$
  $<page_{pageNoReq,j}.id>$_$<j>$_prevPage:
    $<if : \exists page_{pageNoReq,j-1}>$
      loadc $<j-1>$
      loadcr$<page_{pageNoReq,j-1}.id>$_$<j-1>$_main
      page
    $<else>$
      $<if : \exists l \geq 0 : guiCmptsSvIdx_{pageNoReq,l} \neq \emptyset>$
        fcall _svBuf_write
      $<else>$
        fcall _svBufIdx_reset
      $<end>$
      sendrcvpage _pageNo, $<j-1>$
    $<end>$
$<end>$

$<if : \exists page_{p,pageNoReq,j+1}>$
  $<page_{pageNoReq,j}.id>$_$<j>$_nextPage:
    $<if : \exists page_{pageNoReq,j+1}>$
      loadc $<j+1>$
      loadcr$<page_{pageNoReq,j+1}.id>$_$<j+1>$_main
      page
    $<else>$
      $<if : \exists l \geq 0 : guiCmptsSvIdx_{pageNoReq,l} \neq \emptyset>$
        fcall _svBuf_write
      $<else>$
        fcall _svBufIdx_reset
      $<end>$
      sendrcvpage _pageNo, $<j+1>$

5.5. CVM User Interface (CVMUI)

    $<end>$
$<end>$

////////////////////////////
// Service Variables
////////////////////////////

$<if : guiCmptsSvIdx_{pageNoReq,j} \neq \emptyset>$
  .fct $<page_{pageNoReq,j}.id>\_<j>\_$svBuf_write()
  {
  load $<page_{pageNoReq,j}.id>\_<j>\_$bInit
  loadc_0
  loadcr $<page_{pageNoReq,j}.id>\_<j>\_$svBuf_write_$<lblCntr_1>$
  je
    $<\forall guiCmpt \in guiCmptsSvIdx_{pageNoReq,j}>$
    fcall $<page_{pageNoReq,j}.id>\_<j>\_<guiCmpt.id>\_$svBuf_write
    $<end>$
  $<page_{pageNoReq,j}.id>\_<j>\_$svBuf_write_$<lblCntr_1>$:
  return
  }
$<end>$

////////////////
// Events
////////////////

.data
EventTable $<page_{pageNoReq,j}.id>\_<j>\_$et [
  $<if : idxGuiCmptsInteractive_{pageNoReq,j} \neq \emptyset \lor \exists page_{p,pageNoReq,j-1} \lor \exists page_{p,pageNoReq,j+1}>$
    $<if : cvmKeyCodeSet \in cvmProfile.profileItems>$
      key_pressed, $<page_{pageNoReq,j}.id>\_<j>\_$kp
      $<if : cvmMouseButtons \in cvmProfile.profileItems>$, $<end>$
    $<end>$
    $<if : cvmMouseButtons \in cvmProfile.profileItems>$
      mouse_pressed_left, $<page_{pageNoReq,j}.id>\_<j>\_$mpl
    $<end>$
  $<end>$
]

$<if : idxGuiCmptsInteractive_{pageNoReq,j} \neq \emptyset \lor \exists page_{p,pageNoReq,j-1} \lor \exists page_{p,pageNoReq,j+1}>$
  $<if : cvmKeyCodeSet \in cvmProfile.profileItems>$
    .code
    $<page_{pageNoReq,j}.id>\_<j>\_$kp:
      $<if : idxGuiCmptsInteractive_{pageNoReq,j} \neq \emptyset>$
      loadep1
      loadc XK_Tab
      loadcr $<page_{pageNoReq,j}.id>\_<j>\_$kp_tab
      je
      $<end>$
      $<if : \exists page_{p,pageNoReq,j-1}>$
      loadep1

```
            loadc XK_Left
            loadcr <page_{pageNoReq,j}.id>_<j>_kp_left
            je
        <end>
        <if : ∃page_{p,pageNoReq,j+1}>
            loadep1
            loadc XK_Right
            loadcr <page_{pageNoReq,j}.id>_<j>_kp_right
            je
        <end>
            halt
    <if : idxGuiCmptsInteractive_{pageNoReq,j} ≠ ∅>
        <page_{pageNoReq,j}.id>_<j>_kp_tab:
            loadc  <page_{pageNoReq,j}.id>_<j>_prp   push
            loadc  <page_{pageNoReq,j}.id>_<j>_<guiCmpt^{a0}.id>_prp   push
            loadc  libMisc_emptyProc   push
            loadc  libGui<libGuiAbbr(guiCmpt^{a0}.guiCmptType)><libGuiStyle>_drwFcs   push
            fcall libGui_mvFcs
            halt
    <end>
    <if : ∃page_{p,pageNoReq,j-1}>
        <page_{pageNoReq,j}.id>_<j>_kp_left:
            loadcr <page_{pageNoReq,j}.id>_<j>_prevPage
            jmp
    <end>
    <if : ∃page_{p,pageNoReq,j+1}>
        <page_{pageNoReq,j}.id>_<j>_kp_right:
            loadcr <page_{pageNoReq,j}.id>_<j>_nextPage
            jmp
    <end>
<end>

<if : cvmMouseButtons ∈ cvmProfile.profileItems>
    .code
    <page_{pageNoReq,j}.id>_<j>_mpl:
        loadep1  push
        loadep2  push
        loadc  <page_{pageNoReq,j}.id>_<j>_prp   push
        loadc libMisc_emptyProc   push
        fcall  <page_{pageNoReq,j}.id>_<j>_mplFcs
        halt

    .fct  <page_{pageNoReq,j}.id>_<j>_mplFcs (Int x, Int y,
                                Int adrPrpSrc, Int adrUnDrwFcsSrc)
    {
        <∀guiCmpt ∈ page_{pageNoReq,j}.pageItems : guiCmpt is interactive.>
            incsp
            load x  push
            load y  push
            loadc  <page_{pageNoReq,j}.id>_<j>_<guiCmpt.id>_x   push
            loadc  <page_{pageNoReq,j}.id>_<j>_<guiCmpt.id>_y   push
```

5.5. CVM User Interface (CVMUI)

```
            loadc <page_{pageNoReq,j}.id>_<j>_<guiCmpt.id>_w    push
            loadc <page_{pageNoReq,j}.id>_<j>_<guiCmpt.id>_h    push
            fcall libGui_rectIn
            pop  loadc_0  loadcr <page_{pageNoReq,j}.id>_<j>_mplFcs_<lblCntr_2>    je
            load adrPrpSrc  push
            loadc <page_{pageNoReq,j}.id>_<j>_<guiCmpt.id>_prp   push
            load adrUnDrwFcsSrc  push
            loadc libGui<libGuiAbbr(guiCmpt.guiCmptType)>
                     <libGuiStyle>_drwFcs  push
            fcall libGui_mvFcs
            <if : guiCmpt.guiCmptType = Btn>
              fcall  <page_{pageNoReq,j}.id>_<j>_<guiCmpt.id>_evDwn
            <elseif : guiCmpt.guiCmptType = Hlk>
              loadc <page_{pageNoReq,j}.id>_<j>_<guiCmpt.id>_prp   push
              fcall libGuiHlk_dwn
            <end>
            return
          <page_{pageNoReq,j}.id>_<j>_mplFcs_<lblCntr_2>:
        <end>
        <if : ∃page_{p,pageNoReq,j−1}>
          load x
          loadc _cvmScreenWidth  loadc 2  div
          loadcr <page_{pageNoReq,j}.id>_<j>_prevPage
          jl
          <if : ∃page_{p,pageNoReq,j+1}>
            loadcr <page_{pageNoReq,j}.id>_<j>_nextPage
            jmp
          <end>
        <elseif : ∃page_{p,pageNoReq,j+1}>
          loadc _cvmScreenWidth  loadc 2  div
          load x
          loadcr <page_{pageNoReq,j}.id>_<j>_nextPage
          jl
        <end>
        return
        }
    <end>
<end>

///////////////////
// Page Items
///////////////////

<∀k ≥ 0 : ∃pageItem_{i,j,k}>
  <if : pageItem_{i,j,k GuiCmpt}>
    <import : CVMA code for pageItem>    // Refer to sections 5.5.3 – 5.5.7 (pages 177 ff.)
  <elseif : pageItem_{i,j,k CvmAs}>
    <pageItem.cvmAs>
<end>
```

Comments

- $attrName \in page_{pageNoReq,j}.pageItems \equiv$
  $\exists k \geq 0 : page_{pageNoReq,j}.pageItems[k]_{Attr} \land page_{pageNoReq,j}.pageItems[k].attrName = attrName$

- $attr(page_{pageNoReq,j}, attrName)$ returns the value of the attribute with the name $attrName$ that is defined in $page_{pageNoReq,j}$. The data type of an attribute is $Attr$ and is specified in section 5.1.2 (page 147). The value of an attribute is defined by its expression $expr$. Note that the value of a referenced service variable in $expr$ is determined by using the data structure $sessions[k].serviceVars$ instead of $sessions[k].serviceVarsSaved$. Refer to sections 5.1.1 (page 138) and 5.1.1 (page 145) for more information on attributes and service variables.

- $idxGuiCmptsInteractive_{pageNoReq,j} := \{k \geq 0 : page_{pageNoReq,j}.pageItems[k]_{GuiCmpt} \land page_{pageNoReq,j}.pageItems[k]$ is interactive$\}$

  So far, interactive user interface components are of the type Btn, Hlk, or Ixt, i.e., $page_{pageNoReq,j}.pageItems[k].guiCmptType \in \{Btn, Hlk, Ixt\}$. Additional interactive user interface component types may be defined in the future.

- $idxGuiCmptsInteractive^{min}_{pageNoReq,j} \in idxGuiCmptsInteractive_{pageNoReq,j} \land$
  $\forall k \in idxGuiCmptsInteractive_{pageNoReq,j} : idxGuiCmptsInteractive^{min}_{pageNoReq,j} \leq k$

- $guiCmpt^{a0} := page_{pageNoReq,j}.pageItems[idxGuiCmptsInteractive^{min}_{pageNoReq,j}]$

- $libGuiAbbr(guiCmptType)$ returns the short name of the given user interface component type ($guiCmptType$):
  $libGuiAbbr(Btn) = $ Btn
  $libGuiAbbr(Ixt) = $ Ixt
  $libGuiAbbr(Txp) = $ Txp
  $libGuiAbbr(Txt) = $ Txt

  This abbreviation is used in the CVMUI libraries. Refer to section C (page 249) for more information on the CVMUI libraries.

- $libGuiStyle$ defines the appearance of the user interface components. So far, two styles are defined in the CVMUI libraries: Smp and 3D.

- libGui..., libMisc..., e.g., libGuiBtnSmp_drw, libGuiIxt3D_drwFcs, libGuiHlk_dwn, libGui_setFcs, libGui_rectIn, libMisc_emptyProc, etc. These functions are defined in the CVMUI libraries. Refer to section C (pages 249 ff.) for more information on the CVMUI libraries.

- $lblCntr_c$ ($c \geq 0$) is a unique positive integer number that is used within label names so that the labels are unique in the whole CVMA program.

- $page_{p,i,j}$ with $p, i, j \geq 0$ refers to an Aui subpage that meets the following conditions:
  $\exists p, q \geq 0 : (genAuis[p].pages[q] = page_{p,i,j} \land$
  $\qquad genAuis[p].pages[q].pageNo = i \land$
  $\qquad genAuis[p].pages[q].subpageNo = j)$

5.5. CVM User Interface (CVMUI)   177

- cvmKeyCodeSet $\in cvmProfile.profileItems$ $\equiv$
  $\exists r \geq 0 : cvmProfile.profileItems[r].profileItemCode =$ cvmKeyCodeSet

- cvmMouseButtons $\in cvmProfile.profileItems$ $\equiv$
  $\exists r \geq 0 : cvmProfile.profileItems[r].profileItemCode =$ cvmMouseButtons

- XK_Tab, XK_Right: Refer to section 3.3 (page 81), $<X11/keysymdef.h>$.

- $pageItem_{i,j,k} := page_{i,j}.pageItems[k]$

- $pageItem_{i,j,k\,GuiCmpt}$ $\equiv$
  The data type of $pageItem_{i,j,k}$ is $GuiCmpt$.

- $pageItem_{i,j,k\,CvmAs}$ $\equiv$
  The data type of $pageItem_{i,j,k}$ is $CvmAs$.

5.5.3 (Single-Line) Text

The following definition is used in the next CVMA code template:

$GuiCmpt\ \ txt := pageItem_{pageNoReq,j,k}$, with $k \geq 0$ and $txt.guiCmptType =$ Txt

CVMA Code Template   The CVMA code template for the AUI text component txt is follows:

```
///////////////
// Attributes
///////////////
```

.const
$<page_{pageNoReq,j}.id>$_$<j>$_$<txt.id>$_x $<attr(txt, x)>$
$<page_{pageNoReq,j}.id>$_$<j>$_$<txt.id>$_y $<if : y \in txt.guiCmptItems>$
                                                   $<attr(txt, y)>$
                                                   $<else>$
                                                     $<page_{pageNoReq,j}.id>$_$<j>$_$<txt.id>$_yStr -
                                                     $<page_{pageNoReq,j}.id>$_$<j>$_$<txt.id>$_fa + 1 -
                                                     $<page_{pageNoReq,j}.id>$_$<j>$_$<txt.id>$_dy
                                                   $<end>$
$<page_{pageNoReq,j}.id>$_$<j>$_$<txt.id>$_w $<page_{pageNoReq,j}.id>$_$<j>$_$<txt.id>$_wStr +
                                                   $<page_{pageNoReq,j}.id>$_$<j>$_$<txt.id>$_dw
$<page_{pageNoReq,j}.id>$_$<j>$_$<txt.id>$_h $<page_{pageNoReq,j}.id>$_$<j>$_$<txt.id>$_hStr +
                                                   $<page_{pageNoReq,j}.id>$_$<j>$_$<txt.id>$_dh

$<if : fg \in txt.guiCmptItems>$
  $<page_{pageNoReq,j}.id>$_$<j>$_$<txt.id>$_fgr $<(attr(txt, fg) \gg 16)\ \&\ 0xFF>$
  $<page_{pageNoReq,j}.id>$_$<j>$_$<txt.id>$_fgg $<(attr(txt, fg) \gg 8)\ \&\ 0xFF>$
  $<page_{pageNoReq,j}.id>$_$<j>$_$<txt.id>$_fgb $<attr(txt, fg)\ \&\ 0xFF>$
$<else>$
  $<page_{pageNoReq,j}.id>$_$<j>$_$<txt.id>$_fgr $<page_{pageNoReq,j}.id>$_$<j>$_fgr
  $<page_{pageNoReq,j}.id>$_$<j>$_$<txt.id>$_fgg $<page_{pageNoReq,j}.id>$_$<j>$_fgg
  $<page_{pageNoReq,j}.id>$_$<j>$_$<txt.id>$_fgb $<page_{pageNoReq,j}.id>$_$<j>$_fgb

$<end>$

$<if : bg \in txt.guiCmptItems>$
$\quad<page_{pageNoReq,j}.id>\_<j>\_<txt.id>\_\texttt{bgr}\quad <(attr(txt,bg)) \gg 16)\ \&\ 0xFF>$
$\quad<page_{pageNoReq,j}.id>\_<j>\_<txt.id>\_\texttt{bgg}\quad <(attr(txt,bg)) \gg 8)\ \&\ 0xFF>$
$\quad<page_{pageNoReq,j}.id>\_<j>\_<txt.id>\_\texttt{bgb}\quad <attr(txt,bg)\ \&\ 0xFF>$
$<else>$
$\quad<page_{pageNoReq,j}.id>\_<j>\_<txt.id>\_\texttt{bgr}\quad <page_{pageNoReq,j}.id>\_<j>\_\texttt{bgr}$
$\quad<page_{pageNoReq,j}.id>\_<j>\_<txt.id>\_\texttt{bgg}\quad <page_{pageNoReq,j}.id>\_<j>\_\texttt{bgg}$
$\quad<page_{pageNoReq,j}.id>\_<j>\_<txt.id>\_\texttt{bgb}\quad <page_{pageNoReq,j}.id>\_<j>\_\texttt{bgb}$
$<end>$

$<page_{pageNoReq,j}.id>\_<j>\_<txt.id>\_\texttt{fc}\quad <if : fc \in txt.guiCmptItems>$
$\qquad\qquad\qquad\qquad\qquad\qquad\quad <attr(txt,fc)>$
$\qquad\qquad\qquad\qquad\qquad\qquad <else>$
$\qquad\qquad\qquad\qquad\qquad\qquad\quad <page_{pageNoReq,j}.id>\_<j>\_\texttt{fc}$
$\qquad\qquad\qquad\qquad\qquad\qquad <end>$

$<page_{pageNoReq,j}.id>\_<j>\_<txt.id>\_\texttt{fs}\quad <if : fs \in txt.guiCmptItems>$
$\qquad\qquad\qquad\qquad\qquad\qquad\quad <attr(txt,fs)>$
$\qquad\qquad\qquad\qquad\qquad\qquad <else>$
$\qquad\qquad\qquad\qquad\qquad\qquad\quad <page_{pageNoReq,j}.id>\_<j>\_\texttt{fs}$
$\qquad\qquad\qquad\qquad\qquad\qquad <end>$

$<page_{pageNoReq,j}.id>\_<j>\_<txt.id>\_\texttt{str}\quad$ "$<attr(txt,str)>$"
$<page_{pageNoReq,j}.id>\_<j>\_<txt.id>\_\texttt{yStr}\quad <if : yStr \in txt.guiCmptItems>$
$\qquad\qquad\qquad\qquad\qquad\qquad\quad <attr(txt,yStr)>$
$\qquad\qquad\qquad\qquad\qquad\qquad <else>$
$\qquad\qquad\qquad\qquad\qquad\qquad\quad <page_{pageNoReq,j}.id>\_<j>\_<txt.id>\_\texttt{y}\ +$
$\qquad\qquad\qquad\qquad\qquad\qquad\quad <page_{pageNoReq,j}.id>\_<j>\_<txt.id>\_\texttt{fa}\ -\ 1\ +$
$\qquad\qquad\qquad\qquad\qquad\qquad\quad <page_{pageNoReq,j}.id>\_<j>\_<txt.id>\_\texttt{dy}$
$\qquad\qquad\qquad\qquad\qquad\qquad <end>$

$<page_{pageNoReq,j}.id>\_<j>\_<txt.id>\_\texttt{xStr}\quad <page_{pageNoReq,j}.id>\_<j>\_<txt.id>\_\texttt{x}\ +$
$\qquad\qquad\qquad\qquad\qquad\qquad\quad <page_{pageNoReq,j}.id>\_<j>\_<txt.id>\_\texttt{dx}$
$<page_{pageNoReq,j}.id>\_<j>\_<txt.id>\_\texttt{wStr}\quad \texttt{textWidth (}$
$\qquad\qquad\qquad\qquad\qquad\qquad\quad <page_{pageNoReq,j}.id>\_<j>\_<txt.id>\_\texttt{str},$
$\qquad\qquad\qquad\qquad\qquad\qquad\quad <page_{pageNoReq,j}.id>\_<j>\_<txt.id>\_\texttt{fc},$
$\qquad\qquad\qquad\qquad\qquad\qquad\quad <page_{pageNoReq,j}.id>\_<j>\_<txt.id>\_\texttt{fs)}$
$<page_{pageNoReq,j}.id>\_<j>\_<txt.id>\_\texttt{hStr}\quad \texttt{textHeight (}$
$\qquad\qquad\qquad\qquad\qquad\qquad\quad <page_{pageNoReq,j}.id>\_<j>\_<txt.id>\_\texttt{str},$
$\qquad\qquad\qquad\qquad\qquad\qquad\quad <page_{pageNoReq,j}.id>\_<j>\_<txt.id>\_\texttt{fc},$
$\qquad\qquad\qquad\qquad\qquad\qquad\quad <page_{pageNoReq,j}.id>\_<j>\_<txt.id>\_\texttt{fs},$
$\qquad\qquad\qquad\qquad\qquad\qquad\quad \texttt{0)}$

$<page_{pageNoReq,j}.id>\_<j>\_<txt.id>\_\texttt{fa}\quad \texttt{fontAscent (}$
$\qquad\qquad\qquad\qquad\qquad\qquad\quad <page_{pageNoReq,j}.id>\_<j>\_<txt.id>\_\texttt{fc},$
$\qquad\qquad\qquad\qquad\qquad\qquad\quad <page_{pageNoReq,j}.id>\_<j>\_<txt.id>\_\texttt{fs)}$

$<page_{pageNoReq,j}.id>\_<j>\_<txt.id>\_\texttt{dx}\quad \texttt{libGuiTxt}<libGuiStyle>\_\texttt{dx}$
$<page_{pageNoReq,j}.id>\_<j>\_<txt.id>\_\texttt{dy}\quad \texttt{libGuiTxt}<libGuiStyle>\_\texttt{dy}$
$<page_{pageNoReq,j}.id>\_<j>\_<txt.id>\_\texttt{dw}\quad \texttt{libGuiTxt}<libGuiStyle>\_\texttt{dw}$

5.5. CVM User Interface (CVMUI)   179

$<page_{pageNoReq,j}.id>\_<j>\_<txt.id>$_dh   libGuiTxt$<libGuiStyle>$_dh

```
//////////
// Misc
//////////

.code
.fct  <page_{pageNoReq,j}.id>_<j>_<txt.id>_drw()
{
loadc  <page_{pageNoReq,j}.id>_<j>_<txt.id>_fgr
loadc  <page_{pageNoReq,j}.id>_<j>_<txt.id>_fgg
loadc  <page_{pageNoReq,j}.id>_<j>_<txt.id>_fgb
setcolor
loadc  <page_{pageNoReq,j}.id>_<j>_<txt.id>_bgr
loadc  <page_{pageNoReq,j}.id>_<j>_<txt.id>_bgg
loadc  <page_{pageNoReq,j}.id>_<j>_<txt.id>_bgb
setbgcolor
loadc  <page_{pageNoReq,j}.id>_<j>_<txt.id>_fc
loadc  <page_{pageNoReq,j}.id>_<j>_<txt.id>_fs
setfont
loadc  <page_{pageNoReq,j}.id>_<j>_<txt.id>_xStr
loadc  <page_{pageNoReq,j}.id>_<j>_<txt.id>_yStr
textbg  <page_{pageNoReq,j}.id>_<j>_<txt.id>_str
return
}
```

Comments

- *attr(txt, attrName)* returns the value of the attribute with the name *attrName* that is defined in *txt*. The data type of the attribute is *Attr* and is defined in section 5.1.2 (page 147). Refer to section 5.1.1 (page 138) for more information on attributes.

- `fontAscent()`, `textWidth()`, `textHeight()`: Refer to section B.4 (page 227) for more information on these CVMA builtin functions.

5.5.4 Text Paragraph

The following definition is used in the next CVMA code template:
GuiCmpt txp := *pageItem*$_{pageNoReq,j,k}$, with $k \geq 0$ and *txp.guiCmptType* = `Txp`

CVMA Code Template The CVMA code template for the AUI text component *txp* is follows:

```
////////////////
// Attributes
////////////////

.const
```

$<page_{pageNoReq,j}.id>\_<j>\_<txp.id>\_\texttt{x}$ $<attr(txp,x)>$
$<page_{pageNoReq,j}.id>\_<j>\_<txp.id>\_\texttt{y}$ $<if: y \in txp.guiCmptItems>$
                                                  $<attr(txp,y)>$
                                                  $<else>$
                                                  $<page_{pageNoReq,j}.id>\_<j>\_<txp.id>\_\texttt{yStr}$ -
                                                  $<page_{pageNoReq,j}.id>\_<j>\_<txp.id>\_\texttt{fa}$ + 1 -
                                                  $<page_{pageNoReq,j}.id>\_<j>\_<txp.id>\_\texttt{dy}$
                                                  $<end>$
$<page_{pageNoReq,j}.id>\_<j>\_<txp.id>\_\texttt{w}$ $<attr(txp,w)>$
$<page_{pageNoReq,j}.id>\_<j>\_<txp.id>\_\texttt{h}$ $<page_{pageNoReq,j}.id>\_<j>\_<txp.id>\_\texttt{hStr}$ +
                                                  $<page_{pageNoReq,j}.id>\_<j>\_<txp.id>\_\texttt{dh}$

$<if: fg \in txp.guiCmptItems>$
   $<page_{pageNoReq,j}.id>\_<j>\_<txp.id>\_\texttt{fgr}$ $<(attr(txp,fg) \gg 16) \ \& \ 0xFF>$
   $<page_{pageNoReq,j}.id>\_<j>\_<txp.id>\_\texttt{fgg}$ $<(attr(txp,fg) \gg 8) \ \& \ 0xFF>$
   $<page_{pageNoReq,j}.id>\_<j>\_<txp.id>\_\texttt{fgb}$ $<attr(txp,fg) \ \& \ 0xFF>$
$<else>$
   $<page_{pageNoReq,j}.id>\_<j>\_<txp.id>\_\texttt{fgr}$ $<page_{pageNoReq,j}.id>\_<j>\_\texttt{fgr}$
   $<page_{pageNoReq,j}.id>\_<j>\_<txp.id>\_\texttt{fgg}$ $<page_{pageNoReq,j}.id>\_<j>\_\texttt{fgg}$
   $<page_{pageNoReq,j}.id>\_<j>\_<txp.id>\_\texttt{fgb}$ $<page_{pageNoReq,j}.id>\_<j>\_\texttt{fgb}$
$<end>$

$<if: bg \in txp.guiCmptItems>$
   $<page_{pageNoReq,j}.id>\_<j>\_<txp.id>\_\texttt{bgr}$ $<(attr(txp,bg) \gg 16) \ \& \ 0xFF>$
   $<page_{pageNoReq,j}.id>\_<j>\_<txp.id>\_\texttt{bgg}$ $<(attr(txp,bg) \gg 8) \ \& \ 0xFF>$
   $<page_{pageNoReq,j}.id>\_<j>\_<txp.id>\_\texttt{bgb}$ $<attr(txp,bg) \ \& \ 0xFF>$
$<else>$
   $<page_{pageNoReq,j}.id>\_<j>\_<txp.id>\_\texttt{bgr}$ $<page_{pageNoReq,j}.id>\_<j>\_\texttt{bgr}$
   $<page_{pageNoReq,j}.id>\_<j>\_<txp.id>\_\texttt{bgg}$ $<page_{pageNoReq,j}.id>\_<j>\_\texttt{bgg}$
   $<page_{pageNoReq,j}.id>\_<j>\_<txp.id>\_\texttt{bgb}$ $<page_{pageNoReq,j}.id>\_<j>\_\texttt{bgb}$
$<end>$

$<page_{pageNoReq,j}.id>\_<j>\_<txp.id>\_\texttt{fc}$ $<if: fc \in txp.guiCmptItems>$
                                                  $<attr(txp,fc)>$
                                                  $<else>$
                                                  $<page_{pageNoReq,j}.id>\_<j>\_\texttt{fc}$
                                                  $<end>$
$<page_{pageNoReq,j}.id>\_<j>\_<txp.id>\_\texttt{fs}$ $<if: fs \in txp.guiCmptItems>$
                                                  $<attr(txp,fs)>$
                                                  $<else>$
                                                  $<page_{pageNoReq,j}.id>\_<j>\_\texttt{fs}$
                                                  $<end>$

$<page_{pageNoReq,j}.id>\_<j>\_<txp.id>\_\texttt{strInit}$ "$<attr(txp,str)>$"
$<page_{pageNoReq,j}.id>\_<j>\_<txp.id>\_\texttt{str}$ textBreakLines (
                                                  $<page_{pageNoReq,j}.id>\_<j>\_<txp.id>\_\texttt{strInit}$,
                                                  $<page_{pageNoReq,j}.id>\_<j>\_<txp.id>\_\texttt{fc}$,
                                                  $<page_{pageNoReq,j}.id>\_<j>\_<txp.id>\_\texttt{fs}$,
                                                  $<page_{pageNoReq,j}.id>\_<j>\_<txp.id>\_\texttt{w}$)
$<page_{pageNoReq,j}.id>\_<j>\_<txp.id>\_\texttt{yStr}$ $<if: yStr \in txp.guiCmptItems>$
                                                  $<attr(txp,yStr)>$

5.5. CVM User Interface (CVMUI)

	$<else>$
	$\quad<page_{pageNoReq.j}.id>\_<j>\_<txp.id>\_y\ +$
	$\quad<page_{pageNoReq.j}.id>\_<j>\_<txp.id>\_fa\ -\ 1\ +$
	$\quad<page_{pageNoReq.j}.id>\_<j>\_<txp.id>\_dy$
	$<end>$
$<page_{pageNoReq.j}.id>\_<j>\_<txp.id>\_xStr$	$<page_{pageNoReq.j}.id>\_<j>\_<txp.id>\_x\ +$
	$<page_{pageNoReq.j}.id>\_<j>\_<txp.id>\_dx$
$<page_{pageNoReq.j}.id>\_<j>\_<txp.id>\_wStr$	$<page_{pageNoReq.j}.id>\_<j>\_<txp.id>\_w\ -$
	$<page_{pageNoReq.j}.id>\_<j>\_<txp.id>\_dw$
$<page_{pageNoReq.j}.id>\_<j>\_<txp.id>\_hStr$	textHeight (
	$\quad<page_{pageNoReq.j}.id>\_<j>\_<txp.id>\_str,$
	$\quad<page_{pageNoReq.j}.id>\_<j>\_<txp.id>\_fc,$
	$\quad<page_{pageNoReq.j}.id>\_<j>\_<txp.id>\_fs,$
	0)
$<page_{pageNoReq.j}.id>\_<j>\_<txp.id>\_fa$	fontAscent (
	$\quad<page_{pageNoReq.j}.id>\_<j>\_<txp.id>\_fc,$
	$\quad<page_{pageNoReq.j}.id>\_<j>\_<txp.id>\_fs)$
$<page_{pageNoReq.j}.id>\_<j>\_<txp.id>\_dx$	libGuiTxp$<libGuiStyle>$_dx
$<page_{pageNoReq.j}.id>\_<j>\_<txp.id>\_dy$	libGuiTxp$<libGuiStyle>$_dy
$<page_{pageNoReq.j}.id>\_<j>\_<txp.id>\_dw$	libGuiTxp$<libGuiStyle>$_dw
$<page_{pageNoReq.j}.id>\_<j>\_<txp.id>\_dh$	libGuiTxp$<libGuiStyle>$_dh

//////////
// Misc
//////////

```
.code
.fct <page_{pageNoReq.j}.id>_<j>_<txp.id>_drw()
  {
  loadc <page_{pageNoReq.j}.id>_<j>_<txp.id>_fgr
  loadc <page_{pageNoReq.j}.id>_<j>_<txp.id>_fgg
  loadc <page_{pageNoReq.j}.id>_<j>_<txp.id>_fgb
  setcolor
  loadc <page_{pageNoReq.j}.id>_<j>_<txp.id>_bgr
  loadc <page_{pageNoReq.j}.id>_<j>_<txp.id>_bgg
  loadc <page_{pageNoReq.j}.id>_<j>_<txp.id>_bgb
  setbgcolor
  loadc <page_{pageNoReq.j}.id>_<j>_<txp.id>_fc
  loadc <page_{pageNoReq.j}.id>_<j>_<txp.id>_fs
  setfont
  loadc <page_{pageNoReq.j}.id>_<j>_<txp.id>_xStr
  setxtextline
  loadc <page_{pageNoReq.j}.id>_<j>_<txp.id>_yStr
  textpbg <page_{pageNoReq.j}.id>_<j>_<txp.id>_str
  return
  }
```

Comments

- $attr(txp, attrName)$ returns the value of the attribute with the name $attrName$ that is defined in txp. The data type of the attribute is $Attr$ and is defined in section 5.1.2 (page 147). Refer to section 5.1.1 (page 138) for more information on attributes.

- `fontAscent()`, `textBreakLines()`, `textHeight()`: Refer to section B.4 (page 227) for more information on these CVMA builtin functions.

5.5.5 Text Box

The following definition is used in the next CVMA code template:

$GuiCmpt\ ixt := pageItem_{pageNoReq,j,k}$, with $k \geq 0$ and $ixt.guiCmptType = \texttt{Ixt}$

CVMA Code Template The CVMA code template for the AUI text box ixt is as follows:

```
//////////////////
// Attributes
//////////////////

.const
```

$<page_{pageNoReq,j}.id>\_<j>\_<ixt.id>\_\texttt{x}$ $<attr(ixt, x)>$
$<page_{pageNoReq,j}.id>\_<j>\_<ixt.id>\_\texttt{y}$ $<if : y \in ixt.guiCmptItems>$
                                                       $<attr(ixt, y)>$
                                                       $<else>$
                                                       $<page_{pageNoReq,j}.id>\_<j>\_<ixt.id>\_\texttt{yStr}$ -
                                                       $<page_{pageNoReq,j}.id>\_<j>\_<ixt.id>\_\texttt{fa}$ + 1 -
                                                       $<page_{pageNoReq,j}.id>\_<j>\_<ixt.id>\_\texttt{dy}$
                                                       $<end>$
$<page_{pageNoReq,j}.id>\_<j>\_<ixt.id>\_\texttt{w}$ $<attr(ixt, w)>$
$<page_{pageNoReq,j}.id>\_<j>\_<ixt.id>\_\texttt{h}$ $<page_{pageNoReq,j}.id>\_<j>\_<ixt.id>\_\texttt{hStr}$ +
                                                       $<page_{pageNoReq,j}.id>\_<j>\_<ixt.id>\_\texttt{dh}$

$<if : fg \in ixt.guiCmptItems>$
   $<page_{pageNoReq,j}.id>\_<j>\_<ixt.id>\_\texttt{fgr}$ $<(attr(ixt, fg) \gg 16)\ \&\ 0xFF>$
   $<page_{pageNoReq,j}.id>\_<j>\_<ixt.id>\_\texttt{fgg}$ $<(attr(ixt, fg) \gg 8)\ \&\ 0xFF>$
   $<page_{pageNoReq,j}.id>\_<j>\_<ixt.id>\_\texttt{fgb}$ $<attr(ixt, fg)\ \&\ 0xFF>$
$<else>$
   $<page_{pageNoReq,j}.id>\_<j>\_<ixt.id>\_\texttt{fgr}$ $<page_{pageNoReq,j}.id>\_<j>\_\texttt{fgr}$
   $<page_{pageNoReq,j}.id>\_<j>\_<ixt.id>\_\texttt{fgg}$ $<page_{pageNoReq,j}.id>\_<j>\_\texttt{fgg}$
   $<page_{pageNoReq,j}.id>\_<j>\_<ixt.id>\_\texttt{fgb}$ $<page_{pageNoReq,j}.id>\_<j>\_\texttt{fgb}$
$<end>$

$<if : bg \in ixt.guiCmptItems>$
   $<page_{pageNoReq,j}.id>\_<j>\_<ixt.id>\_\texttt{bgr}$ $<(attr(ixt, bg) \gg 16)\ \&\ 0xFF>$
   $<page_{pageNoReq,j}.id>\_<j>\_<ixt.id>\_\texttt{bgg}$ $<(attr(ixt, bg) \gg 8)\ \&\ 0xFF>$
   $<page_{pageNoReq,j}.id>\_<j>\_<ixt.id>\_\texttt{bgb}$ $<attr(ixt, bg)\ \&\ 0xFF>$
$<else>$
   $<page_{pageNoReq,j}.id>\_<j>\_<ixt.id>\_\texttt{bgr}$ $<page_{pageNoReq,j}.id>\_<j>\_\texttt{bgr}$
   $<page_{pageNoReq,j}.id>\_<j>\_<ixt.id>\_\texttt{bgg}$ $<page_{pageNoReq,j}.id>\_<j>\_\texttt{bgg}$

5.5. CVM User Interface (CVMUI)   183

$<page_{pageNoReq.j}.id>\_<j>\_<ixt.id>$_bgb $<page_{pageNoReq.j}.id>\_<j>$_bgb
$<end>$

$<page_{pageNoReq.j}.id>\_<j>\_<ixt.id>$_fc $<if: fc \in ixt.guiCmptItems>$
                                                  $<attr(ixt, fc)>$
                                                  $<else>$
                                                      $<page_{pageNoReq.j}.id>\_<j>$_fc
                                                  $<end>$
$<page_{pageNoReq.j}.id>\_<j>\_<ixt.id>$_fs $<if: fs \in ixt.guiCmptItems>$
                                                  $<attr(ixt, fs)>$
                                                  $<else>$
                                                      $<page_{pageNoReq.j}.id>\_<j>$_fs
                                                  $<end>$

.data
Bytes $<page_{pageNoReq.j}.id>\_<j>\_<ixt.id>$_str
                           $<page_{pageNoReq.j}.id>\_<j>\_<ixt.id>$_strLenMax + 3

.const
$<page_{pageNoReq.j}.id>\_<j>\_<ixt.id>$_yStr $<if: yStr \in ixt.guiCmptItems>$
                                                  $<attr(ixt, yStr)>$
                                                  $<else>$
                                                      $<page_{pageNoReq.j}.id>\_<j>\_<ixt.id>$_y +
                                                      $<page_{pageNoReq.j}.id>\_<j>\_<ixt.id>$_fa - 1 +
                                                      $<page_{pageNoReq.j}.id>\_<j>\_<ixt.id>$_dy
                                                  $<end>$
$<page_{pageNoReq.j}.id>\_<j>\_<ixt.id>$_strLenMax $<attr(ixt, strLenMax)>$

$<if: svIdx \in ixt.guiCmptItems>$
    $<page_{pageNoReq.j}.id>\_<j>\_<ixt.id>$_svIdx
                            svIdx$<genAui.serviceVars[attr(ixt, svIdx)].id>$
    $<page_{pageNoReq.j}.id>\_<j>\_<ixt.id>$_svBufLen
                            $<page_{pageNoReq.j}.id>\_<j>\_<ixt.id>$_strLenMax + 3
$<end>$

$<page_{pageNoReq.j}.id>\_<j>\_<ixt.id>$_xStr $<page_{pageNoReq.j}.id>\_<j>\_<ixt.id>$_x +
                                                  $<page_{pageNoReq.j}.id>\_<j>\_<ixt.id>$_dx
$<page_{pageNoReq.j}.id>\_<j>\_<ixt.id>$_wStr $<page_{pageNoReq.j}.id>\_<j>\_<ixt.id>$_w -
                                                  $<page_{pageNoReq.j}.id>\_<j>\_<ixt.id>$_dw
$<page_{pageNoReq.j}.id>\_<j>\_<ixt.id>$_hStr $<page_{pageNoReq.j}.id>\_<j>\_<ixt.id>$_fh
$<page_{pageNoReq.j}.id>\_<j>\_<ixt.id>$_yaStr $<page_{pageNoReq.j}.id>\_<j>\_<ixt.id>$_y +
                                                  $<page_{pageNoReq.j}.id>\_<j>\_<ixt.id>$_dy

.data
String $<page_{pageNoReq.j}.id>\_<j>\_<ixt.id>$_strIni
                    "$<strPraefix(attr(ixt, str), attr(ixt, strLenMax))>$"

.const
$<page_{pageNoReq.j}.id>\_<j>\_<ixt.id>$_wChar   textWidth (
                                                  " ",
                                                  $<page_{pageNoReq.j}.id>\_<j>\_<ixt.id>$_fc,

$<page_{pageNoReq,j}.id>\_<j>\_<ixt.id>\_$strPos
$<page_{pageNoReq,j}.id>\_<j>\_<ixt.id>\_$fs)
$<strPosInit>$

$<page_{pageNoReq,j}.id>\_<j>\_<ixt.id>\_$fa fontAscent (
$<page_{pageNoReq,j}.id>\_<j>\_<ixt.id>\_$fc,
$<page_{pageNoReq,j}.id>\_<j>\_<ixt.id>\_$fs)
$<page_{pageNoReq,j}.id>\_<j>\_<ixt.id>\_$fh fontHeight (
$<page_{pageNoReq,j}.id>\_<j>\_<ixt.id>\_$fc,
$<page_{pageNoReq,j}.id>\_<j>\_<ixt.id>\_$fs)

$<page_{pageNoReq,j}.id>\_<j>\_<ixt.id>\_$dx libGuiIxt<$libGuiStyle$>_dx
$<page_{pageNoReq,j}.id>\_<j>\_<ixt.id>\_$dy libGuiIxt<$libGuiStyle$>_dy
$<page_{pageNoReq,j}.id>\_<j>\_<ixt.id>\_$dw libGuiIxt<$libGuiStyle$>_dw
$<page_{pageNoReq,j}.id>\_<j>\_<ixt.id>\_$dh libGuiIxt<$libGuiStyle$>_dh

```
.data
Bytes <page_pageNoReq,j.id>_<j>_<ixt.id>_prp [
  <page_pageNoReq,j.id>_<j>_<ixt.id>_et,
  <page_pageNoReq,j.id>_<j>_<ixt.id>_x,
  <page_pageNoReq,j.id>_<j>_<ixt.id>_y,
  <page_pageNoReq,j.id>_<j>_<ixt.id>_w,
  <page_pageNoReq,j.id>_<j>_<ixt.id>_h,
  <page_pageNoReq,j.id>_<j>_<ixt.id>_fgr,
  <page_pageNoReq,j.id>_<j>_<ixt.id>_fgg,
  <page_pageNoReq,j.id>_<j>_<ixt.id>_fgb,
  <page_pageNoReq,j.id>_<j>_<ixt.id>_bgr,
  <page_pageNoReq,j.id>_<j>_<ixt.id>_bgg,
  <page_pageNoReq,j.id>_<j>_<ixt.id>_bgb,
  <page_pageNoReq,j.id>_<j>_<ixt.id>_fc,
  <page_pageNoReq,j.id>_<j>_<ixt.id>_fs,
  <page_pageNoReq,j.id>_<j>_<ixt.id>_str,
  <page_pageNoReq,j.id>_<j>_<ixt.id>_xStr,
  <page_pageNoReq,j.id>_<j>_<ixt.id>_yStr,
  <page_pageNoReq,j.id>_<j>_<ixt.id>_wStr,
  <page_pageNoReq,j.id>_<j>_<ixt.id>_hStr,
  <page_pageNoReq,j.id>_<j>_<ixt.id>_yaStr,
  <page_pageNoReq,j.id>_<j>_<ixt.id>_strLenMax,
  <page_pageNoReq,j.id>_<j>_<ixt.id>_wChar,
  <page_pageNoReq,j.id>_<j>_<ixt.id>_strPos
]
```

////////
// Init
////////

```
.code
.fct <page_pageNoReq,j.id>_<j>_<ixt.id>_init()
  {
  // Reset string cursor position
  loadc <page_pageNoReq,j.id>_<j>_<ixt.id>_strPos
  loadc <page_pageNoReq,j.id>_<j>_<ixt.id>_prp
```

5.5. CVM User Interface (CVMUI)   185

```
    loadc libGui_strPosOfs
    add
    storea
    // Reset string value
    loadc <page_{pageNoReq,j}.id>_<j>_<ixt.id>_str     push
    loadc <page_{pageNoReq,j}.id>_<j>_<ixt.id>_strIni  push
    fcall libMisc_strCp
    return
    }
```

///////////
// *Events*
///////////

```
.data
EventTable <page_{pageNoReq,j}.id>_<j>_<ixt.id>_et [
  <if : cvmKeyCodeSet ∈ cvmProfile.profileItems>
    key_pressed,         <page_{pageNoReq,j}.id>_<j>_<ixt.id>_kp,
    key_pressed_escape,  <page_{pageNoReq,j}.id>_<j>_<ixt.id>_kpes,
  <end>
  <if : cvmMouseButtons ∈ cvmProfile.profileItems>
    mouse_pressed_left,  <page_{pageNoReq,j}.id>_<j>_<ixt.id>_mpl,
  <end>
  1, <page_{pageNoReq,j}.id>_<j>_et
]

<if : cvmKeyCodeSet ∈ cvmProfile.profileItems>
  .code
  <page_{pageNoReq,j}.id>_<j>_<ixt.id>_kp:
    <if : |idxGuiCmptsInteractive_{pageNoReq,j}| > 1>
      loadep1
      loadc XK_Tab
      loadcr <page_{pageNoReq,j}.id>_<j>_<ixt.id>_kp_tab
      je
      loadep1
      loadc XK_ISO_Left_Tab
      loadcr <page_{pageNoReq,j}.id>_<j>_<ixt.id>_kp_leftTab
      je
    <end>
    loadc <page_{pageNoReq,j}.id>_<j>_<ixt.id>_prp  push
    fcall libGuiIxt_kp
    halt

  <if : |idxGuiCmptsInteractive_{pageNoReq,j}| > 1>
    <page_{pageNoReq,j}.id>_<j>_<ixt.id>_kp_tab:
      loadc <page_{pageNoReq,j}.id>_<j>_<ixt.id>_prp           push
      loadc <page_{pageNoReq,j}.id>_<j>_<ixt^{a→}.id>_prp      push
      loadc libGuiIxt<libGuiStyle>_unDrwFcs  push
      loadc libGui<libGuiAbbr(ixt^{a→}.guiCmptType)><libGuiStyle>_drwFcs  push
      fcall libGui_mvFcs
      halt
```

$<page_{pageNoReq,j}.id>\_<j>\_<ixt.id>\_$kp_leftTab:
  loadc $<page_{pageNoReq,j}.id>\_<j>\_<ixt.id>\_$prp push
  loadc $<page_{pageNoReq,j}.id>\_<j>\_<ixt^{a\leftarrow}.id>\_$prp push
  loadc libGuiIxt<$libGuiStyle$>_unDrwFcs push
  loadc libGui<$libGuiAbbr(ixt^{a\leftarrow}.guiCmptType)$><$libGuiStyle$>_drwFcs push
  fcall libGui_mvFcs
  halt
$<end>$

$<page_{pageNoReq,j}.id>\_<j>\_<ixt.id>\_$kpes:
  loadc $<page_{pageNoReq,j}.id>\_<j>\_<ixt.id>\_$prp push
  loadc $<page_{pageNoReq,j}.id>\_<j>\_$prp push
  loadc libGuiIxt<$libGuiStyle$>_unDrwFcs push
  loadc libMisc_emptyProc push
  fcall libGui_mvFcs
  halt
$<end>$

$<if$: cvmMouseButtons $\in$ cvmProfile.profileItems$>$
.code
$<page_{pageNoReq,j}.id>\_<j>\_<ixt.id>\_$mpl:
  loadep1 push
  loadep2 push
  loadc $<page_{pageNoReq,j}.id>\_<j>\_<ixt.id>\_$prp push
  loadc libGuiIxt<$libGuiStyle$>_unDrwFcs push
  fcall $<page_{pageNoReq,j}.id>\_<j>\_$mplFcs
  halt
$<end>$

////////////////////////////
// Service Variables
////////////////////////////

$<if$: svIdx $\in$ ixt.guiCmptItems$>$
.code
.fct $<page_{pageNoReq,j}.id>\_<j>\_<ixt.id>\_$svBuf_write()
{
  loadc $<page_{pageNoReq,j}.id>\_<j>\_<ixt.id>\_$svIdx
  loadc _svBuf
  load _svBufIdx
  astore<$svIdxLen$>
  load _svBufIdx loadc <$svIdxLen$> add store _svBufIdx
  loadc _svBuf load _svBufIdx add push
  loadc $<page_{pageNoReq,j}.id>\_<j>\_<ixt.id>\_$str push
  fcall libMisc_strCp
  load _svBufIdx
  incsp
  loadc $<page_{pageNoReq,j}.id>\_<j>\_<ixt.id>\_$str push
  fcall libMisc_strLen
  pop
  add

```
loadc 3  add
store _svBufIdx
return
}
```
$<end>$

Comments

- $attr(ixt, attrName)$ returns the value of the attribute with the name $attrName$ that is defined in ixt. The data type of the attribute is $Attr$ and is defined in section 5.1.2 (page 147). Refer to section 5.1.1 (page 138) for more information on attributes.

- `Bytes`   ..._$<ixt.id>$_str   ..._$<ixt.id>$_strLenMax + 3
  The longer binary string format is chosen. Refer to section 3.1.1 (page 33) for more information on the CVM string formats.

- $strPraefix(String\ str,\ Nat\ maxChars)$ returns only the available first $maxChars$ characters of the string str. The rest of str is ignored.

- ..._$<ixt.id>$_wChar   textWidth(" ", ..._$<ixt.id>$_fc, ..._$<ixt.id>$_fs)
  Note that ..._$<ixt.id>$_fc must refer to a monospaced font, because the `Ixt` user interface component requires an equal width for all characters. This width is used by the cursor to move back and forth in the input field of the text box.

- `fontAscent()`, `fontHeight()`: Refer to section B.4 (page 227) for more information on these CVMA builtin functions.

- $strPosInit = -s * wChar$, with
  $s = \{\, t \geq 0 \mid t * wChar > strLen * wChar - wStr \,\}_{min}$,
  $wChar = \, <page_{pageNoReq.j}.id>\_<j>\_<ixt.id>\_\texttt{wChar}$,
  $wStr = \, <page_{pageNoReq.j}.id>\_<j>\_<ixt.id>\_\texttt{wStr}$,
  $strLen = \{\,$ number of characters in $<page_{pageNoReq.j}.id>\_<j>\_<ixt.id>\_\texttt{strIni}$,
  $<page_{pageNoReq.j}.id>\_<j>\_<ixt.id>\_\texttt{strLenMax} \,\}_{min}$

- `XK_Tab`, `XK_ISO_Left_Tab`: Refer to section 3.3 (page 81), $<X11/keysymdef.h>$.

- $ixt^{a\rightarrow}$ and $ixt^{a\leftarrow}$ each return the next and previous interactive user interface component of ixt in the list data structure $page_{pageNoReq.j}.pageItems[k]$, respectively. For the successor of the last element the first element is used. For the predecessor of the first element the last element is used. The data type of $ixt^{a\rightarrow}$ and $ixt^{a\leftarrow}$ is $GuiCmpt$. It is specified in section 5.1.2 (page 147). So far, interactive user interface components are of the type `Btn`, `Hlk`, or `Ixt`. Additional interactive user interface component types may be defined in the future.

5.5.6 Hyperlink

The following definition is used in the next CVMA code template:
$GuiCmpt\ \ hlk := pageItem_{pageNoReq.j,k}$, with $k \geq 0$ and $hlk.guiCmptType = \texttt{Hlk}$

CVMA Code Template The CVMA code template for the AUI hyperlink hlk is as follows:

```
///////////////
// Attributes
///////////////
```

.const
$<page_{pageNoReq.j}.id>\_<j>\_<hlk.id>\_\texttt{x}$ $<attr(hlk, x)>$
$<page_{pageNoReq.j}.id>\_<j>\_<hlk.id>\_\texttt{y}$ $<if : y \in hlk.guiCmptItems>$
                                      $<attr(hlk, y)>$
                                      $<else>$
                                      $<page_{pageNoReq.j}.id>\_<j>\_<hlk.id>\_\texttt{yStr}\ -$
                                      $<page_{pageNoReq.j}.id>\_<j>\_<hlk.id>\_\texttt{fa}\ +\ 1\ -$
                                      $<page_{pageNoReq.j}.id>\_<j>\_<hlk.id>\_\texttt{dy}$
                                      $<end>$
$<page_{pageNoReq.j}.id>\_<j>\_<hlk.id>\_\texttt{w}$ $<if : str \in hlk.guiCmptItems>$
                                      $<page_{pageNoReq.j}.id>\_<j>\_<hlk.id>\_\texttt{wStr}\ +$
                                      $<page_{pageNoReq.j}.id>\_<j>\_<hlk.id>\_\texttt{dw}$
                                      $<else>$
                                      $<attr(hlk, w)>$
                                      $<end>$
$<page_{pageNoReq.j}.id>\_<j>\_<hlk.id>\_\texttt{h}$ $<if : str \in hlk.guiCmptItems>$
                                      $<page_{pageNoReq.j}.id>\_<j>\_<hlk.id>\_\texttt{hStr}\ +$
                                      $<page_{pageNoReq.j}.id>\_<j>\_<hlk.id>\_\texttt{dh}$
                                      $<else>$
                                      $<attr(hlk, h)>$
                                      $<end>$

$<if : fg \in hlk.guiCmptItems>$
    $<page_{pageNoReq.j}.id>\_<j>\_<hlk.id>\_\texttt{fgr}$ $<(attr(hlk, fg) \gg 16)\ \&\ 0xFF>$
    $<page_{pageNoReq.j}.id>\_<j>\_<hlk.id>\_\texttt{fgg}$ $<(attr(hlk, fg) \gg 8)\ \&\ 0xFF>$
    $<page_{pageNoReq.j}.id>\_<j>\_<hlk.id>\_\texttt{fgb}$ $<attr(hlk, fg)\ \&\ 0xFF>$
$<else>$
    $<page_{pageNoReq.j}.id>\_<j>\_<hlk.id>\_\texttt{fgr}$ $<page_{pageNoReq.j}.id>\_<j>\_\texttt{fgr}$
    $<page_{pageNoReq.j}.id>\_<j>\_<hlk.id>\_\texttt{fgg}$ $<page_{pageNoReq.j}.id>\_<j>\_\texttt{fgg}$
    $<page_{pageNoReq.j}.id>\_<j>\_<hlk.id>\_\texttt{fgb}$ $<page_{pageNoReq.j}.id>\_<j>\_\texttt{fgb}$
$<end>$

$<if : bg \in hlk.guiCmptItems>$
    $<page_{pageNoReq.j}.id>\_<j>\_<hlk.id>\_\texttt{bgr}$ $<(attr(hlk, bg) \gg 16)\ \&\ 0xFF>$
    $<page_{pageNoReq.j}.id>\_<j>\_<hlk.id>\_\texttt{bgg}$ $<(attr(hlk, bg) \gg 8)\ \&\ 0xFF>$
    $<page_{pageNoReq.j}.id>\_<j>\_<hlk.id>\_\texttt{bgb}$ $<attr(hlk, bg)\ \&\ 0xFF>$
$<else>$
    $<page_{pageNoReq.j}.id>\_<j>\_<hlk.id>\_\texttt{bgr}$ $<page_{pageNoReq.j}.id>\_<j>\_\texttt{bgr}$
    $<page_{pageNoReq.j}.id>\_<j>\_<hlk.id>\_\texttt{bgg}$ $<page_{pageNoReq.j}.id>\_<j>\_\texttt{bgg}$
    $<page_{pageNoReq.j}.id>\_<j>\_<hlk.id>\_\texttt{bgb}$ $<page_{pageNoReq.j}.id>\_<j>\_\texttt{bgb}$
$<end>$

$<page_{pageNoReq.j}.id>\_<j>\_<hlk.id>\_\texttt{fc}$ $<if : fc \in hlk.guiCmptItems>$
                                      $<attr(hlk, fc)>$

5.5. CVM User Interface (CVMUI)   189

                                          $<else>$
                                             $<page_{pageNoReq.j}.id>\_<j>\_\mathtt{fc}$
                                          $<end>$
$<page_{pageNoReq.j}.id>\_<j>\_<hlk.id>\_\mathtt{fs}$ $<if: fs \in hlk.guiCmptItems>$
                                             $<attr(hlk, fs)>$
                                          $<else>$
                                             $<page_{pageNoReq.j}.id>\_<j>\_\mathtt{fs}$
                                          $<end>$

$<page_{pageNoReq.j}.id>\_<j>\_<hlk.id>\_\mathtt{str}$ $<if: str \in hlk.guiCmptItems>$
                                          "$<attr(hlk, img)>$"
                                          $<else>$
                                          ""
                                          $<end>$
$<page_{pageNoReq.j}.id>\_<j>\_<hlk.id>\_\mathtt{yStr}$ $<if: yStr \in hlk.guiCmptItems>$
                                             $<attr(hlk, yStr)>$
                                          $<else>$
                                             $<page_{pageNoReq.j}.id>\_<j>\_<hlk.id>\_\mathtt{y}$ +
                                             $<page_{pageNoReq.j}.id>\_<j>\_<hlk.id>\_\mathtt{fa}$ - 1 +
                                             $<page_{pageNoReq.j}.id>\_<j>\_<hlk.id>\_\mathtt{dy}$
                                          $<end>$

$<page_{pageNoReq.j}.id>\_<j>\_<hlk.id>\_\mathtt{hostAdr}$ "$<attr(hlk, hostAdr)>$"
$<page_{pageNoReq.j}.id>\_<j>\_<hlk.id>\_\mathtt{serviceNo}$ $<attr(hlk, serviceNo)>$

$<page_{pageNoReq.j}.id>\_<j>\_<hlk.id>\_\mathtt{xStr}$ $<page_{pageNoReq.j}.id>\_<j>\_<hlk.id>\_\mathtt{x}$ +
                                             $<page_{pageNoReq.j}.id>\_<j>\_<hlk.id>\_\mathtt{dx}$
$<page_{pageNoReq.j}.id>\_<j>\_<hlk.id>\_\mathtt{wStr}$ $<if: str \in hlk.guiCmptItems>$
                                          textWidth (
                                             $<page_{pageNoReq.j}.id>\_<j>\_<hlk.id>\_\mathtt{str}$,
                                             $<page_{pageNoReq.j}.id>\_<j>\_<hlk.id>\_\mathtt{fc}$,
                                             $<page_{pageNoReq.j}.id>\_<j>\_<hlk.id>\_\mathtt{fs}$)
                                          $<else>$
                                             $<page_{pageNoReq.j}.id>\_<j>\_<hlk.id>\_\mathtt{w}$ -
                                             $<page_{pageNoReq.j}.id>\_<j>\_<hlk.id>\_\mathtt{dw}$
                                          $<end>$
$<page_{pageNoReq.j}.id>\_<j>\_<hlk.id>\_\mathtt{hStr}$ $<if: str \in hlk.guiCmptItems>$
                                          textHeight (
                                             $<page_{pageNoReq.j}.id>\_<j>\_<hlk.id>\_\mathtt{str}$,
                                             $<page_{pageNoReq.j}.id>\_<j>\_<hlk.id>\_\mathtt{fc}$,
                                             $<page_{pageNoReq.j}.id>\_<j>\_<hlk.id>\_\mathtt{fs}$,
                                             0)
                                          $<else>$
                                             $<page_{pageNoReq.j}.id>\_<j>\_<hlk.id>\_\mathtt{fh}$
                                          $<end>$

$<page_{pageNoReq.j}.id>\_<j>\_<hlk.id>\_\mathtt{fa}$ fontAscent (
                                             $<page_{pageNoReq.j}.id>\_<j>\_<hlk.id>\_\mathtt{fc}$,
                                             $<page_{pageNoReq.j}.id>\_<j>\_<hlk.id>\_\mathtt{fs}$)
$<page_{pageNoReq.j}.id>\_<j>\_<hlk.id>\_\mathtt{fh}$ fontHeight (
                                             $<page_{pageNoReq.j}.id>\_<j>\_<hlk.id>\_\mathtt{fc}$,

190   5. CVM Packet Server (CVMPS)

$<page_{pageNoReq.j}.id>$_$<j>$_$<hlk.id>$_fs)

$<page_{pageNoReq.j}.id>$_$<j>$_$<hlk.id>$_dx   libGuiHlk<$libGuiStyle$>_dx
$<page_{pageNoReq.j}.id>$_$<j>$_$<hlk.id>$_dy   libGuiHlk<$libGuiStyle$>_dy
$<page_{pageNoReq.j}.id>$_$<j>$_$<hlk.id>$_dw   libGuiHlk<$libGuiStyle$>_dw
$<page_{pageNoReq.j}.id>$_$<j>$_$<hlk.id>$_dh   libGuiHlk<$libGuiStyle$>_dh

.data
String $<page_{pageNoReq.j}.id>$_$<j>$_$<hlk.id>$_str_
                         $<page_{pageNoReq.j}.id>$_$<j>$_$<hlk.id>$_str
String $<page_{pageNoReq.j}.id>$_$<j>$_$<hlk.id>$_hostAdr_
                         $<page_{pageNoReq.j}.id>$_$<j>$_$<hlk.id>$_hostAdr

Bytes $<page_{pageNoReq.j}.id>$_$<j>$_$<hlk.id>$_prp [
    $<page_{pageNoReq.j}.id>$_$<j>$_$<hlk.id>$_et,
    $<page_{pageNoReq.j}.id>$_$<j>$_$<hlk.id>$_x,
    $<page_{pageNoReq.j}.id>$_$<j>$_$<hlk.id>$_y,
    $<page_{pageNoReq.j}.id>$_$<j>$_$<hlk.id>$_w,
    $<page_{pageNoReq.j}.id>$_$<j>$_$<hlk.id>$_h,
    $<page_{pageNoReq.j}.id>$_$<j>$_$<hlk.id>$_fgr,
    $<page_{pageNoReq.j}.id>$_$<j>$_$<hlk.id>$_fgg,
    $<page_{pageNoReq.j}.id>$_$<j>$_$<hlk.id>$_fgb,
    $<page_{pageNoReq.j}.id>$_$<j>$_$<hlk.id>$_bgr,
    $<page_{pageNoReq.j}.id>$_$<j>$_$<hlk.id>$_bgg,
    $<page_{pageNoReq.j}.id>$_$<j>$_$<hlk.id>$_bgb,
    $<page_{pageNoReq.j}.id>$_$<j>$_$<hlk.id>$_fc,
    $<page_{pageNoReq.j}.id>$_$<j>$_$<hlk.id>$_fs,
    $<page_{pageNoReq.j}.id>$_$<j>$_$<hlk.id>$_str_,
    $<page_{pageNoReq.j}.id>$_$<j>$_$<hlk.id>$_xStr,
    $<page_{pageNoReq.j}.id>$_$<j>$_$<hlk.id>$_yStr,
    $<page_{pageNoReq.j}.id>$_$<j>$_$<hlk.id>$_hostAdr_,
    $<page_{pageNoReq.j}.id>$_$<j>$_$<hlk.id>$_serviceNo
]

////////////
// Events
////////////

.data
EventTable $<page_{pageNoReq.j}.id>$_$<j>$_$<hlk.id>$_et [
    $<if$: cvmKeyCodeSet $\in$ cvmProfile.profileItems$>$
        key_pressed, $<page_{pageNoReq.j}.id>$_$<j>$_$<hlk.id>$_kp,
        key_pressed_escape, $<page_{pageNoReq.j}.id>$_$<j>$_$<hlk.id>$_kpes,
        key_pressed_enter, $<page_{pageNoReq.j}.id>$_$<j>$_$<hlk.id>$_kpe,
    $<end>$
    $<if$: cvmMouseButtons $\in$ cvmProfile.profileItems$>$
        mouse_pressed_left, $<page_{pageNoReq.j}.id>$_$<j>$_$<hlk.id>$_mpl,
    $<end>$
    1, $<page_{pageNoReq.j}.id>$_$<j>$_et
]

5.5. CVM User Interface (CVMUI)	191

$<if: \text{cvmKeyCodeSet} \in cvmProfile.profileItems>$
.code
  $<page_{pageNoReq,j}.id>\_<j>\_<hlk.id>\_$kp:
    $<if: |idxGuiCmptsInteractive_{pageNoReq,j}| > 1>$
      loadep1
      loadc XK_Tab
      loadcr $<page_{pageNoReq,j}.id>\_<j>\_<hlk.id>\_$kp_tab
      je
      loadep1
      loadc XK_ISO_Left_Tab
      loadcr $<page_{pageNoReq,j}.id>\_<j>\_<hlk.id>\_$kp_leftTab
      je
    $<end>$
    loadc $<page_{pageNoReq,j}.id>\_<j>\_<hlk.id>\_$prp
    push
    fcall libGuiHlk_kp
    halt

  $<if: |idxGuiCmptsInteractive_{pageNoReq,j}| > 1>$
    $<page_{pageNoReq,j}.id>\_<j>\_<hlk.id>\_$kp_tab:
      loadc $<page_{pageNoReq,j}.id>\_<j>\_<hlk.id>\_$prp push
      loadc $<page_{pageNoReq,j}.id>\_<j>\_<hlk^{a\rightarrow}.id>\_$prp push
      loadc libGuiHlk$<libGuiStyle>\_$unDrwFcs push
      loadc libGui$<libGuiAbbr(ixt^{a\rightarrow}.guiCmptType)><libGuiStyle>\_$drwFcs push
      fcall libGui_mvFcs
      halt
    $<page_{pageNoReq,j}.id>\_<j>\_<hlk.id>\_$kp_leftTab:
      loadc $<page_{pageNoReq,j}.id>\_<j>\_<hlk.id>\_$prp push
      loadc $<page_{pageNoReq,j}.id>\_<j>\_<ixt^{a\leftarrow}.id>\_$prp push
      loadc libGuiHlk$<libGuiStyle>\_$unDrwFcs push
      loadc libGui$<libGuiAbbr(ixt^{a\leftarrow}.guiCmptType)><libGuiStyle>\_$drwFcs push
      fcall libGui_mvFcs
      halt
  $<end>$

  $<page_{pageNoReq,j}.id>\_<j>\_<hlk.id>\_$kpes:
    loadc $<page_{pageNoReq,j}.id>\_<j>\_<hlk.id>\_$prp push
    loadc $<page_{pageNoReq,j}.id>\_<j>\_$prp push
    loadc libGuiHlk$<libGuiStyle>\_$unDrwFcs push
    loadc libMisc_emptyProc push
    fcall libGui_mvFcs
    halt

  $<page_{pageNoReq,j}.id>\_<j>\_<hlk.id>\_$kpe:
    loadc $<page_{pageNoReq,j}.id>\_<j>\_<hlk.id>\_$prp push
    fcall libGuiHlk_dwn
    halt

$<if: \text{cvmMouseButtons} \in cvmProfile.profileItems>$
.code
  $<page_{pageNoReq,j}.id>\_<j>\_<hlk.id>\_$mpl:

```
        loadep1   push
        loadep2   push
        loadc   <page_{pageNoReq,j}.id>_<j>_<hlk.id>_prp   push
        loadc   libGuiHlk<libGuiStyle>_unDrwFcs   push
        fcall   <page_{pageNoReq,j}.id>_<j>_mplFcs
        halt
<end>
```

Comment

- $attr(hlk, attrName)$ returns the value of the attribute with the name $attrName$ that is defined in hlk. The data type of the attribute is $Attr$ and is defined in section 5.1.2 (page 147). Refer to section 5.1.1 (page 138) for more information on attributes.

- $hlk^{a\rightarrow}$ and $hlk^{a\leftarrow}$ each return the next and previous interactive user interface component of hlk in the list data structure $page_{pageNoReq,j}.pageItems[k]$. For the successor of the last element the first element is used. For the predecessor of the first element the last element is used. The data type of $hlk^{a\rightarrow}$ and $hlk^{a\leftarrow}$ is $GuiCmpt$. It is specified in section 5.1.2 (page 147). So far, interactive user interface components are of the type Btn, Hlk, or Ixt. Additional interactive user interface component types may be defined in the future.

5.5.7 Button

The following definition is used in the next CVMA code template:

$GuiCmpt \quad btn := pageItem_{pageNoReq,j,k}$, with $k \geq 0$ and $btn.guiCmptType = $ Btn

CVMA Code Template The CVMA code template for the AUI button btn is as follows:

```
///////////////
// Attributes
///////////////

.const
<page_{pageNoReq,j}.id>_<j>_<btn.id>_x    <attr(btn, x)>
<page_{pageNoReq,j}.id>_<j>_<btn.id>_y    <if : y ∈ btn.guiCmptItems>
                                              <attr(btn, y)>
                                          <else>
                                              <page_{pageNoReq,j}.id>_<j>_<btn.id>_yStr -
                                              <page_{pageNoReq,j}.id>_<j>_<btn.id>_fa + 1 -
                                              <page_{pageNoReq,j}.id>_<j>_<btn.id>_dy
                                          <end>
<page_{pageNoReq,j}.id>_<j>_<btn.id>_w    <if : str ∈ btn.guiCmptItems>
                                              <page_{pageNoReq,j}.id>_<j>_<btn.id>_wStr +
                                              <page_{pageNoReq,j}.id>_<j>_<btn.id>_dw
                                          <else>
                                              <attr(btn, w)>
                                          <end>
```

5.5. CVM User Interface (CVMUI) 193

$<page_{pageNoReq.j}.id>\_<j>\_<btn.id>\_\text{h}$ $<if : str \in btn.guiCmptItems>$
　　　　　　　　　　　　　　　　　　$<page_{pageNoReq.j}.id>\_<j>\_<btn.id>\_\text{hStr} +$
　　　　　　　　　　　　　　　　　　$<page_{pageNoReq.j}.id>\_<j>\_<btn.id>\_\text{dh}$
　　　　　　　　　　　　　　$<else>$
　　　　　　　　　　　　　　　　$<attr(btn, h)>$
　　　　　　　　　　　　　　$<end>$

$<if : fg \in btn.guiCmptItems>$
　$<page_{pageNoReq.j}.id>\_<j>\_<btn.id>\_\text{fgr}$　$<(attr(btn, fg) \gg 16)\ \&\ 0xFF>$
　$<page_{pageNoReq.j}.id>\_<j>\_<btn.id>\_\text{fgg}$　$<(attr(btn, fg) \gg 8)\ \&\ 0xFF>$
　$<page_{pageNoReq.j}.id>\_<j>\_<btn.id>\_\text{fgb}$　$<attr(btn, fg)\ \&\ 0xFF>$
$<else>$
　$<page_{pageNoReq.j}.id>\_<j>\_<btn.id>\_\text{fgr}$　$<page_{pageNoReq.j}.id>\_<j>\_\text{fgr}$
　$<page_{pageNoReq.j}.id>\_<j>\_<btn.id>\_\text{fgg}$　$<page_{pageNoReq.j}.id>\_<j>\_\text{fgg}$
　$<page_{pageNoReq.j}.id>\_<j>\_<btn.id>\_\text{fgb}$　$<page_{pageNoReq.j}.id>\_<j>\_\text{fgb}$
$<end>$

$<if : bg \in btn.guiCmptItems>$
　$<page_{pageNoReq.j}.id>\_<j>\_<btn.id>\_\text{bgr}$　$<(attr(btn, bg) \gg 16)\ \&\ 0xFF>$
　$<page_{pageNoReq.j}.id>\_<j>\_<btn.id>\_\text{bgg}$　$<(attr(btn, bg) \gg 8)\ \&\ 0xFF>$
　$<page_{pageNoReq.j}.id>\_<j>\_<btn.id>\_\text{bgb}$　$<attr(btn, bg)\ \&\ 0xFF>$
$<else>$
　$<page_{pageNoReq.j}.id>\_<j>\_<btn.id>\_\text{bgr}$　$<page_{pageNoReq.j}.id>\_<j>\_\text{bgr}$
　$<page_{pageNoReq.j}.id>\_<j>\_<btn.id>\_\text{bgg}$　$<page_{pageNoReq.j}.id>\_<j>\_\text{bgg}$
　$<page_{pageNoReq.j}.id>\_<j>\_<btn.id>\_\text{bgb}$　$<page_{pageNoReq.j}.id>\_<j>\_\text{bgb}$
$<end>$

$<page_{pageNoReq.j}.id>\_<j>\_<btn.id>\_\text{fc}$　$<if : fc \in btn.guiCmptItems>$
　　　　　　　　　　　　　　　　$<attr(btn, fc)>$
　　　　　　　　　　　　　　$<else>$
　　　　　　　　　　　　　　　　$<page_{pageNoReq.j}.id>\_<j>\_\text{fc}$
　　　　　　　　　　　　　　$<end>$
$<page_{pageNoReq.j}.id>\_<j>\_<btn.id>\_\text{fs}$　$<if : fs \in btn.guiCmptItems>$
　　　　　　　　　　　　　　　　$<attr(btn, fs)>$
　　　　　　　　　　　　　　$<else>$
　　　　　　　　　　　　　　　　$<page_{pageNoReq.j}.id>\_<j>\_\text{fs}$
　　　　　　　　　　　　　　$<end>$

$<page_{pageNoReq.j}.id>\_<j>\_<btn.id>\_\text{str}$　$<if : str \in btn.guiCmptItems>$
　　　　　　　　　　　　　　　　"$<attr(btn, img)>$"
　　　　　　　　　　　　　　$<else>$
　　　　　　　　　　　　　　　　""
　　　　　　　　　　　　　　$<end>$
$<page_{pageNoReq.j}.id>\_<j>\_<btn.id>\_\text{yStr}$　$<if : yStr \in btn.guiCmptItems>$
　　　　　　　　　　　　　　　　$<attr(btn, yStr)>$
　　　　　　　　　　　　　　$<else>$
　　　　　　　　　　　　　　　　$<page_{pageNoReq.j}.id>\_<j>\_<btn.id>\_\text{y} +$
　　　　　　　　　　　　　　　　$<page_{pageNoReq.j}.id>\_<j>\_<btn.id>\_\text{fa} - 1$
　　　　　　　　　　　　　　　　$+ <page_{pageNoReq.j}.id>\_<j>\_<btn.id>\_\text{dy}$
　　　　　　　　　　　　　　$<end>$

$<page_{pageNoReq,j}.id>\_<j>\_<btn.id>\_$img $<if : img \in btn.guiCmptItems>$
                                                   "$<attr(btn, img)>$"
                                                 $<else>$
                                                   ""
                                                 $<end>$
$<page_{pageNoReq,j}.id>\_<j>\_<btn.id>\_$imgStyle $<attr(btn, imgStyle)>$

$<page_{pageNoReq,j}.id>\_<j>\_<btn.id>\_$xStr $<page_{pageNoReq,j}.id>\_<j>\_<btn.id>\_$x +
                                                 $<page_{pageNoReq,j}.id>\_<j>\_<btn.id>\_$dx
$<page_{pageNoReq,j}.id>\_<j>\_<btn.id>\_$wStr $<if : str \in btn.guiCmptItems>$
                                                   textWidth (
                                                       $<page_{pageNoReq,j}.id>\_<j>\_<btn.id>\_$str,
                                                       $<page_{pageNoReq,j}.id>\_<j>\_<btn.id>\_$fc,
                                                       $<page_{pageNoReq,j}.id>\_<j>\_<btn.id>\_$fs)
                                                 $<else>$
                                                   $<page_{pageNoReq,j}.id>\_<j>\_<btn.id>\_$w -
                                                   $<page_{pageNoReq,j}.id>\_<j>\_<btn.id>\_$dw
                                                 $<end>$
$<page_{pageNoReq,j}.id>\_<j>\_<btn.id>\_$hStr $<if : str \in btn.guiCmptItems>$
                                                   textHeight (
                                                       $<page_{pageNoReq,j}.id>\_<j>\_<btn.id>\_$str,
                                                       $<page_{pageNoReq,j}.id>\_<j>\_<btn.id>\_$fc,
                                                       $<page_{pageNoReq,j}.id>\_<j>\_<btn.id>\_$fs,
                                                       0)
                                                 $<else>$
                                                   $<page_{pageNoReq,j}.id>\_<j>\_<btn.id>\_$fh
                                                 $<end>$

$<page_{pageNoReq,j}.id>\_<j>\_<btn.id>\_$fa   fontAscent (
                                                       $<page_{pageNoReq,j}.id>\_<j>\_<btn.id>\_$fc,
                                                       $<page_{pageNoReq,j}.id>\_<j>\_<btn.id>\_$fs)
$<page_{pageNoReq,j}.id>\_<j>\_<btn.id>\_$fh   fontHeight (
                                                       $<page_{pageNoReq,j}.id>\_<j>\_<btn.id>\_$fc,
                                                       $<page_{pageNoReq,j}.id>\_<j>\_<btn.id>\_$fs)

$<page_{pageNoReq,j}.id>\_<j>\_<btn.id>\_$dx   libGuiBtn$<libGuiStyle>\_$dx
$<page_{pageNoReq,j}.id>\_<j>\_<btn.id>\_$dy   libGuiBtn$<libGuiStyle>\_$dy
$<page_{pageNoReq,j}.id>\_<j>\_<btn.id>\_$dw   libGuiBtn$<libGuiStyle>\_$dw
$<page_{pageNoReq,j}.id>\_<j>\_<btn.id>\_$dh   libGuiBtn$<libGuiStyle>\_$dh

.data
String $<page_{pageNoReq,j}.id>\_<j>\_<btn.id>\_$str_ $<page_{pageNoReq,j}.id>\_<j>\_<btn.id>\_$str
String $<page_{pageNoReq,j}.id>\_<j>\_<btn.id>\_$img_ $<page_{pageNoReq,j}.id>\_<j>\_<btn.id>\_$img

Bytes $<page_{pageNoReq,j}.id>\_<j>\_<btn.id>\_$prp [
   $<page_{pageNoReq,j}.id>\_<j>\_<btn.id>\_$et,
   $<page_{pageNoReq,j}.id>\_<j>\_<btn.id>\_$x,
   $<page_{pageNoReq,j}.id>\_<j>\_<btn.id>\_$y,
   $<page_{pageNoReq,j}.id>\_<j>\_<btn.id>\_$w,
   $<page_{pageNoReq,j}.id>\_<j>\_<btn.id>\_$h,
   $<page_{pageNoReq,j}.id>\_<j>\_<btn.id>\_$fgr,

5.5. CVM User Interface (CVMUI)

$<page_{pageNoReq.j}.id>\_<j>\_<btn.id>\_$fgg,
$<page_{pageNoReq.j}.id>\_<j>\_<btn.id>\_$fgb,
$<page_{pageNoReq.j}.id>\_<j>\_<btn.id>\_$bgr,
$<page_{pageNoReq.j}.id>\_<j>\_<btn.id>\_$bgg,
$<page_{pageNoReq.j}.id>\_<j>\_<btn.id>\_$bgb,
$<page_{pageNoReq.j}.id>\_<j>\_<btn.id>\_$fc,
$<page_{pageNoReq.j}.id>\_<j>\_<btn.id>\_$fs,
$<page_{pageNoReq.j}.id>\_<j>\_<btn.id>\_$str_,
$<page_{pageNoReq.j}.id>\_<j>\_<btn.id>\_$xStr,
$<page_{pageNoReq.j}.id>\_<j>\_<btn.id>\_$yStr,
$<page_{pageNoReq.j}.id>\_<j>\_<btn.id>\_$img_,
$<page_{pageNoReq.j}.id>\_<j>\_<btn.id>\_$imgStyle
]

```
////////////
// Events
////////////
.data
EventTable
```
$<page_{pageNoReq.j}.id>\_<j>\_<btn.id>\_$et [
  $<if$: cvmKeyCodeSet $\in cvmProfile.profileItems>$
    key_pressed, $<page_{pageNoReq.j}.id>\_<j>\_<btn.id>\_$kp,
    key_pressed_escape, $<page_{pageNoReq.j}.id>\_<j>\_<btn.id>\_$kpes,
    key_pressed_enter, $<page_{pageNoReq.j}.id>\_<j>\_<btn.id>\_$kpe,
    key_released, $<page_{pageNoReq.j}.id>\_<j>\_<btn.id>\_$kr,
    key_released_enter, $<page_{pageNoReq.j}.id>\_<j>\_<btn.id>\_$kre,
  $<end>$
  $<if$: cvmMouseButtons $\in cvmProfile.profileItems>$
    mouse_pressed_left, $<page_{pageNoReq.j}.id>\_<j>\_<btn.id>\_$mpl,
    mouse_released_left, $<page_{pageNoReq.j}.id>\_<j>\_<btn.id>\_$mrl,
  $<end>$
  1, $<page_{pageNoReq.j}.id>\_<j>\_$et
]

$<if$: cvmKeyCodeSet $\in cvmProfile.profileItems>$
.code
$<page_{pageNoReq.j}.id>\_<j>\_<btn.id>\_$kp:
  $<if : |idxGuiCmptsInteractive_{pageNoReq.j}| > 1>$
    loadep1
    loadc XK_Tab
    loadcr $<page_{pageNoReq.j}.id>\_<j>\_<btn.id>\_$kp_tab
    je
    loadep1
    loadc XK_ISO_Left_Tab
    loadcr $<page_{pageNoReq.j}.id>\_<j>\_<btn.id>\_$kp_leftTab
    je
  $<end>$
  loadep1
  loadc XK_space
  loadcr $<page_{pageNoReq.j}.id>\_<j>\_<btn.id>\_$kp_space
  je

        halt

    $<if : |idxGuiCmptsInteractive_{pageNoReq,j}| > 1>$
        $<page_{pageNoReq,j}.id>$_$<j>$_$<btn.id>$_kp_tab:
            loadc $<page_{pageNoReq,j}.id>$_$<j>$_$<btn.id>$_prp   push
            loadc $<page_{pageNoReq,j}.id>$_$<j>$_$<btn^{a\rightarrow}.id>$_prp   push
            loadc libGuiBtn$<libGuiStyle>$_unDrwFcs   push
            loadc libGui$<libGuiAbbr(btn^{a\rightarrow}.guiCmptType)>$$<libGuiStyle>$_drwFcs   push
            fcall libGui_mvFcs
            halt
        $<page_{pageNoReq,j}.id>$_$<j>$_$<btn.id>$_kp_leftTab:
            loadc $<page_{pageNoReq,j}.id>$_$<j>$_$<btn.id>$_prp   push
            loadc $<page_{pageNoReq,j}.id>$_$<j>$_$<btn^{a\leftarrow}.id>$_prp   push
            loadc libGuiBtn$<libGuiStyle>$_unDrwFcs   push
            loadc libGui$<libGuiAbbr(btn^{a\leftarrow}.guiCmptType)>$$<libGuiStyle>$_drwFcs   push
            fcall libGui_mvFcs
            halt
    $<end>$

    $<page_{pageNoReq,j}.id>$_$<j>$_$<btn.id>$_kp_space:
        fcall $<page_{pageNoReq,j}.id>$_$<j>$_$<btn.id>$_evDwn
        halt

    $<page_{pageNoReq,j}.id>$_$<j>$_$<btn.id>$_kpes:
        loadc $<page_{pageNoReq,j}.id>$_$<j>$_$<btn.id>$_prp   push
        loadc $<page_{pageNoReq,j}.id>$_$<j>$_prp   push
        loadc libGuiBtn$<libGuiStyle>$_unDrwFcs   push
        loadc libMisc_emptyProc   push
        fcall libGui_mvFcs
        halt

    $<page_{pageNoReq,j}.id>$_$<j>$_$<btn.id>$_kpe:
        fcall $<page_{pageNoReq,j}.id>$_$<j>$_$<btn.id>$_evDwn
        halt

    $<page_{pageNoReq,j}.id>$_$<j>$_$<btn.id>$_kr:
        loadep1
        loadc XK_space
        loadcr $<page_{pageNoReq,j}.id>$_$<j>$_$<btn.id>$_kr_space
        je
        halt

    $<page_{pageNoReq,j}.id>$_$<j>$_$<btn.id>$_kr_space:
        fcall $<page_{pageNoReq,j}.id>$_$<j>$_$<btn.id>$_evUp
        halt

    $<page_{pageNoReq,j}.id>$_$<j>$_$<btn.id>$_kre:
        fcall $<page_{pageNoReq,j}.id>$_$<j>$_$<btn.id>$_evUp
        halt
$<end>$

5.5. CVM User Interface (CVMUI)

$<if$: cvmMouseButtons $\in cvmProfile.profileItems>$
  .code
  $<page_{pageNoReq.j}.id>\_<j>\_<btn.id>\_\texttt{mpl}$:
     loadep1   push
     loadep2   push
     loadc $<page_{pageNoReq.j}.id>\_<j>\_<btn.id>\_\texttt{prp}$ push
     loadc libGuiBtn$<libGuiStyle>\_\texttt{unDrwFcs}$ push
     fcall $<page_{pageNoReq.j}.id>\_<j>\_\texttt{mplFcs}$
     halt

  $<page_{pageNoReq.j}.id>\_<j>\_<btn.id>\_\texttt{mrl}$:
     fcall $<page_{pageNoReq.j}.id>\_<j>\_<btn.id>\_\texttt{evUp}$
     halt
$<end>$

$<if$: cvmKeyCodeSet $\in cvmProfile.profileItems \lor$
       cvmMouseButtons $\in cvmProfile.profileItems>$
  .code
  .fct $<page_{pageNoReq.j}.id>\_<j>\_<btn.id>\_\texttt{evDwn}()$
  {
     loadc $<page_{pageNoReq.j}.id>\_<j>\_<btn.id>\_\texttt{prp}$
     push
     fcall libGuiBtn$<libGuiStyle>\_\texttt{dwn}$
     $<if : \exists l \geq 0 : btn.guiCmptItems[l]_{Event} \land btn.guiCmptItems[l].type = evDwn$
        $<btn.guiCmptItems[l].cvmAs>$
     $<end>$
     return
  }

  .fct $<page_{pageNoReq.j}.id>\_<j>\_<btn.id>\_\texttt{evUp}()$
  {
     loadc $<page_{pageNoReq.j}.id>\_<j>\_<btn.id>\_\texttt{prp}$
     push
     fcall libGuiBtn$<libGuiStyle>\_\texttt{up}$
     $<if : \exists l \geq 0 : btn.guiCmptItems[l]_{Event} \land btn.guiCmptItems[l].type = evUp$
        $<btn.guiCmptItems[l].cvmAs>$
     $<end>$
     return
  }
$<end>$

Comments

- $attr(btn, attrName)$ returns the value of the attribute with the name $attrName$ that is defined in btn. The data type of the attribute is $Attr$ and is defined in section 5.1.2 (page 147). Refer to section 5.1.1 (page 138) for more information on attributes.

- $btn^{a\rightarrow}$ and $btn^{a\leftarrow}$ each return the next and previous interactive user interface component of btn in the list data structure $page_{pageNoReq.j}.pageItems[k]$. For the successor of the last element the first element is used. For the predecessor of the first element the last element is used. The data type of $btn^{a\to}$ and $btn^{a\leftarrow}$ is *GuiCmpt*. It is specified in section 5.1.2 (page 147). So far, interactive user interface components are of the type Btn, Hlk, or Ixt. Additional interactive user interface component types may be defined in the future.

- $btn.guiCmptItems[l]_{Event} \equiv$
The data type of $btn.guiCmptItems[l]$ is *Event*.

5.6 Implementation Notes

The CVM packet server has been implemented with the C [20] programming language under the Linux [43] operating system.

Source Files The C source files for the session manager, the service generator, and the fixed part of the service instance are in the subdirectories Implementation/CvmPacket-Server/Src/ and Implementation/RghLib/Src/. The latter subdirectory contains only source files whose names start with the prefix "rgh".

- cvmps.{h,c}: These source files implement the session manager module of the CVM packet server. The main() function is implemented here as well.

- cvmpsSd.{h,c}, session.{h,c}: These source files implement that part of the session manager module which manages the session data of all sessions.

- svcVar.{h,c}: These source files contain elementary definitions for accessing the service variables of a session.

- cptp.h, cptpSrv.{h,c}: These source files implement the server part of the CPTP protocol. Refer to section 4 (page 127) for more information on the CPTP protocol.

  For the implementation of the TCP/IP [69] network communication the Linux socket interface, which is compatible to the BSD [17] socket interface, has been used. However, this implementation supports only IPv4, but not IPv6.

- svcInstGen.{h,c}: These source files implement the service generator module of the CVM packet server. Here is the function auiTree_generateServiceInstance() defined. The name of the generated C file is *"sessionId_serviceId.c"*. Refer to section 4.1 (page 128) for more information on *sessionId* and to section 5.1.1 (page 145) for more information on *serviceId*. The generated C file is located in the subdirectory Implementation/CvmPacketServer/SvcInst/Gen/.

  The Makefile [34] in the subdirectory Implementation/CvmPacketServer/Svc-Inst/ manages the compilation of the source files to build the executable file of the generated service instance. After the missing C source file of the service instance has been generated, the CVM packet server automatically invokes the make command with the following command: make *sessionId_serviceId* sessionId=*sessionId*

  The name of the built executable file, which represents the service instance, is *"sessionId_serviceId"*. This file is located in the subdirectory Implementation/Cvm-PacketServer/SvcInst/Gen/, as well.

5.6. Implementation Notes

- `svcInst.{h,c}`, `_svcInst.h`: These source files belong to the fixed part of the service instance and contain definitions that are used by all service instances. Note that the missing service-specific parts are generated by the service generator from the given AUI description during the client-server session.

- `rgh*.{h,c}`: These source files contain general utility functions and definitions for managing the heap, list and tree structures, for debugging, and for managing strings and scanner tokens, respectively.

The C source files for the CVM packet generator are in the subdirectories `Implementation/CvmPacketGenerator/Src/` and `Implementation/RghLib/Src/`. The latter subdirectory contains only source files whose names start with the prefix "`rgh`".

- `auiAttrName.h`, `auiBuiltinFct.h`, `auiEventType.h`, `auiImgStyle.h`, `auiServerLng.h`, `auiVarType.h`: These source files contain general definitions that refer to attribute names, builtin functions, event types, etc.

- `cvmui.{h,c}`: These source files contain definitions that refer to CVMUIs.

- `auiNode.{h,c}`: These source files contain node-specific definitions and constructors to build the abstract syntax tree. An AUI description is dealt as an *Aui* tree structure. The *Aui* data type is defined in section 5.1.2 (page 147).

- `auiTree.{h,c}`: These source files contain the core parts of the CVM packet generator. This includes the definitions to perform the semantic check of the context conditions and the generation of the CVM packet. Here are the functions `auiTree_generateAuis()` and `auiTree_2cvmui()` defined.

- `auiParse.y`: This source file contains the syntactic grammar specification for the parser generator `bison`. The parser transforms the AUI description into a syntax tree for further processing.

- `auiScan.l`: This source file contains the lexical grammar specification for the scanner generator `flex`.

- `cvmpg.{h,c}`: These source files contain the function `cvmpg_aui2cvmui()` and other definitions and functions that are needed by the CVM packet generator.

- `test_generateAuis.c`: This source file contains the `main()` function of the test program `test_generateAuis`.

- `test_generateServiceInstance.c`: This source file contains the `main()` function of the test program `test_generateServiceInstance`.

- `test_aui2cvmui.c`: This source file contains the `main()` function of the test program `test_aui2cvmui`.

- `rgh*.{h,c}`: These source files contain general utility functions and definitions for managing the heap, list and tree structures, for debugging, and for managing strings and scanner tokens, respectively.

Building

- `cvmps`: The `Makefile` [34] in the subdirectory `Implementation/CvmPacketServer/` manages the compilation of the source files to build the executable file `cvmps` which represents the CVM packet server. The executable is located in the subdirectory `Implementation/CvmPacketServer/Bin/`. In the same subdirectory where `Makefile` is located, the `make` [34] command must be invoked in a shell [31].

- `test_generateAuis`, `test_generateServiceInstance`, `test_aui2cvmui`: The `Makefile` [34] in the subdirectory `Implementation/CvmPacketGenerator/` manages the compilation of the source files to build the executable files `test_generateAuis`, `test_generateServiceInstance`, and `test_aui2cvmui`. In the same subdirectory where `Makefile` is located, the `make` [34] command must be invoked in a shell [31].

  `test_generateAuis` is a test program that generates from a particular page of a given AUI description the customized intermediate and CVMUI representations. For this, a predefined CVM profile, default initial values for the service variables, and the localhost IP [62] address "127.0.0.1" for the CVM packet server are used.

  `test_generateServiceInstance` is a test program that translates a given AUI description into a readable C [20]-program that contains the generated part of the service instance.

  `test_aui2cvmui` is a test program that translates a particular page of a given AUI description into a readable CVM assembler program that conforms to the CVMUI structure. For this, a predefined CVM profile, default initial values for the service variables, and the localhost IP [62] address "127.0.0.1" for the CVM packet server are used.

  `test_generateAuis`, `test_generateServiceInstance`, and `test_aui2cvmui` are located in the subdirectory `Implementation/CvmPacketGenerator/Bin/`.

Invocation

- `cvmps`: The CVM packet server is started with the command `cvmps`.

- `test_generateAuis`: The invocation syntax of `test_generateAuis` is as follows:

  `test_generateAuis [-p` *auiPageNo*`] [-t] [-i] <` *fileNameAUI*

  `test_generateAuis` reads the AUI description file with the name *fileNameAUI* from the standard input and generates from a particular page of a given AUI description the customized intermediate and CVMUI representations. The output is written in a readable format to the standard output.

  Optional parts are enclosed with [...]. The three options [-p], [-t] and [-i] can appear in any order. [-p *auiPageNo*] specifies the number of the AUI page that will be customized. *auiPageNo* must be an integer number greater than or equal to zero. Its default value is zero. [-t] and [-i] direct `test_aui2cvmui` to produce informative messages onto the standard output. [-t] prints each matched lexical token during the lexical analysis. [-i] prints the completely parsed tree structure of the AUI description in a well-readable and formatted way, after it has been checked.

5.6. Implementation Notes

- `test_generateServiceInstance`: The invocation syntax of `test_generateService-Instance` is as follows:

    `test_generateServiceInstance [-t] [-i] <` *fileNameAUI*

    `test_generateServiceInstance` reads the AUI description file with the name *fileNameAUI* from the standard input and generates a readable C [20]-program that contains the generated part of the service instance. The output is written to the standard output. Optional parts are enclosed with [...]. The two options `[-t]` and `[-i]` can appear in any order. `[-t]` and `[-i]` direct `test_aui2cvmui` to produce informative messages onto the standard output. `[-t]` prints each matched lexical token during the lexical analysis. `[-i]` prints the completely parsed tree structure of the AUI description in a well-readable and formatted way, after it has been checked.

- `test_aui2cvmui`: The invocation syntax of `test_aui2cvmui` is as follows:

    `test_aui2cvmui [-p` *auiPageNo*`] [-t] [-i] <` *fileNameAUI*

    `test_aui2cvmui` reads the AUI description file with the name *fileNameAUI* from the standard input and translates a particular page of a given AUI description into a readable CVM assembler program that conforms to the CVMUI structure. The output is written to the standard output.

    Optional parts are enclosed with [...]. The three options `[-p]`, `[-t]` and `[-i]` can appear in any order. `[-p` *auiPageNo*`]` specifies the number of the AUI page that will be translated. *auiPageNo* must be an integer number greater than or equal to zero. Its default value is zero. `[-t]` and `[-i]` direct `test_aui2cvmui` to produce informative messages onto the standard output. `[-t]` prints each matched lexical token during the lexical analysis. `[-i]` prints the completely parsed tree structure of the AUI description in a well-readable and formatted way, after it has been checked.

Chapter 6

Conclusions

This thesis presents a client-server architecture where customized graphical user interfaces are generated for networked clients with different capabilities. Particularly, it addresses restricted client devices that are mainly characterized by severe limitations in terms of processing power, available memory, and input/output interface. Very low-end and cheap client devices, i.e., devices with very low manufacturing costs per unit, are widely used in the consumer and embedded mass market. For example, typical "thin" clients might be in-car computers in the automotive industry, networked home appliances such as fridges, or wearables like wristwatches.

In addition, by trying to save hardware resources on the client side as much as possible the proposed client-server architecture contributes to the emerging initiative called Green Computing [37].

The generation of graphical user interfaces for networked clients with restricted capabilities imposes technical as well as ergonomic challenges. This thesis focuses on the technical aspects.

6.1 Summary

The main components of the proposed client-server architecture are summarized as follows:

- The **Client Virtual Machine (CVM)** is a new virtual machine that runs on the client device. The main tasks of the CVM are to communicate with the CVM packet server and to interpret the received CVM packets, which contain the user interface descriptions. The main design goal of the CVM is a simple and modular architecture to make it suitable for a variety of cheap low-end devices on the mass market.

- The **CVM packet format** is a new user interface description format and represents the binary executable format for the CVM. CVM packets are generated by the CVM packet generator and sent by the CVM packet server to the requesting CVM to be executed there. Mainly, the CVM packet format contains CVM instructions that encode user interfaces operationally at a low level of abstraction.

- The **CVM profile format** is a binary format that describes the client capabilities of a given CVM at a low level that reflects the configuration parameters of the given CVM implementation, e.g., the CVM's screen dimensions in pixels, its memory size

6.1. Summary

in bytes, etc. The CVM sends its CVM profile to the CVM packet server during a request. The CVM packet generator then uses the CVM's profile data to create CVM packets that are tailored to the capabilities of the client device.

- The **CVM packet transfer protocol (CPTP)** is a very simple application protocol that manages the communication between the CVM and the CVM packet server. It runs on top of the transport layer and is a very "thin" counterpart to the HTTP protocol, which is used in the World Wide Web. The main design idea of CPTP is to shift all application-specific protocol mechanisms, e.g., complex error handling with a variety of different and application-specific error codes, into the control-logic of the network service.

- The **CVM packet server (CVMPS)** performs the customization process and delivers the requesting client with the adapted user interfaces. Note that the proposed client-server architecture does not specify the internal architecture of the CVMPS and its internally used content format. The proposed client-server architecture rather represents a technical platform that leaves the service providers as much flexibility and responsibility in layout-related and other ergonomic issues as possible. Any CVMPS implementation is valid as far as it conforms to the CVM packet format, the CVM profile format, and the CPTP communication protocol. As a proof of concept, an exemplary CVM packet server has been developed and implemented in this thesis. Its main components are summarized as follows:

    - The **Abstract User Interface Description Language (AUI)** is an exemplary language that is designed for specifying interactive network services on the application layer. It provides language constructs to specify the client-side user interface components as well as language constructs to embed code for state-dependent actions that are executed on the client and server side. Client-side actions are specified in CVM assembler whereas server-side actions can be specified in any common programming language. The CVM packet server keeps a collection of AUI descriptions for each offered network service. A given AUI description is used both by the service generator and by the CVM packet generator to generate the client-specific service instance and the client-specific CVM packets, respectively. Instead of AUI, any other description language might be used as well. For example, refer to BOSS [67], EmuGen [14] [15], XForms [24], UIML [86], WSDL [21], HTML [65], etc.

    - A **CVM User Interface (CVMUI)** is a CVM program that is generated by the CVM packet generator from a given AUI description. It contains a whole AUI page or only parts of it. An exemplary structure for a CVMUI is presented. The proposed structure particularly takes the GUI functionality into account, because a CVMUI mostly contains graphical user interface components.

    - The **session manager** processes all incoming client requests and stores the data that is involved during a client-server session.

    - The **service generator** generates from a given AUI description and CVM profile a client-specific service instance that meets the client capabilities and user preferences. For simplification, the CVM profile can be ignored during the generation of the service instance. The generated service instance contains the state machine that implements the control logic of the network service which is specified in the AUI description. As already mentioned, the server-side actions are specified in the AUI description in a common programming language. The client-specific service instance runs as a separate process and its lifetime is limited by the time span of the respective client-server session.

- The **CVM packet generator** generates from a given AUI description and CVM profile CVM packets that meet the client capabilities and user preferences. These CVM packets are called CVMUIs and sent to the requesting client. A customization method for the generation of the CVMUIs has been implemented in this thesis to prove the concept. It is particularly applicable to very small client devices like wrist watches.

6.2 Results

The main results of this thesis are summarized as follows:

- The CVM is very suitable for a variety of cheap low-end devices on the mass market because of its simple and modular architecture. Its architecture is simpler than the architecture of the KVM [79] from J2ME. The KVM executable from the CLDC [73] Reference Implementation Version 1.1 for a Linux platform requires about 280 Kbytes, whereas the CVM executable from this implementation requires only about 70 Kbytes, including already the client-side part of the CPTP protocol. In addition, the CVM is applicable to client devices with sufficient system resources such as PCs and high-end workstations as well.

- The CVM packet format can be executed immediately by the CVM without large efforts in contrast to XML-based formats such as HTML [65] and WML [56], which are declarative and quite abstract. In addition, it does not predefine any particular layout design and thus allows user interface descriptions of different complexities, which enables scalability. The CVM packet format provides as much functionality as HTML, WML, CSS [12], or Java(Script) [27], which are currently mainly used for describing Web user interfaces. Therefore, using the CVM packet format as the only client-side format relieves the client device from handling a variety of different and complex data formats as well. All in all, the CVM packet format takes into account from scratch the different capabilities of the possibly restricted client devices, and it is a compromise that fulfills the requirements of scalability, compactness, and functionality. Therefore, the CVM packet format is suitable for describing user interfaces for a variety of different and possibly resource-limited client devices.

- The CVM profile format allows precise descriptions of the client-side hardware configuration, which is mandatory for the generation of customized CVM packets for the client on the server side.

- The CVM packet transfer protocol (CPTP) is suitable for very low-end devices as well as for PCs and high-end workstations. In contrast to HTTP, it contains only a few elementary protocol methods for requesting and delivering CVM packets, for requesting and sending profile information about the client, and for very basic error handling.

- The proposed client-server architecture enables the generation of very small-sized content for the requesting client device. The customization method that has been implemented in this thesis groups two user interface components into a single CVMUI page. As a result, the sizes of the generated CVM packets are about 1.3 Kbytes and less. By using another customization method, where each CVMUI page contains only one single user interface component, even smaller packet sizes can be achieved.

- The proposed client-server architecture leaves the service providers as much flexibility and responsibility in layout-related and ergonomic issues as possible.

- The proposed concepts do not depend on Java [36]-, XML [16]-, or WAP [54]-based technologies and combine ideas from the areas of client-server architectures, user interfaces, virtual machines, and compiler technology. In addition, the proposed concepts have been implemented in the C [20] programming language and are demonstrated by several examples.

6.3 Future Work

The main perspectives for future work are summarized as follows:

- This thesis covers the specification of the CVM modules Core, Visual, Keyboard, Mouse, Network, Libraries, and Home Menu. The modules Core, Visual, Keyboard, Mouse, and Network have been specified thoroughly. Only particular details might be added such as the definition of additional shortcut events for the input devices or the definition of additional history buffer entries that save the state of a CVMUI page when it was last visited, etc. The modules Libraries and Home Menu, however, have only been been discussed exemplarily and are left for future work. The specification of the Audio module is not covered in this thesis, either, and therefore left for future work. In addition, other CVM modules may be defined in the future as well.

- The exemplarily developed AUI is a full-featured language to specify interactive network services on the application layer which consist of user interfaces for the CVM and state-dependent actions that are executed on the client and server side. Currently, AUI supports several elementary types of user interfaces components, e.g., text fields, buttons, and hyperlinks. More user interface components might be added in the future, e.g., check boxes, combo boxes, list boxes, tables, etc. Note that the CVMUI then has to be extended, accordingly.

- The exemplary generation method that is presented in this thesis for the generation of the service instance does not consider the CVM profile. The investigation of more general and complex methods for the service generator to generate client-specific service instances is left for future work.

- The exemplary generation method that is presented in this thesis for the generation of the CVM packets only considers a particular CVM profile that is typical for very small client devices like wrist watches. The investigation of more general and complex customization methods for the CVM packet generator to generate client-specific CVMUIs is left for future work.

Appendix A

Notations

The following notations are used in this thesis:

A.1 Miscellaneous

Hexadecimal Numbers 0x(0|...|9|a|...|f|A|...|F)+

For example, the hexadecimal numbers 0xFF and 0x12FE32 equal to the decimal numbers 255 and 1244722, respectively.

Bitwise Operators

&   Bitwise AND (conjunction). For example, 0xA63 & 0xC85 = 0x801.

| Bitwise OR (disjunction). For example, 0xA63 | 0xC85 = 0xEE7.

$\oplus$ Bitwise XOR. For example, 0xA63 $\oplus$ 0xC85 = 0x6E6.

$\gg$ Bitwise arithmetic shift right, i.e., with sign extension. For example, 0xF61A $\gg$ 4 = 0xFF61.

$\ggg$ Bitwise logical shift right, i.e., with zero extension. For example, 0xF61A $\ggg$ 4 = 0x0F61.

$\ll$ Bitwise shift left. For example, 0xF61A $\ll$ 4 = 0xF61A0.

Logical Operators

$\neg$ Logical NOT (negation). For example, $\neg$true = false.

$\wedge$ Logical AND (conjunction). For example, true $\wedge$ false = false.

$\vee$ Logical OR (disjunction). For example, true $\vee$ false = true.

Concatenation Operator The concatenation operator "$\circ$" is used to concatenate sequences, e.g., character strings, or single sequence elements. The result is always a sequence. If the sequence is a character string, then a sequence element is a single character. An empty sequence is denoted by the symbol "ϵ".

Comments Comments may appear in pseudo-code, data structure definitions, and grammar definitions. Similar to the common programming languages C(++) [20] [71] and Java [36], the common delimiters // and /∗...∗/ are used for end of line and block comments, respectively.

Data Type and Instruction Grouping Often, similar CVM data types and instructions are grouped together. The alternative parts are delimited by using the notation "<...|...|...>". For example, Int<1|...|4> refers to the data types Int1, Int2, ..., and Int4. loadc<1|...|4> refers to the instructions loadc1, loadc2, ..., and loadc4. loadc<ε|u><1|...|3> refers to the instructions loadc1, loadc2, ..., loadc3, loadcu1, loadcu2, ..., and loadcu3. There might also be only one item in the alternative part listed. For example, Int<i> represents the data type Int3, if the value of the integer variable i equals to 3 in a given context.

A.2 Context Free Grammars

The used notation for defining context free grammars should be generally understandable. Complete examples can be found in the sections B.1 (page 216) and 5.1.1 (page 136). A grammar definition consists of a list of productions, whereas each production consists of a left side, the symbol "::=", and a right side. The left side contains the name of a nonterminal symbol. Nonterminal symbols appear in italic fonts. The right side is an expression that defines a word set for the nonterminal symbol on the left side. The expression consists of terminal characters and character sequences, nonterminal symbols, and the following meta symbols:

- "'": Terminal characters and character sequences appear in teletype font and are enclosed with "'", e.g., 'a', '.16Bit'.

- "(", ")": The opening and closing parentheses are used for grouping syntactical items together, e.g., (',' *DeclVar*).

- "?": An optional syntactical item is marked with a succeeding "?", e.g., 'a'?, *Mode*?.

- "∗": n ($n \geq 0$) times repetition of a syntactical item is marked with a succeeding ∗, e.g., (',' *DeclVar*)∗.

- "+": n ($n > 0$) times repetition of a syntactical item is marked with a succeeding "+", e.g., *Digit*+.

- "|": Alternative syntactical items are specified with "|", e.g., (*DeclConstInt* | *DeclConstString*)∗.

- "..": Ranges of single terminal characters are specified with "..", e.g., 'a'..'z'.

- "\": The "\" symbol represents the set operator *minus*. For example, ASCII \ '"' represents all ASCII characters without the '"' character, and ASCII∗ \ (ASCII∗ '∗/' ASCII∗) represents all ASCII strings that do not contain "∗/" as a substring. However, when used within a terminal character sequence, e.g., '\n', '\\"', etc., "\" serves as an escape character as it is used in the C [20] programming language. Therefore, '\n' represents the new line character, '\f' the form feed character, '\r' the carriage return character, '\t' the horizontal tab character, and '\\' produces the terminal character "\".

A.3 Data Types

Data types are used to specify complex data structures, e.g., the abstract syntax of a given context free grammar as well as binary formats.

A.3.1 Syntax of Data Type Definitions

The used notation for data type and binary format definitions should be generally understandable. Examples can be found throughout the thesis, e.g., in 3.1.1 (page 33), 5.1.2 (page 147), etc. The concrete syntax of a data type definition (*DataTypeDef*) is specified as a context free grammar:

DataTypeDef   ::=   *DataTypeProduction*+
DataTypeProduction   ::=   *DataTypeIdComplex* '=' *DataType*

DataType   ::=   *Variant* | *List* | *Tuple*

Variant   ::=   *DataTypeId* ('|' *DataTypeId*)*

List   ::=   *DataTypeId* ('*' | // non-empty or empty list
                                           '+' | // non-empty list
                                           '[' *NumElems*? ']')   // array

Tuple   ::=   '{' *TupleItem* (';' *TupleItem*)* '}'
TupleItem   ::=   *DataTypeId* *TupleItemIdDef*
TupleItemIdDef   ::=   *TupleItemId* |
                             TupleItemId '=' *ConstVal* |
                             ConstVal

DataTypeId   ::=   *DataTypeIdBase* | *DataTypeIdComplex*
DataTypeIdBase   ::=   'Int' | 'Nat' | 'String' | ...
DataTypeIdComplex   ::=   *Identifier*
TupleItemId   ::=   *Identifier*

ConstVal   ::=   *Expr*   // integer or string expression
NumElems   ::=   *Expr*   // integer expression

Identifier   ::=   ...
Expr   ::=   ...

DataTypeIdBase   *DataTypeIdBase* refers to an elementary data type. Elementary data types are well-known and "simple" data types such as integer, boolean, char, string, or similar types. The identifier of an elementary data type never appears on the left side of a data type definition (*DataTypeDef*).

A.3. Data Types

DataTypeIdComplex *DataTypeIdComplex* refers to a complex data type. Each complex data type may be defined only once, i.e., it may appear on the left side of a data type production (*DataTypeProduction*) at least once. For each *DataTypeIdComplex* that appears on the right side of a production there must exist a *DataTypeProduction* with an equal *DataTypeIdComplex*. For better readability and easier distinction from elementary data types, the identifiers of complex data types appear in data type definitions often in italic fonts.

List A list structure that may be empty, i.e., that may contain no elements, is denoted with the symbol '*'. A list structure that may not be empty is denoted with the symbol '+'. An array is a list that contains exactly *NumElems* elements. If *NumElems* is omitted in an array definition, then the array boundary is dynamic and the array structure equals to a list structure that may be empty ('*'). The index position of the first list element is zero. Arrays are often used in this thesis for specifying binary formats. In addition, list definitions must not contain cycles.

Tuple Tuple definitions must not contain cycles.

TupleItemIdDef The *TupleItemId* is used to access a particular item value. A *TupleItemId* must be unique only within the respective tuple (*Tuple*). If a constant value (*ConstVal*) is given, then the value of this item is predefined and always equal to this constant value in every instance of the specified data type. If the value of a particular item is never accessed explicitly, then the respective *TupleItemId* might be omitted.

Constant values (*ConstVal*) can be specified only for elementary data types (*DataTypeId*). In addition, constant values (*ConstVal*) and missing item ids (*TupleItemId*) are often used in binary format definitions.

Variant Each *DataTypeId* in a *Variant* definition may appear at least once. In addition, *Variant* definitions must not contain cycles.

Syntax Extensions For reasons of convenience, the presented syntax is extended with the following notations in this thesis:

- *Variant* definitions may also contain *List* and *Tuple* definitions in addition to *DataTypeId*, i.e.:

  Variant   ::=   *VariantElem* ('|' *VariantElem*)*
  VariantElem ::=   *DataTypeId* | *List* | *Tuple*

- The data type of a *TupleItem* may also be a *List*, *Tuple*, or *Variant* definition in addition to *DataTypeId*. In addition, more than one *TupleItemIdDef* may appear in a comma separated list in a *TupleItem* definition. Then, several *TupleItemIdDef*s of the same data type can be grouped together into one *TupleItem* declaration.

  TupleItem   ::=   *TupleItemDataType*
                                    TupleItemIdDef (',' *TupleItemIdDef*)*
  TupleItemDataType ::=   *DataTypeId* | *List* | *Tuple* | *Variant*

- The data type of a list element may also be a *Variant* or *Tuple* definition in addition to *DataTypeId*, i.e.:

List ::= *ListElemDataType* ('*' | '+' | '[' *NumElems*? ']')
ListElemDataType ::= *DataTypeId* | '(' *Variant* ')' | *Tuple*

Variant must be enclosed in left and right parentheses to avoid ambiguous data type definitions.

- The brackets '{' and '}' in a *Tuple* definition may be omitted, if the *Tuple* definition consists only of one *TupleItem*.

Note that these extensions do not provide additional semantics. They are just "shortcuts" that can be easily replaced with appropriate definitions using the regular syntax. For example, the first extension implies for each occurring *List* and *Tuple* structure a separate definition that can be referenced then by the respective *DataTypeIdComplex*.

A.3.2 Data Access

Let $DTDef_{DT}$ be the data type definition of a given (complex) data type DT. The access to the components of DT is accomplished by appropriate path expressions.

Syntax A data access path expression has the following syntax:

PathExpr ::= *PathExprElem**
PathExprElem ::= *PathExprElemVariant* | *PathExprElemList* | *PathExprElemTuple*
PathExprElemVariant ::= '.' *DataTypeIdComplex*
PathExprElemList ::= '[' *NatLit* ']'
PathExprElemTuple ::= '.' *TupleItemId*

If a variable of the type DT is defined, then each component of the variable can be accessed by appending the appropriate path expression to the identifier of the variable.

Data Access Path Expression In the following, a data access path expression is formally treated as a sequence of path expression entities.
Let $PathExprElem_{DT}$ be the set of all possible path expression entities of a given data type DT, i.e., $PathExprElem_{DT} = DataTypeIdComplex \cup NatLit \cup TupleItemId$.
Let $PathExpr_{DT}$ be the set of all possible path expressions of a given data type DT, i.e., $PathExpr_{DT} = (PathExprElem_{DT})*$.
In addition, the following notations are used:

- $\exists prodVariant_{DTDef_{DT}}(T, w) \equiv$
  $DTDef_{DT}$ contains a *Variant* definition of the form: "$T = ... | w | ...$"

A.3. Data Types

- $\exists prodList_{DTDef_{DT}}(T, A, w) \equiv$
  $DTDef_{DT}$ contains a *List* definition of the form:
  "$T = A*$", "$T = A+$", "$T = A[\,]$", or "$T = A[N]$" and w is a valid index position. Valid index positions are integer numbers greater than or equal to zero. If the *List* definition is of the form "$T = A[N]$", then the valid index positions additionally must be smaller then N.

- $\exists prodTuple_{DTDef_{DT}}(T, A, w) \equiv$
  $DTDef_{DT}$ contains a *Tuple* definition of the form: "$T = \{\ ...;\ A\ w;\ ...\ \}$"

Type   Let $p, v \in PathExpr_{DT} \wedge w \in PathExprElem_{DT}$. $\mathcal{T}_{DT}(p)$ is the type of the path expression p and defined as follows:

$$\mathcal{T}_{DT}(p) = \begin{array}{ll} DT, & \text{if } p = \epsilon \\ w, & \text{if } p = v \circ w \wedge \exists prodVariant_{DTDef_{DT}}(\mathcal{T}(v), w) \\ A, & \text{if } p = v \circ w \wedge \exists prodList_{DTDef_{DT}}(\mathcal{T}(v), A, w) \\ A, & \text{if } p = v \circ w \wedge \exists prodTuple_{DTDef_{DT}}(\mathcal{T}(v), A, w) \\ \bot, & \text{else} \end{array}$$

Valid Data Access Path Expressions $\mathcal{P}_{DT}$ is the set of all possible and valid path expressions of DT. $\mathcal{P}_{DT}$ is defined as follows:

$p \in \mathcal{P}_{DT} \Leftrightarrow_{def} p = \epsilon$
$\vee$
$p = v \circ w \wedge p \in PathExpr_{DT} \wedge w \in PathExprElem_{DT} \wedge v \in \mathcal{P}_{DT} \wedge$
$(\exists prodVariant_{DTDef_{DT}}(\mathcal{T}(v), w) \vee \exists prodList_{DTDef_{DT}}(\mathcal{T}(v), A, w) \vee$
$\exists prodTuple_{DTDef_{DT}}(\mathcal{T}(v), A, w))$

Data Structure Trees   All valid path expressions can be grouped into *data structure trees*. All tree nodes are path expression entities. A data structure tree is a subset of $\mathcal{P}_{DT}$ where for each variant node exactly one possibility is chosen, i.e., all path expressions in the tree that contain this variant node have the save variant type for this variant node. $\mathcal{TR}_{DT}$ is the set of all possible data structure trees of a given data type DT and defined as follows:

$t \in \mathcal{TR}_{DT} \Leftrightarrow_{def} \epsilon \in t$
$\wedge$
$v \circ w \in t \Rightarrow v \in t$
$\wedge$
$(v \in t \wedge \exists prodVariant_{DTDef_{DT}}(\mathcal{T}(v), w_1) \Rightarrow$
$(\exists prodVariant_{DTDef_{DT}}(\mathcal{T}(v), w_2) : v \circ w_2 \in t)$
$\wedge$
$(\forall w_3 \in PathExprElem_{DT} : v \circ w_3 \in t \Rightarrow w_3 = w_2))$
$\wedge$
$(v \in t \wedge \exists prodTuple_{DTDef_{DT}}(\mathcal{T}(v), A, w_1) \Rightarrow$
$(\forall w_2 \in PathExprElem : \exists prodTuple_{DTDef\,DT}(\mathcal{T}(v), w_2) \Rightarrow v \circ w_2 \in t)$
$\wedge$

$(v \in t \land \exists prodList_{DTDef_{DT}}(\mathcal{T}(v), A, w_1) \Rightarrow$
$(\forall w_2 \in PathExprElem : \exists prodList_{DTDef\,DT}(\mathcal{T}(v), w_2) \Rightarrow v \circ w_2 \in t)$

A.3.3 Example

The following example contains a data type definition for T_0:

$T_0 = \{\, T_1\ s_1;\ T_2\ s_2\, \}$
$T_1 = \text{Int2} \mid T_3$
$T_2 = T_4[2]$
$T_3 = \{\, \text{String}\ s_1;\ \text{Nat1}\ s_2\, \}$
$T_4 = \{\, \text{Int4}\ s_1;\ \text{String}\ s_2\,\}$

Then:

$\mathcal{P}_{T_0} = \{\ \epsilon,$
$\qquad s_1,\ s_1.\text{Int2},\ s_1.T_3,\ s_1.T_3.s_1,\ s_1.T_3.s_2,$
$\qquad s_2,\ s_2[0],\ s_2[0].s_1,\ s_2[0].s_2,\ s_2[1],\ s_2[1].s_1,\ s_2[1].s_2\ \}$

$\mathcal{TR}_{T_0} = \{\ t_1,\ t_2\ \}$
$t_1 = \{\ \epsilon,\ s_1,\ s_1.\text{Int2},\ s_2,\ s_2[0],\ s_2[0].s_1,\ s_2[0].s_2,\ s_2[1],\ s_2[1].s_1,\ s_2[1].s_2\ \}$
$t_2 = \{\ \epsilon,\ s_1,\ s_1.T_3,\ s_1.T_3.s_1;\ s_1.T_3.s_2;\ s_2,\ s_2[0],\ s_2[0].s_1,\ s_2[0].s_2,\ s_2[1],\ s_2[1].s_1,\ s_2[1].s_2\ \}$

For easier readability, a simple dot (".") is used here instead of the sequence operator ("∘").

A.4 Code Templates

Code templates are used to specify generated code. Examples can be found in the sections 5.5 (page 166) and 5.3.2 (page 161).

Fixed Parts Fixed parts of the generated code do not depend on any values that have to be evaluated by the code generator and therefore remain always the same for each code generation process. Fixed parts are expressed in teletype font, e.g.,

```
.data
Int _svBufIdx   0

.code
M1:
   loadc_0  loadc_m1   add   rempty
   halt
```

A.4. Code Templates

Variable Parts Variable parts of the generated code depend on context values that have to be first evaluated by the code generator and therefore might be different after each code generation process. Variable parts are enclosed with "<*Variable Part*>". The description of *Variable Part* is not bound to a particular format, but must be comprehensible from the context.

For example,

.<*cvmProfile.cvmMode*>Bit

results in the generated code

.16Bit

if the value of the term *cvmProfile.cvmMode*, which depends on the requesting client, is evaluated to 16 during the generation process.

Conditional Parts Conditional parts are expressed with

<*if : Condition$_1$*>
  ... // code template
<*elseif : Condition$_2$*>
  ... // code template
...
<*elseif : Condition$_n$*> // $n \geq 1$
  ... // code template
<*else*>
  ... // code template
<*end*>

The code template for *Condition$_i$* ($1 \geq i \geq n$), i.e., the ith condition, is only inserted, if the ith condition is met. The description of the ith condition is not bound to a particular format, but must be comprehensible from the context. Note that the <*elseif : ...*> parts and the <*else*> part are optional.

For example,

printf ("
    <*if : cvmProfile.cvmMode = 16*>
    16
    <*elseif : cvmProfile.cvmMode = 32*>
    32
    <*else*>
    not 16 and not 32
    <*end*>
");

results in the generated code

printf ("16");
or
printf ("32");
or
printf ("not 16 and not 32");

if the term *cvmProfile.cvmMode* evaluates to 16, 32, or any other value, respectively.

Iterative Parts Iterative parts are expressed with

<∀ *Expression*>
 ... // code template
<*end*>

Expression must evaluate to an expression, where an element is selected from a set of elements. The set of elements is defined in *Expression* as well. The inner part of the code template specifies the generated code for each element of the set, whereby the element may appear as a variable. Note that the set is processed in an ascending order.

For example,

<∀ $i : 0 \leq i \leq 2$>
  printf ("<*i*>");
<*end*>

results in the generated code

printf ("0");
printf ("1");
printf ("2");

Imported Parts Imported parts are expressed with

<*import* : *Verbal Description* >

Verbal Description contains the information which code template is inserted here.

For example,

<*import* : Code of the example in the previous subsection "Variable Parts">

results in the generated code

.16Bit

Functions A function definition is expressed with

<*fct* : *id*(*parDeclarations*)>
 ... // code template
<*end*>

id contains the (unique) name of the function. *parDefinitions* contains an optional list of parameter declarations. A formal syntax for the declaration of the parameter list is not specified here.

A function call is expressed with

<*call* : *id*(*parValues*)>

id refers to the defined function with the same *id*. *parValues* defines values for the function parameters, if available.

For example,

<*fct* : *max* (Int *i1*, Int *i2*)>
  <*if* : *i1* > *i2*>
    <*i1*>

A.4. Code Templates

```
    <else>
      <i2>
    <end>
<end>
printf ("<call : max(2, 5)>");
```
results in the generated code
```
printf ("5");
```

Verbal Description of Instruction Blocks A block of CVM instructions that performs a certain task might be described verbally, i.e., without listing the particular CVM instructions in detail, by using the notation "<*Verbal Description*>". Verbal descriptions of instruction blocks are used in code templates for reasons of brevity and clearness, even if the instruction block contains only fixed parts of the generated code.

For example, the CVM assembler code fragment in section 3.1.4.2 (page 39) contains verbal descriptions of instruction blocks. Refer to section B (page 216) for more information on the CVM assembler.

Appendix B

CVM Assembler (CVMA)

In this thesis an assembler for writing CVM programs, called the CVM assembler, has been developed and implemented. The CVM assembler translates readable CVM programs into binary CVM packets that are executed by the CVM. The CVM assembler can be used as a low-level language to write user interfaces or other programs for the CVM. It is also used in the code templates to describe the code that is generated by the CVM packet generator. This section specifies in detail its use. At the end, some example programs and their disassembled binaries are listed.

B.1 Syntax

CVM assembler programs are case sensitive. The grammar for the concrete syntax of the CVM assembler is presented in a generally understandable notation. Refer to section A.2 (page 207) for a short description of the used notation. The grammar of the CVM assembler can be split into a syntactic and a lexical part. First, the grammar is listed, then additional explanations and context conditions are provided for particular syntactic constructs in alphabetical order.

Syntactic Grammar The syntactic part of the grammar with the root *CvmAsProg* is as follows:

CvmAsProg   ::= *Mode*? (*CvmAsEntity*)*
CvmAsEntity ::= *Const* | *Data* | *Code*

Mode   ::= '.16Bit' | '.16BitEmu' | '.32Bit' | '.32BitEmu'

Const   ::= '.const' (*Identifier Expr*)*

Data   ::= '.data' (*DeclVar Expr*?)*
DeclVar   ::= *DataType Identifier*

Code   ::= '.code' (*DeclFct* | *Label* | *Instruction*)*
DeclFct   ::= '.fct' *Identifier* '(' *DeclPars* ')' *DataType*? *Block*
DeclPars   ::= (*DeclVar* (',' *DeclVar*)*)?

216

B.1. Syntax

Block	::=	'{' (*Block* | *DeclVar* | *Label* | *Instruction*)* '}'
Instruction	::=	*Mnemonic* (*Expr* (',' *Expr*)*)?
Expr	::=	*MulExpr* | *Expr* ('+' | '-') *MulExpr*
MulExpr	::=	*Factor* | *MulExpr* ('*' | '/' | '%') *Factor*
Factor	::=	'(' *Expr* ')' | '-' *Factor* | *NatLiteral* | *StringLiteral* | *Identifier* | *EventCode* | *FontCode* | *KeyCode* | *MouseFontCode* | *LibFctCode* | *BuiltinFct* '(' (*Expr* (',' *Expr*)*)? ')' | *ArrayInit*
ArrayInit	::=	'[' (*ArrayElem* (',' *ArrayElem*)*)? ']'
ArrayElem	::=	*Expr* ('#' *Expr*)?

Lexical Grammar The lexical part of the grammar is as follows:

BuiltinFct	::=	...	// refer to section B.4 (page 227), "*builtin_function_name*"
DataType	::=	...	// refer to section B.2 (page 222), "*DataType*"
EventCode	::=	...	// refer to section 3.1.6.4 (page 49), "*event_code_name*"
FontCode	::=	...	// refer to section 3.2.3 (page 79), "*font_code_name*"
KeyCode	::=	...	// refer to section 3.3 (page 81), <*X11/keysymdef.h*>
MouseFontCode	::=	...	// refer to section 3.5 (page 81), <*X11/cursorFont.h*>
LibFctCode	::=	...	// refer to section 3.5 (page 83), "*library_function_name*"
Mnemonic	::=	*CvmMnemonic* | *MacroMnemonic*	
CvmMnemonic	::=	...	// refer to section 3.9.2 (page 100), "*mnemonic*"
MacroMnemonic	::=	...	// refer to section B.3 (page 224), "*macro_mnemonic*"
Identifier	::=	*Alpha* (*Alpha* | *Digit*)*	
Label	::=	*Identifier* ':'	
NatLiteral	::=	*Digit*+	
StringLiteral	::=	'"' (ASCII \ '"')* ('\\"' (ASCII \ '"')*)* '"'	
Alpha	::=	'a'..'z' | 'A'..'Z' | '_'	
Digit	::=	'0'..'9'	
WhiteSpace	::=	' ' | '\f' | '\n' | '\r' | '\t'	
Comment	::=	'/*' ASCII* \ (ASCII* '*/' ASCII*) '*/' | '//' ASCII* \ (ASCII* '\n' ASCII*) '\n'	

To resolve ambiguities within the lexical part of the grammar, the longest possible character sequence of the input program that matches one of the productions in the lexical grammar is selected. For example, the character sequence `'abc12'` is recognized as one *Identifier*, and not as the *Identifier* `'abc'` followed by the *NatLiteral* `'12'`. In addition, the character sequence `'abc12:'` is recognized as a *Label*. If the longest possible character sequence matches more than one production, the production listed first is chosen.

White space characters (*WhiteSpace*) and comments (*Comment*) are discarded at lexical level. They may appear at any place in the CVM program between the syntactic units listed in the syntactic part of the grammar.

ArrayInit This syntactic construct initializes a data array. The value of each array element (*ArrayElem*) might be either an integer number, a string, or the result of the builtin function `stringBytes()`. Nested *ArrayInit*s are not allowed.

If the value of an array element is a string, it consists only of one expression (*Expr*) which might be a single string literal (*StringLiteral*), or a single identifier (*Identifier*) that references a string constant declaration (*DeclConst*), or a single builtin function (*BuiltinFct*) call that returns a string, or a concatenation of two string expressions with the '+' operator.

If the value of an array element is an integer number, the first expression (*Expr*) defines the value whereas the optional second expression (*Expr*) sets the number of bytes that should be reserved for the value of the array element. However, the second expression is not allowed, if the type and length of the array element is already known from the context. For example, this is the case, if *ArrayInit* is used to declare an event table. Refer to `EventTable` in section B.2 (page 223) for more information on declaring event tables. If the second expression is allowed, but not explicitly given, then the default byte length of the array element is defined by the CVM mode (*Mode*). If the CVM mode is '.16Bit' or '.16BitEmu', the byte length is 2. If the CVM mode is '.32Bit' or '.32BitEmu', the byte length is 4. The value of an existent second expression may only be 1 or 2, if the CVM mode is '.16Bit' or '.16BitEmu', and 1, 2, 3, or 4, if the CVM mode is '.32Bit' or '.32BitEmu'. The identifiers (*Identifier*) that appear inside the second expression must not refer to labels (*Label*), functions (*DeclFct*), function parameters, and local or global variables (*DeclVar*). Neither, the byte length of the array element — no matter whether specified explicitly or implicitly — may be less than the minimum number of bytes that are required for the value of the array element, with using one's-complement format for positive integer values and two's-compliment format for negative integer values.

If the value of an array element is the result of the builtin function `stringBytes()`, then it consists only of one expression which contains only the respective builtin function call (*BuiltinFct*). Refer to section B.4 (page 230) for more information on the builtin function `stringBytes()`.

Const This syntactic construct contains integer and string constant declarations. Array constant declarations are not allowed. A declaration of an integer or string constant assigns the integer or string value of the given expression (*Expr*) to the identifier (*Identifier*). The integer or string value is evaluated by the CVM assembler during assembling. A declared constant can be used within the whole CVM assembler program. As in any other programming language, the use of self-defined constants makes programming more convenient and programs more readable.

If the value of the expression (*Expr*) is an integer number, the identifiers that appear inside that expression may only refer to labels (*Label*), functions (*DeclFct*), global variables (*DeclVar*), and other integer constants (*DeclConst*).

If the value of the expression (*Expr*) is a string, the expression may only consist of a single string literal (*StringLiteral*), or of a single identifier that references another string constant declaration (*DeclConst*), or of a single builtin function (*BuiltinFct*) call that returns a string, or of a concatenation of two string expressions with the '+' operator.

B.1. Syntax

Cyclic definitions of integer or string constants are not allowed, either.

Data This syntactic construct contains global variable declarations. Section B.2 (page 222) describes for each CVM assembler data type the purpose of *Expr*, which might represent an initial value or specify the data type further. Variables with an initial value appear in CVM memory in the Declared Data section. Variables with no initial value appear in CVM memory in the Undeclared Data section.

If the CVM mode (*Mode*) is '.16Bit' or '.32Bit', the CVM assembler sorts the declared data automatically in the following order before assembling them into the CVM packet:

1. Uninitialized byte array declarations (`Bytes`)

2. Uninitialized integer declarations (`Int`)

3. Zero-initialized byte array declarations (`Bytesz`)

4. Zero-initialized integer declarations (`Int`)

5. Non-zero initialized byte array declarations (`Bytesz`)

6. Non-zero initialized integer declarations (`Int`)

7. String declarations (`String`)

8. Event table declarations (`EventTable`)

Note that there may be several event table declarations, but at most one event table is active at a moment during execution.

If the initial value of an integer declaration depends on a memory address, i.e., there is an identifier inside the expression (*Expr*) of the initial value that refers to a label (*Label*), function (*DeclFct*), or global variable (*DeclVar*), then this declaration appears in the non-zero initialized integer declaration section. Otherwise, the CVM assembler cannot perform the address resolution correctly.

If the CVM mode (*Mode*) is '.16Bit' or '.32Bit', the CVM assembler does not assemble the uninitialized data items into the CVM packet, which reduces packet size and thus network bandwidth requirements. In addition, the CVM assembler groups the zero-initialized data items into one byte array using one of the `bytesz<1|...|4>` declaration codes and the non-zero initialized data items except for the event table into another byte array using one of the `bytes<1|...|4>` declaration codes. For the event table it uses the `eventtable` declaration code. Refer to section 3.8 (page 96) for a complete list of all CVM data declaration codes.

If the CVM mode (*Mode*) is '.16BitEmu' or '.32BitEmu', the CVM assembler encodes each data item into the CVM packet separately using the appropriate declaration code. Uninitialized data is then declared as zero initialized data in the CVM packet.

DeclFct A function declaration (or equally called procedure declaration) consists mainly of the following parts: the name (*Identifier*) of the function, possibly the declaration of its parameters (*DeclPars*) and return type (*DataType*), and finally the function body (*Block*). As specified in the grammar, nested declarations of functions are not possible. The data type of an existing return value may only be Int. If the function does not have a return value, the return type is Void or may be omitted. Variables (*DeclVar*) declared within a *Block* are local variables. They are located on the CVM's memory stack during execution of the CVM program. The CVM assembler inserts automatically CVM instructions to reserve space for them on the stack. The data type of a parameter or local variable may only be Int. The scope of a parameter is the whole function body. The scope of a local variable is the rest of the block where it is declared, including all nested sub-blocks. A parameter or local variable must not be redeclared within its scope to overwrite or hide its first declaration. The CVM assembler inserts automatically the following CVM instructions at the beginning of the function body to set the new stack frame:

loadc $((byteLen(result) + \sum_{i=1}^{n} byteLen(par_i)) / $ cvmIntLen)
newstackframe
(loadc *numLocalVariables*
addsp)?

$byteLen(result) + \sum_{i=1}^{n} byteLen(par_i)$ represents the total amount of bytes for the return value and the function parameters and cvmIntLen is 2 on a 16-bit CVM and 4 on a 32-bit CVM. *numLocalVariables* represents the total number of stack cells that are reserved for the local variables of the function on the memory stack. If it is zero, than no space is reserved for them with the loadc and addsp instructions. Note that because of the limited scopes of the local variables within the nested block structure, different local variables with different scopes might be mapped to the same memory stack cell.

The instruction ret is not allowed within the function body, whereas the macro return must occur at least once. Refer to section B.3 (page 226) for more information on return.

Function declarations provide a higher means for writing functions (or procedures) in CVM assembler. However, they are not essential because the common low level way of writing functions in assembler is also possible. But used together with appropriate macros the access of parameters, local variables, and the return value gets more convenient to the CVM assembler programmer. This is illustrated by the example program in section B.6 (page 237).

DeclVar *DeclVar* is used for declaring global variables within the *Data* section and local variables and parameters within a function declaration (*DeclFct*). In a variable or parameter declaration first comes the data type (*DataType*) of the variable, then its name (*Identifier*).

Expr The value of an expression (*Expr*) might be an integer number, a string, or a data array and is evaluated by the CVM assembler during assembling.

If its value is a string, then the expression consists of a single string literal (*StringLiteral*), or of a single identifier (*Identifier*) that references a string constant declaration (*DeclConst*), or of a single builtin function (*BuiltinFct*) call that returns a string, or of a concatenation of two string expressions with the '+' operator.

B.1. Syntax

If its value is a data array, then the expression consists only of a single array initialization (*ArrayInit*) or of a single builtin function (*BuiltinFct*) call that returns a data array. Refer to *Identifier* for more information on the values of identifiers that appear as factors (*Factor*) within expressions. The values of *BuiltinFct*, *EventCode*, *FontCode*, *MouseFontCode*, *KeyCode*, and *LibFctCode* are specified in the sections that are referred to in the comments of the respective productions in the lexical grammar specification.

All arithmetic operations with integer numbers are based on integer but not floating point arithmetic.

Identifier Lexically, an identifier (*Identifier*) must not match a *BuiltinFct*, *DataType*, *EventCode*, *FontCode*, *MouseFontCode*, *KeyCode*, *LibFctCode*, and a *Mnemonic*. An identifier is used for declaring constants (*DeclConst*), labels (*Label*), functions (*DeclFct*), global and local variables (*DeclVar*), and function parameters (*DeclVar*). Each identifier of a constant, label, function, and global variable may be used in a declaration only once and must be unique in the whole CVM assembler program. Either it must not be reused to declare a parameter or local variable of a function.

An identifier (*Identifier*) might appear as a factor (*Factor*) within an expression (*Expr*) and refer either to an integer or string constant (*DeclConst*), a label (*Label*), a function (*DeclFct*), a function parameter (*DeclVar*), a global variable (*DeclVar*), or a local variable (*DeclVar*) that is valid where the identifier appears. If it refers to a string constant its value is the declared string. Otherwise, the value of the identifier is an integer value — that will be called in the following *valId* — and is calculated depending on the type of its appropriate declaration:

- *DeclConst*
  valId is the value of the expression (*Expr*) within the integer constant declaration *DeclConst*.

- *DeclFct*
  This declaration type is treated like a *Label*. Refer to *Label*.

- *DeclVar*
  If the variable is global, *valId* is the absolute memory address of the variable in the Declared or Undeclared Data section in CVM memory. If the variable is a parameter or local variable, then *valId* is the relative memory address of the parameter or local variable on the current stack frame starting from the address given by the special register `regBP`. Refer also to section 3.1.4.2 (page 39). Note that because of the limited scopes of the local variables within the nested block structure, different local variables with different scopes might be mapped to the same memory stack cell.

- *Label*:
  valId is the memory address of the next following instruction. If there is no instruction following this label, then *valId* is the memory address of the previous instruction plus its byte length. If there is no previous instruction, either, then *valId* is equal to `codeSegmentAdr`. Refer to section 3.8 (page 95) for more information on `codeSegmentAdr`.

Instruction The grammar for *Instruction* defines the general syntax of an instruction. Instructions can be classified into CVM instructions and macros which act as pseudo instructions. The operands and additional context conditions of the CVM instructions are explained in section 3.9.2 (page 100), of the macros in section B.3 (page 224).

Label As usual, a label declares symbolically the memory address of its next following instruction.

Mode This syntactic construct specifies the CVM mode. If it is not explicitly specified, '.32BitEmu' is used as default. Refer to section 3.1.2 (page 33) for more information on CVM modes. In the following, the term "16-bit CVM" is used to refer that *Mode* is '.16Bit' or '.16BitEmu', and the term "32-bit CVM" is used to refer that *Mode* is '.32Bit' or '.32BitEmu'.

NatLiteral If the positive integer number specified by *NatLiteral* exceeds the maximum value $2^{31} - 1$, it is truncated automatically to that limit by the CVM assembler.

StringLiteral A string literal is a sequence of ASCII [7] characters. The number of ASCII characters in the ASCII sequence need not equal to the number of characters in the produced string. For example, the escape characters for line feed, carriage return, and horizontal tab are represented by the ASCII character sequences "\n", "\r", and "\t", respectively. The """ character is represented by the ASCII character sequence "\"". In addition, each character in a string literal may also be represented by its Unicode [88] number in the form \U{*hexadecimal_unicode_number*}. For example, the string literal "K\U{F6}nig" produces the string "König". Note that the binary UTF-8 representation of the produced string must not exceed 65535 bytes.

B.2 Data Types

The CVM assembler provides the following data types: Bytes, Bytesz, EventTable, Int, and Void. In the following, the purpose of the syntactic unit *Expr* from the grammar specification to declare and possibly initialize variables within the *Data* section will be described by using the following description format:

data_type *value*
verbose_description

value is shown in the form *ident*$_{type}$. *ident* can be any identifier and is chosen to characterize the usage of *value*. *type* specifies the syntactic type of *value* and must be a syntactic subtype of *Expr*, i.e., it can be derived from *Expr* according to the grammar specification in section B.1 (page 216). *value* must match the production for *type*. For example, num_{Expr} might be used to specify a number that matches the production for *Expr*. Afterwards, some additional explanations are given.

Note that for some data types several different kinds of values are possible. Each possibility is listed separately.

B.2. Data Types

Bytes $numBytes_{Expr}$
The data type **Bytes** declares a byte array without initializing it. The value of the expression $numBytes$ specifies the byte length of the array. It must be an unsigned integer number in the range of $[1; 2^{16}-1]$ on a 16-bit CVM or $[1; 2^{32}-1]$ on a 32-bit CVM, respectively, and must not depend on labels (*Label*), functions (*DeclFct*), function parameters, and local or global variables (*DeclVar*).

Bytes $text_{Expr}$
The data type **Bytes** declares an UTF-8 string and initializes it with the string expression $text_{Expr}$.

Bytes $array_{ArrayInit}$
The data type **Bytes** declares a byte array and initializes it with *array*.

Bytes $builtinFctName_{BuiltinFct}$
The data type **Bytes** declares a byte array and initializes it with the byte array that is returned by the builtin function with the name *builtinFct*. Refer to section B.4 (page 227 for more information on builtin functions.

Bytesz $numBytes_{Expr}$
The data type **Bytesz** declares a byte array and initializes all elements with zero. The integer value of the expression $numBytes$ specifies the byte length of the array. It must be an unsigned integer number in the range of $[1; 2^{16}-1]$ on a 16-bit CVM or $[1; 2^{32}-1]$ on a 32-bit CVM, respectively, and must not depend on labels (*Label*), functions (*DeclFct*), function parameters, and local or global variables (*DeclVar*).

EventTable $array_{ArrayInit}$
The data type **EventTable** declares an event table. Here, the syntactic structure of *array* is a special form of an initialized byte array and must be '[' ($eventCode_{Expr}$ ',' $memAdr_{Expr}$)* ']'. The value of *eventCode* must be an integer number greater than zero. If the value of *eventCode* is 1, then *eventCode* must be the second last element in the array. The value of *memAdr* must be an integer number greater than zero. Refer to sections 3.8 (page 96) and 3.1.6.2 (page 48) for more information on event tables.

Int num_{Expr}?
The data type **Int** declares a signed (two's complement) 2-byte integer number on a 16-bit CVM or a 4-byte integer number on a 32-bit CVM, respectively, with the optional initial value *num*. The value of *num* must be a signed (two's complement) integer number in the range of $[-2^{15}; 2^{15}-1]$ on a 16-bit CVM or $[-2^{31}; 2^{31}-1]$ on a 32-bit CVM, respectively.

String $text_{Expr}$
The data type **String** declares an UTF-8 string and initializes it with the string expression $text_{Expr}$. If the CVM mode (*Mode*) is '.16Bit' or '.32Bit', this declaration equals to the "**Bytes** $text_{Expr}$" declaration. Otherwise, the CVM assembler uses the CVM declaration code **string** when assembling this data item into the CVM packet.

B.3 Macros

For reasons of convenience, the CVM assembler provides some predefined macros to simplify programming in CVM assembler. A predefined macro contains several successive CVM instructions and is used as a pseudo instruction. However, the predefined macros are still quite low-level. The CVM assembler expands them into CVM instructions before it generates the binary code. In the following, the predefined macros are listed alphabetically and described using the following description format:

macro_mnemonic *operands* $\longrightarrow$ *target_instructions*
verbose_description

The left side contains the mnemonic of the macro and its (possibly empty) operand list. Each operand is shown in the form $ident_{type}$. *ident* can be any identifier and is chosen to characterize the usage of the operand. *type* determines the syntactic type of the operand according to the grammar specification in section B.1 (page 216). The operand must match the production for *type*. For example, $var_{Identifier}$ might be used to specify a variable whose name matches the production for *Identifier*. The right side contains the instruction sequence into which the macro is expanded. Afterwards, some additional explanations are given.

fcall $fctId_{Identifier}$ $\longrightarrow$ loadcr $fctId_{Identifier}$
call
(loadc $-numPars$
addsp)?

The macro fcall first calls a declared function and then pops the function parameters — if available — from the memory stack and discards them. Therefore, it assumes a function declaration with *fctId* being the name of the function. *numPars* represents the total number of stack cells occupied by the parameters on the memory stack. Each stack cell occupies cvmIntLen number of bytes. Refer to sections B.3 (page 225) and 3.1.2 (page 33) for more information on loadcr and cvmIntLen, respectively.

fcall_I $fctId_{Identifier}$, num_{Expr} $\longrightarrow$ loadc num_{Expr}
push
fcall $fctId_{Identifier}$

The macro fcall_I calls a declared function with an integer parameter. The value of *num* must be an integer number.

load $var_{Identifier}$ $\longrightarrow$ loadc $adr(var)$
load<a|r>

The macro load loads the value of the signed 2- or 4-byte integer (Int) variable *var* onto the register stack, depending on whether the CVM mode (*Mode*) is set to 16-bit ('.16Bit', '.16BitEmu') or 32-bit ('.32Bit', '.32BitEmu'). *var* must be a declared function parameter, local variable, or global variable. $adr(var)$ represents the memory address of *var*, which is absolute, if *var* is a global variable, otherwise relative. Section B.1 (page 221) explains how the correct memory address of the identifier *var* is determined. If *var* is a

B.3. Macros

global variable, the instruction loada is used, otherwise loadr. The benefit of this macro is that the CVM assembler programmer does not need to hardcode explicitly the load instruction, the memory address of the variable *var*, and the byte length of the memory address of the variable *var* when retrieving its value from memory. All these informations are included automatically by the CVM assembler into the resulting instructions.

loadc num_{Expr} $\longrightarrow$ loadc<ε|u><$byteLen(val(num))$> $val(num)$
| loadc_0 | loadc_1 | loadc_m1

The macro loadc loads the immediate integer number $val(num)$ onto the register stack with $val(num)$ representing the integer value of the expression num and $byteLen(val(num)) \in \{1, 2, 3, 4\}$ representing the minimum byte length that is required for $val(num)$. If $val(num)$ is negative, $val(num)$ is encoded as a two's-complement integer number, otherwise as a one's-complement integer number. Depending on the algebraic sign of $val(num)$ and its byte length, the CVM assembler expands this macro into one of the appropriate load instructions. $byteLen(val(num))$ must not exceed 2 on a 16-bit CVM or 4 on a 32-bit CVM, respectively. The benefit of this macro is that the CVM assembler programmer does not need to hardcode explicitly the algebraic sign and the required byte length of $val(num)$ into the load instruction. Note that this macro must not be the last instruction in a CVM assembler program, which simplifies address resolution for the CVM assembler and does not cause any considerable restriction.

loadcr num_{Expr} $\longrightarrow$ loadc<ε|u><$byteLen(relAdr)$> $relAdr$
| loadc_0 | loadc_1 | loadc_m1

The macro loadcr loads the immediate integer number $relAdr$ onto the register stack with $relAdr = val(num) - memAdr(nextInst)$. $val(num)$ represents the integer value of the expression num, $memAdr(nextInst)$ represents the absolute memory address of the next instruction, and $byteLen(relAdr) \in \{1, 2, 3, 4\}$ represents the minimum byte length that is required for $relAdr$. If $relAdr$ is negative, $relAdr$ is encoded as a two's-complement integer number, otherwise as a one's-complement integer number. Depending on the algebraic sign of $relAdr$ and its byte length, the CVM assembler expands this macro into one of the appropriate load instructions. $byteLen(relAdr)$ must not exceed 2 on a 16-bit CVM or 4 on a 32-bit CVM, respectively. The benefit of this macro is that the CVM assembler programmer does not need to hardcode explicitly the algebraic sign and the required byte length of $relAdr$ into the load instruction. This macro is used right before a jump or call instruction to load the relative memory address of the jump target. Note that this macro must not be the last instruction in a CVM assembler program.

rcvpage $pageNo_{Expr}, subpageNo_{Expr}$ $\longrightarrow$ loadc _hostAdrSrv
loadc $pageNo$
loadc $subpageNo$
rcv

The macro rcvpage contacts the CVM packet server that serves the client and requests from it the CVMUI page with the AUI page number $pageNo$ and the AUI subpage number $subpageNo$. The values of $pageNo$ and $subpageNo$ must be integer numbers. Refer also to section 5.5.1 (page 166) for more information on _hostAdrSrv.

rcvpage_a $pageNo_{Expr}$, $subpageNoMemAdr_{Expr}$ ⟶   loadc _hostAdrSrv
                                                                                                              loadc $pageNo$
                                                                                                              loadc $subpageNoMemAdr$
                                                                                                              loada
                                                                                                              rcv

The macro rcvpage_a is similar to the macro rcvpage. However, $subpageNoMemAdr$ represents the absolute memory address of $subpageNo$.

rcvsvc $hostAdrMemAdr_{Expr}$, $serviceNo_{Expr}$ ⟶   sidzero
                                                                                                              loadc $hostAdrMemAdr$
                                                                                                              loadc $serviceNo$
                                                                                                              loadc_0
                                                                                                              rcv

The macro rcvsvc starts a new client-server session with the addressed CVM packet server and requests a CVMUI page that belongs to the interactive network service with the service number $serviceNo_{Expr}$. The AUI page and subpage numbers of the requested CVMUI page are zero, each. The values of $hostAdrMemAdr$ and $serviceNo$ must be integer numbers.

retload   ⟶   loadc_0
                     loadr

The macro retload loads the current return value of the function from the memory stack onto the register stack for further processing. Therefore, it can only appear within the body of a function declaration that has a return value. The benefit of this macro is that the CVM assembler programmer does not need to hardcode explicitly the relative memory address of the return value.

retstore   ⟶   loadc_0
                     storer

The macro retstore pops the top-most value from the register stack and assigns it to the return value of the function in the memory stack. Therefore, it can only appear within the body of a function declaration that has a return value. The benefit of this macro is that the CVM assembler programmer does not need to hardcode explicitly the relative memory address of the return value.

return   ⟶   (loadc $-numLocVars$
                   addsp)?
                   oldstackframe
                   ret

The macro return first pops the current available local variables from the memory stack and discards them. Then it sets back the previous stack frame and returns to the caller of this function. Therefore, it can only appear within the body of a function declaration. In addition, there must be at least one return instruction in each function body. $numLocVars$ represents the total number of stack cells that are occupied by the local variables on the memory stack. The benefit of this macro is that the CVM assembler programmer can return with one instruction conveniently back to the caller of the function.

B.4. Builtin Functions   227

sendrcvpage $pageNo_{Expr}$, $subpageNo_{Expr}$ ⟶   loadc _hostAdrSrv
                                                         loadc $pageNo$
                                                         loadc $subpageNo$
                                                         load _svBufIdx
                                                         loadc _svBuf
                                                         sendrcv

The macro **sendrcvpage** contacts the CVM packet server that serves the client, sends data to it and requests the CVMUI page with the AUI page number $pageNo$ and the AUI subpage number $subpageNo$. The values of $pageNo$ and $subpageNo$ must be integer numbers. Refer also to section 5.5.1 (page 166) for more information on _hostAdrSrv, _svBufIdx, and _svBuf.

sendrcvpage_a $pageNo_{Expr}$, $subpageNoMemAdr_{Expr}$ ⟶   loadc _hostAdrSrv
                                                                  loadc $pageNo$
                                                                  loadc $subpageNoMemAdr$
                                                                  loada
                                                                  load _svBufIdx
                                                                  loadc _svBuf
                                                                  sendrcv

The macro **sendrcvpage_a** is similar to the macro **sendrcvpage**. However, $subpageNoMemAdr$ represents the absolute memory address of $subpageNo$.

store $var_{Identifier}$ ⟶   loadc $adr(var)$
                                    store<a|r>

The macro **store** stores the value on the top of the register stack into the integer (Int) variable var. var must be a declared function parameter, local variable, or global variable. $adr(var)$ represents the memory address of var, which is absolute, if var is a global variable, or relative, if var is a parameter or local variable. Section B.1 (page 221) explains how the correct memory address of var ($Identifier$) is determined. Depending on the specified CVM mode ($Mode$), the byte length of the variable var is 2 on a 16-bit CVM and 4 on a 32-bit CVM. If var is a global variable, the instruction **storea** is used, otherwise **storer**. The benefit of this macro is that the CVM assembler programmer does not need to hardcode explicitly the store instruction, the memory address of the variable var, and the byte length of the memory address of the variable var when storing a value into it. All these informations are included automatically by the CVM assembler into the resulting instructions.

B.4 Builtin Functions

For reasons of convenience, the CVM assembler also provides some builtin functions to simplify programming in CVM assembler. The CVM assembler processes a builtin function during assembling and writes the result into the binary code. In the following, the builtin functions are listed alphabetically and described using the following description format:

builtin_function_name   (*parameters*) :   *return_type*

verbose_description

builtin_function_name serves as a one-word description of the purpose of the function. *parameters* is a (comma separated and possibly empty) list of function parameters. Each parameter is shown in the form *ident$_{type}$*. *ident* can be any identifier and is usually chosen to characterize the meaning of the parameter. *type* determines the syntactic type of the parameter according to the grammar specification in section B.1 (page 216). The parameter must match the production for *type*. For example, *val$_{Expr}$* might be used to specify a value that matches the production for *Expr*. *return_type* specifies the data type of the result and is one of the CVM data types Int, Nat, String, or a tuple structure. Afterwards, a verbose description of the builtin function is given.

bitmapFile (*fileName$_{Expr}$*) : { Nat<2|4> width, height;
                                     Nat1[width * height] data }
The builtin function bitmapFile reads a bitmap image file that complies to the X11 BitMap format XBM [96]. The name of the bitmap file is the value of the string expression *fileName*. This builtin function returns the width and height of the bitmap image and the image data as a byte array. If the CVM mode is set to a 32-bit CVM, i.e., *Mode* = '.32Bit' or '.32BitEmu', the data types of width and height are each Nat4 and the width and height of the bitmap image must fit into the Nat4 data type. If the CVM mode is set to a 16-bit CVM, i.e., *Mode* = '.16Bit' or '.16BitEmu', the data types of width and height are each Nat2 and the width and height of the bitmap image must fit into the Nat2 data type. width and height are specified in pixels.

bitmapHeight (*fileName$_{Expr}$*) : Int
bitmapWidth   (*fileName$_{Expr}$*) : Int
The builtin functions bitmapHeight and bitmapWidth read a bitmap image file and return its height and width in pixels, respectively. The bitmap image complies to the X11 BitMap format XBM [96]. The name of the bitmap file is the value of the string expression *fileName*.

font (*fontCode$_{Expr}$*, *fontSize$_{Expr}$*) : Int4
The builtin function font encodes the given font components into an appropriate Int4 number according to the following format: (*fontSize* $\ll$ 16) | *fontCode*. This builtin function can only be used, if the specified CVM mode is set to a 32-bit CVM, i.e., *Mode* = '.32Bit' or '.32BitEmu'. The values of the expressions *fontCode* and *fontSize* must be unsigned integer numbers in the range of [0; 65535] and each of them must not depend on labels (*Label*), functions (*DeclFct*), function parameters, and local or global variables (*DeclVar*). *fontSize* is specified in pixels. Refer to section 3.2.3 (page 79) for a list of the currently supported font codes and their respective valid font sizes. Refer also to the CVM instruction setfont32 (page 113).

fontPt (*fontCode$_{Expr}$*, *fontSize$_{Expr}$*) : Int4
Same functionality as font(). However, *fontSize* is specified in tenths of a Point (*pt*), but not in pixels.

B.4. Builtin Functions

fontAscent $(fontCode_{Expr}, fontSize_{Expr})$: Int
fontDescent $(fontCode_{Expr}, fontSize_{Expr})$: Int
fontHeight $(fontCode_{Expr}, fontSize_{Expr})$: Int
The builtin functions fontAscent, fontDescent, and fontHeight return the ascent, descent, and height of a font in pixels. The height is the sum of its ascent and descent. The font is specified by *fontCode* and *fontSize*. The values of the expressions *fontCode* and *fontSize* must be unsigned integer numbers in the range of [0; 65535] and each of them must not depend on labels (*Label*), functions (*DeclFct*), function parameters, and local or global variables (*DeclVar*). *fontSize* is specified in pixels. Refer to section 3.2.3 (page 79) for a list of the currently supported font codes and their respective valid font sizes.

fontAscentPt $(fontCode_{Expr}, fontSize_{Expr})$: Int
fontDescentPt $(fontCode_{Expr}, fontSize_{Expr})$: Int
fontHeightPt $(fontCode_{Expr}, fontSize_{Expr})$: Int
Same functionality as fontAscent(), fontDescent(), and fontHeight(), respectively. However, *fontSize* and the return value are specified in tenths of a Point (*pt*), but not in pixels.

MAX $(num1_{Expr}, num2_{Expr})$: Int
MIN $(num1_{Expr}, num2_{Expr})$: Int
The builtin functions MAX and MIN return the maximum and the minimum of the two integer values *num1* and *num2*, respectively.

pixmapFile $(fileName_{Expr})$: Nat1[] data
The builtin function pixmapFile reads a pixmap image file that complies to the X11 PixMap format XPM [38]. The name of the pixmap file is the value of the string expression *fileName*. This builtin function returns an ASCII [7] character string as a byte array that represents an exact copy of the X PixMap (XPM) [38] file in memory. Note that the byte array data does not contain the terminating null character.

pixmapHeight $(fileName_{Expr})$: Int
pixmapWidth $(fileName_{Expr})$: Int
The builtin functions pixmapHeight and pixmapWidth read a pixmap image file and return its height and width in pixels, respectively. The pixmap image complies to the X11 PixMap format XPM [38]. The name of the pixmap file is the value of the string expression *fileName*.

rgb $(red_{Expr}, green_{Expr}, blue_{Expr})$: Int4
The builtin function rgb encodes the given red, green, and blue color components into an appropriate Int4 number according to the following format: $(red \ll 16) \mid (green \ll 8) \mid blue$. This builtin function can only be used, if the specified CVM mode is set to a 32-bit CVM, i.e., *Mode* = '.32Bit' or '.32BitEmu'. The values of the expressions *red*, *green*, and *blue* must be unsigned integer numbers in the range of [0; 255] and each of them must not depend on labels (*Label*), functions (*DeclFct*), function parameters, and local or global variables (*DeclVar*). Refer also to the CVM instruction setcolor32 (page 112).

sizeof (val_{Expr}) : Int
The builtin function sizeof returns the byte length of the value of the expression val. It is similar to the sizeof operator of the C [20] programming language. If val is an integer expression, then the builtin function returns 2 on a 16-bit CVM and 4 on a 32-bit CVM, respectively. If val is a string expression, then the builtin function returns the byte length of the corresponding String structure. Refer to section 3.1.1 (page 33) for more information on the CVM type String. If val is an array expression, then the builtin function returns the number of bytes of the corresponding byte array. However, if val consists only of an identifier (*Identifier*) that directly or indirectly refers to a variable declaration (*DeclVar*), then the builtin function returns the byte length of the declared data.

For example, in the following CVM assembler code fragment

```
.32Bit

.data
String   d1    "123456789"

.const
c1    d1
c2    sizeof (c1)
c3    sizeof ([32, 165, "Hello", 5321, sizeof ([9294, 12431, "World!", 4325]),
              stringBytes ("Hello World!")])
```

the values of the integer constants c2 and c3 are 10 and 34, respectively.

stringBytes ($text_{Expr}$) : Nat1[] data
The builtin function stringBytes returns the value of the string expression text as a byte array of UTF-8 characters. Compared to the CVM type String, the returned byte array data equals to the bytes field of the corresponding String structure, but not to the whole String structure. Refer to section 3.1.1 (page 33) for more information on the CVM type String. For example, stringBytes("Hello World!\n") returns the byte array [72, 101, 108, 108, 111, 32, 87, 111, 114, 108, 100, 33, 10], with each byte value represented here in decimal notation and separated by a comma. The whole corresponding String structure, however, equals to the byte array [13, 72, 101, 108, 108, 111, 32, 87, 111, 114, 108, 100, 33, 10], again with each byte value represented here in decimal notation and separated by a comma. The first byte with the value 13 indicates the number of the following bytes within the String structure.

textBreakLines ($text_{Expr}$, $fontCode_{Expr}$, $fontSize_{Expr}$, $maxWidth_{Expr}$) : String
The builtin function textBreakLines formats the text paragraph *text*, which is a string expression, by inserting single line break characters ("\n"), so that the maximum width of the resulting text paragraph, which is also a string, does not exceed the value of the integer expression *maxWidth*. A text paragraph consists of one or more text lines that are separated by the "\n" character. The width of a text paragraph is the maximum width of all its text lines. A "\n" character can only be inserted right before a space character (" "), i.e., the words within *text* are not truncated. Note that no "\n" characters that are already contained in *text* are removed in the resulting text paragraph. In addition, textBreakLines also truncates successive " " characters within *text* to one " " character

B.4. Builtin Functions

and ignores all " " characters right at the beginning and at the end of a text line in *text*. The used font is specified by *fontCode* and *fontSize*. The values of the expressions *fontCode* and *fontSize* must be unsigned integer numbers in the range of [0; 65535] and each of them must not depend on labels (*Label*), functions (*DeclFct*), function parameters, and local or global variables (*DeclVar*). *fontSize* and *maxWidth* are specified in pixels. Refer to section 3.2.3 (page 79) for a list of the currently supported font codes and their respective valid font sizes.

For example, in the following CVM assembler code fragment

```
.const
str1    textBreakLines (
        "  This CVM   program computes the nth Fibonacci number. \n  " +
        "  During the computation it     counts the     elapsed time. \n  ",
        fontCourier, 12, 242)
```

the value of the string constant `str1` is "This CVM program computes the nth\nFibonacci number.\nDuring the computation it counts\nthe elapsed time.\n". When drawn on the CVM display with the instruction `textp` (page 116), this string corresponds to the following text paragraph:

```
This CVM program computes the nth
Fibonacci number.
During the computation it counts
the elapsed time.
```

textBreakLinesPt ($text_{Expr}$, $fontCode_{Expr}$, $fontSize_{Expr}$, $maxWidthPt_{Expr}$) : **String**
Same functionality as `textBreakLines()`. However, *fontSize* and *maxWidthPt* are specified in tenths of a Point (*pt*), but not in pixels.

textHeight ($text_{Expr}$, $fontCode_{Expr}$, $fontSize_{Expr}$, $lineHeight_{Expr}$) : **Int**
The builtin function `textHeight` returns the height of the text paragraph *text* which consists of one or more text lines that are separated by the "\n" character. The height of the text paragraph is the number of its text lines multiplied by *height*. If the value of *lineHeight* is less than or equal to zero, then *height* equals to the height of the used font. Otherwise, *height* equals to the value of *lineHeight*. The font is specified by *fontCode* and *fontSize*. The height of the font is the sum of its ascent and descent. *text* must be a string expression. The values of the expressions *fontCode* and *fontSize* must be unsigned integer numbers in the range of [0; 65535] and each of them must not depend on labels (*Label*), functions (*DeclFct*), function parameters, and local or global variables (*DeclVar*). *fontSize*, *lineHeight*, and the return value are specified in pixels. Refer to section 3.2.3 (page 79) for a list of the currently supported font codes and their respective valid font sizes.

textHeightPt ($text_{Expr}$, $fontCode_{Expr}$, $fontSize_{Expr}$, $lineHeight_{Expr}$) : **Int**
Same functionality as `textHeight()`. However, *fontSize*, *lineHeight*, and the return value are specified in tenths of a Point (*pt*), but not in pixels.

textWidth ($text_{Expr}$, $fontCode_{Expr}$, $fontSize_{Expr}$) : Int
The builtin function **textWidth** returns the width of the text paragraph *text* which consists of one or more text lines that are separated by the "\n" character. The width of the text paragraph is the maximum width of all its text lines. The used font is specified by *fontCode* and *fontSize*. *text* must be a string expression. The values of the expressions *fontCode* and *fontSize* must be unsigned integer numbers in the range of [0; 65535] and each of them must not depend on labels (*Label*), functions (*DeclFct*), function parameters, and local or global variables (*DeclVar*). *fontSize* and the return value are specified in pixels. Refer to section 3.2.3 (page 79) for a list of the currently supported font codes and their respective valid font sizes.

textWidthPt ($text_{Expr}$, $fontCode_{Expr}$, $fontSize_{Expr}$) : Int
Same functionality as **textWidth()**. However, *fontSize* and the return value are specified in tenths of a Point (*pt*), but not in pixels.

B.5 Implementation Notes

The CVM assembler has been implemented with the C [20] programming language under the Linux [43] operating system. The used C compiler is **gcc** [32]. For the lexical and syntactic analysis the scanner generator **flex** [33] and the parser generator **bison** [30] have been used, respectively. In addition to the CVM assembler, a CVM disassembler has been implemented, as well. The implemented CVM assembler checks an input program thoroughly and produces a meaningful message for each detected error.

Source Files The C source files for the CVM assembler and disassembler are in the subdirectories `Implementation/CvmAssembler/Src/` and `Implementation/RghLib/Src/`. The latter subdirectory contains only source files whose names start with the prefix "rgh".

- `cvmAs.{h,c}`: These source files contain the function `cvmAs_ascii2cvmp()` and other definitions and functions that are needed by the CVM assembler.

- `cvmAsDisAs.{h,c}`: These source files contain definitions and functions that are needed both by the CVM assembler and by the CVM disassembler.

- `cvmAsMain.c`: This source file contains the `main()` function of the CVM assembler. It invokes the `cvmAs_ascii2cvmp()` function.

- `cvmAsNode.{h,c}`: These source files contain the core parts of the CVM assembler. This includes the tree node constructors to build the syntax tree, the semantic check of the context conditions, and the generation of the CVM packet, which contains the CVM binary code. The CVM program is dealt as a tree structure.

- `cvmAsParse.y`: This source file contains the syntactic grammar specification for the parser generator **bison**. The parser transforms the CVM assembler program into a syntax tree for further processing.

- `cvmAsScan.l`: This source file contains the lexical grammar specification for the scanner generator **flex**.

B.5. Implementation Notes

- cvmDisAs.{h,c}: These source files contain the function cvmDisAs_cvmp2ascii() and other functions that are needed by the CVM disassembler.

- cvmDisAsMain.c: This source file contains the main() function of the CVM disassembler. It invokes the cvmDisAs_cvmp2ascii() function.

- rghHeap.{h,c}, rghList.{h,c}, rghNode.{h,c}, rghStd.{h,c}, rghString.{h,c}, rghToken.h: These source files contain general utility functions and definitions for managing the heap, list and tree structures, for debugging, and for managing strings and scanner tokens, respectively.

Building The Makefile [34] file, which is in the subdirectory Implementation/CvmAssembler/, manages the compilation of the source files to build the executable files cvmAs2cvmp and cvmp2ascii. cvmAs2cvmp ("cvm Assembler to cvm packet") represents the CVM assembler and cvmp2ascii ("cvm packet to ascii") represents the CVM disassembler. Both executables are located in the subdirectory Implementation/CvmAssembler/Bin/. In the same subdirectory where Makefile is located, the make [34] command must be invoked in a shell [31] with the following options to start successful compilation:

```
make [CFLAGS="[-DDEBUG]"]
```

Optional parts are enclosed with [...]. The CFLAGS option -DDEBUG directs the CVM assembler cvmAs2cvmp and the disassembler cvmp2ascii to produce debugging messages onto the standard output. For example, the name of each called and executed C function is printed each time at the beginning of its execution.

Invocation The invocation syntax of cvmAs2cvmp is as follows:

```
cvmAs2cvmp [-t] [-i] < fileName
```

cvmAs2cvmp reads the CVM assembler program file with the name *fileName* from the standard input and translates it into the output file cvmp.bin, which represents the corresponding binary CVM packet. Note that the file cvmp.bin is created, if it does not exist, or overwritten, if it already exists. Optional parts are enclosed with [...]. The two options [-t] and [-i] can appear in any order. They direct the CVM assembler cvmAs2cvmp to produce informative messages onto the standard output. [-t] prints each matched lexical token during the lexical analysis. [-i] prints the completely parsed tree structure of the input CVM assembler program in a well-readable and formatted way, after it has been checked, restructured, and after all symbolic references have been resolved.

The invocation syntax of cvmp2ascii is as follows:

```
cvmp2ascii < fileName
```

cvmp2ascii disassembles the binary CVM packet file with the name *fileName* and writes the readable output in a formatted way to the standard output.

B.6 Examples

Not Implemented Parts Except for some restrictions concerning string literals (*String-Literal*) the CVM assembler has been implemented completely. String literals may only contain ASCII [7] characters. Unicode numbers are not supported within string literals, either. As these parts are not necessarily needed for the demonstration purpose of this implementation, they can be added later.

B.6 Examples

The following example programs illustrate the use of the CVM assembler. More examples can be found in the subdirectory `Implementation/CvmAssembler/Examples/`.

testAs.cvm Useless, but syntactically well-formed CVM assembler program. The only purpose is to demonstrate the syntax of the CVM assembler. However, if you run this program with the CVM, it will result in a runtime error.

```
.32BitEmu                                String  d11    "Hello World!"
                                         Bytes   d12    ""
.const                                   Bytesz  d13    9
c1   -128
c2   12345678901234567890 // will be     .code
     // truncated by the CVM Assembler           loadc 15
c3   c1 + c2 / 4                                 push
                                                 loadc -2
c4   "A multiline      example string            push
with \, \n, \r, \t, \" inside."                  fcall f1
                                                 halt
c5   rgb (1, 2+4,  -c1 + 2*16)
c6   font (fcHelveticaBold, 12)          .fct f1 (Int p1, Int p2) Int
                                         {
c7   f1                                     load p1
c8   d1                                     loadc p2
                                            Int loc1
.data                                       { Int loc2   Int loc3
Int   d1                                    load loc2  load loc3 }
Int   d2   c1 + c3                          Int loc2
EventTable d99  [ 5, 2, 6, 13 ]             load loc1
Int   d3   0                                load loc2
Int   d4   label1 - d4                      load d3
Bytes d5   15 - c1
Bytes d6   c4                            label1:
Bytes d7   [ 4, 255#1, -32768#2, c1#1,      retload
           "Hello", c2/c3#4, c4, d5#4 ]     retstore
Bytesz d8  5                             hallo:
EventTable d9   [ 3, 1, 2, c2 / c3 ]        {}
Int   d10  d10 - 320 + d5                }
```

The invocation of `cvmAs2cvmp -i` produces besides the binary CVM packet `cvmp.bin` the following readable and informative output during assembling:

B.6. Examples

```
.32BitEmu

.const
c1    -128
c2    2147483647
c3    c1 /*-128*/ + c2 /*2147483647*/ /
      4
c4    "A multiline \texample string
      \nwith \, \n, \r, \t, \"
      inside."
c5    rgb(1, 2 + 4, -c1 /*-128*/ + 2 *
      16) /*67232*/
c6    font(12, 12) /*786444*/
c7    f1 /*393*/
c8    d1 /*0*/

.data
/*   0*/   Int     d1
/*   4*/   Int     d2    c1 /*-128*/ + c3
                         /*536870783*/
/*   8*/   EventTable  d99   [
/*   8*/     5, 2,
/*  16*/     6, 13 ]
/*  28*/   Int     d3    0
/*  32*/   Int     d4    label1 /*419*/ - d4
                         /*32*/
/*  36*/   Bytes   d5    15 - c1 /*-128*/
/*180*/    Bytes   d6    c4 /*"A multiline
                         \texample string \nwith \,
                         \n, \r, \t, \" inside."*/
/*236*/    Bytes   d7    [ 4, 255#1,
                         -32768#2, c1 /*-128*/#1,
                         "Hello", c2 /*2147483647*/ /
                         c3 /*536870783*/#4, c4 /*"A
                         multiline \texample string
                         \nwith \, \n, \r, \t, \"
                         inside."*/, d5 /*36*/#4 ]
/*316*/    Bytesz  d8    5
/*324*/    EventTable  d9   [
/*324*/      3, 1,
/*332*/      2, c2 /*2147483647*/ / c3
             /*536870783*/ ]
/*344*/    Int     d10   d10 /*344*/ - 320
                         + d5 /*36*/
/*348*/    String  d11   "Hello World!"
/*364*/    Bytes   d12   ""
/*368*/    Bytesz  d13   9

.code
/*380*/    loadcu1 15
/*382*/    push
/*383*/    loadc1 -2
/*385*/    push
/*386*/    loadcu1 5
/*388*/    call
/*389*/    loadc1 -2
/*391*/    addsp
/*392*/    halt
/*393*/    .fct f1 (Int p1, Int p2) Int
           {
/*393*/    loadcu1 3
/*395*/    newstackframe
/*396*/    loadcu1 3
/*398*/    addsp
/*399*/    loadcu1 4
/*401*/    loadr
/*402*/    loadcu1 8
           Int   loc1
           {
           Int   loc2
           Int   loc3
/*404*/    loadcu1 24
/*406*/    loadr
/*407*/    loadcu1 28
/*409*/    loadr
           }
           Int   loc2
/*410*/    loadcu1 20
/*412*/    loadr
/*413*/    loadcu1 24
/*415*/    loadr
/*416*/    loadcu1 28
/*418*/    loada
/*419*/    label1:
/*419*/    loadc_0
/*420*/    loadr
/*421*/    loadc_0
/*422*/    storer
/*423*/    loadc1 -3
/*425*/    addsp
/*426*/    oldstackframe
/*427*/    ret
/*428*/    hallo:
           {}
           }
```

The numbers that are embedded within comments at the beginning of the relevant lines in the .data and .code sections represent absolute memory addresses where the respective data or code items are located in CVM memory, respectively.

The byte size of the generated CVM packet `cvmp.bin` is 254. During disassembling of `cvmp.bin`, the disassembler `cvmp2ascii` produces the following output:

```
magic = 0x63766D70                                      0 }
attrs = 19  // cvmDisAs_cvmMode =       /*344*/     nat1 = 60
    32BitEmu, cvmDisAs_cvmpAdrLen = 2   /*348*/     string = "Hello World!"
dataDeclSegmentAdr = 0                  /*364*/     bytes1 = 3, [ 0, 0, 0 ]
codeSegmentAdr = 380                    /*368*/     bytesz1 = 9
stackSegmentAdr = 428
lenData = 380                           instructions:
lenInsts = 48                           /*380*/     loadcu1 15
                                        /*382*/     push
data declarations:                      /*383*/     loadc1 -2
/*   0*/    intz                        /*385*/     push
/*   4*/    int4 = 536870655            /*386*/     loadcu1 5
/*   8*/    eventTable = {              /*388*/     call
              history_reload, 2,        /*389*/     loadc1 -2
              input_hostAdr, 13,        /*391*/     addsp
              0 }                       /*392*/     halt
/*  28*/    intz                        /*393*/     loadcu1 3
/*  32*/    nat2 = 387                  /*395*/     newstackframe
/*  36*/    bytesz1 = 143               /*396*/     loadcu1 3
/* 180*/    bytes1 = 56, [ 55, 65, 32,  /*398*/     addsp
    109, 117, 108, 116, 105, 108, 105,  /*399*/     loadcu1 4
    110, 101, 32, 9, 101, 120, 97, 109, /*401*/     loadr
    112, 108, 101, 32, 115, 116, 114,   /*402*/     loadcu1 8
    105, 110, 103, 32, 10, 119, 105,    /*404*/     loadcu1 24
    116, 104, 32, 92, 44, 32, 10, 44,   /*406*/     loadr
    32, 13, 44, 32, 9, 44, 32, 34, 32,  /*407*/     loadcu1 28
    105, 110, 115, 105, 100, 101, 46 ]  /*409*/     loadr
/* 236*/    bytes1 = 78, [ 0, 0, 0, 4,  /*410*/     loadcu1 20
    255, 128, 0, 128, 5, 72, 101, 108,  /*412*/     loadr
    108, 111, 0, 0, 0, 4, 55, 65, 32,   /*413*/     loadcu1 24
    109, 117, 108, 116, 105, 108, 105,  /*415*/     loadr
    110, 101, 32, 9, 101, 120, 97, 109, /*416*/     loadcu1 28
    112, 108, 101, 32, 115, 116, 114,   /*418*/     loada
    105, 110, 103, 32, 10, 119, 105,    /*419*/     loadc_0
    116, 104, 32, 92, 44, 32, 10, 44,   /*420*/     loadr
    32, 13, 44, 32, 9, 44, 32, 34, 32,  /*421*/     loadc_0
    105, 110, 115, 105, 100, 101, 46, 0,/*422*/     storer
    0, 0, 36 ]                          /*423*/     loadc1 -3
/* 316*/    bytesz1 = 5                 /*425*/     addsp
/* 324*/    eventTable = {              /*426*/     oldstackframe
              history_back, 1,          /*427*/     ret
              cvm_quit, 4,
```

If the first line of `testAs.cvm` is replaced with ".32Bit" to set the CVM mode to a not emulated 32-bit CVM, then the byte size of the corresponding CVM packet `cvmp.bin` is 248 and `cvmp.bin` has the following structure:

B.6. Examples

```
magic = 0x63766D70
attrs = 18    // cvmDisAs_cvmMode =
  32Bit, cvmDisAs_cvmpAdrLen = 2
dataDeclSegmentAdr = 148
codeSegmentAdr = 380
stackSegmentAdr = 428
lenData = 232
lenInsts = 48

data declarations:
/*148*/   bytesz1 = 24
/*172*/   bytes1 = 165, [ 55, 65, 32,
  109, 117, 108, 116, 105, 108, 105,
  110, 101, 32, 9, 101, 120, 97, 109,
  112, 108, 101, 32, 115, 116, 114,
  105, 110, 103, 32, 10, 119, 105,
  116, 104, 32, 92, 44, 32, 10, 44,
  32, 13, 44, 32, 9, 44, 32, 34, 32,
  105, 110, 115, 105, 100, 101, 46, 0,
  0, 0, 4, 255, 128, 0, 128, 5, 72,
  101, 108, 108, 111, 0, 0, 0, 4, 55,
  65, 32, 109, 117, 108, 116, 105,
  108, 105, 110, 101, 32, 9, 101, 120, 120,
  97, 109, 112, 108, 101, 32, 115,
  116, 114, 105, 110, 103, 32, 10,
  119, 105, 116, 104, 32, 92, 44, 32,
  10, 44, 32, 13, 44, 32, 9, 44, 32,
  34, 32, 105, 110, 115, 105, 100, 101,
  46, 0, 0, 0, 0, 0, 0, 0, 0, 0, 0, 0,
  0, 31, 255, 254, 255, 0, 0, 0, 103,
  0, 0, 0, 0, 12, 72, 101, 108, 108, 111,
  111, 32, 87, 111, 114, 108, 100, 33
  ]
/*340*/   eventTable = {
    history_reload, 2,
    input_hostAdr, 13,
    0 }
/*360*/   eventTable = {
    history_back, 1,
```

```
                         cvm_quit, 4,
                         0 }

instructions:
/*380*/   loadcu1 15
/*382*/   push
/*383*/   loadc1 -2
/*385*/   push
/*386*/   loadcu1 5
/*388*/   call
/*389*/   loadc1 -2
/*391*/   addsp
/*392*/   halt
/*393*/   loadcu1 3
/*395*/   newstackframe
/*396*/   loadcu1 3
/*398*/   addsp
/*399*/   loadcu1 4
/*401*/   loadr
/*402*/   loadcu1 8
/*404*/   loadcu1 24
/*406*/   loadr
/*407*/   loadcu1 28
/*409*/   loadr
/*410*/   loadcu1 20
/*412*/   loadr
/*413*/   loadcu1 24
/*415*/   loadr
/*416*/   loadcu1 168
/*418*/   loada
/*419*/   loadc_0
/*420*/   loadr
/*421*/   loadc_0
/*422*/   storer
/*423*/   loadc1 -3
/*425*/   addsp
/*426*/   oldstackframe
/*427*/   ret
```

fibTimer.cvm   Fibonacci Numbers. This example program computes recursively the Nth (N ≥ 0) Fibonacci number and displays the result on the screen. During the computation it also counts and displays the elapsed time. In addition, if the user presses a key, it displays a short message on the screen. Figure 3.8 (page 122) contains a screen shot of this program when it is executed with the CVM interpreter.

```
.32Bit

///////
// Main

///////
.code
main:
```

```
// Draw Root Window
  fcall drawRt

// Enable Event Handling
  loadc eventTable   seteventtableadr
  enableevents

// Set Interval Timer
  loadc timerHandle  settimerhandleadr
  loadc 10   settimerinterval

// Compute Fib(N)
  incsp
  loadc N   push
  fcall Fib
  pop

// Display Result
  loadc xFib + wFib   loadc yFib
    loadc printInt   lib

// Stop Interval Timer
  loadc 0   settimerinterval
  halt


//////////////
// Event Table
//////////////

.data
EventTable   eventTable  [
  key_pressed, eventMessageOn,
  key_pressed_enter, eventMessageOn,
  key_pressed_escape, eventMessageOn,
  key_released, eventMessageOff,
  key_released_enter, eventMessageOff,
  key_released_escape, eventMessageOff
]

.const
strEvMessage   "Key Pressed !"

.code
eventMessageOn:
  loadc 255   loadc 0   loadc 0
    setcolor
  loadc xiRt   loadc hRt - fdRt
    textbg strEvMessage
  loadc 0   loadc 0   loadc 0   setcolor
  halt

eventMessageOff:
  loadc 255   loadc 255   loadc 255
    setcolor
  loadc xiRt   loadc hRt - fdRt
    textbg strEvMessage
  loadc 0   loadc 0   loadc 0   setcolor
  halt


///////
// Root {Window}
///////

.const
// Screen Dimensions: Width, Height
wRt   250
hRt   150

// Font
fcRt   fcHelvetica   // Code
fsRt   12  // Size
fdRt   fontDescent (fcRt, fsRt)

// Indent: Horizontal x, Vertical y
xiRt   (5 * fsRt) / sF
yiRt   0

// Colors: Foreground, Background
fgRedRt     0
fgGreenRt   0
fgBlueRt    0
bgRedRt     255
bgGreenRt   255
bgBlueRt    255

// Scale Factor
sF   14

.code
.fct drawRt () Void
{
  loadc bgRedRt   loadc bgGreenRt
    loadc bgBlueRt   setcolor
  loadc 0   loadc 0   loadc wRt
    loadc hRt   rectfill
  loadc fgRedRt   loadc fgGreenRt
    loadc fgBlueRt   setcolor
  fcall drawHeadLine
  loadc xiRt   setxtextline
  fcall drawIntro
  fcall drawPar
```

B.6. Examples

```
    fcall drawFib
    fcall drawElapse
    return
  }

//////////
// HeadLine {Text}
//////////

.const
strHeadLine  "Fibonacci"
fcHeadLine   fcHelveticaBoldItalic
fsHeadLine   18
fhHeadLine   fontHeight (fcHeadLine,
                         fsHeadLine)
xHeadLine    xiRt +
             (wIntro - wHeadLine) / 2
yHeadLine    yiRt + fhHeadLine
wHeadLine    textWidth (strHeadLine,
                        fcHeadLine, fsHeadLine)
hHeadLine    textHeight (strHeadLine,
                         fcHeadLine, fsHeadLine, 0)
.code
.fct drawHeadLine () Void
  {
    loadc fcHeadLine  loadc fsHeadLine
      setfont
    loadc xHeadLine  loadc yHeadLine
      text strHeadLine
    return
  }


////////
// Intro {Text}
////////

.const
strIntro   textBreakLines (
             "This CVM program computes "
           + "recursively the Nth Fibonacci "
           + "number. During the computation "
           + "it counts the elapsed time.",
             fcRt, fsRt, wRt - 2 * xiRt)
xIntro     xiRt
yIntro     yHeadLine + hHeadLine
wIntro     textWidth (strIntro, fcRt,
                      fsRt)
hIntro     textHeight (strIntro, fcRt,
```

```
                       fsRt, 0)
.code
.fct drawIntro () Void
  {
    loadc fcRt   loadc fsRt  setfont
    loadc yIntro  textp strIntro
    return
  }


//////
// Par {Text}
//////

.const
strPar    "N = "
xPar      xiRt
yPar      yIntro + hIntro +
          (3 * fsRt) / sF
wPar      textWidth (strPar, fcRt,
                     fsRt)
hPar      textHeight (strPar, fcRt,
                      fsRt, 0)
.code
.fct drawPar () Void
  {
    loadc yPar  textp strPar
    loadc N    loadc xPar + wPar
      loadc yPar  loadc printInt  lib
    return
  }


//////
// Fib {Text}
//////

.const
strFib    "Fib(N) = "
xFib      xiRt
yFib      yPar + hPar
wFib      textWidth (strFib, fcRt, fsRt)
hFib      textHeight (strFib, fcRt, fsRt,
                      0)
N   18
.code
.fct drawFib () Void
```

B. CVM Assembler (CVMA)

```
  {
    loadc yFib  textp strFib
    return
  }


//////////
// Elapse {Text}
//////////

.const
strElapse  "Elapsed Time (1/100 s) = "
xElapse    xiRt
yElapse    yFib + hFib +
           (3 * fsRt) / sF
wElapse    textWidth (strElapse, fcRt,
                      fsRt)
hElapse    textHeight (strElapse, fcRt,
                      fsRt, 0)
.code
.fct drawElapse () Void
  {
    loadc yElapse  textp strElapse
    return
  }


///////////////////////
// Fibonacci Function
///////////////////////

.code
```

```
.fct Fib (Int n) Int
  {
    loadc 1  load n  loadcr Fib_1  jl
    loadc 1  retstore
    return
Fib_1:
    incsp
    load n   dec  push
    fcall Fib
    incsp
    load n   loadc 2   sub  push
    fcall Fib
    pop  pop  add  retstore
    return
  }

////////
// Timer
////////

.data
Int    elapsedTime   0

.code
timerHandle:
    load elapsedTime  inc
    store elapsedTime
    load elapsedTime
    loadc xElapse + wElapse
    loadc yElapse  loadc printIntBg
    lib
    halt
```

During disassembling of the generated CVM packet file cvmp.bin, the disassembler cvmp2ascii produces the following output:

```
magic = 0x63766D70                         key_pressed_escape, 91,
attrs = 18  // cvmDisAs_cvmMode =          key_released, 120,
   32Bit, cvmDisAs_cvmpAdrLen = 2          key_released_enter, 120,
dataDeclSegmentAdr = 0                     key_released_escape, 120,
codeSegmentAdr = 56                        0 }
stackSegmentAdr = 476
lenData = 56                            instructions:
lenInsts = 418                          /* 56*/   loadcu1 93
                                        /* 58*/   call
data declarations:                      /* 59*/   loadcu1 4
/*  0*/   bytesz1 = 4                   /* 61*/   seteventtableadr
/*  4*/   eventTable = {                /* 62*/   enableevents
    key_pressed, 91,                    /* 63*/   loadcu2 459
    key_pressed_enter, 91,              /* 66*/   settimerhandleadr
```

B.6. Examples

```
/* 67*/   loadcu1 10
/* 69*/   settimerinterval
/* 70*/   incsp
/* 71*/   loadcu1 18
/* 73*/   push
/* 74*/   loadcu2 336
/* 77*/   call
/* 78*/   loadc_m1
/* 79*/   addsp
/* 80*/   pop
/* 81*/   loadcu1 54
/* 83*/   loadcu1 100
/* 85*/   loadcu1 6
/* 87*/   lib
/* 88*/   loadc_0
/* 89*/   settimerinterval
/* 90*/   halt
/* 91*/   loadcu1 255
/* 93*/   loadc_0
/* 94*/   loadc_0
/* 95*/   setcolor
/* 96*/   loadcu1 4
/* 98*/   loadcu1 147
/*100*/   textbg "Key Pressed !"
/*115*/   loadc_0
/*116*/   loadc_0
/*117*/   loadc_0
/*118*/   setcolor
/*119*/   halt
/*120*/   loadcu1 255
/*122*/   loadcu1 255
/*124*/   loadcu1 255
/*126*/   setcolor
/*127*/   loadcu1 4
/*129*/   loadcu1 147
/*131*/   textbg "Key Pressed !"
/*146*/   loadc_0
/*147*/   loadc_0
/*148*/   loadc_0
/*149*/   setcolor
/*150*/   halt
/*151*/   loadc_0
/*152*/   newstackframe
/*153*/   loadcu1 255
/*155*/   loadcu1 255
/*157*/   loadcu1 255
/*159*/   setcolor
/*160*/   loadc_0
/*161*/   loadc_0
/*162*/   loadcu1 250
/*164*/   loadcu1 150

/*166*/   rectfill
/*167*/   loadc_0
/*168*/   loadc_0
/*169*/   loadc_0
/*170*/   setcolor
/*171*/   loadcu1 18
/*173*/   call
/*174*/   loadcu1 4
/*176*/   setxtextline
/*177*/   loadcu1 36
/*179*/   call
/*180*/   loadcu1 160
/*182*/   call
/*183*/   loadcu1 178
/*185*/   call
/*186*/   loadcu1 192
/*188*/   call
/*189*/   oldstackframe
/*190*/   ret
/*191*/   loadc_0
/*192*/   newstackframe
/*193*/   loadcu1 14
/*195*/   loadcu1 18
/*197*/   setfont
/*198*/   loadcu1 76
/*200*/   loadcu1 21
/*202*/   text "Fibonacci"
/*213*/   oldstackframe
/*214*/   ret
/*215*/   loadc_0
/*216*/   newstackframe
/*217*/   loadcu1 11
/*219*/   loadcu1 12
/*221*/   setfont
/*222*/   loadcu1 42
/*224*/   textp "This CVM program
          computes recursively\nthe Nth
          Fibonacci number. During
          the\ncomputation it counts the
          elapsed time."
/*340*/   oldstackframe
/*341*/   ret
/*342*/   loadc_0
/*343*/   newstackframe
/*344*/   loadcu1 86
/*346*/   textp "N = "
/*352*/   loadcu1 18
/*354*/   loadcu1 28
/*356*/   loadcu1 86
/*358*/   loadcu1 6
/*360*/   lib
```

```
/*361*/   oldstackframe              /*436*/   call
/*362*/   ret                        /*437*/   loadc_m1
/*363*/   loadc_0                    /*438*/   addsp
/*364*/   newstackframe              /*439*/   incsp
/*365*/   loadcu1 100                /*440*/   loadcu1 4
/*367*/   textp "Fib(N) = "          /*442*/   loadr
/*378*/   oldstackframe              /*443*/   loadcu1 2
/*379*/   ret                        /*445*/   sub
/*380*/   loadc_0                    /*446*/   push
/*381*/   newstackframe              /*447*/   loadc1 -36
/*382*/   loadcu1 116                /*449*/   call
/*384*/   textp "Elapsed Time (1/100 /*450*/   loadc_m1
          s) = "                     /*451*/   addsp
/*411*/   oldstackframe              /*452*/   pop
/*412*/   ret                        /*453*/   pop
/*413*/   loadcu1 2                  /*454*/   add
/*415*/   newstackframe              /*455*/   loadc_0
/*416*/   loadc_1                    /*456*/   storer
/*417*/   loadcu1 4                  /*457*/   oldstackframe
/*419*/   loadr                      /*458*/   ret
/*420*/   loadcu1 6                  /*459*/   loadc_0
/*422*/   jl                         /*460*/   loada
/*423*/   loadc_1                    /*461*/   inc
/*424*/   loadc_0                    /*462*/   loadc_0
/*425*/   storer                     /*463*/   storea
/*426*/   oldstackframe              /*464*/   loadc_0
/*427*/   ret                        /*465*/   loada
/*428*/   incsp                      /*466*/   loadcu1 148
/*429*/   loadcu1 4                  /*468*/   loadcu1 116
/*431*/   loadr                      /*470*/   loadcu1 7
/*432*/   dec                        /*472*/   lib
/*433*/   push                       /*473*/   halt
/*434*/   loadc1 -23
```

Note that the CVM instructions of the recursive Fib() function start at the memory address /*413*/ and end at the address /*458*/.

simpleGui.cvm   A simple graphical user interface. This example program represents the small user interface program from section 2.2.1.2 (page 21).

```
.16Bit                                  str1   "An example user interface"
                                        fc1    fcHelveticaBoldItalic
.const                                  fs1    18
xMax      249                           fh1    fontHeight (fc1, fs1)
yMax      149                           xStr1  (5 * fs2) / 14
                                        yStr1  fh1
lenCursor textWidth ("_", fc2, fs2)
delta     1                             str2   "Here a list with 2 items:"
                                        fc2    fcHelvetica
                                        fs2    14
```

B.6. Examples   243

```
fa2     fontAscent (fc2, fs2)                    // state of the button
fd2     fontDescent (fc2, fs2)                   Int     currentlyPressed 0
fh2     fontHeight (fc2, fs2)
yStr2   yStr1 + fh1                              // mixed
                                                 Int     x2    0
xDot    xStr1 + (5 * fs2) / 14
yDot    yStr3 - (fontAscent (fc2, fs2)           EventTable    eventTable    [
        + dDot) / 2 + 1                              key_pressed, keyPressed,
dDot    (4 * fs2) / 14                               key_pressed_enter, keyPressedEnter,
                                                     key_released_enter, keyReleasedEnter ]
str3    "First item"
xStr3   xDot + (10 * fs2) / 14                   .code
yStr3   yStr2 + fh2 + (3 * fs2) / 14             main:
                                                     loadcr paintUserInterface  call
str4    "Second item"                                loadcr paintCursor  call
yStr4   yStr3 + fh2                                  loadc eventTable  seteventtableadr
                                                     enableevents
str5    "A hyperlink:"                               halt
yStr5   yStr4 + fh2 + (8 * fs2) / 14
                                                 // paint procedures
str6    "http://www.w3.org"
xStr6   xStr1 + textWidth (str5, fc2,            paintUserInterface:
        fs2) + (15 * fs2) / 14                       loadc fc1   loadc fs1   setfont
                                                     loadc xStr1  loadc yStr1  text str1
str7    "Finally a button:"                          loadc fc2   loadc fs2   setfont
yStr7   yStr5 + fh2 + (13 * fs2) / 14                loadc xStr1  loadc yStr2  text str2
                                                     loadc xDot   loadc yDot  loadc dDot
str8    "Click me"                                     circlefill
xStr8   xStr1 + textWidth (str7, fc2,                loadc xStr3  loadc yStr3  text str3
        fs2) + (15 * fs2) / 14                       loadc xDot   loadc yDot + fh2
                                                     loadc dDot   circlefill
wHyperlink  textWidth (str6, fc2, fs2)               loadc xStr3  loadc yStr4  text str4
                                                     loadc xStr1  loadc yStr5  text str5
xButton    xStr8 - (4 * fs2) / 14                    loadcr paintHyperlink call
yButton    yStr7 - fontAscent (fc2, fs2)             loadc xStr1  loadc yStr7  text str7
           + 1 - (4 * fs2) / 14                      loadcr paintButton  call
wButton    textWidth (str8, fc2, fs2) +              ret
           (9 * fs2) / 14
hButton    fontAscent (fc2, fs2) + (9 *          paintHyperlink:
           fs2) / 14                                 load visited   loadc 0  loadcr isVisited
                                                     jne
.data                                                loadc 0   loadc 0   loadc 255   setcolor
Bytes   cursorBgPixmap   lenCursor * 4               loadcr paintHyperlink_1  jmp
                                                 isVisited:
// x-y position of cursor                            loadc 255  loadc 0   loadc 0   setcolor
Int     xPos    (150 * fs2) / 14                 paintHyperlink_1:
Int     yPos    (70 * fs2) / 14                      loadc xStr6  loadc yStr5  text str6
                                                     loadc xStr6  loadc yStr5 + 2
// state of the hyperlink                            loadc wHyperlink   linehoriz
Int     visited   0                                  loadc 0   loadc 0   loadc 0   setcolor
                                                     ret
```

```
paintButton:
  load currentlyPressed  loadc 0
  loadcr isCurrentlyPressed  jne
  loadc 0  loadc 255  loadc 0  setcolor
  loadcr paintButton_1  jmp
isCurrentlyPressed:
  loadc 255  loadc 0  loadc 0  setcolor
paintButton_1:
  loadc xButton  loadc yButton
    loadc wButton  loadc hButton
    rectfill
  loadc 0  loadc 0  loadc 0  setcolor
  loadc xButton  loadc yButton
    loadc wButton  loadc hButton  rect
  loadc xStr8  loadc yStr7  text str8
  ret

paintCursor:
  load xPos  load yPos  loadc lenCursor
    loadc 1
    loadc cursorBgPixmap
    screen2mem
  load xPos  load yPos  loadc lenCursor
    linehoriz
  ret

// event handling

keyPressed:
  loadep1  loadc XK_Left
    loadcr keyPressedLeft  je
  loadep1  loadc XK_Up
    loadcr keyPressedUp  je
  loadep1  loadc XK_Down
    loadcr keyPressedDown  je
  loadep1  loadc XK_Right
    loadcr keyPressedRight  je
keyPressedIgnore:
  halt
keyPressedLeft:
  load xPos  loadc delta  sub  loadc 0
    loadcr keyPressedIgnore  jl
  load xPos  load yPos  loadc lenCursor
    loadc 1  loadc cursorBgPixmap
    mem2screen
  load xPos  loadc delta  sub
    store xPos
  loadcr paintCursor  call
  halt
keyPressedRight:
  loadc xMax  load xPos
```

```
    loadc lenCursor  add  dec
    loadc delta  add
    loadcr keyPressedIgnore  jl
  load xPos  load yPos  loadc lenCursor
    loadc 1  loadc cursorBgPixmap
    mem2screen
  load xPos  loadc delta  add
    store xPos
  loadcr paintCursor  call
  halt
keyPressedUp:
  load yPos  loadc delta  sub  loadc 0
    loadcr keyPressedIgnore  jl
  load xPos  load yPos  loadc lenCursor
    loadc 1
    loadc cursorBgPixmap
    mem2screen
  load yPos  loadc delta  sub
    store yPos
  loadcr paintCursor  call
  halt
keyPressedDown:
  loadc yMax  load yPos  loadc delta
    add  loadcr keyPressedIgnore  jl
  load xPos  load yPos  loadc lenCursor
    loadc 1
    loadc cursorBgPixmap
    mem2screen
  loadc delta  load yPos  add
    store yPos
  loadcr paintCursor  call
  halt

keyPressedEnter:
keyPressedEnterIfHyperlink:
  load xPos  loadc xStr6
    loadcr keyPressedEnterIfButton  jl
  loadc xStr6 + wHyperlink - lenCursor
    load xPos
    loadcr keyPressedEnterIfButton  jl
  load yPos  loadc yStr5 - fa2
    loadcr keyPressedEnterIfButton  jl
  loadc yStr5 + fd2  load yPos
    loadcr keyPressedEnterIfButton  jl
keyPressedEnterHyperlink:
  loadc 1  store visited
  load xPos  load yPos  loadc lenCursor
    loadc 1
    loadc cursorBgPixmap
    mem2screen
  loadcr paintHyperlink  call
```

B.6. Examples

```
    loadcr paintCursor  call
    halt
keyPressedEnterIfButton:
    load xPos   loadc xButton
        loadcr keyPressedIgnore  jl
    loadc xButton + wButton - lenCursor
        load xPos   loadc keyPressedIgnore
        jl
    load yPos   loadc yButton
        loadcr keyPressedIgnore  jl
    loadc yButton + hButton   load yPos
        loadcr keyPressedIgnore  jl
keyPressedEnterButton:
    loadc 1   store currentlyPressed
    loadcr paintButton  call
    loadcr paintCursor  call
    halt
```

```
keyReleasedEnter:
keyReleasedEnterIfButton:
    load xPos   loadc xButton
        loadcr keyReleasedEnterIgnore  jl
    loadc xButton + wButton - lenCursor
        load xPos   loadc keyReleasedEnterIgnore
        jl
    load yPos   loadc yButton
        loadcr keyReleasedEnterIgnore  jl
    loadc yButton + hButton   load yPos
        loadcr keyReleasedEnterIgnore  jl
keyReleasedEnterButton:
    loadc 0   store currentlyPressed
    loadcr paintButton  call
    loadcr paintCursor  call
keyReleasedEnterIgnore:
    halt
```

The byte size of the generated CVM packet cvmp.bin is 663. During disassembling of cvmp.bin, the disassembler cvmp2ascii produces the following output:

```
magic = 0x63766D70
attrs = 16   // cvmDisAs_cvmMode =
    16Bit, cvmDisAs_cvmpAdrLen = 2
dataDeclSegmentAdr = 32
codeSegmentAdr = 56
stackSegmentAdr = 686
lenData = 24
lenInsts = 629

data declarations:
/* 32*/   bytesz1 = 6
/* 38*/   bytes1 = 4, [ 0, 150, 0, 70
    ]
/* 42*/   eventTable = {
          key_pressed, 369,
          key_pressed_enter, 534,
          key_released_enter, 639,
          0 }

instructions:
/* 56*/   loadcu1 10
/* 58*/   call
/* 59*/   loadc2 286
/* 62*/   call
/* 63*/   loadcu1 42
/* 65*/   seteventtableadr
/* 66*/   enableevents
/* 67*/   halt
/* 68*/   loadcu1 14
```

```
/* 70*/   loadcu1 18
/* 72*/   setfont
/* 73*/   loadcu1 5
/* 75*/   loadcu1 21
/* 77*/   text "An example user
    interface"
/*104*/   loadcu1 11
/*106*/   loadcu1 14
/*108*/   setfont
/*109*/   loadcu1 5
/*111*/   loadcu1 42
/*113*/   text "Here a list with 2
    items:"
/*140*/   loadcu1 10
/*142*/   loadcu1 54
/*144*/   loadcu1 4
/*146*/   circlefill
/*147*/   loadcu1 20
/*149*/   loadcu1 61
/*151*/   text "First item"
/*163*/   loadcu1 10
/*165*/   loadcu1 70
/*167*/   loadcu1 4
/*169*/   circlefill
/*170*/   loadcu1 20
/*172*/   loadcu1 77
/*174*/   text "Second item"
/*187*/   loadcu1 5
/*189*/   loadcu1 101
```

```
/*191*/   text "A hyperlink:"         /*311*/   loadcu1 116
/*205*/   loadcu1 28                  /*313*/   loadcu1 114
/*207*/   call                        /*315*/   loadcu1 63
/*208*/   loadcu1 5                   /*317*/   loadcu1 22
/*210*/   loadcu1 130                 /*319*/   rectfill
/*212*/   text "Finally a button:"    /*320*/   loadc_0
/*231*/   loadcu1 58                  /*321*/   loadc_0
/*233*/   call                        /*322*/   loadc_0
/*234*/   ret                         /*323*/   setcolor
/*235*/   loadcu1 32                  /*324*/   loadcu1 116
/*237*/   loada                       /*326*/   loadcu1 114
/*238*/   loadc_0                     /*328*/   loadcu1 63
/*239*/   loadcu1 9                   /*330*/   loadcu1 22
/*241*/   jne                         /*332*/   rect
/*242*/   loadc_0                     /*333*/   loadcu1 120
/*243*/   loadc_0                     /*335*/   loadcu1 130
/*244*/   loadcu1 255                 /*337*/   text "Click me"
/*246*/   setcolor                    /*347*/   ret
/*247*/   loadcu1 6                   /*348*/   loadcu1 38
/*249*/   jmp                         /*350*/   loada
/*250*/   loadcu1 255                 /*351*/   loadcu1 40
/*252*/   loadc_0                     /*353*/   loada
/*253*/   loadc_0                     /*354*/   loadcu1 8
/*254*/   setcolor                    /*356*/   loadc_1
/*255*/   loadcu1 95                  /*357*/   loadc_0
/*257*/   loadcu1 101                 /*358*/   screen2mem
/*259*/   text "http://www.w3c.org"   /*359*/   loadcu1 38
/*279*/   loadcu1 95                  /*361*/   loada
/*281*/   loadcu1 103                 /*362*/   loadcu1 40
/*283*/   loadcu1 118                 /*364*/   loada
/*285*/   linehoriz                   /*365*/   loadcu1 8
/*286*/   loadc_0                     /*367*/   linehoriz
/*287*/   loadc_0                     /*368*/   ret
/*288*/   loadc_0                     /*369*/   loadep1
/*289*/   setcolor                    /*370*/   loadc2 -175
/*290*/   ret                         /*373*/   loadcu1 23
/*291*/   loadcu1 34                  /*375*/   je
/*293*/   loada                       /*376*/   loadep1
/*294*/   loadc_0                     /*377*/   loadc2 -174
/*295*/   loadcu1 9                   /*380*/   loadcu1 85
/*297*/   jne                         /*382*/   je
/*298*/   loadc_0                     /*383*/   loadep1
/*299*/   loadcu1 255                 /*384*/   loadc2 -172
/*301*/   loadc_0                     /*387*/   loadcu1 111
/*302*/   setcolor                    /*389*/   je
/*303*/   loadcu1 6                   /*390*/   loadep1
/*305*/   jmp                         /*391*/   loadc2 -173
/*306*/   loadcu1 255                 /*394*/   loadcu1 34
/*308*/   loadc_0                     /*396*/   je
/*309*/   loadc_0                     /*397*/   halt
/*310*/   setcolor                    /*398*/   loadcu1 38
```

B.6. Examples

```
/*400*/   loada
/*401*/   loadc_1
/*402*/   sub
/*403*/   loadc_0
/*404*/   loadc1 -9
/*406*/   jl
/*407*/   loadcu1 38
/*409*/   loada
/*410*/   loadcu1 40
/*412*/   loada
/*413*/   loadcu1 8
/*415*/   loadc_1
/*416*/   loadc_0
/*417*/   mem2screen
/*418*/   loadcu1 38
/*420*/   loada
/*421*/   loadc_1
/*422*/   sub
/*423*/   loadcu1 38
/*425*/   storea
/*426*/   loadc1 -80
/*428*/   call
/*429*/   halt
/*430*/   loadcu1 249
/*432*/   loadcu1 38
/*434*/   loada
/*435*/   loadcu1 8
/*437*/   add
/*438*/   dec
/*439*/   loadc_1
/*440*/   add
/*441*/   loadc1 -46
/*443*/   jl
/*444*/   loadcu1 38
/*446*/   loada
/*447*/   loadcu1 40
/*449*/   loada
/*450*/   loadcu1 8
/*452*/   loadc_1
/*453*/   loadc_0
/*454*/   mem2screen
/*455*/   loadcu1 38
/*457*/   loada
/*458*/   loadc_1
/*459*/   add
/*460*/   loadcu1 38
/*462*/   storea
/*463*/   loadc1 -117
/*465*/   call
/*466*/   halt
/*467*/   loadcu1 40

/*469*/   loada
/*470*/   loadc_1
/*471*/   sub
/*472*/   loadc_0
/*473*/   loadc1 -78
/*475*/   jl
/*476*/   loadcu1 38
/*478*/   loada
/*479*/   loadcu1 40
/*481*/   loada
/*482*/   loadcu1 8
/*484*/   loadc_1
/*485*/   loadc_0
/*486*/   mem2screen
/*487*/   loadcu1 40
/*489*/   loada
/*490*/   loadc_1
/*491*/   sub
/*492*/   loadcu1 40
/*494*/   storea
/*495*/   loadc2 -150
/*498*/   call
/*499*/   halt
/*500*/   loadcu1 149
/*502*/   loadcu1 40
/*504*/   loada
/*505*/   loadc_1
/*506*/   add
/*507*/   loadc1 -112
/*509*/   jl
/*510*/   loadcu1 38
/*512*/   loada
/*513*/   loadcu1 40
/*515*/   loada
/*516*/   loadcu1 8
/*518*/   loadc_1
/*519*/   loadc_0
/*520*/   mem2screen
/*521*/   loadc_1
/*522*/   loadcu1 40
/*524*/   loada
/*525*/   add
/*526*/   loadcu1 40
/*528*/   storea
/*529*/   loadc2 -184
/*532*/   call
/*533*/   halt
/*534*/   loadcu1 38
/*536*/   loada
/*537*/   loadcu1 95
/*539*/   loadcu1 49
```

```
/*541*/   jl
/*542*/   loadcu1 205
/*544*/   loadcu1 38
/*546*/   loada
/*547*/   loadcu1 41
/*549*/   jl
/*550*/   loadcu1 40
/*552*/   loada
/*553*/   loadcu1 88
/*555*/   loadcu1 33
/*557*/   jl
/*558*/   loadcu1 104
/*560*/   loadcu1 40
/*562*/   loada
/*563*/   loadcu1 25
/*565*/   jl
/*566*/   loadc_1
/*567*/   loadcu1 32
/*569*/   storea
/*570*/   loadcu1 38
/*572*/   loada
/*573*/   loadcu1 40
/*575*/   loada
/*576*/   loadcu1 8
/*578*/   loadc_1
/*579*/   loadc_0
/*580*/   mem2screen
/*581*/   loadc2 -349
/*584*/   call
/*585*/   loadc2 -240
/*588*/   call
/*589*/   halt
/*590*/   loadcu1 38
/*592*/   loada
/*593*/   loadcu1 116
/*595*/   loadc2 -201
/*598*/   jl
/*599*/   loadcu1 171
/*601*/   loadcu1 38
/*603*/   loada
/*604*/   loadc2 397
/*607*/   jl
/*608*/   loadcu1 40
/*610*/   loada

/*611*/   loadcu1 114
/*613*/   loadc2 -219
/*616*/   jl
/*617*/   loadcu1 136
/*619*/   loadcu1 40
/*621*/   loada
/*622*/   loadc2 -228
/*625*/   jl
/*626*/   loadc_1
/*627*/   loadcu1 34
/*629*/   storea
/*630*/   loadc2 -342
/*633*/   call
/*634*/   loadc2 -289
/*637*/   call
/*638*/   halt
/*639*/   loadcu1 38
/*641*/   loada
/*642*/   loadcu1 116
/*644*/   loadcu1 38
/*646*/   jl
/*647*/   loadcu1 171
/*649*/   loadcu1 38
/*651*/   loada
/*652*/   loadc2 684
/*655*/   jl
/*656*/   loadcu1 40
/*658*/   loada
/*659*/   loadcu1 114
/*661*/   loadcu1 21
/*663*/   jl
/*664*/   loadcu1 136
/*666*/   loadcu1 40
/*668*/   loada
/*669*/   loadcu1 13
/*671*/   jl
/*672*/   loadc_0
/*673*/   loadcu1 34
/*675*/   storea
/*676*/   loadc2 -388
/*679*/   call
/*680*/   loadc2 -335
/*683*/   call
/*684*/   halt
```

Appendix C
CVMUI Library (CVMUI Lib)

The CVMUI library contains constant and function definitions that are imported by CVM-UI programs. Note that the CVMUI libraries that are presented in this thesis serve only as an example to demonstrate the concept. Additional libraries may be defined in the future.

C.1 libMisc.cvm

This CVMUI library contains basic definitions about strings, etc.

libMisc_emptyProc This "trivial" procedure does nothing, but returns immediately.

```
.code                           ret
libMisc_emptyProc:
```

libMisc_bytesCp This function copies `len` bytes from the memory address `adrSrc` to `adrTgt`.

```
.code                              load len   dec
.fct libMisc_bytesCp                rdup   store len
  (Int adrTgt, Int adrSrc, Int len) aload1
  {                                load adrTgt
libMisc_bytesCp_1:                 load len
  load len                         astore1
    loadc 0                        loadcr libMisc_bytesCp_1  jmp
    loadcr libMisc_bytesCp_       libMisc_bytesCp_:
    jle                            return
  load adrSrc                    }
```

libMisc_strCp This function copies the CVM string at the memory address `adrSrc` to the memory address `adrTgt`. Note that for the target string always the longer **String** format is chosen. Refer to section 3.1.1 (page 33) for more information on the CVM string formats.

```
.code                                   jne
// strTgt = [0#1, len#2, ...]           libMisc_strCp_g255:
.fct libMisc_strCp                        rskip
(Int adrTgt, Int adrSrc)                  load adrSrc  loadc 0  aload2
{                                         load adrSrc  loadc 2  add
  loadc 0                                 store adrSrc
    load adrTgt                         libMisc_strCp_le255:
    loadc 0                               rdup
    astore1                               load adrTgt  loadc 0  astore2
  load adrTgt  inc  store adrTgt          load adrTgt  loadc 2  add  push
  load adrSrc  loadc 0  aload1            load adrSrc  push
    rdup                                  push
    load adrSrc  inc  store adrSrc        fcall libMisc_bytesCp
    loadc 0                               return
    loadcr libMisc_strCp_le255          }
```

libMisc_strAppChar   This function appends the character **char** to the CVM string at the memory address **adrStr**, if the string has less then **maxLen** characters before the operation. Note that the **String** format of the string must be the longer one. Refer to section 3.1.1 (page 33) for more information on the CVM string formats.

```
.code                                   jle
// adrStr = [0#1, len#2, ...]             load char
.fct libMisc_strAppChar                   load adrStr
(Int adrStr, Int maxLen, Int char)        loadc 3  add
{                                         load strLen  add
  Int strLen                              loadc 0  astore1
  incsp  load adrStr  push                load adrStr  push
    fcall libMisc_strLen                  load strLen  inc  push
    pop  store strLen                     fcall libMisc_strLenSet
  load maxLen                           libMisc_strAppChar_1:
    load strLen                           return
    loadcr libMisc_strAppChar_1         }
```

libMisc_strLen   This function returns the length of the CVM string at the memory address **adrStr**, which is the value of the **length** item in the tuple structure **String**, but not the byte length of the whole tuple structure. Refer to section 3.1.1 (page 33) for more information on the CVM string formats.

```
.code                                   rskip
.fct libMisc_strLen (Int adrStr) Int      load adrStr  inc  loadc 0  aload2
{                                       libMisc_strLen_1:
  load adrStr  loadc 0  aload1  rdup      retstore
    loadc 0  loadcr libMisc_strLen_1  jne return
libMisc_strLen_g255:                    }
```

libMisc_strLenSet   This function writes the value of **strLen** into the **length** item of the CVM string at the memory address **adrStr**. Note that the **String** format of the string must be the longer one. Refer to section 3.1.1 (page 33) for more information on the CVM string formats.

```
.code                               astore1
   // [0, strLen#2, ...]            load strLen
   .fct libMisc_strLenSet              load adrStr   inc
     (Int adrStr, Int strLen)          loadc 0
   {                                   astore2
     loadc 0                           return
       load adrStr                  }
       loadc 0
```

C.2 libGui.cvm

This CVMUI library contains definitions for all user interface components.

Property Offsets of User Interface Components The property values of the user interface components are stored in memory in appropriate tuple structures. The following constants are used to address these property values relatively within the respective tuple structure:

```
.const                                      //////
                                            // Btn {Button}
   //////                                   //////
   // Btn {Button}, Hlk {Hyperlink},
   // Ixt {Text Box}                        libGui_img          16 * _cil
   //////                                   libGui_imgStyle     17 * _cil

   libGui_etOfs        0
   libGui_xOfs         1 * _cil             //////
   libGui_yOfs         2 * _cil             // Hlk {Hyperlink}
   libGui_wOfs         3 * _cil             //////
   libGui_hOfs         4 * _cil
   libGui_fgRedOfs     5 * _cil             libGui_hostAdrOfs     16 * _cil
   libGui_fgGreenOfs   6 * _cil             libGui_serviceNoOfs   17 * _cil
   libGui_fgBlueOfs    7 * _cil
   libGui_bgRedOfs     8 * _cil             //////
   libGui_bgGreenOfs   9 * _cil             // Ixt {Text Box}
   libGui_bgBlueOfs   10 * _cil             //////

   libGui_fcOfs       11 * _cil             libGui_wStrOfs        16 * _cil
   libGui_fsOfs       12 * _cil             libGui_hStrOfs        17 * _cil
   libGui_adrStrOfs   13 * _cil             libGui_yaStrOfs       18 * _cil
   libGui_xStrOfs     14 * _cil             libGui_strLenMaxOfs   19 * _cil
   libGui_yStrOfs     15 * _cil             libGui_wCharOfs       20 * _cil
                                            libGui_strPosOfs      21 * _cil
```

_cil ("CVM integer length") is an integer constant and must be defined in the main CVM-As program that imports these constant definitions. It is equal to the value of cvmIntLen.

Refer to section 3.1.2 (page 33) for more information on cvmIntLen.

The tuple structures for the different user interface component types are defined as follows:

- Page: { Int et; }
  Refer to section 3.1.1 (page 33) for the CVM data type Int. Refer to $<page_{pageNoReq.j}.id>\_<j>\_$prp in the CVMA code template in section 5.5.2 (pages 170 ff.) for the property value et.

- Button (Btn):

  { Int et,
      x, y, w, h,
      fgr, fgb, fgg,
      bgr, bgb, bgg,
      fc, fs,
      str, xStr, yStr,
      img, imgStyle; }

  Refer to $<page_{pageNoReq.j}.id>\_<j>\_<btn.id>\_$prp in the CVMA code template in section 5.5.7 (pages 192 ff.) for the property values.

- Hyperlink (Hlk):

  { Int et,
      x, y, w, h,
      fgr, fgb, fgg,
      bgr, bgb, bgg,
      fc, fs,
      str, xStr, yStr,
      hostAdr, serviceNo; }

  Refer to $<hlk.id>\_$prp in the CVMA code template in section 5.5.6 (pages 187 ff.) for the property values.

- Text Box (Ixt):

  { Int et,
      x, y, w, h,
      fgr, fgb, fgg,
      bgr, bgb, bgg,
      fc, fs,
      str, xStr, yStr,
      wStr, hStr, yaStr,
      strLenMax, wChar, strPos; }

  Refer to $<ixt.id>\_$prp in the CVMA code template in section 5.5.5 (page 182) for the property values.

- Text (Txt): So far, Txt user interface components have no property values.

libGui_linehorizDash This function draws a horizontal dashed line from start point (x, y) to end point (x + w − 1, y).

C.2. libGui.cvm

```
.code                                        linehoriz
.fct libGui_linehorizDash                      load x   inc   inc   store x
  (Int x, Int y, Int w)                        load w   dec   dec   store w
  {                                            loadcr libGui_linehorizDash_1  jmp
libGui_linehorizDash_1:                      libGui_linehorizDash_2:
  load w  loadc 0                              return
    loadcr libGui_linehorizDash_2  jle       }
  load x  load y  loadc 1
```

libGui_linevertDash This function draws a vertical dashed line from start point (x, y) to end point (x, y + h − 1).

```
.code                                        linevert
.fct libGui_linevertDash                       load y   inc   inc   store y
  (Int x, Int y, Int h)                        load h   dec   dec   store h
  {                                            loadcr libGui_linevertDash_1  jmp
libGui_linevertDash_1:                       libGui_linevertDash_2:
  load h  loadc 0                              return
    loadcr libGui_linevertDash_2  jle        }
  load x  load y  loadc 1
```

libGui_rectDash This function draws a dashed rectangle with the upper-left corner at (x, y) and the lower-right corner at (x + w − 1, y + h − 1).

```
.const                                       load x1  push
libGui_rectCornerDash  1                     load y   push
                                             load w1  push
.code                                        fcall libGui_linehorizDash
.fct libGui_rectDash                         load x   push
  (Int x, Int y, Int w, Int h)               load y1  push
  {                                          load h1  push
  Int x1                                     fcall libGui_linevertDash
  Int y1                                     load x1  push
  Int w1                                     load y
  Int h1                                       load h
  load x                                       add   dec   push
    loadc libGui_rectCornerDash  add         load w1  push
    store x1                                 fcall libGui_linehorizDash
  load y                                     load x
    loadc libGui_rectCornerDash  add           load w
    store y1                                   add   dec   push
  load w                                     load y1  push
    loadc 2 * libGui_rectCornerDash          load h1  push
    sub  store w1                            fcall libGui_linevertDash
  load h                                     return
    loadc 2 * libGui_rectCornerDash          }
    sub  store h1
```

libGui_rectIn   This function checks whether the xy coordinate position (x, y) is inside the rectangular area with the upper-left corner at (xr, yr) and the lower-right corner at (xr + wr − 1, yr + hr − 1). If yes, then the function returns 1, otherwise 0.

```
.code                                    load yr   load hr   add  load y
.fct libGui_rectIn                         loadcr libGui_rectIn_0  jle
  (Int x, Int y, Int xr, Int yr,         libGui_rectIn_1:
   Int wr, Int hr) Int                     loadc_1
{                                          loadcr libGui_rectIn_   jmp
  load x   load xr                       libGui_rectIn_0:
    loadcr libGui_rectIn_0  jl             loadc_0
  load xr  load wr  add  load x          libGui_rectIn_:
    loadcr libGui_rectIn_0  jle            retstore
  load y   load yr                         return
    loadcr libGui_rectIn_0  jl           }
```

libGui_mvFcs   This function moves the input focus from the current user interface component to the specified next one. **adrPrpSrc** contains the memory address of the properties of the current user interface component. **adrPrpTgt** contains the memory address of the properties of the next user interface component. **adrUnDrwFcsSrc** contains the memory address of the undraw-focus function of the current user interface component. **adrDrwFcsTgt** contains the memory address of the draw-focus function of the next user interface component.

```
.code                                    sub
.fct libGui_mvFcs                        libGui_mvFcs_1:
  (Int adrPrpSrc, Int adrPrpTgt,           call
   Int adrUnDrwFcsSrc,                     pop  rskip
   Int adrDrwFcsTgt)                       load adrPrpTgt  push
{                                          load adrDrwFcsTgt
  getbp  push                              loadc libGui_mvFcs_2
  load adrPrpTgt  setbp                    sub
  loadc libGui_etOfs  loadr              libGui_mvFcs_2:
    seteventtableadr                       call
  pop  setbp                               pop  rskip
  load adrPrpSrc  push                     return
  load adrUnDrwFcsSrc                    }
  loadc libGui_mvFcs_1
```

libGui_setFcs   This function sets the input focus to the specified user interface component. **adrPrp** contains the memory address of the properties of that user interface component. **adrDrwFcs** contains the memory address of the draw-focus function of that user interface component.

```
.code                                    getbp  push
.fct libGui_setFcs                       load adrPrp  setbp
  (Int adrPrp, Int adrDrwFcs)            loadc libGui_etOfs  loadr
{                                          seteventtableadr
```

```
    pop   setbp                              libGui_setFcs_1:
    load  adrPrp  push                          call
    load  adrDrwFcs                             pop   rskip
    loadc libGui_setFcs_1                       return
    sub                                      }
```

C.3 libGui3D.cvm

This CVMUI library contains definitions for all user interface components with a 3D look.

Constants

```
.const                                    libGui3D_shadeBright  50
libGui3D_shadeDark   40                   libGui3D_shadeNorm   100
```

libGui3D_colorShadeDark This function returns on the register stack the RGB values of the darker shadow color from the color that is given by the RGB values red, green, and blue. The darker shadow color is used together with the brighter shadow color to provide a 3D look for the user interface components.

```
.code                                        loadc libGui3D_shadeNorm -
.fct libGui3D_colorShadeDark                       libGui3D_shadeDark
  (Int red, Int green, Int blue)             mul  loadc libGui3D_shadeNorm  div
  {                                          load blue
  load red                                   loadc libGui3D_shadeNorm -
    loadc libGui3D_shadeNorm -                     libGui3D_shadeDark
          libGui3D_shadeDark                 mul  loadc libGui3D_shadeNorm  div
    mul   loadc libGui3D_shadeNorm   div     return
  load green                                 }
```

libGui3D_colorShadeBright This function returns on the register stack the RGB values of the brighter shadow color from the color that is given by the RGB values red, green, and blue. The brighter shadow color is used together with the darker shadow color to provide a 3D look for the user interface components.

```
.code                                        loadc libGui3D_shadeBright  mul
.fct libGui3D_colorShadeBright               loadc libGui3D_shadeNorm   div
  (Int red, Int green, Int blue)             add
  {                                          load blue
  load red                                     loadc 255  load blue  sub
    loadc 255  load red   sub                  loadc libGui3D_shadeBright  mul
    loadc libGui3D_shadeBright  mul            loadc libGui3D_shadeNorm   div
    loadc libGui3D_shadeNorm   div             add
    add                                        return
  load green                                 }
    loadc 255  load green  sub
```

C.4 libGuiTxtSmp.cvm

This CVMUI library contains definitions for all Txt user interface components with a "simple" (Smp) look.

Constants   The ..._dx and ..._dy constants define the horizontal and vertical space between the borders of the user interface component and its containing text.

```
.const
libGuiTxtSmp_dx   0              libGuiTxtSmp_dw   2 * libGuiTxtSmp_dx
libGuiTxtSmp_dy   0              libGuiTxtSmp_dh   2 * libGuiTxtSmp_dy
```

C.5 libGuiTxt3D.cvm

This CVMUI library contains definitions for all Txt user interface components with a 3D look.

Constants   The ..._dx and ..._dy constants define the horizontal and vertical space between the borders of the user interface component and its containing text.

```
.const
libGuiTxt3D_dx   0               libGuiTxt3D_dw   2 * libGuiTxt3D_dx
libGuiTxt3D_dy   0               libGuiTxt3D_dh   2 * libGuiTxt3D_dy
```

C.6 libGuiTxpSmp.cvm

This CVMUI library contains definitions for all Txp user interface components with a "simple" (Smp) look.

Constants   The ..._dx and ..._dy constants define the horizontal and vertical space between the borders of the user interface component and its containing text.

```
.const
libGuiTxpSmp_dx   0              libGuiTxpSmp_dw   2 * libGuiTxpSmp_dx
libGuiTxpSmp_dy   0              libGuiTxpSmp_dh   2 * libGuiTxpSmp_dy
```

C.7 libGuiTxp3D.cvm

This CVMUI library contains definitions for all Txp user interface components with a 3D look.

Constants   The ..._dx and ..._dy constants define the horizontal and vertical space between the borders of the user interface component and its containing text.

```
.const                                    libGuiTxp3D_dw    2 * libGuiTxp3D_dx
libGuiTxp3D_dx   0                        libGuiTxp3D_dh    2 * libGuiTxp3D_dy
libGuiTxp3D_dy   0
```

C.8 libGuiHlk.cvm

This CVMUI library contains definitions for all `Hlk` user interface components.

libGuiHlk_kp This function defines the implicit event behavior of an `Hlk` user interface component when a `key_pressed` event occurs. `adrPrp` contains the memory address of the properties of that user interface component. Refer to the sections 3.1.6 (pages 45 ff.) and 5.1.1 (page 140) for more information on CVM events and AUI events.

```
.code                                     return
.fct libGuiHlk_kp (Int adrPrp)            libGuiHlk_kp_dwn:
{                                           load adrPrp  push
  loadep1                                   fcall libGuiHlk_dwn
    loadc XK_space                          return
    loadcr libGuiHlk_kp_dwn               }
    je
```

libGuiHlk_dwn This function defines the implicit event behavior of an `Hlk` user interface component after it has been activated by the user of the CVM. `adrPrp` contains the memory address of the properties of that user interface component.

```
.code                                     loadc libGui_serviceNoOfs  loadr
.fct libGuiHlk_dwn (Int adrPrp)           loadc 0
{                                         rcv
  load adrPrp  setbp                      return
  sidzero                                 }
  loadc libGui_hostAdrOfs  loadr
```

C.9 libGuiHlkSmp.cvm

This CVMUI library contains definitions for all `Hlk` user interface components with a "simple" (`Smp`) look.

Constants The ..._dx and ..._dy constants define the horizontal and vertical space between the borders of the user interface component and its containing text.

```
.const                                    libGuiHlkSmp_dw   2 * libGuiHlkSmp_dx
libGuiHlkSmp_dx   0                       libGuiHlkSmp_dh   2 * libGuiHlkSmp_dy
libGuiHlkSmp_dy   0
```

libGuiHlkSmp_drw This function draws an Hlk user interface component. **adrPrp** contains the memory address of the properties of that user interface component.

```
.code                                      loadc libGui_fgGreenOfs  loadr
.fct libGuiHlkSmp_drw (Int adrPrp)         loadc libGui_fgBlueOfs  loadr
{                                          setcolor
  load adrPrp  setbp                       loadc libGui_fcOfs  loadr
////////////                               loadc libGui_fsOfs  loadr
// Background                              setfont
////////////                               loadc libGui_xStrOfs  loadr
  loadc libGui_bgRedOfs  loadr             loadc libGui_yStrOfs  loadr
    loadc libGui_bgGreenOfs  loadr         loadc libGui_adrStrOfs  loadr
    loadc libGui_bgBlueOfs  loadr          textm
  setcolor                               ////////////
  loadc libGui_xOfs  loadr               // Underline
    loadc libGui_yOfs  loadr             ////////////
    loadc libGui_wOfs  loadr               loadc libGui_xOfs  loadr
    loadc libGui_hOfs  loadr               loadc libGui_yStrOfs  loadr  inc
  rectfill                                 loadc libGui_wOfs  loadr
///////                                    linehoriz
// Text                                    return
///////                                  }
  loadc libGui_fgRedOfs  loadr
```

libGuiHlkSmp_drwFcs This function performs on the given Hlk user interface component some drawing operations that indicate to the user that this user interface component currently has input focus. **adrPrp** contains the memory address of the properties of that user interface component.

```
.code                                      setcolor
.fct libGuiHlkSmp_drwFcs (Int adrPrp)      loadc libGui_xOfs  loadr
{                                          loadc libGui_yStrOfs  loadr  inc  inc
  load adrPrp  setbp                       loadc libGui_wOfs  loadr
  loadc libGui_fgRedOfs  loadr             linehoriz
    loadc libGui_fgGreenOfs  loadr         return
    loadc libGui_fgBlueOfs  loadr        }
```

libGuiHlkSmp_unDrwFcs This function performs on the given Hlk user interface component some drawing operations that indicate to the user that this user interface component currently has not input focus any more. **adrPrp** contains the memory address of the properties of that user interface component.

```
.code                                      setcolor
.fct libGuiHlkSmp_unDrwFcs (Int adrPrp)    loadc libGui_xOfs  loadr
{                                          loadc libGui_yStrOfs  loadr  inc  inc
  load adrPrp  setbp                       loadc libGui_wOfs  loadr
  loadc libGui_bgRedOfs  loadr             linehoriz
    loadc libGui_bgGreenOfs  loadr         return
    loadc libGui_bgBlueOfs  loadr        }
```

C.10 libGuiHlk3D.cvm

This CVMUI library contains definitions for all `Hlk` user interface components with a 3D look.

Constants The ..._dx and ..._dy constants define the horizontal and vertical space between the borders of the user interface component and its containing text.

```
.const
libGuiHlk3D_dx   0          libGuiHlk3D_dw   2 * libGuiHlk3D_dx
libGuiHlk3D_dy   0          libGuiHlk3D_dh   2 * libGuiHlk3D_dy
```

libGuiHlk3D_drw This function draws an `Hlk` user interface component. `adrPrp` contains the memory address of the properties of that user interface component.

```
.code                              loadc libGui_yOfs  loadr
.fct libGuiHlk3D_drwFcs (Int adrPrp)  dec  dec  push
{                                  loadc libGui_wOfs  loadr
  load adrPrp  setbp                 loadc 4  add  push
  loadc libGui_fgRedOfs   loadr    loadc libGui_hOfs  loadr
    loadc libGui_fgGreenOfs loadr    loadc 4  add  push
    loadc libGui_fgBlueOfs  loadr    fcall libGui_rectDash
  setcolor                         return
  loadc libGui_xStrOfs  loadr      }
    dec  dec  push
```

libGuiHlk3D_drwFcs This function performs on the given `Hlk` user interface component some drawing operations that indicate to the user that this user interface component currently has input focus. `adrPrp` contains the memory address of the properties of that user interface component.

```
.code                              loadc libGui_yOfs  loadr
.fct libGuiHlk3D_drwFcs (Int adrPrp)  dec  dec  push
{                                  loadc libGui_wOfs  loadr
  load adrPrp  setbp                 loadc 4  add  push
  loadc libGui_fgRedOfs   loadr    loadc libGui_hOfs  loadr
    loadc libGui_fgGreenOfs loadr    loadc 4  add  push
    loadc libGui_fgBlueOfs  loadr    fcall libGui_rectDash
  setcolor                         return
  loadc libGui_xStrOfs  loadr      }
    dec  dec  push
```

libGuiHlk3D_unDrwFcs This function performs on the given `Hlk` user interface component some drawing operations that indicate to the user that this user interface component currently has not input focus any more. `adrPrp` contains the memory address of the properties of that user interface component.

```
.code
.fct libGuiHlk3D_undrwFcs (Int adrPrp)
{
  load adrPrp  setbp
  loadc libGui_bgRedOfs  loadr
    loadc libGui_bgGreenOfs  loadr
    loadc libGui_bgBlueOfs  loadr
  setcolor
  loadc libGui_xStrOfs  loadr
    dec  dec  push
```
```
  loadc libGui_yOfs  loadr
    dec  dec  push
  loadc libGui_wOfs  loadr
    loadc 4  add  push
  loadc libGui_hOfs  loadr
    loadc 4  add  push
  fcall libGui_rectDash
  return
}
```

C.11 libGuiIxt.cvm

This CVMUI library contains definitions for all Ixt user interface components.

libGuiIxt_drwTxt This function draws the text of an Ixt user interface component. adrPrp contains the memory address of the properties of that user interface component. The str property contains the memory address of the text.

```
.code
.fct libGuiIxt_drwTxt (Int adrPrp)
{
  load adrPrp  setbp
  loadc  libGui_fcOfs  loadr
    loadc libGui_fsOfs  loadr
  setfont
  loadc libGui_fgRedOfs  loadr
    loadc libGui_fgGreenOfs  loadr
    loadc libGui_fgBlueOfs  loadr
  setcolor
  loadc libGui_bgRedOfs  loadr
    loadc libGui_bgGreenOfs  loadr
    loadc libGui_bgBlueOfs  loadr
  setbgcolor
  loadc libGui_xStrOfs  loadr
    loadc libGui_yaStrOfs  loadr
```
```
  loadc libGui_wStrOfs  loadr
  loadc libGui_hStrOfs  loadr
  setclip
  loadc libGui_xStrOfs  loadr
    loadc libGui_strPosOfs  loadr
    add
  loadc libGui_yStrOfs  loadr
  loadc  libGui_adrStrOfs  loadr
  textmbg
  loadc 0
  loadc 0
  loadc _cvmScreenWidth
  loadc _cvmScreenHeight
  setclip
  return
}
```

libGuiIxt_drwCr This function draws the text cursor of an Ixt user interface component with its foreground color. adrPrp contains the memory address of the properties of that user interface component.

```
.code
.fct libGuiIxt_drwCr (Int adrPrp)
{
  getbp  push
  load adrPrp  setbp
  loadc libGui_fgRedOfs  loadr
    loadc libGui_fgGreenOfs  loadr
```
```
  loadc libGui_fgBlueOfs  loadr
  setcolor
  pop  setbp
  load adrPrp  push
  fcall libGuiIxt_drwCr_1
  return
}
```

C.11. libGuiIxt.cvm 261

libGuiIxt_unDrwCr This function draws the text cursor of an Ixt user interface component with its background color, i.e., it erases it. adrPrp contains the memory address of the properties of that user interface component.

```
.code                                    loadc libGui_bgBlueOfs   loadr
.fct libGuiIxt_unDrwCr (Int adrPrp)      setcolor
{                                        pop   setbp
  getbp  push                            load adrPrp  push
  load adrPrp  setbp                     fcall libGuiIxt_drwCr_1
  loadc libGui_bgRedOfs    loadr         return
    loadc libGui_bgGreenOfs loadr       }
```

libGuiIxt_drwCr_1 This auxiliary function is called by the functions libGuiIxt_drwCr and libGuiIxt_unDrwCr. adrPrp contains the memory address of the properties of that user interface component.

```
.code                                    mul
.fct libGuiIxt_drwCr_1 (Int adrPrp)      loadc libGui_xStrOfs   loadr  add
{                                        loadc libGui_strPosOfs loadr
  load adrPrp  setbp                     add
  incsp                                  loadc libGui_yaStrOfs  loadr
    loadc libGui_adrStrOfs  loadr        loadc libGui_hStrOfs   loadr
    push                                 linevert
    fcall libMisc_strLen  pop            return
  loadc libGui_wCharOfs  loadr          }
```

libGuiIxt_kp This function defines the implicit event behavior of an Ixt user interface component when a key_pressed event occurs. adrPrp contains the memory address of the properties of that user interface component. Refer to the sections 3.1.6 (pages 45 ff.) and 5.1.1 (page 140) for more information on CVM events and AUI events.

```
.code                                    load adrPrp  setbp
.fct libGuiIxt_kp (Int adrPrp)           incsp
{                                          loadc libGui_adrStrOfs  loadr
  loadep1                                  push
    loadc XK_BackSpace                     fcall libMisc_strLen
    loadcr libGuiIxt_kp_backSpace        pop
    je                                     loadc libGui_strLenMaxOfs  loadr
  loadep1                                  loadcr libGuiIxt_kp_lMaxStrLen
    loadc XK_space                       jl
    loadcr libGuiIxt_kp_notPrintable     pop  return
    jl                                   libGuiIxt_kp_lMaxStrLen:
  loadc XK_asciitilde                      pop  setbp
    loadep1                                load adrPrp  push
    loadcr libGuiIxt_kp_notPrintable       fcall libGuiIxt_unDrwCr
    jl                                     getbp  push
libGuiIxt_kp_printable:                    load adrPrp  setbp
  getbp  push                              loadc libGui_adrStrOfs  loadr  push
```

```
    loadc libGui_strLenMaxOfs  loadr        fcall libGuiIxt_unDrwCr
    push                                    pop
    loadep1  push                           getbp  push
    fcall libMisc_strAppChar                load adrPrp  setbp
  incsp                                     dec rdup
    loadc libGui_adrStrOfs  loadr           loadc libGui_adrStrOfs  loadr
    push                                    push
    fcall libMisc_strLen                    push
    pop                                     fcall libMisc_strLenSet
    loadc libGui_wCharOfs  loadr            loadc libGui_fcOfs  loadr
    mul                                     loadc libGui_fsOfs  loadr
    loadc libGui_wStrOfs  loadr             setfont
    loadcr libGuiIxt_kp_leWidth             loadc libGui_wCharOfs  loadr  mul
    jle                                     loadc libGui_xStrOfs  loadr  add
    loadc libGui_strPosOfs  loadr           loadc libGui_strPosOfs  loadr  add
    loadc libGui_wCharOfs  loadr  sub       loadc libGui_yStrOfs  loadr
    loadc libGui_strPosOfs  storer          textbg " "
libGuiIxt_kp_leWidth:                       loadc 0
    pop  setbp                              loadc libGui_strPosOfs  loadr
    load adrPrp  push                       loadcr libGuiIxt_kp_ge0
    fcall libGuiIxt_drwTxt                  jle
    load adrPrp  push                       loadc libGui_strPosOfs  loadr
    fcall libGuiIxt_drwCr                   loadc libGui_wCharOfs  loadr  add
    return                                  loadc libGui_strPosOfs  storer
libGuiIxt_kp_backSpace:                   libGuiIxt_kp_ge0:
    getbp  push                             pop  setbp
    load adrPrp  setbp                      load adrPrp  push
  incsp                                     fcall libGuiIxt_drwTxt
    loadc libGui_adrStrOfs  loadr           load adrPrp  push
    push                                    fcall libGuiIxt_drwCr
    fcall libMisc_strLen                    return
    pop                                   libGuiIxt_kp_le0:
    rdup                                    rskip
    loadc 0                                 pop  setbp
    loadcr libGuiIxt_kp_le0                 return
    jle                                   libGuiIxt_kp_notPrintable:
    pop  setbp                              return
    push                                  }
    load adrPrp  push
```

C.12 libGuiIxtSmp.cvm

This CVMUI library contains definitions for all Ixt user interface components with a "simple" (Smp) look.

Constants The ..._dx and ..._dy constants define the horizontal and vertical space between the borders of the user interface component and its containing text.

C.12. libGuiIxtSmp.cvm

```
.const
libGuiIxtSmp_dx    2                  libGuiIxtSmp_dw    2 * libGuiIxtSmp_dx
libGuiIxtSmp_dy    2                  libGuiIxtSmp_dh    2 * libGuiIxtSmp_dy
```

libGuiIxtSmp_drw This function draws an `Ixt` user interface component. `adrPrp` contains the memory address of the properties of that user interface component.

```
.code                                 //////////
.fct libGuiIxtSmp_drw (Int adrPrp)      loadc libGui_fgRedOfs    loadr
  {                                       loadc libGui_fgGreenOfs  loadr
  getbp  push                             loadc libGui_fgBlueOfs   loadr
  load adrPrp  setbp                      setcolor
//////////////                          loadc libGui_xOfs    loadr
// Background                             loadc libGui_yOfs    loadr
//////////////                            loadc libGui_wOfs    loadr
  loadc libGui_bgRedOfs    loadr          loadc libGui_hOfs    loadr
    loadc libGui_bgGreenOfs  loadr        rect
    loadc libGui_bgBlueOfs   loadr    //////////////
    setcolor                          // Caption Text
  loadc libGui_xOfs    loadr   inc    //////////////
    loadc libGui_yOfs    loadr   inc    pop  setbp
    loadc libGui_wOfs    loadr   dec  dec   load adrPrp  push
    loadc libGui_hOfs    loadr   dec  dec   fcall libGuiIxt_drwTxt
    rectfill                              return
//////////                                }
// Borders
```

libGuiIxtSmp_drwFcs This function performs on the given `Ixt` user interface component some drawing operations that indicate to the user that this user interface component currently has input focus. `adrPrp` contains the memory address of the properties of that user interface component.

```
.code                                   fcall libGuiIxt_drwCr
.fct libGuiIxtSmp_drwFcs (Int adrPrp)   return
  {                                     }
  load adrPrp  push
```

libGuiIxtSmp_unDrwFcs This function performs on the given `Ixt` user interface component some drawing operations that indicate to the user that this user interface component currently has not input focus. `adrPrp` contains the memory address of the properties of that user interface component.

```
.code                                   fcall libGuiIxt_unDrwCr
.fct libGuiIxtSmp_unDrwFcs (Int adrPrp) return
  {                                     }
  load adrPrp  push
```

C.13 libGuiIxt3D.cvm

This CVMUI library contains definitions for all Ixt user interface components with a 3D look.

Constants The ..._dx and ..._dy constants define the horizontal and vertical space between the borders of the user interface component and its containing text.

```
.const
libGuiIxt3D_dx    4                    libGuiIxt3D_dw    2 * libGuiIxt3D_dx
libGuiIxt3D_dy    4                    libGuiIxt3D_dh    2 * libGuiIxt3D_dy
```

libGuiIxt3D_drw This function draws an Ixt user interface component. `adrPrp` contains the memory address of the properties of that user interface component.

```
.code                                  loadc 1    store libGuiIxt3D_crIsVisible
.fct libGuiIxt3D_drwFcs (Int adrPrp)   loadc libGuiIxt3D_crTimer
  {                                      settimerhandleadr
  load adrPrp   push                   loadc 500  settimerinterval
    fcall libGuiIxt_drwCr              return
  load adrPrp   store libGuiIxt3D_adrPrp }
```

libGuiIxt3D_drwFcs This function performs on the given Ixt user interface component some drawing operations that indicate to the user that this user interface component currently has input focus. `adrPrp` contains the memory address of the properties of that user interface component.

```
.code                                  loadc 1    store libGuiIxt3D_crIsVisible
.fct libGuiIxt3D_drwFcs (Int adrPrp)   loadc libGuiIxt3D_crTimer
  {                                      settimerhandleadr
  load adrPrp   push                   loadc 500  settimerinterval
    fcall libGuiIxt_drwCr              return
  load adrPrp   store libGuiIxt3D_adrPrp }
```

libGuiIxt3D_unDrwFcs This function performs on the given Ixt user interface component some drawing operations that indicate to the user that this user interface component currently has not input focus. `adrPrp` contains the memory address of the properties of that user interface component.

```
.code                                  load adrPrp   push
.fct libGuiIxt3D_unDrwFcs (Int adrPrp)   fcall libGuiIxt_unDrwCr
  {                                    return
  loadc 0   settimerinterval           }
```

libGuiIxt3D_crTimer   This function is called on a timer interrupt. Ixt user interface components with a 3D look are supplied with a blinking cursor. An interval timer is used to make the text cursor blink. Refer to section 3.1.9 (page 57) for more information on the CVM interval timer.

```
.data                                   libGuiIxt3D_crTimer_notVisible:
Int libGuiIxt3D_adrPrp                    loadc 1   store libGuiIxt3D_crIsVisible
Int libGuiIxt3D_crIsVisible               load libGuiIxt3D_adrPrp   push
                                          fcall libGuiIxt_drwCr
.code                                     halt
libGuiIxt3D_crTimer:                    libGuiIxt3D_crTimer_isVisible:
  load libGuiIxt3D_crIsVisible            loadc 0   store libGuiIxt3D_crIsVisible
  loadc 0                                 load libGuiIxt3D_adrPrp   push
  loadcr libGuiIxt3D_crTimer_isVisible    fcall libGuiIxt_unDrwCr
  jne                                     halt
```

C.14 libGuiBtnSmp.cvm

This CVMUI library contains definitions for all **Btn** user interface components with a "simple" (**Smp**) look.

Constants   The ..._dx and ..._dy constants define the horizontal and vertical space between the borders of the user interface component and its containing text.

```
.const                                  libGuiBtnSmp_dw   2 * libGuiBtnSmp_dx
libGuiBtnSmp_dx   3                     libGuiBtnSmp_dh   2 * libGuiBtnSmp_dy
libGuiBtnSmp_dy   2
```

libGuiBtnSmp_drw   This function draws a **Btn** user interface component in the normal, i.e., unpressed, state. **adrPrp** contains the memory address of the properties of that user interface component.

```
.code                                     rectfill
.fct libGuiBtnSmp_drw (Int adrPrp)        //////////
{                                         // Borders
  load adrPrp   setbp                     //////////
//////////////                            loadc libGui_fgRedOfs   loadr
// Background                             loadc libGui_fgGreenOfs loadr
//////////////                            loadc libGui_fgBlueOfs  loadr
  loadc libGui_bgRedOfs   loadr           setcolor
    loadc libGui_bgGreenOfs loadr         loadc libGui_xOfs   loadr
    loadc libGui_bgBlueOfs  loadr         loadc libGui_yOfs   loadr
    setcolor                              loadc libGui_wOfs   loadr
  loadc libGui_xOfs   loadr               loadc libGui_hOfs   loadr
    loadc libGui_yOfs   loadr             rect
    loadc libGui_wOfs   loadr           ////////////////
    loadc libGui_hOfs   loadr           // Caption Text
```

```
//////////////                          loadc libGui_yStrOfs   loadr
  loadc libGui_fcOfs  loadr             loadc libGui_adrStrOfs loadr
  loadc libGui_fsOfs  loadr             textm
  setfont                               return
  loadc libGui_xStrOfs  loadr         }
```

libGuiBtnSmp_drwDwn   This function draws a `Btn` user interface component in the pressed state. `adrPrp` contains the memory address of the properties of that user interface component.

```
.code                                   loadc libGui_bgGreenOfs  loadr
.fct libGuiBtnSmp_drwDwn (Int adrPrp)   loadc libGui_bgBlueOfs   loadr
{                                       setcolor
  load adrPrp  setbp                    loadc libGui_xOfs  loadr
//////////////                          loadc libGui_yOfs  loadr
// Background                           loadc libGui_wOfs  loadr
//////////////                          loadc libGui_hOfs  loadr
  loadc libGui_fgRedOfs    loadr        rect
    loadc libGui_fgGreenOfs  loadr    ///////////////
    loadc libGui_fgBlueOfs   loadr    // Caption Text
  setcolor                            ///////////////
  loadc libGui_xOfs  loadr              loadc libGui_fcOfs  loadr
    loadc libGui_yOfs  loadr            loadc libGui_fsOfs  loadr
    loadc libGui_wOfs  loadr            setfont
    loadc libGui_hOfs  loadr            loadc libGui_xStrOfs    loadr
  rectfill                              loadc libGui_yStrOfs    loadr
//////////                              loadc libGui_adrStrOfs  loadr
// Borders                              textm
//////////                              return
  loadc libGui_bgRedOfs  loadr        }
```

libGuiBtnSmp_drwFcs   This function performs on the given `Btn` user interface component some drawing operations that indicate to the user that this user interface component currently has input focus. `adrPrp` contains the memory address of the properties of that user interface component.

```
.code                                   loadc libGui_xOfs  loadr  inc
.fct libGuiBtnSmp_drwFcs (Int adrPrp)   loadc libGui_yOfs  loadr  inc
{                                       loadc libGui_wOfs  loadr  dec  dec
  load adrPrp  setbp                    loadc libGui_hOfs  loadr  dec  dec
  loadc libGui_fgRedOfs    loadr        rect
    loadc libGui_fgGreenOfs  loadr      return
    loadc libGui_fgBlueOfs   loadr    }
  setcolor
```

libGuiBtnSmp_unDrwFcs   This function performs on the given `Btn` user interface component some drawing operations that indicate to the user that this user interface component currently has not input focus. `adrPrp` contains the memory address of the properties of that user interface component.

```
.code                                    loadc libGui_xOfs  loadr  inc
.fct libGuiBtnSmp_unDrwFcs (Int adrPrp)  loadc libGui_yOfs  loadr  inc
{                                        loadc libGui_wOfs  loadr  dec  dec
  load adrPrp  setbp                     loadc libGui_hOfs  loadr  dec  dec
  loadc libGui_bgRedOfs    loadr         rect
    loadc libGui_bgGreenOfs  loadr       return
    loadc libGui_bgBlueOfs   loadr       }
  setcolor
```

libGuiBtnSmp_dwn This function defines the implicit event behavior of a `Btn` user interface component when an `evDwn` event occurs. `adrPrp` contains the memory address of the properties of that user interface component. Refer to section 5.1.1 (page 140) for more information on AUI events.

```
.code                               load adrPrp  push
.fct libGuiBtnSmp_dwn (Int adrPrp)    fcall libGuiBtnSmp_drwFcs
{                                   return
  load adrPrp  push                 }
  fcall libGuiBtnSmp_drwDwn
```

libGuiBtnSmp_up This function defines the implicit event behavior of a `Btn` user interface component when an `evUp` event occurs. `adrPrp` contains the memory address of the properties of that user interface component. Refer to section 5.1.1 (page 140) for more information on AUI events.

```
.code                              load adrPrp  push
.fct libGuiBtnSmp_up (Int adrPrp)    fcall libGuiBtnSmp_drwFcs
{                                  return
  load adrPrp  push                }
  fcall libGuiBtnSmp_drw
```

C.15 libGuiBtn3D.cvm

This CVMUI library contains definitions for all `Btn` user interface components with a 3D look.

Constants The ..._dx and ..._dy constants define the horizontal and vertical space between the borders of the user interface component and its containing text.

```
.const                          libGuiBtn3D_dh     2 * libGuiBtn3D_dy
libGuiBtn3D_dx      4
libGuiBtn3D_dy      4           libGuiBtn3D_dxFcs  3
                                libGuiBtn3D_dyFcs  3
libGuiBtn3D_dw      2 * libGuiBtn3D_dx
```

libGuiBtn3D_drw   This function draws a Btn user interface component in the normal, i.e., unpressed, state. adrPrp contains the memory address of the properties of that user interface component.

```
.code
.fct libGuiBtn3D_drw (Int adrPrp)
{
  load adrPrp  setbp
  //////////////
  // Background
  //////////////
    loadc libGui_bgRedOfs   loadr
    loadc libGui_bgGreenOfs loadr
    loadc libGui_bgBlueOfs  loadr
    setcolor
    loadc libGui_xOfs loadr
    loadc libGui_yOfs loadr
    loadc libGui_wOfs loadr
    loadc libGui_hOfs loadr
    rectfill
  //////////
  // Borders
  //////////
    loadc libGui_bgRedOfs   loadr push
    loadc libGui_bgGreenOfs loadr push
    loadc libGui_bgBlueOfs  loadr push
    fcall libGui3D_colorShadeDark
    setcolor
    loadc libGui_xOfs loadr
    loadc libGui_yOfs loadr
    loadc libGui_hOfs loadr
    add dec
    loadc libGui_wOfs loadr
    linehoriz
    loadc libGui_xOfs loadr inc
    loadc libGui_yOfs loadr
    loadc libGui_hOfs loadr
    add dec dec
    loadc libGui_wOfs loadr dec
    linehoriz
    loadc libGui_xOfs loadr
    loadc libGui_wOfs loadr
    add dec
    loadc libGui_yOfs loadr
    loadc libGui_hOfs loadr
    linevert
    loadc libGui_xOfs loadr
    loadc libGui_wOfs loadr
    add dec dec
    loadc libGui_yOfs loadr inc
    loadc libGui_hOfs loadr dec
    linevert
    loadc libGui_bgRedOfs   loadr push
    loadc libGui_bgGreenOfs loadr push
    loadc libGui_bgBlueOfs  loadr push
    fcall libGui3D_colorShadeBright
    setcolor
    loadc libGui_xOfs loadr
    loadc libGui_yOfs loadr
    loadc libGui_wOfs loadr dec
    linehoriz
    loadc libGui_xOfs loadr
    loadc libGui_yOfs loadr inc
    loadc libGui_wOfs loadr dec dec
    linehoriz
    loadc libGui_xOfs loadr
    loadc libGui_yOfs loadr
    loadc libGui_hOfs loadr dec
    linevert
    loadc libGui_xOfs loadr inc
    loadc libGui_yOfs loadr
    loadc libGui_hOfs loadr dec dec
    linevert
  //////////////////
  // Caption Text
  //////////////////
    loadc  libGui_fcOfs loadr
    loadc  libGui_fsOfs loadr
    setfont
    loadc libGui_fgRedOfs   loadr
    loadc libGui_fgGreenOfs loadr
    loadc libGui_fgBlueOfs  loadr
    setcolor
    loadc libGui_xStrOfs loadr
    loadc libGui_yStrOfs loadr
    loadc  libGui_adrStrOfs loadr
    textm
    return
}
```

libGuiBtn3D_drwDwn   This function draws a Btn user interface component in the pressed state. adrPrp contains the memory address of the properties of that user interface

C.15. libGuiBtn3D.cvm

component.

```
.code
.fct libGuiBtn3D_drwDwn (Int adrPrp)
{
load adrPrp    setbp
//////////////
// Background
//////////////
  loadc libGui_bgRedOfs   loadr
    loadc libGui_bgGreenOfs loadr
    loadc libGui_bgBlueOfs  loadr
    setcolor
  loadc libGui_xOfs   loadr
    loadc libGui_yOfs   loadr
    loadc libGui_wOfs   loadr
    loadc libGui_hOfs   loadr
    rectfill
//////////
// Borders
//////////
  loadc libGui_bgRedOfs   loadr  push
    loadc libGui_bgGreenOfs loadr  push
    loadc libGui_bgBlueOfs  loadr  push
    fcall libGui3D_colorShadeBright
    setcolor
  loadc libGui_xOfs   loadr
    loadc libGui_yOfs   loadr
    loadc libGui_hOfs   loadr
    add dec
    loadc libGui_wOfs   loadr
    linehoriz
  loadc libGui_xOfs   loadr  inc
    loadc libGui_yOfs   loadr
    loadc libGui_hOfs   loadr
    add dec dec
    loadc libGui_wOfs   loadr  dec
    linehoriz
  loadc libGui_xOfs   loadr
    loadc libGui_wOfs   loadr
    add dec
    loadc libGui_yOfs   loadr
    loadc libGui_hOfs   loadr
    linevert
  loadc libGui_xOfs   loadr
    loadc libGui_wOfs   loadr
    add dec dec
    loadc libGui_yOfs   loadr
    loadc libGui_hOfs   loadr   loadr   dec
    linevert
  loadc libGui_bgRedOfs   loadr  push
    loadc libGui_bgGreenOfs loadr  push
    loadc libGui_bgBlueOfs  loadr  push
    fcall libGui3D_colorShadeDark
    setcolor
  loadc libGui_xOfs   loadr
    loadc libGui_yOfs   loadr
    loadc libGui_wOfs   loadr  dec
    linehoriz
  loadc libGui_xOfs   loadr
    loadc libGui_yOfs   loadr  inc
    loadc libGui_wOfs   loadr  dec dec
    linehoriz
  loadc libGui_xOfs   loadr
    loadc libGui_yOfs   loadr
    loadc libGui_hOfs   loadr  dec
    linevert
  loadc libGui_xOfs   loadr  inc
    loadc libGui_yOfs   loadr
    loadc libGui_hOfs   loadr  dec dec
    linevert
////////////////
// Caption Text
////////////////
  loadc libGui_fcOfs   loadr
    loadc libGui_fsOfs   loadr
    setfont
  loadc libGui_fgRedOfs   loadr
    loadc libGui_fgGreenOfs loadr
    loadc libGui_fgBlueOfs  loadr
    setcolor
  loadc libGui_xStrOfs   loadr  inc
    loadc libGui_yStrOfs   loadr  inc
    loadc libGui_adrStrOfs loadr
    textm
  return
}
```

libGuiBtn3D_drwFcs This function performs on the given Btn user interface component some drawing operations that indicate to the user that this user interface component currently has input focus. adrPrp contains the memory address of the properties of that user interface component.

```
.code
.fct libGuiBtn3D_drwFcs (Int adrPrp)
{
  load adrPrp  setbp
//////////
// Borders
//////////
  loadc libGui_fgRedOfs  loadr
    loadc libGui_fgGreenOfs  loadr
    loadc libGui_fgBlueOfs  loadr
    setcolor
  loadc libGui_xOfs  loadr
    loadc libGui_yOfs  loadr
    loadc libGui_wOfs  loadr
    loadc libGui_hOfs  loadr
    rect
//////////////////
```

```
// Caption Text
//////////////////
  loadc libGui_xOfs  loadr
    loadc libGuiBtn3D_dxFcs
    add  push
  loadc libGui_yOfs  loadr
    loadc libGuiBtn3D_dyFcs
    add  push
  loadc libGui_wOfs  loadr
    loadc libGuiBtn3D_dxFcs
    loadc 2  mul  sub  push
  loadc libGui_hOfs  loadr
    loadc libGuiBtn3D_dyFcs
    loadc 2  mul  sub  push
    fcall libGui_rectDash
  return
}
```

libGuiBtn3D_unDrwFcs This function performs on the given **Btn** user interface component some drawing operations that indicate to the user that this user interface component currently has not input focus. **adrPrp** contains the memory address of the properties of that user interface component.

```
.code
.fct libGuiBtn3D_unDrwFcs (Int adrPrp)
{
  load adrPrp  setbp
//////////
// Borders
//////////
  loadc libGui_bgRedOfs  loadr  push
    loadc libGui_bgGreenOfs  loadr  push
    loadc libGui_bgBlueOfs  loadr  push
    fcall libGui3D_colorShadeDark
    setcolor
  loadc libGui_xOfs  loadr
    loadc libGui_yOfs  loadr
      loadc libGui_hOfs  loadr  add  dec
    loadc libGui_wOfs  loadr
    linehoriz
  loadc libGui_xOfs  loadr
      loadc libGui_wOfs  loadr  add  dec
    loadc libGui_yOfs  loadr
    loadc libGui_hOfs  loadr
    linevert
  loadc libGui_bgRedOfs  loadr  push
    loadc libGui_bgGreenOfs  loadr  push
    loadc libGui_bgBlueOfs  loadr  push
    fcall libGui3D_colorShadeBright
    setcolor
```

```
  loadc libGui_xOfs  loadr
    loadc libGui_yOfs  loadr
    loadc libGui_wOfs  loadr  dec
    linehoriz
  loadc libGui_xOfs  loadr
    loadc libGui_yOfs  loadr
    loadc libGui_hOfs  loadr  dec
    linevert
//////////////////
// Caption Text
//////////////////
  loadc libGui_xOfs  loadr
    loadc libGuiBtn3D_dxFcs
    add  push
  loadc libGui_yOfs  loadr
    loadc libGuiBtn3D_dyFcs
    add  push
  loadc libGui_wOfs  loadr
    loadc libGuiBtn3D_dxFcs
    loadc 2  mul  sub  push
  loadc libGui_hOfs  loadr
    loadc libGuiBtn3D_dyFcs
    loadc 2  mul  sub  push
    fcall libGui_rectDash
  return
}
```

C.15. libGuiBtn3D.cvm 271

libGuiBtn3D_dwn   This function defines the implicit event behavior of a `Btn` user interface component when an `evDwn` event occurs. `adrPrp` contains the memory address of the properties of that user interface component. Refer to section 5.1.1 (page 140) for more information on AUI events.

```
.code                                    load adrPrp  push
.fct libGuiBtn3D_dwn (Int adrPrp)          fcall libGuiBtn3D_drwFcs
{                                        return
  load adrPrp  push                      }
    fcall libGuiBtn3D_drwDwn
```

libGuiBtn3D_up   This function defines the implicit event behavior of a `Btn` user interface component when an `evUp` event occurs. `adrPrp` contains the memory address of the properties of that user interface component. Refer to section 5.1.1 (page 140) for more information on AUI events.

```
.code                                    load adrPrp  push
.fct libGuiBtn3D_up (Int adrPrp)           fcall libGuiBtn3D_drwFcs
{                                        return
  load adrPrp  push                      }
    fcall libGuiBtn3D_drw
```

Appendix D

CVM Packet Server: Example

The following code listings and screen shots refer to the example in section 5.1.4 (page 149).

D.1 Generated Part of the Service Instance

The generated part of the service instance is as follows:

```
#include "_svcInst.h"

//////////////
// Page Numbers
//////////////

enum { _svcInst_p0,
       _svcInst_p1,
       _svcInst_pNotExist,
       _svcInst_pIllegal };

/////////////////
// ServerCodeMisc
/////////////////

///////////////////
// ServerActionsCmd
///////////////////

#define _svcInst_svcCmd_Reset   0
#define _svcInst_svcCmd_Submit  1

int _svcInst_actionsCmd (int svcCmdIdx)
  { dprint {
    switch (svcCmdIdx)
      {
      case _svcInst_svcCmd_Reset:
{
```

D.1. Generated Part of the Service Instance 273

```
  printf("svcCmd_Reset\n");
  svcVar_reset();
  printf("name = \"%s\", email = \"%s\"\n",
         svcVarStr_get("name"), svcVarStr_get("email"));
}
      break;

    case _svcInst_svcCmd_Submit:
{
printf ("svcCmd_Submit\n");
  svcVar_save();
  printf("name = \"%s\", email = \"%s\"\n",
         svcVarStr_get("name"), svcVarStr_get("email"));
}
      break;
    }
  }}


////////////////////
// ServerActionsPage
////////////////////

int _svcInst_actionsPage (int pageNow, int pageReq)
  { dprint {
  int pageNext = pageReq;
  if (pageNow == _svcInst_pageNoNull &&
      pageReq == _svcInst_p0)
    {
    printf("-> p0\n");
    }
    else if (pageNow == _svcInst_p0 &&
             pageReq == _svcInst_p1)
    {
    printf("p0 -> p1\n");
    }
    else if (true &&
             pageReq < _svcInst_p0 || pageReq > _svcInst_pIllegal)
    {
    pageNext = _svcInst_pNotExist;
    }
    else if (true &&
             pageReq == _svcInst_pNotExist)
    {
    pageNext = _svcInst_pIllegal;
    }
    else if (true &&
             true)
    {
    }
    if (pageNext < _svcInst_p0 || pageNext > _svcInst_pIllegal)
    { pageNext = _svcInst_pageNoNull; }
```

```
    return pageNext;
}}
```

D.2 Generated CVM Packets

It depends on the client capabilities whether the AUI pages are customized during the generation of the CVM packets, or not. In the following, both cases are illustrated:

D.2.1 Without Customization

Without customization, for each AUI page only one subpage is generated which is identical to the respective AUI page. Each generated subpage is translated into a CVMUI page using the 3D look. CVM screenshots of the two AUI pages can be found in section 5.1 (pages 149 ff.).

AUI page p0: CVMUI page p0_0 The generated CVM packet for the AUI page p0 contains 3792 bytes and is as follows:

```
.16Bit                                    .data
                                          Int   _subpageNo
.code
   loadcr p0_0_main                       /////////////////////
   jmp                                    // Service Commands
                                          /////
/////////////////////
// Misc                                   .const
/////                                     svcCmd_Reset    0
                                          svcCmd_Submit   1
.const
_cil              2                       /////////////////////
_cvmScreenWidth   250                     // Service Variables
_cvmScreenHeight  150                     /////

.data                                     .const
String  _hostAdrSrv    "127.0.0.1"        _svIdxLen       1
                                          _svIdx_name     1
/////////////////////                     _svIdx_email    2
// Page Numbers
/////                                     .data
                                          Int   _svBufIdx    0
.const                                    Bytes _svBuf      _svIdxLen +
_pageNo       0                              p0_0_ixtName_svBufLen + _svIdxLen
_p0           0                              + p0_0_ixtEmail_svBufLen +
_p1           1                              _svIdxLen + 2
_pNotExist    2
_pIllegal     3                           .code
                                          .fct _svBufIdx_reset ()
```

```
{
loadc_0
store _svBufIdx
return
}

.code
.fct _svBuf_svcCmd_write (Int
    svcCmdIdx)
{
loadc_0
loadc _svBuf
load _svBufIdx
astore1
load _svBufIdx
loadc _svIdxLen
add
store _svBufIdx
load svcCmdIdx
loadc _svBuf
load _svBufIdx
astore2
load _svBufIdx
loadc 2
add
store _svBufIdx
return
}

.code
.fct _svBuf_write ()
{
fcall _svBufIdx_reset
fcall p0_0_svBuf_write
return
}

//////////////////////
// p0_0: Attributes
/////

.const
p0_0_x      0
p0_0_y      0
p0_0_w      _cvmScreenWidth
p0_0_h      _cvmScreenHeight
p0_0_fgr    0
p0_0_fgg    0
p0_0_fgb    0
p0_0_bgr    222
p0_0_bgg    218
p0_0_bgb    210
p0_0_fc     fcHelvetica
p0_0_fs     12
p0_0_img    ""
p0_0_imgStyle  0

.data
Bytes p0_0_prp   [ p0_0_et ]
Int   p0_0_bInit  0

//////////////////////
// p0_0: Misc
/////

.code
p0_0_main:
  loadc_0
  store _subpageNo
  fcall p0_0_init
  fcall p0_0_drw
  loadc p0_0_ixtName_prp
  push
  loadc libGuiIxt3D_drwFcs
  push
  fcall libGui_setFcs
  enableevents
  halt

.code
.fct p0_0_init ()
{
  load p0_0_bInit
  loadc_0
  loadcr p0_0_init_1
  jne
  fcall p0_0_ixtName_init
  fcall p0_0_ixtEmail_init
  loadc_1
  store p0_0_bInit
p0_0_init_1:
  return
}

.code
.fct p0_0_drw ()
{
  loadc p0_0_bgr
  loadc p0_0_bgg
  loadc p0_0_bgb
  setcolor
  loadc p0_0_x
```

```
loadc p0_0_y
loadc p0_0_w
loadc p0_0_h
rectfill
fcall p0_0_txtTitle_drw
fcall p0_0_txpIntro_drw
fcall p0_0_txtName_drw
loadc p0_0_ixtName_prp
push
fcall libGuiIxt3D_drw
fcall p0_0_txtEmail_drw
loadc p0_0_ixtEmail_prp
push
fcall libGuiIxt3D_drw
loadc p0_0_btnReset_prp
push
fcall libGuiBtn3D_drw
loadc p0_0_btnSubmit_prp
push
fcall libGuiBtn3D_drw
return
}

//////////////////
// p0_0: Service Variables
/////

.code
.fct p0_0_svBuf_write ()
{
fcall p0_0_ixtName_svBuf_write
fcall p0_0_ixtEmail_svBuf_write
return
}

//////////////////
// p0_0: Events
/////

.data
EventTable p0_0_et   [
  key_pressed, p0_0_kp,
  mouse_pressed_left, p0_0_mpl ]

.code
p0_0_kp:
  loadep1
  loadc XK_Tab
  loadcr p0_0_kp_tab
  je
  halt

p0_0_kp_tab:
  loadc p0_0_prp
  push
  loadc p0_0_ixtName_prp
  push
  loadc libMisc_emptyProc
  push
  loadc libGuiIxt3D_drwFcs
  push
  fcall libGui_mvFcs
  halt

.code
p0_0_mpl:
  loadep1
  push
  loadep2
  push
  loadc p0_0_prp
  push
  loadc libMisc_emptyProc
  push
  fcall p0_0_mplFcs
  halt

.code
.fct p0_0_mplFcs (Int x, Int y, Int
       adrPrpSrc, Int adrUnDrwFcsSrc)
{
incsp
load x
push
load y
push
loadc p0_0_ixtName_x
push
loadc p0_0_ixtName_y
push
loadc p0_0_ixtName_w
push
loadc p0_0_ixtName_h
push
fcall libGui_rectIn
pop
loadc_0
loadcr p0_0_mplFcs_35
je
load adrPrpSrc
push
loadc p0_0_ixtName_prp
push
```

D.2. Generated CVM Packets

```
load adrUnDrwFcsSrc
push
loadc libGuiIxt3D_drwFcs
push
fcall libGui_mvFcs
return
p0_0_mplFcs_35:
  incsp
  load x
  push
  load y
  push
  loadc p0_0_ixtEmail_x
  push
  loadc p0_0_ixtEmail_y
  push
  loadc p0_0_ixtEmail_w
  push
  loadc p0_0_ixtEmail_h
  push
  fcall libGui_rectIn
  pop
  loadc_0
  loadcr p0_0_mplFcs_36
  je
  load adrPrpSrc
  push
  loadc p0_0_ixtEmail_prp
  push
  load adrUnDrwFcsSrc
  push
  loadc libGuiIxt3D_drwFcs
  push
  fcall libGui_mvFcs
  return
p0_0_mplFcs_36:
  incsp
  load x
  push
  load y
  push
  loadc p0_0_btnReset_x
  push
  loadc p0_0_btnReset_y
  push
  loadc p0_0_btnReset_w
  push
  loadc p0_0_btnReset_h
  push
  fcall libGui_rectIn
  pop
  loadc_0
  loadcr p0_0_mplFcs_37
  je
  load adrPrpSrc
  push
  loadc p0_0_btnReset_prp
  push
  load adrUnDrwFcsSrc
  push
  loadc libGuiBtn3D_drwFcs
  push
  fcall libGui_mvFcs
  fcall p0_0_btnReset_evDwn
  return
p0_0_mplFcs_37:
  incsp
  load x
  push
  load y
  push
  loadc p0_0_btnSubmit_x
  push
  loadc p0_0_btnSubmit_y
  push
  loadc p0_0_btnSubmit_w
  push
  loadc p0_0_btnSubmit_h
  push
  fcall libGui_rectIn
  pop
  loadc_0
  loadcr p0_0_mplFcs_38
  je
  load adrPrpSrc
  push
  loadc p0_0_btnSubmit_prp
  push
  load adrUnDrwFcsSrc
  push
  loadc libGuiBtn3D_drwFcs
  push
  fcall libGui_mvFcs
  fcall p0_0_btnSubmit_evDwn
  return
p0_0_mplFcs_38:
  return
}

////////////////////
// p0_0_txtTitle: Attributes
/////
```

```
.const
p0_0_txtTitle_x    82
p0_0_txtTitle_y    5
p0_0_txtTitle_w    p0_0_txtTitle_wStr +
    p0_0_txtTitle_dw
p0_0_txtTitle_h    p0_0_txtTitle_hStr +
    p0_0_txtTitle_dh
p0_0_txtTitle_fgr    p0_0_fgr
p0_0_txtTitle_fgg    p0_0_fgg
p0_0_txtTitle_fgb    p0_0_fgb
p0_0_txtTitle_bgr    p0_0_bgr
p0_0_txtTitle_bgg    p0_0_bgg
p0_0_txtTitle_bgb    p0_0_bgb
p0_0_txtTitle_fc     fcHelveticaBold
p0_0_txtTitle_fs     14
p0_0_txtTitle_str    "Registration"
p0_0_txtTitle_yStr   p0_0_txtTitle_y +
    p0_0_txtTitle_fa - 1 +
    p0_0_txtTitle_dy
p0_0_txtTitle_xStr   p0_0_txtTitle_x +
    p0_0_txtTitle_dx
p0_0_txtTitle_wStr
    textWidth(p0_0_txtTitle_str,
    p0_0_txtTitle_fc,
    p0_0_txtTitle_fs)
p0_0_txtTitle_hStr
    textHeight(p0_0_txtTitle_str,
    p0_0_txtTitle_fc,
    p0_0_txtTitle_fs, 0)
p0_0_txtTitle_fa
    fontAscent(p0_0_txtTitle_fc,
    p0_0_txtTitle_fs)
p0_0_txtTitle_dx    libGuiTxt3D_dx
p0_0_txtTitle_dy    libGuiTxt3D_dy
p0_0_txtTitle_dw    libGuiTxt3D_dw
p0_0_txtTitle_dh    libGuiTxt3D_dh

///////////////////
// p0_0_txtTitle: Misc
/////

.code
.fct p0_0_txtTitle_drw ()
  {
  loadc p0_0_txtTitle_fgr
  loadc p0_0_txtTitle_fgg
  loadc p0_0_txtTitle_fgb
  setcolor
  loadc p0_0_txtTitle_bgr
  loadc p0_0_txtTitle_bgg
  loadc p0_0_txtTitle_bgb
  setbgcolor
  loadc p0_0_txtTitle_fc
  loadc p0_0_txtTitle_fs
  setfont
  loadc p0_0_txtTitle_xStr
  loadc p0_0_txtTitle_yStr
  textbg p0_0_txtTitle_str
  return
  }

///////////////////
// p0_0_txpIntro: Attributes
/////

.const
p0_0_txpIntro_x    10
p0_0_txpIntro_y    26
p0_0_txpIntro_w    230
p0_0_txpIntro_h    p0_0_txpIntro_hStr +
    p0_0_txpIntro_dh
p0_0_txpIntro_fgr    p0_0_fgr
p0_0_txpIntro_fgg    p0_0_fgg
p0_0_txpIntro_fgb    p0_0_fgb
p0_0_txpIntro_bgr    p0_0_bgr
p0_0_txpIntro_bgg    p0_0_bgg
p0_0_txpIntro_bgb    p0_0_bgb
p0_0_txpIntro_fc     p0_0_fc
p0_0_txpIntro_fs     p0_0_fs
p0_0_txpIntro_strInit    "Welcome to
    the registration form. Please
    enter your name and email
    address:"
p0_0_txpIntro_str
    textBreakLines(p0_0_txpIntro_strInit,
    p0_0_txpIntro_fc,
    p0_0_txpIntro_fs,
    p0_0_txpIntro_w)
p0_0_txpIntro_yStr   p0_0_txpIntro_y +
    p0_0_txpIntro_fa - 1 +
    p0_0_txpIntro_dy
p0_0_txpIntro_xStr   p0_0_txpIntro_x +
    p0_0_txpIntro_dx
p0_0_txpIntro_wStr   p0_0_txpIntro_w -
    p0_0_txpIntro_dw
p0_0_txpIntro_hStr
    textHeight(p0_0_txpIntro_str,
    p0_0_txpIntro_fc,
    p0_0_txpIntro_fs, 0)
p0_0_txpIntro_fa
    fontAscent(p0_0_txpIntro_fc,
    p0_0_txpIntro_fs)
```

D.2. Generated CVM Packets

```
p0_0_txpIntro_dx     libGuiTxp3D_dx
p0_0_txpIntro_dy     libGuiTxp3D_dy
p0_0_txpIntro_dw     libGuiTxp3D_dw
p0_0_txpIntro_dh     libGuiTxp3D_dh

///////////////////
// p0_0_txpIntro: Misc
/////

.code
.fct p0_0_txpIntro_drw ()
 {
  loadc p0_0_txpIntro_fgr
  loadc p0_0_txpIntro_fgg
  loadc p0_0_txpIntro_fgb
  setcolor
  loadc p0_0_txpIntro_bgr
  loadc p0_0_txpIntro_bgg
  loadc p0_0_txpIntro_bgb
  setbgcolor
  loadc p0_0_txpIntro_fc
  loadc p0_0_txpIntro_fs
  setfont
  loadc p0_0_txpIntro_xStr
  setxtextline
  loadc p0_0_txpIntro_yStr
  textpbg p0_0_txpIntro_str
  return
 }

///////////////////
// p0_0_txtName: Attributes
/////

.const
p0_0_txtName_x    10
p0_0_txtName_y    p0_0_txtName_yStr -
    p0_0_txtName_fa + 1 -
    p0_0_txtName_dy
p0_0_txtName_w    p0_0_txtName_wStr +
    p0_0_txtName_dw
p0_0_txtName_h    p0_0_txtName_hStr +
    p0_0_txtName_dh
p0_0_txtName_fgr    p0_0_fgr
p0_0_txtName_fgg    p0_0_fgg
p0_0_txtName_fgb    p0_0_fgb
p0_0_txtName_bgr    p0_0_bgr
p0_0_txtName_bgg    p0_0_bgg
p0_0_txtName_bgb    p0_0_bgb
p0_0_txtName_fc     p0_0_fc
p0_0_txtName_fs     p0_0_fs

p0_0_txtName_str   "Name"
p0_0_txtName_yStr   72
p0_0_txtName_xStr   p0_0_txtName_x +
    p0_0_txtName_dx
p0_0_txtName_wStr
    textWidth(p0_0_txtName_str,
    p0_0_txtName_fc, p0_0_txtName_fs)
p0_0_txtName_hStr
    textHeight(p0_0_txtName_str,
    p0_0_txtName_fc, p0_0_txtName_fs,
    0)
p0_0_txtName_fa
    fontAscent(p0_0_txtName_fc,
    p0_0_txtName_fs)
p0_0_txtName_dx    libGuiTxt3D_dx
p0_0_txtName_dy    libGuiTxt3D_dy
p0_0_txtName_dw    libGuiTxt3D_dw
p0_0_txtName_dh    libGuiTxt3D_dh

///////////////////
// p0_0_txtName: Misc
/////

.code
.fct p0_0_txtName_drw ()
 {
  loadc p0_0_txtName_fgr
  loadc p0_0_txtName_fgg
  loadc p0_0_txtName_fgb
  setcolor
  loadc p0_0_txtName_bgr
  loadc p0_0_txtName_bgg
  loadc p0_0_txtName_bgb
  setbgcolor
  loadc p0_0_txtName_fc
  loadc p0_0_txtName_fs
  setfont
  loadc p0_0_txtName_xStr
  loadc p0_0_txtName_yStr
  textbg p0_0_txtName_str
  return
 }

///////////////////
// p0_0_ixtName: Attributes
/////

.const
p0_0_ixtName_x    52
p0_0_ixtName_y    59
p0_0_ixtName_w    150
```

```
p0_0_ixtName_h      p0_0_ixtName_hStr +
    p0_0_ixtName_dh
p0_0_ixtName_fgr    p0_0_fgr
p0_0_ixtName_fgg    p0_0_fgg
p0_0_ixtName_fgb    p0_0_fgb
p0_0_ixtName_bgr    255
p0_0_ixtName_bgg    255
p0_0_ixtName_bgb    255
p0_0_ixtName_fc     fcCourier
p0_0_ixtName_fs     p0_0_fs

.data
Bytes  p0_0_ixtName_str
    p0_0_ixtName_strLenMax + 3

.const
p0_0_ixtName_yStr   p0_0_ixtName_y +
    p0_0_ixtName_fa - 1 +
    p0_0_ixtName_dy
p0_0_ixtName_strLenMax    80
p0_0_ixtName_svIdx    _svIdx_name
p0_0_ixtName_svBufLen
    p0_0_ixtName_strLenMax + 3
p0_0_ixtName_xStr   p0_0_ixtName_x +
    p0_0_ixtName_dx
p0_0_ixtName_wStr   p0_0_ixtName_w -
    p0_0_ixtName_dw
p0_0_ixtName_hStr   p0_0_ixtName_fh
p0_0_ixtName_yaStr  p0_0_ixtName_y +
    p0_0_ixtName_dy

.data
String p0_0_ixtName_strInit    "your
    name"

.const
p0_0_ixtName_wChar   textWidth(" ",
    p0_0_ixtName_fc, p0_0_ixtName_fs)
p0_0_ixtName_strPos   0
p0_0_ixtName_fa
    fontAscent(p0_0_ixtName_fc,
    p0_0_ixtName_fs)
p0_0_ixtName_fh
    fontHeight(p0_0_ixtName_fc,
    p0_0_ixtName_fs)
p0_0_ixtName_dx     libGuiIxt3D_dx
p0_0_ixtName_dy     libGuiIxt3D_dy
p0_0_ixtName_dw     libGuiIxt3D_dw
p0_0_ixtName_dh     libGuiIxt3D_dh

.data

Bytes  p0_0_ixtName_prp  [
    p0_0_ixtName_et, p0_0_ixtName_x,
    p0_0_ixtName_y, p0_0_ixtName_w,
    p0_0_ixtName_h, p0_0_ixtName_fgr,
    p0_0_ixtName_fgg,
    p0_0_ixtName_fgb,
    p0_0_ixtName_bgr,
    p0_0_ixtName_bgg,
    p0_0_ixtName_bgb,
    p0_0_ixtName_fc, p0_0_ixtName_fs,
    p0_0_ixtName_str,
    p0_0_ixtName_xStr,
    p0_0_ixtName_yStr,
    p0_0_ixtName_wStr,
    p0_0_ixtName_hStr,
    p0_0_ixtName_yaStr,
    p0_0_ixtName_strLenMax,
    p0_0_ixtName_wChar,
    p0_0_ixtName_strPos ]

////////////////////
// p0_0_ixtName: Init
/////

.code
.fct p0_0_ixtName_init ()
{
    loadc p0_0_ixtName_strPos
    loadc p0_0_ixtName_prp
    loadc libGui_strPosOfs
    add
    storea
    loadc p0_0_ixtName_str
    push
    loadc p0_0_ixtName_strInit
    push
    fcall libMisc_strCp
    return
}

////////////////////
// p0_0_ixtName: Events
/////

.data
EventTable  p0_0_ixtName_et   [
    key_pressed, p0_0_ixtName_kp,
    key_pressed_escape,
        p0_0_ixtName_kpes,
    mouse_pressed_left,
        p0_0_ixtName_mpl,
```

D.2. Generated CVM Packets

```
1, p0_0_et ]

.code
p0_0_ixtName_kp:
  loadep1
  loadc XK_Tab
  loadcr p0_0_ixtName_kp_tab
  je
  loadep1
  loadc XK_ISO_Left_Tab
  loadcr p0_0_ixtName_kp_leftTab
  je
  loadc p0_0_ixtName_prp
  push
  fcall libGuiIxt_kp
  halt

p0_0_ixtName_kp_tab:
  loadc p0_0_ixtName_prp
  push
  loadc p0_0_ixtEmail_prp
  push
  loadc libGuiIxt3D_unDrwFcs
  push
  loadc libGuiIxt3D_drwFcs
  push
  fcall libGui_mvFcs
  halt
p0_0_ixtName_kp_leftTab:
  loadc p0_0_ixtName_prp
  push
  loadc p0_0_btnSubmit_prp
  push
  loadc libGuiIxt3D_unDrwFcs
  push
  loadc libGuiBtn3D_drwFcs
  push
  fcall libGui_mvFcs
  halt

p0_0_ixtName_kpes:
  loadc p0_0_ixtName_prp
  push
  loadc p0_0_prp
  push
  loadc libGuiIxt3D_unDrwFcs
  push
  loadc libMisc_emptyProc
  push
  fcall libGui_mvFcs
  halt
```

```
.code
p0_0_ixtName_mpl:
  loadep1
  push
  loadep2
  push
  loadc p0_0_ixtName_prp
  push
  loadc libGuiIxt3D_unDrwFcs
  push
  fcall p0_0_mplFcs
  halt

///////////////////
// p0_0_ixtName: Service Variables
/////

.code
.fct p0_0_ixtName_svBuf_write ()
{
  loadc p0_0_ixtName_svIdx
  loadc _svBuf
  load _svBufIdx
  astore1
  load _svBufIdx
  loadc 1
  add
  store _svBufIdx
  loadc _svBuf
  load _svBufIdx
  add
  push
  loadc p0_0_ixtName_str
  push
  fcall libMisc_strCp
  load _svBufIdx
  incsp
  loadc p0_0_ixtName_str
  push
  fcall libMisc_strLen
  pop
  add
  loadc 3
  add
  store _svBufIdx
  return
}

///////////////////
// p0_0_txtEmail: Attributes
/////
```

```
.const
p0_0_txtEmail_x    10
p0_0_txtEmail_y    p0_0_txtEmail_yStr -
    p0_0_txtEmail_fa + 1 -
    p0_0_txtEmail_dy
p0_0_txtEmail_w    p0_0_txtEmail_wStr +
    p0_0_txtEmail_dw
p0_0_txtEmail_h    p0_0_txtEmail_hStr +
    p0_0_txtEmail_dh
p0_0_txtEmail_fgr    p0_0_fgr
p0_0_txtEmail_fgg    p0_0_fgg
p0_0_txtEmail_fgb    p0_0_fgb
p0_0_txtEmail_bgr    p0_0_bgr
p0_0_txtEmail_bgg    p0_0_bgg
p0_0_txtEmail_bgb    p0_0_bgb
p0_0_txtEmail_fc     p0_0_fc
p0_0_txtEmail_fs     p0_0_fs
p0_0_txtEmail_str    "Email"
p0_0_txtEmail_yStr   98
p0_0_txtEmail_xStr   p0_0_txtEmail_x +
    p0_0_txtEmail_dx
p0_0_txtEmail_wStr
    textWidth(p0_0_txtEmail_str,
    p0_0_txtEmail_fc,
    p0_0_txtEmail_fs)
p0_0_txtEmail_hStr
    textHeight(p0_0_txtEmail_str,
    p0_0_txtEmail_fc,
    p0_0_txtEmail_fs, 0)
p0_0_txtEmail_fa
    fontAscent(p0_0_txtEmail_fc,
    p0_0_txtEmail_fs)
p0_0_txtEmail_dx    libGuiTxt3D_dx
p0_0_txtEmail_dy    libGuiTxt3D_dy
p0_0_txtEmail_dw    libGuiTxt3D_dw
p0_0_txtEmail_dh    libGuiTxt3D_dh

///////////////////
// p0_0_txtEmail: Misc
/////

.code
.fct p0_0_txtEmail_drw ()
{
  loadc p0_0_txtEmail_fgr
  loadc p0_0_txtEmail_fgg
  loadc p0_0_txtEmail_fgb
  setcolor
  loadc p0_0_txtEmail_bgr
  loadc p0_0_txtEmail_bgg
  loadc p0_0_txtEmail_bgb
  setbgcolor
  loadc p0_0_txtEmail_fc
  loadc p0_0_txtEmail_fs
  setfont
  loadc p0_0_txtEmail_xStr
  loadc p0_0_txtEmail_yStr
  textbg p0_0_txtEmail_str
  return
}

///////////////////
// p0_0_ixtEmail: Attributes
/////

.const
p0_0_ixtEmail_x    52
p0_0_ixtEmail_y    85
p0_0_ixtEmail_w    150
p0_0_ixtEmail_h    p0_0_ixtEmail_hStr +
    p0_0_ixtEmail_dh
p0_0_ixtEmail_fgr    p0_0_fgr
p0_0_ixtEmail_fgg    p0_0_fgg
p0_0_ixtEmail_fgb    p0_0_fgb
p0_0_ixtEmail_bgr    255
p0_0_ixtEmail_bgg    255
p0_0_ixtEmail_bgb    255
p0_0_ixtEmail_fc     fcCourier
p0_0_ixtEmail_fs     p0_0_fs

.data
Bytes  p0_0_ixtEmail_str
    p0_0_ixtEmail_strLenMax + 3

.const
p0_0_ixtEmail_yStr   p0_0_ixtEmail_y +
    p0_0_ixtEmail_fa - 1 +
    p0_0_ixtEmail_dy
p0_0_ixtEmail_strLenMax    80
p0_0_ixtEmail_svIdx    _svIdx_email
p0_0_ixtEmail_svBufLen
    p0_0_ixtEmail_strLenMax + 3
p0_0_ixtEmail_xStr    p0_0_ixtEmail_x +
    p0_0_ixtEmail_dx
p0_0_ixtEmail_wStr    p0_0_ixtEmail_w -
    p0_0_ixtEmail_dw
p0_0_ixtEmail_hStr    p0_0_ixtEmail_fh
p0_0_ixtEmail_yaStr   p0_0_ixtEmail_y
    + p0_0_ixtEmail_dy

.data
String  p0_0_ixtEmail_strInit    "your
```

D.2. Generated CVM Packets

```
        email"

.const
p0_0_ixtEmail_wChar  textWidth(" ",
    p0_0_ixtEmail_fc,
    p0_0_ixtEmail_fs)
p0_0_ixtEmail_strPos  0
p0_0_ixtEmail_fa
    fontAscent(p0_0_ixtEmail_fc,
    p0_0_ixtEmail_fs)
p0_0_ixtEmail_fh
    fontHeight(p0_0_ixtEmail_fc,
    p0_0_ixtEmail_fs)
p0_0_ixtEmail_dx    libGuiIxt3D_dx
p0_0_ixtEmail_dy    libGuiIxt3D_dy
p0_0_ixtEmail_dw    libGuiIxt3D_dw
p0_0_ixtEmail_dh    libGuiIxt3D_dh

.data
Bytes  p0_0_ixtEmail_prp  [
    p0_0_ixtEmail_et,
    p0_0_ixtEmail_x, p0_0_ixtEmail_y,
    p0_0_ixtEmail_w, p0_0_ixtEmail_h,
    p0_0_ixtEmail_fgr,
    p0_0_ixtEmail_fgg,
    p0_0_ixtEmail_fgb,
    p0_0_ixtEmail_bgr,
    p0_0_ixtEmail_bgg,
    p0_0_ixtEmail_bgb,
    p0_0_ixtEmail_fc,
    p0_0_ixtEmail_fs,
    p0_0_ixtEmail_str,
    p0_0_ixtEmail_xStr,
    p0_0_ixtEmail_yStr,
    p0_0_ixtEmail_wStr,
    p0_0_ixtEmail_hStr,
    p0_0_ixtEmail_yaStr,
    p0_0_ixtEmail_strLenMax,
    p0_0_ixtEmail_wChar,
    p0_0_ixtEmail_strPos ]

/////////////////////
// p0_0_ixtEmail: Init
/////

.code
.fct p0_0_ixtEmail_init ()
{
  loadc p0_0_ixtEmail_strPos
  loadc p0_0_ixtEmail_prp
  loadc libGui_strPosOfs
  add
  storea
  loadc p0_0_ixtEmail_str
  push
  loadc p0_0_ixtEmail_strInit
  push
  fcall libMisc_strCp
  return
}

/////////////////////
// p0_0_ixtEmail: Events
/////

.data
EventTable p0_0_ixtEmail_et  [
    key_pressed, p0_0_ixtEmail_kp,
    key_pressed_escape,
        p0_0_ixtEmail_kpes,
    mouse_pressed_left,
        p0_0_ixtEmail_mpl,
    1, p0_0_et ]

.code
p0_0_ixtEmail_kp:
    loadep1
    loadc XK_Tab
    loadcr p0_0_ixtEmail_kp_tab
    je
    loadep1
    loadc XK_ISO_Left_Tab
    loadcr p0_0_ixtEmail_kp_leftTab
    je
    loadc p0_0_ixtEmail_prp
    push
    fcall libGuiIxt_kp
    halt

p0_0_ixtEmail_kp_tab:
    loadc p0_0_ixtEmail_prp
    push
    loadc p0_0_btnReset_prp
    push
    loadc libGuiIxt3D_unDrwFcs
    push
    loadc libGuiBtn3D_drwFcs
    push
    fcall libGui_mvFcs
    halt
p0_0_ixtEmail_kp_leftTab:
    loadc p0_0_ixtEmail_prp
```

```
  push
  loadc p0_0_ixtName_prp
  push
  loadc libGuiIxt3D_unDrwFcs
  push
  loadc libGuiIxt3D_drwFcs
  push
  fcall libGui_mvFcs
  halt

p0_0_ixtEmail_kpes:
  loadc p0_0_ixtEmail_prp
  push
  loadc p0_0_prp
  push
  loadc libGuiIxt3D_unDrwFcs
  push
  loadc libMisc_emptyProc
  push
  fcall libGui_mvFcs
  halt

.code
p0_0_ixtEmail_mpl:
  loadep1
  push
  loadep2
  push
  loadc p0_0_ixtEmail_prp
  push
  loadc libGuiIxt3D_unDrwFcs
  push
  fcall p0_0_mplFcs
  halt

//////////////////
// p0_0_ixtEmail: Service Variables
/////

.code
.fct p0_0_ixtEmail_svBuf_write ()
  {
  loadc p0_0_ixtEmail_svIdx
  loadc _svBuf
  load _svBufIdx
  astore1
  load _svBufIdx
  loadc 1
  add
  store _svBufIdx
  loadc _svBuf
```

```
  load _svBufIdx
  add
  push
  loadc p0_0_ixtEmail_str
  push
  fcall libMisc_strCp
  load _svBufIdx
  incsp
  loadc p0_0_ixtEmail_str
  push
  fcall libMisc_strLen
  pop
  add
  loadc 3
  add
  store _svBufIdx
  return
  }

//////////////////
// p0_0_btnReset: Attributes
/////

.const
p0_0_btnReset_x      10
p0_0_btnReset_y      116
p0_0_btnReset_w      p0_0_btnReset_wStr +
                     p0_0_btnReset_dw
p0_0_btnReset_h      p0_0_btnReset_hStr +
                     p0_0_btnReset_dh
p0_0_btnReset_fgr    51
p0_0_btnReset_fgg    51
p0_0_btnReset_fgb    51
p0_0_btnReset_bgr    210
p0_0_btnReset_bgg    218
p0_0_btnReset_bgb    230
p0_0_btnReset_fc     p0_0_fc
p0_0_btnReset_fs     p0_0_fs
p0_0_btnReset_str    "Reset"
p0_0_btnReset_yStr   p0_0_btnReset_y +
                     p0_0_btnReset_fa - 1 +
                     p0_0_btnReset_dy
p0_0_btnReset_img    ""
p0_0_btnReset_imgStyle  0
p0_0_btnReset_xStr   p0_0_btnReset_x +
                     p0_0_btnReset_dx
p0_0_btnReset_wStr
     textWidth(p0_0_btnReset_str,
     p0_0_btnReset_fc,
     p0_0_btnReset_fs)
p0_0_btnReset_hStr   p0_0_btnReset_fh
```

D.2. Generated CVM Packets

```
p0_0_btnReset_fa
    fontAscent(p0_0_btnReset_fc,
    p0_0_btnReset_fs)
p0_0_btnReset_fh
    fontHeight(p0_0_btnReset_fc,
    p0_0_btnReset_fs)
p0_0_btnReset_dx    libGuiBtn3D_dx
p0_0_btnReset_dy    libGuiBtn3D_dy
p0_0_btnReset_dw    libGuiBtn3D_dw
p0_0_btnReset_dh    libGuiBtn3D_dh

.data
String  p0_0_btnReset_str_
    p0_0_btnReset_str
String  p0_0_btnReset_img_
    p0_0_btnReset_img
Bytes   p0_0_btnReset_prp   [
    p0_0_btnReset_et,
    p0_0_btnReset_x, p0_0_btnReset_y,
    p0_0_btnReset_w, p0_0_btnReset_h,
    p0_0_btnReset_fgr,
    p0_0_btnReset_fgg,
    p0_0_btnReset_fgb,
    p0_0_btnReset_bgr,
    p0_0_btnReset_bgg,
    p0_0_btnReset_bgb,
    p0_0_btnReset_fc,
    p0_0_btnReset_fs,
    p0_0_btnReset_str_,
    p0_0_btnReset_xStr,
    p0_0_btnReset_yStr,
    p0_0_btnReset_img_,
    p0_0_btnReset_imgStyle ]

////////////////////
// p0_0_btnReset: Events
/////

.data
EventTable  p0_0_btnReset_et    [
  key_pressed, p0_0_btnReset_kp,
  key_pressed_escape,
    p0_0_btnReset_kpes,
  key_pressed_enter,
    p0_0_btnReset_kpe,
  key_released, p0_0_btnReset_kr,
  key_released_enter,
    p0_0_btnReset_kre,
  mouse_pressed_left,
    p0_0_btnReset_mpl,
  mouse_released_left,
    p0_0_btnReset_mrl,
  1, p0_0_et ]

.code
p0_0_btnReset_kp:
    loadep1
    loadc XK_Tab
    loadcr p0_0_btnReset_kp_tab
    je
    loadep1
    loadc XK_ISO_Left_Tab
    loadcr p0_0_btnReset_kp_leftTab
    je
    loadep1
    loadc XK_space
    loadcr p0_0_btnReset_kp_space
    je
    halt

p0_0_btnReset_kp_tab:
    loadc p0_0_btnReset_prp
    push
    loadc p0_0_btnSubmit_prp
    push
    loadc libGuiBtn3D_unDrwFcs
    push
    loadc libGuiBtn3D_drwFcs
    push
    fcall libGui_mvFcs
    halt
p0_0_btnReset_kp_leftTab:
    loadc p0_0_btnReset_prp
    push
    loadc p0_0_ixtEmail_prp
    push
    loadc libGuiBtn3D_unDrwFcs
    push
    loadc libGuiIxt3D_drwFcs
    push
    fcall libGui_mvFcs
    halt

p0_0_btnReset_kp_space:
    fcall p0_0_btnReset_evDwn
    halt

p0_0_btnReset_kpes:
    loadc p0_0_btnReset_prp
    push
    loadc p0_0_prp
    push
```

```
  loadc libGuiBtn3D_unDrwFcs
  push
  loadc libMisc_emptyProc
  push
  fcall libGui_mvFcs
  halt

p0_0_btnReset_kpe:
  fcall p0_0_btnReset_evDwn
  halt

p0_0_btnReset_kr:
  loadep1
  loadc XK_space
  loadcr p0_0_btnReset_kr_space
  je
  halt

p0_0_btnReset_kr_space:
  fcall p0_0_btnReset_evUp
  halt

p0_0_btnReset_kre:
  fcall p0_0_btnReset_evUp
  halt

.code
p0_0_btnReset_mpl:
  loadep1
  push
  loadep2
  push
  loadc p0_0_btnReset_prp
  push
  loadc libGuiBtn3D_unDrwFcs
  push
  fcall p0_0_mplFcs
  halt

p0_0_btnReset_mrl:
  fcall p0_0_btnReset_evUp
  halt

.code
.fct p0_0_btnReset_evDwn ()
{
  loadc p0_0_btnReset_prp
  push
  fcall libGuiBtn3D_dwn
fcall _svBufIdx_reset
      fcall_I _svBuf_svcCmd_write,
      svcCmd_Reset
  sendrcvpage_a _pageNo,
      _subpageNo
  return
}

.fct p0_0_btnReset_evUp ()
{
  loadc p0_0_btnReset_prp
  push
  fcall libGuiBtn3D_up
  return
}

////////////////////
// p0_0_btnSubmit: Attributes
/////

.const
p0_0_btnSubmit_x    54
p0_0_btnSubmit_y    116
p0_0_btnSubmit_w    p0_0_btnSubmit_wStr
    + p0_0_btnSubmit_dw
p0_0_btnSubmit_h    p0_0_btnSubmit_hStr
    + p0_0_btnSubmit_dh
p0_0_btnSubmit_fgr    51
p0_0_btnSubmit_fgg    51
p0_0_btnSubmit_fgb    51
p0_0_btnSubmit_bgr    210
p0_0_btnSubmit_bgg    218
p0_0_btnSubmit_bgb    230
p0_0_btnSubmit_fc     p0_0_fc
p0_0_btnSubmit_fs     p0_0_fs
p0_0_btnSubmit_str    "Submit"
p0_0_btnSubmit_yStr   p0_0_btnSubmit_y
    + p0_0_btnSubmit_fa - 1 +
    p0_0_btnSubmit_dy
p0_0_btnSubmit_img    ""
p0_0_btnSubmit_imgStyle   0
p0_0_btnSubmit_xStr   p0_0_btnSubmit_x
    + p0_0_btnSubmit_dx
p0_0_btnSubmit_wStr
    textWidth(p0_0_btnSubmit_str,
    p0_0_btnSubmit_fc,
    p0_0_btnSubmit_fs)
p0_0_btnSubmit_hStr
    p0_0_btnSubmit_fh
p0_0_btnSubmit_fa
    fontAscent(p0_0_btnSubmit_fc,
    p0_0_btnSubmit_fs)
p0_0_btnSubmit_fh
```

D.2. Generated CVM Packets

```
        fontHeight(p0_0_btnSubmit_fc,
        p0_0_btnSubmit_fs)
p0_0_btnSubmit_dx    libGuiBtn3D_dx
p0_0_btnSubmit_dy    libGuiBtn3D_dy
p0_0_btnSubmit_dw    libGuiBtn3D_dw
p0_0_btnSubmit_dh    libGuiBtn3D_dh

.data
String  p0_0_btnSubmit_str_
    p0_0_btnSubmit_str
String  p0_0_btnSubmit_img_
    p0_0_btnSubmit_img
Bytes   p0_0_btnSubmit_prp    [
    p0_0_btnSubmit_et,
    p0_0_btnSubmit_x,
    p0_0_btnSubmit_y,
    p0_0_btnSubmit_w,
    p0_0_btnSubmit_h,
    p0_0_btnSubmit_fgr,
    p0_0_btnSubmit_fgg,
    p0_0_btnSubmit_fgb,
    p0_0_btnSubmit_bgr,
    p0_0_btnSubmit_bgg,
    p0_0_btnSubmit_bgb,
    p0_0_btnSubmit_fc,
    p0_0_btnSubmit_fs,
    p0_0_btnSubmit_str_,
    p0_0_btnSubmit_xStr,
    p0_0_btnSubmit_yStr,
    p0_0_btnSubmit_img_,
    p0_0_btnSubmit_imgStyle ]

//////////////////
// p0_0_btnSubmit: Events
/////

.data
EventTable p0_0_btnSubmit_et   [
  key_pressed, p0_0_btnSubmit_kp,
  key_pressed_escape,
    p0_0_btnSubmit_kpes,
  key_pressed_enter,
    p0_0_btnSubmit_kpe,
  key_released, p0_0_btnSubmit_kr,
  key_released_enter,
    p0_0_btnSubmit_kre,
  mouse_pressed_left,
    p0_0_btnSubmit_mpl,
  mouse_released_left,
    p0_0_btnSubmit_mrl,
  1, p0_0_et ]

.code
p0_0_btnSubmit_kp:
  loadep1
  loadc XK_Tab
  loadcr p0_0_btnSubmit_kp_tab
  je
  loadep1
  loadc XK_ISO_Left_Tab
  loadcr p0_0_btnSubmit_kp_leftTab
  je
  loadep1
  loadc XK_space
  loadcr p0_0_btnSubmit_kp_space
  je
  halt

p0_0_btnSubmit_kp_tab:
  loadc p0_0_btnSubmit_prp
  push
  loadc p0_0_ixtName_prp
  push
  loadc libGuiBtn3D_unDrwFcs
  push
  loadc libGuiIxt3D_drwFcs
  push
  fcall libGui_mvFcs
  halt
p0_0_btnSubmit_kp_leftTab:
  loadc p0_0_btnSubmit_prp
  push
  loadc p0_0_btnReset_prp
  push
  loadc libGuiBtn3D_unDrwFcs
  push
  loadc libGuiBtn3D_drwFcs
  push
  fcall libGui_mvFcs
  halt

p0_0_btnSubmit_kp_space:
  fcall p0_0_btnSubmit_evDwn
  halt

p0_0_btnSubmit_kpes:
  loadc p0_0_btnSubmit_prp
  push
  loadc p0_0_prp
  push
  loadc libGuiBtn3D_unDrwFcs
  push
  loadc libMisc_emptyProc
```

```
    push
    fcall libGui_mvFcs
    halt

p0_0_btnSubmit_kpe:
    fcall p0_0_btnSubmit_evDwn
    halt

p0_0_btnSubmit_kr:
    loadep1
    loadc XK_space
    loadcr p0_0_btnSubmit_kr_space
    je
    halt

p0_0_btnSubmit_kr_space:
    fcall p0_0_btnSubmit_evUp
    halt

p0_0_btnSubmit_kre:
    fcall p0_0_btnSubmit_evUp
    halt

.code
p0_0_btnSubmit_mpl:
    loadep1
    push
    loadep2
    push
    loadc p0_0_btnSubmit_prp
    push
    loadc libGuiBtn3D_unDrwFcs
    push
```

```
    fcall p0_0_mplFcs
    halt

p0_0_btnSubmit_mrl:
    fcall p0_0_btnSubmit_evUp
    halt

.code
.fct p0_0_btnSubmit_evDwn ()
{
    loadc p0_0_btnSubmit_prp
    push
    fcall libGuiBtn3D_dwn
    fcall _svBuf_write
        fcall_I _svBuf_svcCmd_write,
        svcCmd_Submit
        sendrcvpage _p1, 0
    return
}

.fct p0_0_btnSubmit_evUp ()
{
    loadc p0_0_btnSubmit_prp
    push
    fcall libGuiBtn3D_up
    return
}

/////////////////////
// CVMUI Lib
/////

...
```

AUI page p1: CVMUI page p1_0 The generated CVM packet for the AUI page p1 contains 1138 bytes and is as follows:

```
.16Bit

.code
    loadcr p1_0_main
    jmp

/////////////////////
// Misc
/////

.const
_cil          2
_cvmScreenWidth   250
```

```
_cvmScreenHeight  150

.data
String  _hostAdrSrv   "127.0.0.1"

/////////////////////
// Page Numbers
/////

.const
_pageNo     1
_p0         0
_pNotExist  2
```

D.2. Generated CVM Packets

```
_pIllegal   3

.data
Int   _subpageNo

////////////////////
// Service Commands
/////

.const
svcCmd_Reset    0
svcCmd_Submit   1

////////////////////
// Service Variables
/////

.const
_svIdxLen    1
_svIdx_name  1
_svIdx_email 2

.data
Int   _svBufIdx   0
Bytes _svBuf      _svIdxLen + 2

////////////////////
// p1_0: Attributes
/////

.const
p1_0_x    0
p1_0_y    0
p1_0_w    _cvmScreenWidth
p1_0_h    _cvmScreenHeight
p1_0_fgr  0
p1_0_fgg  0
p1_0_fgb  0
p1_0_bgr  222
p1_0_bgg  218
p1_0_bgb  210
p1_0_fc   fcHelvetica
p1_0_fs   12
p1_0_img  ""
p1_0_imgStyle  0

.data
Bytes p1_0_prp  [ p1_0_et ]
Int   p1_0_bInit   0

////////////////////
// p1_0: Misc
/////

.code
p1_0_main:
  loadc_0
  store _subpageNo
  fcall p1_0_init
  fcall p1_0_drw
  loadc p1_0_hlkService_prp
  push
  loadc libGuiHlk3D_drwFcs
  push
  fcall libGui_setFcs
  enableevents
  halt

.code
.fct p1_0_init ()
{
  load p1_0_bInit
  loadc_0
  loadcr p1_0_init_1
  jne
  loadc_1
  store p1_0_bInit
p1_0_init_1:
  return
}

.code
.fct p1_0_drw ()
{
  loadc p1_0_bgr
  loadc p1_0_bgg
  loadc p1_0_bgb
  setcolor
  loadc p1_0_x
  loadc p1_0_y
  loadc p1_0_w
  loadc p1_0_h
  rectfill
  fcall p1_0_txtTitle_drw
  fcall p1_0_txtName_drw
  fcall p1_0_txtNameVal_drw
  fcall p1_0_txtEmail_drw
  fcall p1_0_txtEmailVal_drw
  loadc p1_0_hlkService_prp
  push
  fcall libGuiHlk3D_drw
  return
```

```
}

///////////////////
// p1_0: Service Variables
/////

///////////////////
// p1_0: Events
/////

.data
EventTable p1_0_et    [
  key_pressed, p1_0_kp,
  mouse_pressed_left, p1_0_mpl ]

.code
p1_0_kp:
  loadep1
  loadc XK_Tab
  loadcr p1_0_kp_tab
  je
  halt
p1_0_kp_tab:
  loadc p1_0_prp
  push
  loadc p1_0_hlkService_prp
  push
  loadc libMisc_emptyProc
  push
  loadc libGuiHlk3D_drwFcs
  push
  fcall libGui_mvFcs
  halt

.code
p1_0_mpl:
  loadep1
  push
  loadep2
  push
  loadc p1_0_prp
  push
  loadc libMisc_emptyProc
  push
  fcall p1_0_mplFcs
  halt

.code
.fct p1_0_mplFcs (Int x, Int y, Int
    adrPrpSrc, Int adrUnDrwFcsSrc)
  {
    incsp
    load x
    push
    load y
    push
    loadc p1_0_hlkService_x
    push
    loadc p1_0_hlkService_y
    push
    loadc p1_0_hlkService_w
    push
    loadc p1_0_hlkService_h
    push
    fcall libGui_rectIn
    pop
    loadc_0
    loadcr p1_0_mplFcs_39
    je
    load adrPrpSrc
    push
    loadc p1_0_hlkService_prp
    push
    load adrUnDrwFcsSrc
    push
    loadc libGuiHlk3D_drwFcs
    push
    fcall libGui_mvFcs
    loadc p1_0_hlkService_prp
    push
    fcall libGuiHlk_dwn
    return
p1_0_mplFcs_39:
    return
  }

///////////////////
// p1_0_txtTitle: Attributes
/////

.const
p1_0_txtTitle_x    34
p1_0_txtTitle_y    5
p1_0_txtTitle_w    p1_0_txtTitle_wStr +
       p1_0_txtTitle_dw
p1_0_txtTitle_h    p1_0_txtTitle_hStr +
       p1_0_txtTitle_dh
p1_0_txtTitle_fgr    p1_0_fgr
p1_0_txtTitle_fgg    p1_0_fgg
p1_0_txtTitle_fgb    p1_0_fgb
p1_0_txtTitle_bgr    p1_0_bgr
p1_0_txtTitle_bgg    p1_0_bgg
```

D.2. Generated CVM Packets

```
p1_0_txtTitle_bgb    p1_0_bgb
p1_0_txtTitle_fc     fcHelveticaBold
p1_0_txtTitle_fs     14
p1_0_txtTitle_str    "Confirmation of
    Your Data"
p1_0_txtTitle_yStr   p1_0_txtTitle_y +
    p1_0_txtTitle_fa - 1 +
    p1_0_txtTitle_dy
p1_0_txtTitle_xStr   p1_0_txtTitle_x +
    p1_0_txtTitle_dx
p1_0_txtTitle_wStr
    textWidth(p1_0_txtTitle_str,
    p1_0_txtTitle_fc,
    p1_0_txtTitle_fs)
p1_0_txtTitle_hStr
    textHeight(p1_0_txtTitle_str,
    p1_0_txtTitle_fc,
    p1_0_txtTitle_fs, 0)
p1_0_txtTitle_fa
    fontAscent(p1_0_txtTitle_fc,
    p1_0_txtTitle_fs)
p1_0_txtTitle_dx     libGuiTxt3D_dx
p1_0_txtTitle_dy     libGuiTxt3D_dy
p1_0_txtTitle_dw     libGuiTxt3D_dw
p1_0_txtTitle_dh     libGuiTxt3D_dh

///////////////////
// p1_0_txtTitle: Misc
/////

.code
.fct p1_0_txtTitle_drw ()
{
  loadc p1_0_txtTitle_fgr
  loadc p1_0_txtTitle_fgg
  loadc p1_0_txtTitle_fgb
  setcolor
  loadc p1_0_txtTitle_bgr
  loadc p1_0_txtTitle_bgg
  loadc p1_0_txtTitle_bgb
  setbgcolor
  loadc p1_0_txtTitle_fc
  loadc p1_0_txtTitle_fs
  setfont
  loadc p1_0_txtTitle_xStr
  loadc p1_0_txtTitle_yStr
  textbg p1_0_txtTitle_str
  return
}
///////////////////

// p1_0_txtName: Attributes
/////

.const
p1_0_txtName_x       10
p1_0_txtName_y       31
p1_0_txtName_w       p1_0_txtName_wStr +
    p1_0_txtName_dw
p1_0_txtName_h       p1_0_txtName_hStr +
    p1_0_txtName_dh
p1_0_txtName_fgr     p1_0_fgr
p1_0_txtName_fgg     p1_0_fgg
p1_0_txtName_fgb     p1_0_fgb
p1_0_txtName_bgr     p1_0_bgr
p1_0_txtName_bgg     p1_0_bgg
p1_0_txtName_bgb     p1_0_bgb
p1_0_txtName_fc      p1_0_fc
p1_0_txtName_fs      p1_0_fs
p1_0_txtName_str     "Name:"
p1_0_txtName_yStr    p1_0_txtName_y +
    p1_0_txtName_fa - 1 +
    p1_0_txtName_dy
p1_0_txtName_xStr    p1_0_txtName_x +
    p1_0_txtName_dx
p1_0_txtName_wStr
    textWidth(p1_0_txtName_str,
    p1_0_txtName_fc, p1_0_txtName_fs)
p1_0_txtName_hStr
    textHeight(p1_0_txtName_str,
    p1_0_txtName_fc, p1_0_txtName_fs,
    0)
p1_0_txtName_fa
    fontAscent(p1_0_txtName_fc,
    p1_0_txtName_fs)
p1_0_txtName_dx      libGuiTxt3D_dx
p1_0_txtName_dy      libGuiTxt3D_dy
p1_0_txtName_dw      libGuiTxt3D_dw
p1_0_txtName_dh      libGuiTxt3D_dh

///////////////////
// p1_0_txtName: Misc
/////

.code
.fct p1_0_txtName_drw ()
{
  loadc p1_0_txtName_fgr
  loadc p1_0_txtName_fgg
  loadc p1_0_txtName_fgb
  setcolor
  loadc p1_0_txtName_bgr
```

```
    loadc p1_0_txtName_bgg
    loadc p1_0_txtName_bgb
    setbgcolor
    loadc p1_0_txtName_fc
    loadc p1_0_txtName_fs
    setfont
    loadc p1_0_txtName_xStr
    loadc p1_0_txtName_yStr
    textbg p1_0_txtName_str
    return
    }

///////////////////
// p1_0_txtNameVal: Attributes
/////

.const
p1_0_txtNameVal_x       55
p1_0_txtNameVal_y       31
p1_0_txtNameVal_w
    p1_0_txtNameVal_wStr +
    p1_0_txtNameVal_dw
p1_0_txtNameVal_h
    p1_0_txtNameVal_hStr +
    p1_0_txtNameVal_dh
p1_0_txtNameVal_fgr     p1_0_fgr
p1_0_txtNameVal_fgg     p1_0_fgg
p1_0_txtNameVal_fgb     p1_0_fgb
p1_0_txtNameVal_bgr     p1_0_bgr
p1_0_txtNameVal_bgg     p1_0_bgg
p1_0_txtNameVal_bgb     p1_0_bgb
p1_0_txtNameVal_fc      p1_0_fc
p1_0_txtNameVal_fs      p1_0_fs
p1_0_txtNameVal_str     "Max Mustermann"
p1_0_txtNameVal_yStr
    p1_0_txtNameVal_y +
    p1_0_txtNameVal_fa - 1 +
    p1_0_txtNameVal_dy
p1_0_txtNameVal_xStr
    p1_0_txtNameVal_x +
    p1_0_txtNameVal_dx
p1_0_txtNameVal_wStr
    textWidth(p1_0_txtNameVal_str,
    p1_0_txtNameVal_fc,
    p1_0_txtNameVal_fs)
p1_0_txtNameVal_hStr
    textHeight(p1_0_txtNameVal_str,
    p1_0_txtNameVal_fc,
    p1_0_txtNameVal_fs, 0)
p1_0_txtNameVal_fa
    fontAscent(p1_0_txtNameVal_fc,
    p1_0_txtNameVal_fs)
p1_0_txtNameVal_dx      libGuiTxt3D_dx
p1_0_txtNameVal_dy      libGuiTxt3D_dy
p1_0_txtNameVal_dw      libGuiTxt3D_dw
p1_0_txtNameVal_dh      libGuiTxt3D_dh

///////////////////
// p1_0_txtNameVal: Misc
/////

.code
.fct p1_0_txtNameVal_drw ()
    {
    loadc p1_0_txtNameVal_fgr
    loadc p1_0_txtNameVal_fgg
    loadc p1_0_txtNameVal_fgb
    setcolor
    loadc p1_0_txtNameVal_bgr
    loadc p1_0_txtNameVal_bgg
    loadc p1_0_txtNameVal_bgb
    setbgcolor
    loadc p1_0_txtNameVal_fc
    loadc p1_0_txtNameVal_fs
    setfont
    loadc p1_0_txtNameVal_xStr
    loadc p1_0_txtNameVal_yStr
    textbg p1_0_txtNameVal_str
    return
    }

///////////////////
// p1_0_txtEmail: Attributes
/////

.const
p1_0_txtEmail_x     10
p1_0_txtEmail_y     50
p1_0_txtEmail_w     p1_0_txtEmail_wStr +
    p1_0_txtEmail_dw
p1_0_txtEmail_h     p1_0_txtEmail_hStr +
    p1_0_txtEmail_dh
p1_0_txtEmail_fgr   p1_0_fgr
p1_0_txtEmail_fgg   p1_0_fgg
p1_0_txtEmail_fgb   p1_0_fgb
p1_0_txtEmail_bgr   p1_0_bgr
p1_0_txtEmail_bgg   p1_0_bgg
p1_0_txtEmail_bgb   p1_0_bgb
p1_0_txtEmail_fc    p1_0_fc
p1_0_txtEmail_fs    p1_0_fs
p1_0_txtEmail_str   "Email:"
p1_0_txtEmail_yStr  p1_0_txtEmail_y +
```

D.2. Generated CVM Packets

```
        p1_0_txtEmail_fa - 1 +
        p1_0_txtEmail_dy
p1_0_txtEmail_xStr    p1_0_txtEmail_x +
        p1_0_txtEmail_dx
p1_0_txtEmail_wStr
        textWidth(p1_0_txtEmail_str,
        p1_0_txtEmail_fc,
        p1_0_txtEmail_fs)
p1_0_txtEmail_hStr
        textHeight(p1_0_txtEmail_str,
        p1_0_txtEmail_fc,
        p1_0_txtEmail_fs, 0)
p1_0_txtEmail_fa
        fontAscent(p1_0_txtEmail_fc,
        p1_0_txtEmail_fs)
p1_0_txtEmail_dx      libGuiTxt3D_dx
p1_0_txtEmail_dy      libGuiTxt3D_dy
p1_0_txtEmail_dw      libGuiTxt3D_dw
p1_0_txtEmail_dh      libGuiTxt3D_dh

////////////////////
// p1_0_txtEmail: Misc
/////

.code
.fct p1_0_txtEmail_drw ()
{
  loadc p1_0_txtEmail_fgr
  loadc p1_0_txtEmail_fgg
  loadc p1_0_txtEmail_fgb
  setcolor
  loadc p1_0_txtEmail_bgr
  loadc p1_0_txtEmail_bgg
  loadc p1_0_txtEmail_bgb
  setbgcolor
  loadc p1_0_txtEmail_fc
  loadc p1_0_txtEmail_fs
  setfont
  loadc p1_0_txtEmail_xStr
  loadc p1_0_txtEmail_yStr
  textbg p1_0_txtEmail_str
  return
}

////////////////////
// p1_0_txtEmailVal: Attributes
/////

.const
p1_0_txtEmailVal_x    55
p1_0_txtEmailVal_y    50
```

```
p1_0_txtEmailVal_w
        p1_0_txtEmailVal_wStr +
        p1_0_txtEmailVal_dw
p1_0_txtEmailVal_h
        p1_0_txtEmailVal_hStr +
        p1_0_txtEmailVal_dh
p1_0_txtEmailVal_fgr    p1_0_fgr
p1_0_txtEmailVal_fgg    p1_0_fgg
p1_0_txtEmailVal_fgb    p1_0_fgb
p1_0_txtEmailVal_bgr    p1_0_bgr
p1_0_txtEmailVal_bgg    p1_0_bgg
p1_0_txtEmailVal_bgb    p1_0_bgb
p1_0_txtEmailVal_fc     p1_0_fc
p1_0_txtEmailVal_fs     p1_0_fs
p1_0_txtEmailVal_str
        "MaxMustermann@xyz.de"
p1_0_txtEmailVal_yStr
        p1_0_txtEmailVal_y +
        p1_0_txtEmailVal_fa - 1 +
        p1_0_txtEmailVal_dy
p1_0_txtEmailVal_xStr
        p1_0_txtEmailVal_x +
        p1_0_txtEmailVal_dx
p1_0_txtEmailVal_wStr
        textWidth(p1_0_txtEmailVal_str,
        p1_0_txtEmailVal_fc,
        p1_0_txtEmailVal_fs)
p1_0_txtEmailVal_hStr
        textHeight(p1_0_txtEmailVal_str,
        p1_0_txtEmailVal_fc,
        p1_0_txtEmailVal_fs, 0)
p1_0_txtEmailVal_fa
        fontAscent(p1_0_txtEmailVal_fc,
        p1_0_txtEmailVal_fs)
p1_0_txtEmailVal_dx     libGuiTxt3D_dx
p1_0_txtEmailVal_dy     libGuiTxt3D_dy
p1_0_txtEmailVal_dw     libGuiTxt3D_dw
p1_0_txtEmailVal_dh     libGuiTxt3D_dh

////////////////////
// p1_0_txtEmailVal: Misc
/////

.code
.fct p1_0_txtEmailVal_drw ()
{
  loadc p1_0_txtEmailVal_fgr
  loadc p1_0_txtEmailVal_fgg
  loadc p1_0_txtEmailVal_fgb
  setcolor
  loadc p1_0_txtEmailVal_bgr
```

```
        loadc p1_0_txtEmailVal_bgg
        loadc p1_0_txtEmailVal_bgb
        setbgcolor
        loadc p1_0_txtEmailVal_fc
        loadc p1_0_txtEmailVal_fs
        setfont
        loadc p1_0_txtEmailVal_xStr
        loadc p1_0_txtEmailVal_yStr
        textbg p1_0_txtEmailVal_str
        return
        }

//////////////////
// p1_0_hlkService: Attributes
/////

.const
p1_0_hlkService_x    10
p1_0_hlkService_y    74
p1_0_hlkService_w
    p1_0_hlkService_wStr +
    p1_0_hlkService_dw
p1_0_hlkService_h
    p1_0_hlkService_hStr +
    p1_0_hlkService_dh
p1_0_hlkService_fgr    p1_0_fgr
p1_0_hlkService_fgg    p1_0_fgg
p1_0_hlkService_fgb    p1_0_fgb
p1_0_hlkService_bgr    p1_0_bgr
p1_0_hlkService_bgg    p1_0_bgg
p1_0_hlkService_bgb    p1_0_bgb
p1_0_hlkService_fc     p1_0_fc
p1_0_hlkService_fs     p1_0_fs
p1_0_hlkService_str    "Exit and return
    to the Registration Form"
p1_0_hlkService_yStr
    p1_0_hlkService_y +
    p1_0_hlkService_fa - 1 +
    p1_0_hlkService_dy
p1_0_hlkService_hostAdr    "127.0.0.1"
p1_0_hlkService_serviceNo    1
p1_0_hlkService_xStr
    p1_0_hlkService_x +
    p1_0_hlkService_dx
p1_0_hlkService_wStr
    textWidth(p1_0_hlkService_str,
    p1_0_hlkService_fc,
    p1_0_hlkService_fs)
p1_0_hlkService_hStr
    p1_0_hlkService_fh
p1_0_hlkService_fa
```
```
        fontAscent(p1_0_hlkService_fc,
        p1_0_hlkService_fs)
p1_0_hlkService_fh
        fontHeight(p1_0_hlkService_fc,
        p1_0_hlkService_fs)
p1_0_hlkService_dx    libGuiHlk3D_dx
p1_0_hlkService_dy    libGuiHlk3D_dy
p1_0_hlkService_dw    libGuiHlk3D_dw
p1_0_hlkService_dh    libGuiHlk3D_dh

.data
String  p1_0_hlkService_str_
        p1_0_hlkService_str
String  p1_0_hlkService_hostAdr_
        p1_0_hlkService_hostAdr
Bytes   p1_0_hlkService_prp    [
        p1_0_hlkService_et,
        p1_0_hlkService_x,
        p1_0_hlkService_y,
        p1_0_hlkService_w,
        p1_0_hlkService_h,
        p1_0_hlkService_fgr,
        p1_0_hlkService_fgg,
        p1_0_hlkService_fgb,
        p1_0_hlkService_bgr,
        p1_0_hlkService_bgg,
        p1_0_hlkService_bgb,
        p1_0_hlkService_fc,
        p1_0_hlkService_fs,
        p1_0_hlkService_str_,
        p1_0_hlkService_xStr,
        p1_0_hlkService_yStr,
        p1_0_hlkService_hostAdr_,
        p1_0_hlkService_serviceNo ]

//////////////////
// p1_0_hlkService: Events
/////

.data
EventTable p1_0_hlkService_et    [
    key_pressed, p1_0_hlkService_kp,
    key_pressed_escape,
        p1_0_hlkService_kpes,
    key_pressed_enter,
        p1_0_hlkService_kpe,
    mouse_pressed_left,
        p1_0_hlkService_mpl,
    1, p1_0_et ]

.code
```

```
p1_0_hlkService_kp:                 fcall libGuiHlk_dwn
  loadc p1_0_hlkService_prp           halt
  push
  fcall libGuiHlk_kp                .code
  halt                              p1_0_hlkService_mpl:
                                      loadep1
p1_0_hlkService_kpes:                 push
  loadc p1_0_hlkService_prp           loadep2
  push                                push
  loadc p1_0_prp                      loadc p1_0_hlkService_prp
  push                                push
  loadc libGuiHlk3D_unDrwFcs          loadc libGuiHlk3D_unDrwFcs
  push                                push
  loadc libMisc_emptyProc             fcall p1_0_mplFcs
  push                                halt
  fcall libGui_mvFcs
  halt                              //////////////////
                                    // CVMUI Lib
p1_0_hlkService_kpe:                /////
  loadc p1_0_hlkService_prp
  push                              ...
```

D.2.2 With Customization

The implemented customization method is only for demonstration purpose and therefore will not be specified in detail. Instead, CVM screenshots and some selected CVMA code samples of the generated CVM packets will be presented. The implemented customization method is particularly applicable to very small client devices like wrist watches that may have the following exemplary CVM profile:

```
{ cvmMode = 16Bit;
  profileId = 483721;
  cvmNumGeneralRegs = 10;
  cvmMemMaxAdr = 2 Kbytes - 1;
  cvmScreenWidth = 50;
  cvmScreenHeight = 19;
  cvmFonts = 1;
  cvmKeyCodeSet = 0;
  0 }}
```

During the generation of the CVMUIs the "simple" (Smp) look is used. The tables D.1 (page 296) and D.2 (page 297) give an overview of the generated CVM packets for the AUI pages p0 and p1 and also contain CVM screenshots, respectively.

AUI page p0: CVMUI pages p0_0 and p0_1 The CVM packet for the CVMUI pages p0_0 and p0_1 is as follows:

CVM packet	CVM packet size [Bytes]	CVMUI page	CVM Screenshot
0	320	p0_0	Registra
		p0_1	tion
1	348	p0_2	Welcome
		p0_3	to the r
2	349	p0_4	egistrat
		p0_5	ion form
3	349	p0_6	, Please
		p0_7	enter y
4	349	p0_8	our name
		p0_9	and ema
5	344	p0_10	il addre
		p0_11	ss:
6	1291	p0_12	Name
		p0_13	ur name
7	1293	p0_14	Email
		p0_15	r email
8	999	p0_16	Reset
		p0_17	Submit

Table D.1: **Customized CVM Packets:** registration.aui, CVMUI pages for AUI page p0

D.2. Generated CVM Packets

CVM packet	CVM packet size [Bytes]	CVMUI page	CVM Screenshot
0	324	p1_0	Confirma
		p1_1	tion of
1	341	p1_2	Your Dat
		p1_3	a
2	346	p1_4	Name:
		p1_5	Max Must
3	345	p1_6	ermann
		p1_7	Email:
4	349	p1_8	MaxMuste
		p1_9	rmann@xy
5	661	p1_10	z.de
		p1_11	Exit and
6	780	p1_12	return
		p1_13	to the R
7	756	p1_14	egistrat
		p1_15	ion Form

Table D.2: **Customized CVM Packets:** registration.aui, CVMUI pages for AUI page p1

```
.16Bit

.code
  loadcr p0_0_main
  jmp

///////////////////
// Misc
/////

.const
_cil    2
_cvmScreenWidth    50
_cvmScreenHeight   19

.data
String  _hostAdrSrv   "127.0.0.1"

///////////////////
// Page Numbers
/////

.const
_pageNo    0
_p0        0
_p1        1
_pNotExist 2
_pIllegal  3

.data
Int  _subpageNo

///////////////////
// Service Commands
/////

.const
svcCmd_Reset   0
svcCmd_Submit  1

///////////////////
// Service Variables
/////

.const
_svIdxLen     1
_svIdx_name   1
_svIdx_email  2

.data
Int  _svBufIdx   0
```

```
Bytes  _svBuf   _svIdxLen + 2

.code
.fct _svBufIdx_reset ()
{
  loadc_0
  store _svBufIdx
  return
}

///////////////////
// p0_0: Attributes
/////

.const
p0_0_x     0
p0_0_y     0
p0_0_w     _cvmScreenWidth
p0_0_h     _cvmScreenHeight
p0_0_fgr   0
p0_0_fgg   0
p0_0_fgb   0
p0_0_bgr   255
p0_0_bgg   255
p0_0_bgb   255
p0_0_fc    fcFixedStandard
p0_0_fs    13
p0_0_img   ""
p0_0_imgStyle  0

.data
Bytes  p0_0_prp  [ p0_0_et ]
Int    p0_0_bInit   0

///////////////////
// p0_0: Misc
/////

.code
p0_0_main:
  loadc_0
  store _subpageNo
  fcall p0_0_init
  fcall p0_0_drw
  loadc p0_0_prp
  push
  loadc libMisc_emptyProc
  push
  fcall libGui_setFcs
  enableevents
  halt
```

D.2. Generated CVM Packets

```
.code
.fct p0_0_init ()
{
  load p0_0_bInit
  loadc_0
  loadcr p0_0_init_1
  jne
  loadc_1
  store p0_0_bInit
p0_0_init_1:
  return
}

.code
.fct p0_0_drw ()
{
  loadc p0_0_bgr
  loadc p0_0_bgg
  loadc p0_0_bgb
  setcolor
  loadc p0_0_x
  loadc p0_0_y
  loadc p0_0_w
  loadc p0_0_h
  rectfill
  fcall p0_0_txtTitle_drw
  return
}

.code
p0_0_nextPage:
  loadc 1
  loadcr p0_1_main
  page

///////////////////
// p0_0: Service Variables
/////

///////////////////
// p0_0: Events
/////

.data
EventTable p0_0_et  [
  key_pressed, p0_0_kp ]

.code
p0_0_kp:
  loadep1
  loadc XK_Right
  loadcr p0_0_kp_right
  je
  halt
p0_0_kp_right:
  loadcr p0_0_nextPage
  jmp

///////////////////
// p0_0_txtTitle: Attributes
/////

.const
p0_0_txtTitle_x    1
p0_0_txtTitle_y    1
p0_0_txtTitle_w    p0_0_txtTitle_wStr +
                   p0_0_txtTitle_dw
p0_0_txtTitle_h    p0_0_txtTitle_hStr +
                   p0_0_txtTitle_dh
p0_0_txtTitle_fgr   p0_0_fgr
p0_0_txtTitle_fgg   p0_0_fgg
p0_0_txtTitle_fgb   p0_0_fgb
p0_0_txtTitle_bgr   p0_0_bgr
p0_0_txtTitle_bgg   p0_0_bgg
p0_0_txtTitle_bgb   p0_0_bgb
p0_0_txtTitle_fc    p0_0_fc
p0_0_txtTitle_fs    p0_0_fs
p0_0_txtTitle_str   "Registra"
p0_0_txtTitle_yStr  p0_0_txtTitle_y +
                    p0_0_txtTitle_fa - 1 +
                    p0_0_txtTitle_dy
p0_0_txtTitle_xStr  p0_0_txtTitle_x +
                    p0_0_txtTitle_dx
p0_0_txtTitle_wStr
     textWidth(p0_0_txtTitle_str,
               p0_0_txtTitle_fc,
               p0_0_txtTitle_fs)
p0_0_txtTitle_hStr
     textHeight(p0_0_txtTitle_str,
                p0_0_txtTitle_fc,
                p0_0_txtTitle_fs, 0)
p0_0_txtTitle_fa
     fontAscent(p0_0_txtTitle_fc,
                p0_0_txtTitle_fs)
p0_0_txtTitle_dx    libGuiTxtSmp_dx
p0_0_txtTitle_dy    libGuiTxtSmp_dy
p0_0_txtTitle_dw    libGuiTxtSmp_dw
p0_0_txtTitle_dh    libGuiTxtSmp_dh

///////////////////
// p0_0_txtTitle: Misc
/////
```

```
.code
.fct p0_0_txtTitle_drw ()
{
  loadc p0_0_txtTitle_fgr
  loadc p0_0_txtTitle_fgg
  loadc p0_0_txtTitle_fgb
  setcolor
  loadc p0_0_txtTitle_bgr
  loadc p0_0_txtTitle_bgg
  loadc p0_0_txtTitle_bgb
  setbgcolor
  loadc p0_0_txtTitle_fc
  loadc p0_0_txtTitle_fs
  setfont
  loadc p0_0_txtTitle_xStr
  loadc p0_0_txtTitle_yStr
  textbg p0_0_txtTitle_str
  return
}

/////////////////////
// p0_1: Attributes
/////

.const
p0_1_x     0
p0_1_y     0
p0_1_w     _cvmScreenWidth
p0_1_h     _cvmScreenHeight
p0_1_fgr   0
p0_1_fgg   0
p0_1_fgb   0
p0_1_bgr   255
p0_1_bgg   255
p0_1_bgb   255
p0_1_fc    fcFixedStandard
p0_1_fs    13
p0_1_img   ""
p0_1_imgStyle   0

.data
Bytes  p0_1_prp   [ p0_1_et ]
Int    p0_1_bInit    0

/////////////////////
// p0_1: Misc
/////

.code
p0_1_main:
  loadc_0
  store _subpageNo
  fcall p0_1_init
  fcall p0_1_drw
  loadc p0_1_prp
  push
  loadc libMisc_emptyProc
  push
  fcall libGui_setFcs
  enableevents
  halt

.code
.fct p0_1_init ()
{
  load p0_1_bInit
  loadc_0
  loadcr p0_1_init_1
  jne
  loadc_1
  store p0_1_bInit
p0_1_init_1:
  return
}

.code
.fct p0_1_drw ()
{
  loadc p0_1_bgr
  loadc p0_1_bgg
  loadc p0_1_bgb
  setcolor
  loadc p0_1_x
  loadc p0_1_y
  loadc p0_1_w
  loadc p0_1_h
  rectfill
  fcall p0_1_txtTitle_drw
  return
}

.code
p0_1_prevPage:
  loadc 0
  loadcr p0_0_main
  page

.code
p0_1_nextPage:
  fcall _svBufIdx_reset
  sendrcvpage _pageNo, 2
```

D.2. Generated CVM Packets

```
////////////////////
// p0_1: Service Variables
/////

////////////////////
// p0_1: Events
/////

.data
EventTable  p0_1_et   [
  key_pressed, p0_1_kp ]

.code
p0_1_kp:
  loadep1
  loadc XK_Left
  loadcr p0_1_kp_left
  je
  loadep1
  loadc XK_Right
  loadcr p0_1_kp_right
  je
  halt
p0_1_kp_left:
  loadcr p0_1_prevPage
  jmp
p0_1_kp_right:
  loadcr p0_1_nextPage
  jmp

////////////////////
// p0_1_txtTitle: Attributes
/////

.const
p0_1_txtTitle_x    1
p0_1_txtTitle_y    1
p0_1_txtTitle_w    p0_1_txtTitle_wStr +
    p0_1_txtTitle_dw
p0_1_txtTitle_h    p0_1_txtTitle_hStr +
    p0_1_txtTitle_dh
p0_1_txtTitle_fgr    p0_1_fgr
p0_1_txtTitle_fgg    p0_1_fgg
p0_1_txtTitle_fgb    p0_1_fgb
p0_1_txtTitle_bgr    p0_1_bgr
p0_1_txtTitle_bgg    p0_1_bgg
p0_1_txtTitle_bgb    p0_1_bgb
p0_1_txtTitle_fc     p0_1_fc
p0_1_txtTitle_fs     p0_1_fs
p0_1_txtTitle_str    "tion"

p0_1_txtTitle_yStr   p0_1_txtTitle_y +
    p0_1_txtTitle_fa - 1 +
    p0_1_txtTitle_dy
p0_1_txtTitle_xStr   p0_1_txtTitle_x +
    p0_1_txtTitle_dx
p0_1_txtTitle_wStr
    textWidth(p0_1_txtTitle_str,
    p0_1_txtTitle_fc,
    p0_1_txtTitle_fs)
p0_1_txtTitle_hStr
    textHeight(p0_1_txtTitle_str,
    p0_1_txtTitle_fc,
    p0_1_txtTitle_fs, 0)
p0_1_txtTitle_fa
    fontAscent(p0_1_txtTitle_fc,
    p0_1_txtTitle_fs)
p0_1_txtTitle_dx     libGuiTxtSmp_dx
p0_1_txtTitle_dy     libGuiTxtSmp_dy
p0_1_txtTitle_dw     libGuiTxtSmp_dw
p0_1_txtTitle_dh     libGuiTxtSmp_dh

////////////////////
// p0_1_txtTitle: Misc
/////

.code
.fct p0_1_txtTitle_drw ()
{
  loadc p0_1_txtTitle_fgr
  loadc p0_1_txtTitle_fgg
  loadc p0_1_txtTitle_fgb
  setcolor
  loadc p0_1_txtTitle_bgr
  loadc p0_1_txtTitle_bgg
  loadc p0_1_txtTitle_bgb
  setbgcolor
  loadc p0_1_txtTitle_fc
  loadc p0_1_txtTitle_fs
  setfont
  loadc p0_1_txtTitle_xStr
  loadc p0_1_txtTitle_yStr
  textbg p0_1_txtTitle_str
  return
}

////////////////////
// CVMUI Lib
/////

...
```

AUI page p0: CVMUI pages p0_2 and p0_3

The CVM packet for the CVMUI pages p0_2 and p0_3 is as follows:

```
.16Bit

.code
  loadcr p0_2_main
  jmp

/////////////////
// Misc
/////

.const
_cil     2
_cvmScreenWidth     50
_cvmScreenHeight    19

.data
String  _hostAdrSrv   "127.0.0.1"

/////////////////
// Page Numbers
/////

.const
_pageNo    0
_p0        0
_p1        1
_pNotExist 2
_pIllegal  3

.data
Int   _subpageNo

/////////////////
// Service Commands
/////

.const
svcCmd_Reset    0
svcCmd_Submit   1

/////////////////
// Service Variables
/////

.const
_svIdxLen       1
_svIdx_name     1
_svIdx_email    2

.data
Int    _svBufIdx   0
Bytes  _svBuf     _svIdxLen + 2

.code
.fct _svBufIdx_reset ()
{
  loadc_0
  store _svBufIdx
  return
}

/////////////////
// p0_2: Attributes
/////

.const
p0_2_x     0
p0_2_y     0
p0_2_w     _cvmScreenWidth
p0_2_h     _cvmScreenHeight
p0_2_fgr   0
p0_2_fgg   0
p0_2_fgb   0
p0_2_bgr   255
p0_2_bgg   255
p0_2_bgb   255
p0_2_fc    fcFixedStandard
p0_2_fs    13
p0_2_img   ""
p0_2_imgStyle   0

.data
Bytes  p0_2_prp   [ p0_2_et ]
Int    p0_2_bInit   0

/////////////////
// p0_2: Misc
/////

.code
p0_2_main:
  loadc_0
  store _subpageNo
  fcall p0_2_init
  fcall p0_2_drw
  loadc p0_2_prp
```

D.2. Generated CVM Packets

```
    push
    loadc libMisc_emptyProc
    push
    fcall libGui_setFcs
    enableevents
    halt
.code
.fct p0_2_init ()
{
    load p0_2_bInit
    loadc_0
    loadcr p0_2_init_1
    jne
    loadc_1
    store p0_2_bInit
p0_2_init_1:
    return
}

.code
.fct p0_2_drw ()
{
    loadc p0_2_bgr
    loadc p0_2_bgg
    loadc p0_2_bgb
    setcolor
    loadc p0_2_x
    loadc p0_2_y
    loadc p0_2_w
    loadc p0_2_h
    rectfill
    fcall p0_2_txpIntro_drw
    return
}

.code
p0_2_prevPage:
    fcall _svBufIdx_reset
    sendrcvpage _pageNo, 1

.code
p0_2_nextPage:
    loadc 3
    loadcr p0_3_main
    page

////////////////////////
// p0_2: Service Variables
/////
```

```
////////////////////////
// p0_2: Events
/////

.data
EventTable p0_2_et  [
    key_pressed, p0_2_kp ]

.code
p0_2_kp:
    loadep1
    loadc XK_Left
    loadcr p0_2_kp_left
    je
    loadep1
    loadc XK_Right
    loadcr p0_2_kp_right
    je
    halt
p0_2_kp_left:
    loadcr p0_2_prevPage
    jmp
p0_2_kp_right:
    loadcr p0_2_nextPage
    jmp

////////////////////////
// p0_2_txpIntro: Attributes
/////

.const
p0_2_txpIntro_x    1
p0_2_txpIntro_y    1
p0_2_txpIntro_w    p0_2_txpIntro_wStr +
    p0_2_txpIntro_dw
p0_2_txpIntro_h    p0_2_txpIntro_hStr +
    p0_2_txpIntro_dh
p0_2_txpIntro_fgr  p0_2_fgr
p0_2_txpIntro_fgg  p0_2_fgg
p0_2_txpIntro_fgb  p0_2_fgb
p0_2_txpIntro_bgr  p0_2_bgr
p0_2_txpIntro_bgg  p0_2_bgg
p0_2_txpIntro_bgb  p0_2_bgb
p0_2_txpIntro_fc   p0_2_fc
p0_2_txpIntro_fs   p0_2_fs
p0_2_txpIntro_str    "Welcome "
p0_2_txpIntro_yStr   p0_2_txpIntro_y +
    p0_2_txpIntro_fa - 1 +
    p0_2_txpIntro_dy
p0_2_txpIntro_xStr   p0_2_txpIntro_x +
    p0_2_txpIntro_dx
```

```
p0_2_txpIntro_wStr
    textWidth(p0_2_txpIntro_str,
    p0_2_txpIntro_fc,
    p0_2_txpIntro_fs)
p0_2_txpIntro_hStr
    textHeight(p0_2_txpIntro_str,
    p0_2_txpIntro_fc,
    p0_2_txpIntro_fs, 0)
p0_2_txpIntro_fa
    fontAscent(p0_2_txpIntro_fc,
    p0_2_txpIntro_fs)
p0_2_txpIntro_dx    libGuiTxtSmp_dx
p0_2_txpIntro_dy    libGuiTxtSmp_dy
p0_2_txpIntro_dw    libGuiTxtSmp_dw
p0_2_txpIntro_dh    libGuiTxtSmp_dh

/////////////////
// p0_2_txpIntro: Misc
/////

.code
.fct p0_2_txpIntro_drw ()
  {
  loadc p0_2_txpIntro_fgr
  loadc p0_2_txpIntro_fgg
  loadc p0_2_txpIntro_fgb
  setcolor
  loadc p0_2_txpIntro_bgr
  loadc p0_2_txpIntro_bgg
  loadc p0_2_txpIntro_bgb
  setbgcolor
  loadc p0_2_txpIntro_fc
  loadc p0_2_txpIntro_fs
  setfont
  loadc p0_2_txpIntro_xStr
  loadc p0_2_txpIntro_yStr
  textbg p0_2_txpIntro_str
  return
  }

/////////////////
// p0_3: Attributes
/////

.const
p0_3_x    0
p0_3_y    0
p0_3_w    _cvmScreenWidth
p0_3_h    _cvmScreenHeight
p0_3_fgr  0
p0_3_fgg  0

p0_3_fgb  0
p0_3_bgr  255
p0_3_bgg  255
p0_3_bgb  255
p0_3_fc   fcFixedStandard
p0_3_fs   13
p0_3_img  ""
p0_3_imgStyle  0

.data
Bytes p0_3_prp    [ p0_3_et ]
Int   p0_3_bInit  0

/////////////////
// p0_3: Misc
/////

.code
p0_3_main:
  loadc_0
  store _subpageNo
  fcall p0_3_init
  fcall p0_3_drw
  loadc p0_3_prp
  push
  loadc libMisc_emptyProc
  push
  fcall libGui_setFcs
  enableevents
  halt

.code
.fct p0_3_init ()
  {
  load p0_3_bInit
  loadc_0
  loadcr p0_3_init_1
  jne
  loadc_1
  store p0_3_bInit
p0_3_init_1:
  return
  }

.code
.fct p0_3_drw ()
  {
  loadc p0_3_bgr
  loadc p0_3_bgg
  loadc p0_3_bgb
  setcolor
```

```
    loadc p0_3_x
    loadc p0_3_y
    loadc p0_3_w
    loadc p0_3_h
    rectfill
    fcall p0_3_txpIntro_drw
    return
  }

.code
p0_3_prevPage:
    loadc 2
    loadcr p0_2_main
    page

.code
p0_3_nextPage:
    fcall _svBufIdx_reset
    sendrcvpage _pageNo, 4

////////////////////
// p0_3: Service Variables
/////

////////////////////
// p0_3: Events
/////

.data
EventTable p0_3_et    [
    key_pressed, p0_3_kp ]

.code
p0_3_kp:
    loadep1
    loadc XK_Left
    loadcr p0_3_kp_left
    je
    loadep1
    loadc XK_Right
    loadcr p0_3_kp_right
    je
    halt
p0_3_kp_left:
    loadcr p0_3_prevPage
    jmp
p0_3_kp_right:
    loadcr p0_3_nextPage
    jmp

////////////////////

// p0_3_txpIntro: Attributes
/////

.const
p0_3_txpIntro_x     1
p0_3_txpIntro_y     1
p0_3_txpIntro_w     p0_3_txpIntro_wStr +
                    p0_3_txpIntro_dw
p0_3_txpIntro_h     p0_3_txpIntro_hStr +
                    p0_3_txpIntro_dh
p0_3_txpIntro_fgr   p0_3_fgr
p0_3_txpIntro_fgg   p0_3_fgg
p0_3_txpIntro_fgb   p0_3_fgb
p0_3_txpIntro_bgr   p0_3_bgr
p0_3_txpIntro_bgg   p0_3_bgg
p0_3_txpIntro_bgb   p0_3_bgb
p0_3_txpIntro_fc    p0_3_fc
p0_3_txpIntro_fs    p0_3_fs
p0_3_txpIntro_str   "to the r"
p0_3_txpIntro_yStr  p0_3_txpIntro_y +
                    p0_3_txpIntro_fa - 1 +
                    p0_3_txpIntro_dy
p0_3_txpIntro_xStr  p0_3_txpIntro_x +
                    p0_3_txpIntro_dx
p0_3_txpIntro_wStr
    textWidth(p0_3_txpIntro_str,
    p0_3_txpIntro_fc,
    p0_3_txpIntro_fs)
p0_3_txpIntro_hStr
    textHeight(p0_3_txpIntro_str,
    p0_3_txpIntro_fc,
    p0_3_txpIntro_fs, 0)
p0_3_txpIntro_fa
    fontAscent(p0_3_txpIntro_fc,
    p0_3_txpIntro_fs)
p0_3_txpIntro_dx    libGuiTxtSmp_dx
p0_3_txpIntro_dy    libGuiTxtSmp_dy
p0_3_txpIntro_dw    libGuiTxtSmp_dw
p0_3_txpIntro_dh    libGuiTxtSmp_dh

////////////////////
// p0_3_txpIntro: Misc
/////

.code
.fct p0_3_txpIntro_drw ()
  {
    loadc p0_3_txpIntro_fgr
    loadc p0_3_txpIntro_fgg
    loadc p0_3_txpIntro_fgb
    setcolor
```

```
    loadc p0_3_txpIntro_bgr              textbg p0_3_txpIntro_str
    loadc p0_3_txpIntro_bgg              return
    loadc p0_3_txpIntro_bgb          }
    setbgcolor
    loadc p0_3_txpIntro_fc           //////////////////////
    loadc p0_3_txpIntro_fs           // CVMUI Lib
    setfont                          /////
    loadc p0_3_txpIntro_xStr
    loadc p0_3_txpIntro_yStr             ...
```

AUI page p0: CVMUI pages p0_12 and p0_13 The CVM packet for the CVMUI pages p0_12 and p0_13 is as follows:

```
.16Bit                               svcCmd_Reset    0
                                     svcCmd_Submit   1
.code
    loadcr p0_12_main                //////////////////////
    jmp                              // Service Variables
                                     /////
//////////////////////
// Misc                              .const
/////                                _svIdxLen   1
                                     _svIdx_name   1
.const                               _svIdx_email  2
_cil   2
_cvmScreenWidth    50                .data
_cvmScreenHeight   19                Int    _svBufIdx    0
                                     Bytes  _svBuf     _svIdxLen +
.data                                       p0_13_ixtName_svBufLen +
String  _hostAdrSrv   "127.0.0.1"           _svIdxLen + 2

//////////////////////                .code
// Page Numbers                       .fct _svBufIdx_reset ()
/////                                 {
                                        loadc_0
.const                                  store _svBufIdx
_pageNo   0                             return
_p0   0                               }
_p1   1
_pNotExist   2                        .code
_pIllegal    3                        .fct _svBuf_write ()
                                      {
.data                                   fcall _svBufIdx_reset
Int    _subpageNo                       fcall p0_13_svBuf_write
                                        return
//////////////////////                 }
// Service Commands
/////                                 //////////////////////
                                      // p0_12: Attributes
.const                                /////
```

```
.const
p0_12_x      0
p0_12_y      0
p0_12_w      _cvmScreenWidth
p0_12_h      _cvmScreenHeight
p0_12_fgr    0
p0_12_fgg    0
p0_12_fgb    0
p0_12_bgr    255
p0_12_bgg    255
p0_12_bgb    255
p0_12_fc     fcFixedStandard
p0_12_fs     13
p0_12_img    ""
p0_12_imgStyle  0

.data
Bytes  p0_12_prp   [ p0_12_et ]
Int    p0_12_bInit    0

////////////////////
// p0_12: Misc
/////

.code
p0_12_main:
  loadc_0
  store _subpageNo
  fcall p0_12_init
  fcall p0_12_drw
  loadc p0_12_prp
  push
  loadc libMisc_emptyProc
  push
  fcall libGui_setFcs
  enableevents
  halt

.code
.fct p0_12_init ()
{
  load p0_12_bInit
  loadc_0
  loadcr p0_12_init_1
  jne
  loadc_1
  store p0_12_bInit
p0_12_init_1:
  return
}

.code
.fct p0_12_drw ()
{
  loadc p0_12_bgr
  loadc p0_12_bgg
  loadc p0_12_bgb
  setcolor
  loadc p0_12_x
  loadc p0_12_y
  loadc p0_12_w
  loadc p0_12_h
  rectfill
  fcall p0_12_txtName_drw
  return
}

.code
p0_12_prevPage:
  fcall _svBuf_write
  sendrcvpage _pageNo, 11

.code
p0_12_nextPage:
  loadc 13
  loadcr p0_13_main
  page

////////////////////
// p0_12: Service Variables
/////

////////////////////
// p0_12: Events
/////

.data
EventTable p0_12_et   [
  key_pressed, p0_12_kp ]

.code
p0_12_kp:
  loadep1
  loadc XK_Left
  loadcr p0_12_kp_left
  je
  loadep1
  loadc XK_Right
  loadcr p0_12_kp_right
  je
  halt
p0_12_kp_left:
```

```
    loadcr p0_12_prevPage
    jmp
p0_12_kp_right:
    loadcr p0_12_nextPage
    jmp

////////////////////
// p0_12_txtName: Attributes
/////

.const
p0_12_txtName_x     1
p0_12_txtName_y     1
p0_12_txtName_w     p0_12_txtName_wStr +
    p0_12_txtName_dw
p0_12_txtName_h     p0_12_txtName_hStr +
    p0_12_txtName_dh
p0_12_txtName_fgr   p0_12_fgr
p0_12_txtName_fgg   p0_12_fgg
p0_12_txtName_fgb   p0_12_fgb
p0_12_txtName_bgr   p0_12_bgr
p0_12_txtName_bgg   p0_12_bgg
p0_12_txtName_bgb   p0_12_bgb
p0_12_txtName_fc    p0_12_fc
p0_12_txtName_fs    p0_12_fs
p0_12_txtName_str   "Name"
p0_12_txtName_yStr  p0_12_txtName_y +
    p0_12_txtName_fa - 1 +
    p0_12_txtName_dy
p0_12_txtName_xStr  p0_12_txtName_x +
    p0_12_txtName_dx
p0_12_txtName_wStr
    textWidth(p0_12_txtName_str,
    p0_12_txtName_fc,
    p0_12_txtName_fs)
p0_12_txtName_hStr
    textHeight(p0_12_txtName_str,
    p0_12_txtName_fc,
    p0_12_txtName_fs, 0)
p0_12_txtName_fa
    fontAscent(p0_12_txtName_fc,
    p0_12_txtName_fs)
p0_12_txtName_dx    libGuiTxtSmp_dx
p0_12_txtName_dy    libGuiTxtSmp_dy
p0_12_txtName_dw    libGuiTxtSmp_dw
p0_12_txtName_dh    libGuiTxtSmp_dh

////////////////////
// p0_12_txtName: Misc
/////

.code
.fct p0_12_txtName_drw ()
{
    loadc p0_12_txtName_fgr
    loadc p0_12_txtName_fgg
    loadc p0_12_txtName_fgb
    setcolor
    loadc p0_12_txtName_bgr
    loadc p0_12_txtName_bgg
    loadc p0_12_txtName_bgb
    setbgcolor
    loadc p0_12_txtName_fc
    loadc p0_12_txtName_fs
    setfont
    loadc p0_12_txtName_xStr
    loadc p0_12_txtName_yStr
    textbg p0_12_txtName_str
    return
}

////////////////////
// p0_13: Attributes
/////

.const
p0_13_x         0
p0_13_y         0
p0_13_w         _cvmScreenWidth
p0_13_h         _cvmScreenHeight
p0_13_fgr       0
p0_13_fgg       0
p0_13_fgb       0
p0_13_bgr       255
p0_13_bgg       255
p0_13_bgb       255
p0_13_fc        fcFixedStandard
p0_13_fs        13
p0_13_img       ""
p0_13_imgStyle  0

.data
Bytes   p0_13_prp   [ p0_13_et ]
Int     p0_13_bInit    0

////////////////////
// p0_13: Misc
/////

.code
p0_13_main:
    loadc_0
```

D.2. Generated CVM Packets

```
    store _subpageNo
    fcall p0_13_init
    fcall p0_13_drw
    loadc p0_13_ixtName_prp
    push
    loadc libGuiIxtSmp_drwFcs
    push
    fcall libGui_setFcs
    enableevents
    halt
.code
.fct p0_13_init ()
{
    load p0_13_bInit
    loadc_0
    loadcr p0_13_init_1
    jne
    fcall p0_13_ixtName_init
    loadc_1
    store p0_13_bInit
p0_13_init_1:
    return
}

.code
.fct p0_13_drw ()
{
    loadc p0_13_bgr
    loadc p0_13_bgg
    loadc p0_13_bgb
    setcolor
    loadc p0_13_x
    loadc p0_13_y
    loadc p0_13_w
    loadc p0_13_h
    rectfill
    loadc p0_13_ixtName_prp
    push
    fcall libGuiIxtSmp_drw
    return
}

.code
p0_13_prevPage:
    loadc 12
    loadcr p0_12_main
    page

.code
p0_13_nextPage:
```

```
    fcall _svBuf_write
    sendrcvpage _pageNo, 14

///////////////////
// p0_13: Service Variables
/////
.code
.fct p0_13_svBuf_write ()
{
    fcall p0_13_ixtName_svBuf_write
    return
}

///////////////////
// p0_13: Events
/////
.data
EventTable p0_13_et [
    key_pressed, p0_13_kp ]
.code
p0_13_kp:
    loadep1
    loadc XK_Tab
    loadcr p0_13_kp_tab
    je
    loadep1
    loadc XK_Left
    loadcr p0_13_kp_left
    je
    loadep1
    loadc XK_Right
    loadcr p0_13_kp_right
    je
    halt
p0_13_kp_tab:
    loadc p0_13_prp
    push
    loadc p0_13_ixtName_prp
    push
    loadc libMisc_emptyProc
    push
    loadc libGuiIxtSmp_drwFcs
    push
    fcall libGui_mvFcs
    halt
p0_13_kp_left:
    loadcr p0_13_prevPage
    jmp
```

```
p0_13_kp_right:
    loadcr p0_13_nextPage
    jmp

////////////////////
// p0_13_ixtName: Attributes
/////

.const
p0_13_ixtName_x     1
p0_13_ixtName_y     1
p0_13_ixtName_w     48
p0_13_ixtName_h     p0_13_ixtName_hStr +
    p0_13_ixtName_dh
p0_13_ixtName_fgr   p0_13_fgr
p0_13_ixtName_fgg   p0_13_fgg
p0_13_ixtName_fgb   p0_13_fgb
p0_13_ixtName_bgr   p0_13_bgr
p0_13_ixtName_bgg   p0_13_bgg
p0_13_ixtName_bgb   p0_13_bgb
p0_13_ixtName_fc    p0_13_fc
p0_13_ixtName_fs    p0_13_fs

.data
Bytes  p0_13_ixtName_str
    p0_13_ixtName_strLenMax + 3

.const
p0_13_ixtName_yStr   p0_13_ixtName_y +
    p0_13_ixtName_fa - 1 +
    p0_13_ixtName_dy
p0_13_ixtName_strLenMax   80
p0_13_ixtName_svIdx    _svIdx_name
p0_13_ixtName_svBufLen
    p0_13_ixtName_strLenMax + 3
p0_13_ixtName_xStr   p0_13_ixtName_x +
    p0_13_ixtName_dx
p0_13_ixtName_wStr   p0_13_ixtName_w -
    p0_13_ixtName_dw
p0_13_ixtName_hStr   p0_13_ixtName_fh
p0_13_ixtName_yaStr  p0_13_ixtName_y
    + p0_13_ixtName_dy

.data
String  p0_13_ixtName_strInit   "your
    name"

.const
p0_13_ixtName_wChar   textWidth(" ",
    p0_13_ixtName_fc,
    p0_13_ixtName_fs)

p0_13_ixtName_strPos   -12
p0_13_ixtName_fa
    fontAscent(p0_13_ixtName_fc,
    p0_13_ixtName_fs)
p0_13_ixtName_fh
    fontHeight(p0_13_ixtName_fc,
    p0_13_ixtName_fs)
p0_13_ixtName_dx    libGuiIxtSmp_dx
p0_13_ixtName_dy    libGuiIxtSmp_dy
p0_13_ixtName_dw    libGuiIxtSmp_dw
p0_13_ixtName_dh    libGuiIxtSmp_dh

.data
Bytes  p0_13_ixtName_prp   [
    p0_13_ixtName_et,
    p0_13_ixtName_x, p0_13_ixtName_y,
    p0_13_ixtName_w, p0_13_ixtName_h,
    p0_13_ixtName_fgr,
    p0_13_ixtName_fgg,
    p0_13_ixtName_fgb,
    p0_13_ixtName_bgr,
    p0_13_ixtName_bgg,
    p0_13_ixtName_bgb,
    p0_13_ixtName_fc,
    p0_13_ixtName_fs,
    p0_13_ixtName_str,
    p0_13_ixtName_xStr,
    p0_13_ixtName_yStr,
    p0_13_ixtName_wStr,
    p0_13_ixtName_hStr,
    p0_13_ixtName_yaStr,
    p0_13_ixtName_strLenMax,
    p0_13_ixtName_wChar,
    p0_13_ixtName_strPos ]

////////////////////
// p0_13_ixtName: Init
/////

.code
.fct p0_13_ixtName_init ()
{
    loadc p0_13_ixtName_strPos
    loadc p0_13_ixtName_prp
    loadc libGui_strPosOfs
    add
    storea
    loadc p0_13_ixtName_str
    push
    loadc p0_13_ixtName_strInit
    push
```

D.2. Generated CVM Packets

```
      fcall libMisc_strCp
      return
    }

    ///////////////////
    // p0_13_ixtName: Events
    /////

    .data
    EventTable p0_13_ixtName_et    [
      key_pressed, p0_13_ixtName_kp,
      key_pressed_escape,
        p0_13_ixtName_kpes,
      1, p0_13_et ]

    .code
    p0_13_ixtName_kp:
      loadc p0_13_ixtName_prp
      push
      fcall libGuiIxt_kp
      halt


    p0_13_ixtName_kpes:
      loadc p0_13_ixtName_prp
      push
      loadc p0_13_prp
      push
      loadc libGuiIxtSmp_unDrwFcs
      push
      loadc libMisc_emptyProc
      push
      fcall libGui_mvFcs
      halt

    ///////////////////
    // p0_13_ixtName: Service Variables
    /////
```

```
    .code
    .fct p0_13_ixtName_svBuf_write ()
    {
      loadc p0_13_ixtName_svIdx
      loadc _svBuf
      load _svBufIdx
      astore1
      load _svBufIdx
      loadc 1
      add
      store _svBufIdx
      loadc _svBuf
      load _svBufIdx
      add
      push
      loadc p0_13_ixtName_str
      push
      fcall libMisc_strCp
      load _svBufIdx
      incsp
      loadc p0_13_ixtName_str
      push
      fcall libMisc_strLen
      pop
      add
      loadc 3
      add
      store _svBufIdx
      return
    }

    ///////////////////
    // CVMUI Lib
    /////

    ...
```

AUI page p0: CVMUI pages p0_16 and p0_17 The CVM packet for the CVMUI pages p0_16 and p0_17 is as follows:

```
    .16Bit

    .code
      loadcr p0_16_main
      jmp

    ///////////////////
    // Misc
    /////
```

```
    .const
    _cil   2
    _cvmScreenWidth   50
    _cvmScreenHeight  19

    .data
    String _hostAdrSrv   "127.0.0.1"

    ///////////////////
```

```
// Page Numbers
/////

.const
_pageNo     0
_p0         0
_p1         1
_pNotExist  2
_pIllegal   3

.data
Int _subpageNo

////////////////////
// Service Commands
/////

.const
svcCmd_Reset   0
svcCmd_Submit  1

////////////////////
// Service Variables
/////

.const
_svIdxLen     1
_svIdx_name   1
_svIdx_email  2

.data
Int   _svBufIdx  0
Bytes _svBuf     _svIdxLen + 2

.code
.fct _svBufIdx_reset ()
 {
  loadc_0
  store _svBufIdx
  return
 }

.code
.fct _svBuf_svcCmd_write (Int
    svcCmdIdx)
 {
  loadc_0
  loadc _svBuf
  load _svBufIdx
  astore1
  load _svBufIdx
  loadc _svIdxLen
  add
  store _svBufIdx
  load svcCmdIdx
  loadc _svBuf
  load _svBufIdx
  astore2
  load _svBufIdx
  loadc 2
  add
  store _svBufIdx
  return
 }

.code
.fct _svBuf_write ()
 {
  fcall _svBufIdx_reset
  return
 }

////////////////////
// p0_16: Attributes
/////

.const
p0_16_x         0
p0_16_y         0
p0_16_w         _cvmScreenWidth
p0_16_h         _cvmScreenHeight
p0_16_fgr       0
p0_16_fgg       0
p0_16_fgb       0
p0_16_bgr       255
p0_16_bgg       255
p0_16_bgb       255
p0_16_fc        fcFixedStandard
p0_16_fs        13
p0_16_img       ""
p0_16_imgStyle  0

.data
Bytes p0_16_prp  [ p0_16_et ]
Int   p0_16_bInit   0

////////////////////
// p0_16: Misc
/////

.code
p0_16_main:
```

D.2. Generated CVM Packets

```
  loadc_0
  store _subpageNo
  fcall p0_16_init
  fcall p0_16_drw
  loadc p0_16_btnReset_prp
  push
  loadc libGuiBtnSmp_drwFcs
  push
  fcall libGui_setFcs
  enableevents
  halt
.code
.fct p0_16_init ()
{
  load p0_16_bInit
  loadc_0
  loadcr p0_16_init_1
  jne
  loadc_1
  store p0_16_bInit
p0_16_init_1:
  return
}

.code
.fct p0_16_drw ()
{
  loadc p0_16_bgr
  loadc p0_16_bgg
  loadc p0_16_bgb
  setcolor
  loadc p0_16_x
  loadc p0_16_y
  loadc p0_16_w
  loadc p0_16_h
  rectfill
  loadc p0_16_btnReset_prp
  push
  fcall libGuiBtnSmp_drw
  return
}

.code
p0_16_prevPage:
  fcall _svBufIdx_reset
  sendrcvpage _pageNo, 15

.code
p0_16_nextPage:
  loadc 17
```

```
  loadcr p0_17_main
  page

////////////////////
// p0_16: Service Variables
/////

////////////////////
// p0_16: Events
/////

.data
EventTable p0_16_et  [
  key_pressed, p0_16_kp ]

.code
p0_16_kp:
  loadep1
  loadc XK_Tab
  loadcr p0_16_kp_tab
  je
  loadep1
  loadc XK_Left
  loadcr p0_16_kp_left
  je
  loadep1
  loadc XK_Right
  loadcr p0_16_kp_right
  je
  halt
p0_16_kp_tab:
  loadc p0_16_prp
  push
  loadc p0_16_btnReset_prp
  push
  loadc libMisc_emptyProc
  push
  loadc libGuiBtnSmp_drwFcs
  push
  fcall libGui_mvFcs
  halt
p0_16_kp_left:
  loadcr p0_16_prevPage
  jmp
p0_16_kp_right:
  loadcr p0_16_nextPage
  jmp

////////////////////
// p0_16_btnReset: Attributes
/////
```

```
.const
p0_16_btnReset_x    1
p0_16_btnReset_y    1
p0_16_btnReset_w    p0_16_btnReset_wStr
    + p0_16_btnReset_dw
p0_16_btnReset_h    p0_16_btnReset_hStr
    + p0_16_btnReset_dh
p0_16_btnReset_fgr    p0_16_fgr
p0_16_btnReset_fgg    p0_16_fgg
p0_16_btnReset_fgb    p0_16_fgb
p0_16_btnReset_bgr    p0_16_bgr
p0_16_btnReset_bgg    p0_16_bgg
p0_16_btnReset_bgb    p0_16_bgb
p0_16_btnReset_fc     p0_16_fc
p0_16_btnReset_fs     p0_16_fs
p0_16_btnReset_str    "Reset"
p0_16_btnReset_yStr    p0_16_btnReset_y
    + p0_16_btnReset_fa - 1 +
    p0_16_btnReset_dy
p0_16_btnReset_img    ""
p0_16_btnReset_imgStyle    0
p0_16_btnReset_xStr    p0_16_btnReset_x
    + p0_16_btnReset_dx
p0_16_btnReset_wStr
    textWidth(p0_16_btnReset_str,
    p0_16_btnReset_fc,
    p0_16_btnReset_fs)
p0_16_btnReset_hStr
    p0_16_btnReset_fh
p0_16_btnReset_fa
    fontAscent(p0_16_btnReset_fc,
    p0_16_btnReset_fs)
p0_16_btnReset_fh
    fontHeight(p0_16_btnReset_fc,
    p0_16_btnReset_fs)
p0_16_btnReset_dx    libGuiBtnSmp_dx
p0_16_btnReset_dy    libGuiBtnSmp_dy
p0_16_btnReset_dw    libGuiBtnSmp_dw
p0_16_btnReset_dh    libGuiBtnSmp_dh

.data
String  p0_16_btnReset_str_
    p0_16_btnReset_str
String  p0_16_btnReset_img_
    p0_16_btnReset_img
Bytes   p0_16_btnReset_prp    [
    p0_16_btnReset_et,
    p0_16_btnReset_x,
    p0_16_btnReset_y,
    p0_16_btnReset_w,
    p0_16_btnReset_h,
    p0_16_btnReset_fgr,
    p0_16_btnReset_fgg,
    p0_16_btnReset_fgb,
    p0_16_btnReset_bgr,
    p0_16_btnReset_bgg,
    p0_16_btnReset_bgb,
    p0_16_btnReset_fc,
    p0_16_btnReset_fs,
    p0_16_btnReset_str_,
    p0_16_btnReset_xStr,
    p0_16_btnReset_yStr,
    p0_16_btnReset_img_,
    p0_16_btnReset_imgStyle ]

///////////////////
// p0_16_btnReset: Events
/////

.data
EventTable p0_16_btnReset_et    [
    key_pressed, p0_16_btnReset_kp,
    key_pressed_escape,
        p0_16_btnReset_kpes,
    key_pressed_enter,
        p0_16_btnReset_kpe,
    key_released, p0_16_btnReset_kr,
    key_released_enter,
        p0_16_btnReset_kre,
    1, p0_16_et ]

.code
p0_16_btnReset_kp:
    loadep1
    loadc XK_space
    loadcr p0_16_btnReset_kp_space
    je
    halt

p0_16_btnReset_kp_space:
    fcall p0_16_btnReset_evDwn
    halt

p0_16_btnReset_kpes:
    loadc p0_16_btnReset_prp
    push
    loadc p0_16_prp
    push
    loadc libGuiBtnSmp_unDrwFcs
    push
    loadc libMisc_emptyProc
    push
```

```
      fcall libGui_mvFcs
      halt

p0_16_btnReset_kpe:
      fcall p0_16_btnReset_evDwn
      halt

p0_16_btnReset_kr:
      loadep1
      loadc XK_space
      loadcr p0_16_btnReset_kr_space
      je
      halt

p0_16_btnReset_kr_space:
      fcall p0_16_btnReset_evUp
      halt

p0_16_btnReset_kre:
      fcall p0_16_btnReset_evUp
      halt

.code
.fct p0_16_btnReset_evDwn ()
   {
   loadc p0_16_btnReset_prp
   push
   fcall libGuiBtnSmp_dwn
fcall _svBufIdx_reset
       fcall_I _svBuf_svcCmd_write,
       svcCmd_Reset
        sendrcvpage_a _pageNo,
        _subpageNo
   return
   }

.fct p0_16_btnReset_evUp ()
   {
   loadc p0_16_btnReset_prp
   push
   fcall libGuiBtnSmp_up
   return
   }

////////////////////
// p0_17: Attributes
/////

.const
p0_17_x    0
p0_17_y    0
```

```
p0_17_w    _cvmScreenWidth
p0_17_h    _cvmScreenHeight
p0_17_fgr  0
p0_17_fgg  0
p0_17_fgb  0
p0_17_bgr  255
p0_17_bgg  255
p0_17_bgb  255
p0_17_fc   fcFixedStandard
p0_17_fs   13
p0_17_img  ""
p0_17_imgStyle   0

.data
Bytes  p0_17_prp    [ p0_17_et ]
Int    p0_17_bInit   0

////////////////////
// p0_17: Misc
/////

.code
p0_17_main:
   loadc_0
   store _subpageNo
   fcall p0_17_init
   fcall p0_17_drw
   loadc p0_17_btnSubmit_prp
   push
   loadc libGuiBtnSmp_drwFcs
   push
   fcall libGui_setFcs
   enableevents
   halt

.code
.fct p0_17_init ()
   {
   load p0_17_bInit
   loadc_0
   loadcr p0_17_init_1
   jne
   loadc_1
   store p0_17_bInit
p0_17_init_1:
   return
   }

.code
.fct p0_17_drw ()
   {
```

```
    loadc p0_17_bgr
    loadc p0_17_bgg
    loadc p0_17_bgb
    setcolor
    loadc p0_17_x
    loadc p0_17_y
    loadc p0_17_w
    loadc p0_17_h
    rectfill
    loadc p0_17_btnSubmit_prp
    push
    fcall libGuiBtnSmp_drw
    return
}

.code
p0_17_prevPage:
    loadc 16
    loadcr p0_16_main
    page

////////////////////
// p0_17: Service Variables
/////

////////////////////
// p0_17: Events
/////

.data
EventTable p0_17_et    [
    key_pressed, p0_17_kp ]

.code
p0_17_kp:
    loadep1
    loadc XK_Tab
    loadcr p0_17_kp_tab
    je
    loadep1
    loadc XK_Left
    loadcr p0_17_kp_left
    je
    halt
p0_17_kp_tab:
    loadc p0_17_prp
    push
    loadc p0_17_btnSubmit_prp
    push
    loadc libMisc_emptyProc
    push
    loadc libGuiBtnSmp_drwFcs
    push
    fcall libGui_mvFcs
    halt
p0_17_kp_left:
    loadcr p0_17_prevPage
    jmp

////////////////////
// p0_17_btnSubmit: Attributes
/////

.const
p0_17_btnSubmit_x    1
p0_17_btnSubmit_y    1
p0_17_btnSubmit_w
    p0_17_btnSubmit_wStr +
    p0_17_btnSubmit_dw
p0_17_btnSubmit_h
    p0_17_btnSubmit_hStr +
    p0_17_btnSubmit_dh
p0_17_btnSubmit_fgr    p0_17_fgr
p0_17_btnSubmit_fgg    p0_17_fgg
p0_17_btnSubmit_fgb    p0_17_fgb
p0_17_btnSubmit_bgr    p0_17_bgr
p0_17_btnSubmit_bgg    p0_17_bgg
p0_17_btnSubmit_bgb    p0_17_bgb
p0_17_btnSubmit_fc     p0_17_fc
p0_17_btnSubmit_fs     p0_17_fs
p0_17_btnSubmit_str    "Submit"
p0_17_btnSubmit_yStr
    p0_17_btnSubmit_y +
    p0_17_btnSubmit_fa - 1 +
    p0_17_btnSubmit_dy
p0_17_btnSubmit_img    ""
p0_17_btnSubmit_imgStyle    0
p0_17_btnSubmit_xStr
    p0_17_btnSubmit_x +
    p0_17_btnSubmit_dx
p0_17_btnSubmit_wStr
    textWidth(p0_17_btnSubmit_str,
    p0_17_btnSubmit_fc,
    p0_17_btnSubmit_fs)
p0_17_btnSubmit_hStr
    p0_17_btnSubmit_fh
p0_17_btnSubmit_fa
    fontAscent(p0_17_btnSubmit_fc,
    p0_17_btnSubmit_fs)
p0_17_btnSubmit_fh
    fontHeight(p0_17_btnSubmit_fc,
    p0_17_btnSubmit_fs)
```

D.2. Generated CVM Packets

```
p0_17_btnSubmit_dx     libGuiBtnSmp_dx
p0_17_btnSubmit_dy     libGuiBtnSmp_dy
p0_17_btnSubmit_dw     libGuiBtnSmp_dw
p0_17_btnSubmit_dh     libGuiBtnSmp_dh

.data
String  p0_17_btnSubmit_str_
    p0_17_btnSubmit_str
String  p0_17_btnSubmit_img_
    p0_17_btnSubmit_img
Bytes   p0_17_btnSubmit_prp  [
    p0_17_btnSubmit_et,
    p0_17_btnSubmit_x,
    p0_17_btnSubmit_y,
    p0_17_btnSubmit_w,
    p0_17_btnSubmit_h,
    p0_17_btnSubmit_fgr,
    p0_17_btnSubmit_fgg,
    p0_17_btnSubmit_fgb,
    p0_17_btnSubmit_bgr,
    p0_17_btnSubmit_bgg,
    p0_17_btnSubmit_bgb,
    p0_17_btnSubmit_fc,
    p0_17_btnSubmit_fs,
    p0_17_btnSubmit_str_,
    p0_17_btnSubmit_xStr,
    p0_17_btnSubmit_yStr,
    p0_17_btnSubmit_img_,
    p0_17_btnSubmit_imgStyle ]

////////////////////
// p0_17_btnSubmit: Events
/////

.data
EventTable  p0_17_btnSubmit_et  [
  key_pressed, p0_17_btnSubmit_kp,
  key_pressed_escape,
    p0_17_btnSubmit_kpes,
  key_pressed_enter,
    p0_17_btnSubmit_kpe,
  key_released, p0_17_btnSubmit_kr,
  key_released_enter,
    p0_17_btnSubmit_kre,
  1, p0_17_et ]

.code
p0_17_btnSubmit_kp:
  loadep1
  loadc XK_space
  loadcr p0_17_btnSubmit_kp_space
  je
  halt

p0_17_btnSubmit_kp_space:
  fcall p0_17_btnSubmit_evDwn
  halt

p0_17_btnSubmit_kpes:
  loadc p0_17_btnSubmit_prp
  push
  loadc p0_17_prp
  push
  loadc libGuiBtnSmp_unDrwFcs
  push
  loadc libMisc_emptyProc
  push
  fcall libGui_mvFcs
  halt

p0_17_btnSubmit_kpe:
  fcall p0_17_btnSubmit_evDwn
  halt

p0_17_btnSubmit_kr:
  loadep1
  loadc XK_space
  loadcr p0_17_btnSubmit_kr_space
  je
  halt

p0_17_btnSubmit_kr_space:
  fcall p0_17_btnSubmit_evUp
  halt

p0_17_btnSubmit_kre:
  fcall p0_17_btnSubmit_evUp
  halt

.code
.fct p0_17_btnSubmit_evDwn ()
{
  loadc p0_17_btnSubmit_prp
  push
  fcall libGuiBtnSmp_dwn
fcall _svBuf_write
    fcall_I _svBuf_svcCmd_write,
  svcCmd_Submit
  sendrcvpage _p1, 0
  return
}
```

318   D. CVM Packet Server: Example

```
.fct p0_17_btnSubmit_evUp ()                //////////////////
{                                           // CVMUI Lib
  loadc p0_17_btnSubmit_prp                 /////
  push
  fcall libGuiBtnSmp_up                     ...
  return
}
```

AUI page p1: CVMUI pages p1_12 and p1_13 The CVM packet for the CVMUI pages p1_12 and p1_13 is as follows:

```
.16Bit                              //////////////////
                                    // Service Variables
.code                               /////
  loadcr p1_12_main
  jmp                               .const
                                    _svIdxLen    1
//////////////////                  _svIdx_name  1
// Misc                             _svIdx_email 2
/////
                                    .data
.const                              Int   _svBufIdx   0
_cil 2                              Bytes _svBuf     _svIdxLen + 2
_cvmScreenWidth   50
_cvmScreenHeight  19                .code
                                    .fct _svBufIdx_reset ()
.data                               {
String _hostAdrSrv "127.0.0.1"        loadc_0
                                      store _svBufIdx
//////////////////                    return
// Page Numbers                     }
/////
                                    //////////////////
.const                              // p1_12: Attributes
_pageNo    1                        /////
_p0        0
_pNotExist 2                        .const
_pIllegal  3                        p1_12_x    0
                                    p1_12_y    0
.data                               p1_12_w    _cvmScreenWidth
Int _subpageNo                      p1_12_h    _cvmScreenHeight
                                    p1_12_fgr  0
//////////////////                  p1_12_fgg  0
// Service Commands                 p1_12_fgb  0
/////                               p1_12_bgr  255
                                    p1_12_bgg  255
.const                              p1_12_bgb  255
svcCmd_Reset   0                    p1_12_fc   fcFixedStandard
svcCmd_Submit  1                    p1_12_fs   13
                                    p1_12_img  ""
```

D.2. Generated CVM Packets

```
p1_12_imgStyle   0

.data
Bytes  p1_12_prp   [ p1_12_et ]
Int    p1_12_bInit    0

//////////////////
// p1_12: Misc
/////

.code
p1_12_main:
  loadc_0
  store _subpageNo
  fcall p1_12_init
  fcall p1_12_drw
  loadc p1_12_hlkService_prp
  push
  loadc libGuiHlkSmp_drwFcs
  push
  fcall libGui_setFcs
  enableevents
  halt

.code
.fct p1_12_init ()
{
  load p1_12_bInit
  loadc_0
  loadcr p1_12_init_1
  jne
  loadc_1
  store p1_12_bInit
p1_12_init_1:
  return
}

.code
.fct p1_12_drw ()
{
  loadc p1_12_bgr
  loadc p1_12_bgg
  loadc p1_12_bgb
  setcolor
  loadc p1_12_x
  loadc p1_12_y
  loadc p1_12_w
  loadc p1_12_h
  rectfill
  loadc p1_12_hlkService_prp
  push
```

```
  fcall libGuiHlkSmp_drw
  return
}

.code
p1_12_prevPage:
  fcall _svBufIdx_reset
  sendrcvpage _pageNo, 11

.code
p1_12_nextPage:
  loadc 13
  loadcr p1_13_main
  page

//////////////////
// p1_12: Service Variables
/////

//////////////////
// p1_12: Events
/////

.data
EventTable  p1_12_et   [
  key_pressed, p1_12_kp ]

.code
p1_12_kp:
  loadep1
  loadc XK_Tab
  loadcr p1_12_kp_tab
  je
  loadep1
  loadc XK_Left
  loadcr p1_12_kp_left
  je
  loadep1
  loadc XK_Right
  loadcr p1_12_kp_right
  je
  halt
p1_12_kp_tab:
  loadc p1_12_prp
  push
  loadc p1_12_hlkService_prp
  push
  loadc libMisc_emptyProc
  push
  loadc libGuiHlkSmp_drwFcs
  push
```

```
    fcall libGui_mvFcs                      p1_12_hlkService_fs)
    halt                              p1_12_hlkService_dx    libGuiHlkSmp_dx
p1_12_kp_left:                        p1_12_hlkService_dy    libGuiHlkSmp_dy
    loadcr p1_12_prevPage             p1_12_hlkService_dw    libGuiHlkSmp_dw
    jmp                               p1_12_hlkService_dh    libGuiHlkSmp_dh
p1_12_kp_right:
    loadcr p1_12_nextPage             .data
    jmp                               String  p1_12_hlkService_str_
                                              p1_12_hlkService_str
/////////////////////                 String  p1_12_hlkService_hostAdr_
// p1_12_hlkService: Attributes               p1_12_hlkService_hostAdr
/////                                 Bytes   p1_12_hlkService_prp   [
                                              p1_12_hlkService_et,
.const                                        p1_12_hlkService_x,
p1_12_hlkService_x    1                       p1_12_hlkService_y,
p1_12_hlkService_y    1                       p1_12_hlkService_w,
p1_12_hlkService_w                            p1_12_hlkService_h,
    p1_12_hlkService_wStr +                   p1_12_hlkService_fgr,
    p1_12_hlkService_dw                       p1_12_hlkService_fgg,
p1_12_hlkService_h                            p1_12_hlkService_fgb,
    p1_12_hlkService_hStr +                   p1_12_hlkService_bgr,
    p1_12_hlkService_dh                       p1_12_hlkService_bgg,
p1_12_hlkService_fgr   p1_12_fgr              p1_12_hlkService_bgb,
p1_12_hlkService_fgg   p1_12_fgg              p1_12_hlkService_fc,
p1_12_hlkService_fgb   p1_12_fgb              p1_12_hlkService_fs,
p1_12_hlkService_bgr   p1_12_bgr              p1_12_hlkService_str_,
p1_12_hlkService_bgg   p1_12_bgg              p1_12_hlkService_xStr,
p1_12_hlkService_bgb   p1_12_bgb              p1_12_hlkService_yStr,
p1_12_hlkService_fc    p1_12_fc               p1_12_hlkService_hostAdr_,
p1_12_hlkService_fs    p1_12_fs               p1_12_hlkService_serviceNo ]
p1_12_hlkService_str   " return "
p1_12_hlkService_yStr                 /////////////////////
    p1_12_hlkService_y +              // p1_12_hlkService: Events
    p1_12_hlkService_fa - 1 +         /////
    p1_12_hlkService_dy
p1_12_hlkService_hostAdr   "127.0.0.1"   .data
p1_12_hlkService_serviceNo   1        EventTable p1_12_hlkService_et   [
p1_12_hlkService_xStr                     key_pressed, p1_12_hlkService_kp,
    p1_12_hlkService_x +                  key_pressed_escape,
    p1_12_hlkService_dx                       p1_12_hlkService_kpes,
p1_12_hlkService_wStr                     key_pressed_enter,
    textWidth(p1_12_hlkService_str,           p1_12_hlkService_kpe,
    p1_12_hlkService_fc,                  1, p1_12_et ]
    p1_12_hlkService_fs)
p1_12_hlkService_hStr                 .code
    p1_12_hlkService_fh               p1_12_hlkService_kp:
p1_12_hlkService_fa                       loadc p1_12_hlkService_prp
    fontAscent(p1_12_hlkService_fc,       push
    p1_12_hlkService_fs)                  fcall libGuiHlk_kp
p1_12_hlkService_fh                       halt
    fontHeight(p1_12_hlkService_fc,
```

D.2. Generated CVM Packets

```
p1_12_hlkService_kpes:
  loadc p1_12_hlkService_prp
  push
  loadc p1_12_prp
  push
  loadc libGuiHlkSmp_unDrwFcs
  push
  loadc libMisc_emptyProc
  push
  fcall libGui_mvFcs
  halt

p1_12_hlkService_kpe:
  loadc p1_12_hlkService_prp
  push
  fcall libGuiHlk_dwn
  halt

////////////////////
// p1_13: Attributes
/////

.const
p1_13_x         0
p1_13_y         0
p1_13_w         _cvmScreenWidth
p1_13_h         _cvmScreenHeight
p1_13_fgr       0
p1_13_fgg       0
p1_13_fgb       0
p1_13_bgr       255
p1_13_bgg       255
p1_13_bgb       255
p1_13_fc        fcFixedStandard
p1_13_fs        13
p1_13_img       ""
p1_13_imgStyle  0

.data
Bytes p1_13_prp   [ p1_13_et ]
Int   p1_13_bInit   0

////////////////////
// p1_13: Misc
/////

.code
p1_13_main:
  loadc_0
  store _subpageNo
  fcall p1_13_init
```

```
  fcall p1_13_drw
  loadc p1_13_hlkService_prp
  push
  loadc libGuiHlkSmp_drwFcs
  push
  fcall libGui_setFcs
  enableevents
  halt

.code
.fct p1_13_init ()
{
  load p1_13_bInit
  loadc_0
  loadcr p1_13_init_1
  jne
  loadc_1
  store p1_13_bInit
p1_13_init_1:
  return
}

.code
.fct p1_13_drw ()
{
  loadc p1_13_bgr
  loadc p1_13_bgg
  loadc p1_13_bgb
  setcolor
  loadc p1_13_x
  loadc p1_13_y
  loadc p1_13_w
  loadc p1_13_h
  rectfill
  loadc p1_13_hlkService_prp
  push
  fcall libGuiHlkSmp_drw
  return
}

.code
p1_13_prevPage:
  loadc 12
  loadcr p1_12_main
  page

.code
p1_13_nextPage:
  fcall _svBufIdx_reset
  sendrcvpage _pageNo, 14
```

```
////////////////////
// p1_13: Service Variables
/////

////////////////////
// p1_13: Events
/////

.data
EventTable p1_13_et  [
  key_pressed, p1_13_kp ]

.code
p1_13_kp:
  loadep1
  loadc XK_Tab
  loadcr p1_13_kp_tab
  je
  loadep1
  loadc XK_Left
  loadcr p1_13_kp_left
  je
  loadep1
  loadc XK_Right
  loadcr p1_13_kp_right
  je
  halt
p1_13_kp_tab:
  loadc p1_13_prp
  push
  loadc p1_13_hlkService_prp
  push
  loadc libMisc_emptyProc
  push
  loadc libGuiHlkSmp_drwFcs
  push
  fcall libGui_mvFcs
  halt
p1_13_kp_left:
  loadcr p1_13_prevPage
  jmp
p1_13_kp_right:
  loadcr p1_13_nextPage
  jmp

////////////////////
// p1_13_hlkService: Attributes
/////

.const
p1_13_hlkService_x    1

p1_13_hlkService_y    1
p1_13_hlkService_w
       p1_13_hlkService_wStr +
       p1_13_hlkService_dw
p1_13_hlkService_h
       p1_13_hlkService_hStr +
       p1_13_hlkService_dh
p1_13_hlkService_fgr     p1_13_fgr
p1_13_hlkService_fgg     p1_13_fgg
p1_13_hlkService_fgb     p1_13_fgb
p1_13_hlkService_bgr     p1_13_bgr
p1_13_hlkService_bgg     p1_13_bgg
p1_13_hlkService_bgb     p1_13_bgb
p1_13_hlkService_fc      p1_13_fc
p1_13_hlkService_fs      p1_13_fs
p1_13_hlkService_str     "to the R"
p1_13_hlkService_yStr
       p1_13_hlkService_y +
       p1_13_hlkService_fa - 1 +
       p1_13_hlkService_dy
p1_13_hlkService_hostAdr  "127.0.0.1"
p1_13_hlkService_serviceNo   1
p1_13_hlkService_xStr
       p1_13_hlkService_x +
       p1_13_hlkService_dx
p1_13_hlkService_wStr
       textWidth(p1_13_hlkService_str,
       p1_13_hlkService_fc,
       p1_13_hlkService_fs)
p1_13_hlkService_hStr
       p1_13_hlkService_fh
p1_13_hlkService_fa
       fontAscent(p1_13_hlkService_fc,
       p1_13_hlkService_fs)
p1_13_hlkService_fh
       fontHeight(p1_13_hlkService_fc,
       p1_13_hlkService_fs)
p1_13_hlkService_dx      libGuiHlkSmp_dx
p1_13_hlkService_dy      libGuiHlkSmp_dy
p1_13_hlkService_dw      libGuiHlkSmp_dw
p1_13_hlkService_dh      libGuiHlkSmp_dh

.data
String  p1_13_hlkService_str_
        p1_13_hlkService_str
String  p1_13_hlkService_hostAdr_
        p1_13_hlkService_hostAdr
Bytes   p1_13_hlkService_prp   [
        p1_13_hlkService_et,
        p1_13_hlkService_x,
        p1_13_hlkService_y,
```

D.2. Generated CVM Packets

```
            p1_13_hlkService_w,              p1_13_hlkService_kp:
            p1_13_hlkService_h,                loadc p1_13_hlkService_prp
            p1_13_hlkService_fgr,              push
            p1_13_hlkService_fgg,              fcall libGuiHlk_kp
            p1_13_hlkService_fgb,              halt
            p1_13_hlkService_bgr,
            p1_13_hlkService_bgg,            p1_13_hlkService_kpes:
            p1_13_hlkService_bgb,              loadc p1_13_hlkService_prp
            p1_13_hlkService_fc,               push
            p1_13_hlkService_fs,               loadc p1_13_prp
            p1_13_hlkService_str_,             push
            p1_13_hlkService_xStr,             loadc libGuiHlkSmp_unDrwFcs
            p1_13_hlkService_yStr,             push
            p1_13_hlkService_hostAdr_,         loadc libMisc_emptyProc
            p1_13_hlkService_serviceNo ]      push
                                               fcall libGui_mvFcs
///////////////////                          halt
// p1_13_hlkService: Events
/////                                        p1_13_hlkService_kpe:
                                               loadc p1_13_hlkService_prp
.data                                          push
EventTable  p1_13_hlkService_et    [           fcall libGuiHlk_dwn
  key_pressed, p1_13_hlkService_kp,            halt
  key_pressed_escape,
    p1_13_hlkService_kpes,                   ///////////////////
  key_pressed_enter,                         // CVMUI Lib
    p1_13_hlkService_kpe,                    /////
  1, p1_13_et ]
                                             ...
.code
```

Bibliography

[1] M. Adler et al. *Portable Network Graphics (PNG) Specification*. W3C, 2nd edition, 2003. http://www.w3.org/Graphics/PNG. 3, 86

[2] S. Adler et al. *Extensible Stylesheet Language (XSL)*. W3C, 2001. http://www.w3.org/TR/xsl. 6, 126

[3] Adobe Systems Incorporated. http://www.adobe.com. 79

[4] Adobe Systems Incorporated. *PostScript Language Reference*, 3rd edition, 1999. http://partners.adobe.com/asn/tech/ps/specifications.jsp. 24

[5] Adobe Systems Incorporated. *PDF Reference*, 4th edition, 2001. http://partners.adobe.com/asn/tech/pdf/specifications.jsp. 3

[6] M. Altheim et al. *XHTML 1.1 - Module-based XHTML*. W3C, 2001. http://www.w3.org/TR/xhtml11. 6

[7] *American Standard Code for Information Interchange (ASCII)*. http://www.asciitable.com. 118, 222, 229, 234

[8] M. Baker et al. *XHTML Basic*. W3C, 2000. http://www.w3.org/TR/xhtml-basic. 6, 126

[9] A. Berger. *Embedded Systems Design*. CMP Books, 1st edition, 2001. 2

[10] T. Berners-Lee et al. *Hypertext Transfer Protocol - HTTP/1.1*. IETF, 1999. RFC 2616. 3, 4, 13, 29, 82, 126, 127, 128, 130

[11] S. Björk et al. *WEST: A Web Browser for Small Terminals*. In Proceedings of UIST, ACM Press, 1999. 9

[12] B. Bos et al. *Cascading Style Sheets, level 2 revision 1, CSS 2.1 Specification*. W3C, 2004. http://www.w3.org/TR/CSS21. 3, 6, 126, 204

[13] L. Bouillon et al. *Flexible Re-engineering of Web Sites*. In Proceedings of IUI, ACM Press, 2004. 9

[14] A. Brandl. *EmuGen: A Generator for Multiple-User Interfaces*. In Proceedings of HCI International, 2001. 28, 203

[15] A. Brandl. *Generierung interaktiver Informationssysteme und ihrer Benutzungsoberflächen für mehrere Benutzer*. PhD thesis, Technische Universität München, 2002. http://tumb1.biblio.tu-muenchen.de/publ/diss/in/2002/brandl.html. 28, 203

[16] T. Bray et al. *Extensible Markup Language (XML) 1.0*. W3C, 3rd edition, 2004. http://www.w3.org/TR/REC-xml. 3, 4, 6, 7, 18, 126, 205

[17] Berkeley Software Design (BSD). http://www.bsd.org. 118, 131, 198

[18] D.R. Butenhof. *Programming with POSIX Threads*. Addison-Wesley, 1st edition, 1997. 83

[19] O. Buyukkokten et al. *Power Browser: Efficient Web Browsing for PDAs*. In Proceedings of CHI, ACM Press, 2000. 9

[20] B.W. Kernighan, D.M. Ritchie. *The C Programming Language*. Prentice Hall, 2nd edition, 1988. 16, 117, 161, 198, 200, 201, 205, 207, 230, 232

[21] R. Chinnici et al. *Web Services Description Language (WSDL) Version 2.0 Part 1: Core Language*. W3C, 2004. http://www.w3.org/TR/wsdl20/. 28, 203

[22] J. Clark et al. *XSL Transformations (XSLT)*. W3C, 1999. http://www.w3.org/TR/xslt. 4, 6

[23] W. Dees. *Handling Device Diversity through Multi-Level Stylesheets*. In Proceedings of IUI, ACM Press, 2004. 9

[24] M. Dubinko et al. *XForms 1.0*. W3C, 2003. http://www.w3.org/TR/xforms. 6, 28, 126, 203

[25] J. Eisenstein et al. *Applying Model-Based Techniques to the Development of UIs for Mobile Computers*. In Proceedings of IUI, ACM Press, 2001. 9

[26] R. Fielding. *Relative Uniform Resource Locators*. IETF, 1995. RFC 1808. 14

[27] D. Flanagan. *JavaScript: The Definitive Guide*. O'Reilly, 4th edition, 2001. 3, 13, 15, 21, 204

[28] *Flash and Shockwave*. http://www.macromedia.com. 3

[29] *Graphics Interchange Format (GIF), Version 89a*. CompuServe Incorporated, 1990. 3, 17, 75, 78

[30] *GNU Bison*. http://www.gnu.org/software/bison/manual. 136, 232

[31] *GNU Bourne-Again Shell (bash)*. http://www.gnu.org/software/bash/manual. 118, 200, 233

[32] *GNU Compiler Collection (GCC)*. http://gcc.gnu.org. 117, 232

[33] *GNU Flex — A Scanner Generator*. http://www.gnu.org/software/flex/manual. 136, 232

[34] *GNU make*. http://www.gnu.org/software/make/manual/make.html. 118, 198, 200, 233

[35] *GNU zip (gzip)*. http://www.gzip.org. 85

[36] J. Gosling et al. *The Java Language Specification.* Addison-Wesley, 2nd edition, 2000. http://java.sun.com/docs/books/jls/index.html. 13, 205, 207

[37] *Green Computing.* http://en.wikipedia.org/wiki/Green_computing. 2, 202

[38] A. Le Hors. *X PixMap Format (XPM)*, 1994. http://www.dcs.ed.ac.uk/home/mxr/gfx/2d-hi.html. 78, 85, 229

[39] *Joint Photographic Experts Group (JPEG).* http://www.jpeg.org. 3, 17, 75, 78

[40] G. Klyne et al. *Composite Capability/Preference Profiles (CC/PP): Structure and Vocabularies 1.0.* W3C, 2004. http://www.w3.org/TR/CCPP-struct-vocab. 7

[41] D.E. Knuth. *T_EX: The Program*, chapter 31. Addison Wesley, 1986. 24

[42] T. Lindholm et al. *The Java Virtual Machine Specification.* Addison-Wesley, 2nd edition, 1999. http://java.sun.com/docs/books/jvms/second_edition/html/VMSpecTOC.doc.html. 3

[43] *Linux.* http://www.linux.org. 117, 198, 232

[44] F. Manola et al. *RDF Primer.* W3C, 2004. http://www.w3.org/TR/rdf-primer. 7, 126

[45] P. Mockapetris. *Domain Names — Concepts and Facilities.* IETF, 1987. RFC 1034. 44, 51, 53, 56, 71, 72, 74, 90, 108, 110, 120, 139, 155, 158, 169

[46] *MPEG Layer III (MP3).* http://www.mpeg.org. 3, 4

[47] *Moving Picture Experts Group (MPEG).* http://www.mpeg.org. 3, 4, 75, 78

[48] H. Nielsen et al. *HTTP Extension Framework.* IETF, 2000. RFC 2774. 7

[49] M. Nilsson et al. *Composite Capability/Preference Profiles: Requirements and Architecture.* W3C, 2000. http://www.w3.org/TR/CCPP-ra. 7

[50] A. Nye. *Volume 0: XProtocol Reference Manual.* O'Reilly, 3rd edition, 1992. 79, 81

[51] A. Nye. *Volume 1: Xlib Programming Manual.* O'Reilly, 3rd edition, 1992. 79, 81, 85, 117

[52] A. Nye. *Volume 2: Xlib Reference Manual.* O'Reilly, 3rd edition, 1992. 75, 81, 85, 117

[53] H. Ohto et al. *CC/PP exchange protocol based on HTTP Extension Framework.* W3C, 1999. http://www.w3.org/TR/NOTE-CCPPexchange. 7, 126

[54] *Wireless Application Protocol Forum (WAP).* http://www.wapforum.org. 3, 5, 7, 205

[55] *Open Mobile Alliance (OMA).* http://www.openmobilealliance.org. 7

[56] Open Mobile Alliance. *Wireless Markup Language (WML)*, 2001. http://www.openmobilealliance.org/tech/affiliates/wap/wapindex.html. 3, 5, 7, 9, 125, 204

[57] Open Mobile Alliance. *Wireless Session Protocol (WSP)*, 2001. http://www.openmobilealliance.org/tech/affiliates/wap/wapindex.html. 4, 7, 127

[58] Open Mobile Alliance. *WMLScript*, 2001. http://www.openmobilealliance.org/tech/affiliates/wap/wapindex.html. 7, 125

[59] Open Mobile Alliance. *User Agent Profile*, 2003. http://www.openmobilealliance.org/tech/affiliates/wap/wapindex.html. 7, 126

[60] S. Pemberton et al. *XHTML 1.0: The Extensible HyperText Markup Language*. W3C, 2002. http://www.w3.org/TR/xhtml1. 6

[61] Ch. Perkins. *Ad Hoc Networking*. Addison-Wesley, 1st edition, 2000. 2, 82

[62] J. Postel. *Internet Protocol (IP)*. IETF, 1981. RFC 791. 51, 53, 56, 71, 72, 74, 90, 108, 110, 120, 128, 139, 155, 158, 169, 200

[63] J. Postel et al. *Telnet Protocol Specification*. IETF, 1983. RFC 854. 1

[64] J. Postel et al. *File Transfer Protocol (FTP)*. IETF, 1985. RFC 959. 1

[65] D. Raggett et al. *HTML 4.01 Specification*. W3C, 1999. http://www.w3.org/TR/html4. 3, 6, 9, 13, 15, 126, 142, 203, 204

[66] F. Reynolds et al. *Composite Capability/Preference Profiles (CC/PP): A user side framework for content negotiation*. W3C, 1999. http://www.w3.org/TR/NOTE-CCPP. 7

[67] S. Schreiber. *Spezifikationstechniken und Generierungswerkzeuge für graphische Benutzungsoberflächen*. PhD thesis, Technische Universität München, 1997. Herber Utz Verlag Wissenschaft (in German). 28, 203

[68] W. Stallings. *Wireless Communications & Networks*. Prentice Hall, 1st edition, 2001. 2

[69] W.R. Stevens. *TCP/IP Illustrated*. Addison-Wesley, 1st edition, 1994. 1, 5, 82, 117, 118, 131, 198

[70] M. Stokes et al. *A Standard Default Color Space for the Internet - sRGB*, 1996. http://www.w3.org/Graphics/Color/sRGB. 17, 76

[71] B. Stroustrup. *The C++ Programming Language*. Addison-Wesley, 3rd edition, 1997. 207

[72] Sun Microsystems. *Connected Device Configuration (CDC)*. http://java.sun.com/products/cdc. 7

[73] Sun Microsystems. *Connected, Limited Device Configuration (CLDC)*. http://java.sun.com/products/cldc. 7, 8, 125, 204

[74] Sun Microsystems. *Java 2 Platform, Micro Edition (J2ME)*. http://java.sun.com/j2me. 7, 125

[75] Sun Microsystems. *Java API Specifications*. http://java.sun.com/reference/api/index.html. 24

[76] Sun Microsystems. *Java HotSpot Technology.*
     http://java.sun.com/products/hotspot. 98

[77] Sun Microsystems. *Java Technologies.* http://java.sun.com. 7

[78] Sun Microsystems. *Mobile Information Device Profile (MIDP).*
     http://java.sun.com/products/midp. 8, 125

[79] Sun Microsystems. *J2ME Building Blocks for Mobile Devices*, 2000.
     http://java.sun.com/products/kvm/wp/KVMwp.pdf. 8, 24, 204

[80] F. Yellin T. Lindholm. *Java Virtual Machine.* Addison-Wesley, 2nd edition, 1999.
     http://java.sun.com/docs/books/vmspec/2nd-edition/html/VMSpecTOC.doc.html.
     24, 123

[81] A.S. Tannenbaum. *Computer Networks.* Prentice Hall, 4th edition, 2002. 3, 5

[82] Th. Rappaport Th.S. Rappaport. *Wireless Communications: Principles and Practice.*
     Prentice Hall, 2nd edition, 2001. 2

[83] C.-K. Toh. *Ad Hoc Mobile Wireless Networks: Protocols and Systems.* Addison-Wesley, 1st edition, 2001. 2

[84] J. Trevor et al. *From Desktop to Phonetop: A UI For Web Interaction On Very Small Devices.* In Proceedings of UIST, ACM Press, 2001. 9

[85] *TrueType.* http://www.truetype.com. 79

[86] *User Interface Markup Language (UIML).* http://www.uiml.org/. 28, 203

[87] *Universal Mobile Telecommunications System (UMTS).* http://www.umtsworld.com. 17

[88] *Unicode.* www.unicode.org. 92, 222

[89] *UTF-8, a transformation format of ISO 10646.* IETF, 2003. RFC 3629. 33, 36, 118

[90] *CC/PP Working Group.* W3C. http://www.w3.org/Mobile/CCPP. 7

[91] *Device Independence Working Group.* W3C. http://www.w3.org/2001/di. 7

[92] *World Wide Web Consortium (W3C).* http://www.w3.org. 1, 3, 6

[93] *Windows Media Audio.* http://www.microsoft.com. 3, 4

[94] J.O. Wobbrock et al. *WebThumb: Interaction Techniques for Small-Screen Browsers.*
     In Proceedings of UIST, ACM Press, 2002. 9

[95] T. Wugofski et al. *CSS Mobile Profile 1.0.* W3C, 2002.
     http://www.w3.org/TR/css-mobile. 6, 126

[96] *X BitMap Format (XBM).* http://www.dcs.ed.ac.uk/home/mxr/gfx/2d-hi.html. 78, 103, 228

Index

0-address code, 34
16-bit CVM, 34
16Bit, 89
16BitEmu, 89
32-bit CVM, 34
32Bit, 89
32BitEmu, 89

absolute memory address, 36
Abstract User Interface Description (AUI), 135
add, 101
addsp, 101
aload1, 102
aload2, aload4, 102
and, 102
astore1, 102
astore2, astore4, 102
attributes, 94

background color, 76
Base Pointer, 37
Big Point, 20, 77
bitmap, bitmapbg, 102
bitmapFile, 228
bitmapHeight, 228
bitmapWidth, 228
bookmarks menu, 56
builtin events, 49
builtin events (device specific), 49
builtin functions, 148, 227
Bytes, 223
bytes, 96
Bytesz, 223
bytesz, 96

call, 103
circle, circlefill, 103
Client Virtual Machine (CVM), 31
Code section, 37
codeSegmentAdr, 95
Core module, 32

CoreMisc, 84
CPTP, 127
CptpGET, 58
current history buffer position, 53
CVM, 31
CVM memory, 36
CVM mode, 34
CVM packet, 93
CVM packet generator, 27
CVM packet transfer protocol (CPTP), 127
CVM packet verifier, 98
CVM profile, 89
CVM program, 93
CVM runtime behavior, 58
CVM state machine, 58
CVM state transitions, 58
CVM states, 58
CVM user interface, 27
cvm_quit, 50
cvmAudioAvailable, 90
cvmDNSLookup, 90
cvmFonts, 90
cvmHeapAvailable, 91
cvmIntLen, 33
cvmKeyCodeSet, 91
cvmLibraries, 91
cvmMeasure, 91
cvmMemMaxAdr, 34, 36, 91
cvmMode, 89, 94
cvmMouseButtons, 92
cvmNumGeneralRegs, 34, 92
cvmOutputCharSet, 92
CVMP, 129
cvmpAdrLen, 94
cvmpNo, 53, 129
cvmScreenHeight, 92
cvmScreenHeightMM, 92
cvmScreenWidth, 93
cvmScreenWidthMM, 93
cvmTimerAvailable, 93
CVMUI Lib Misc, 249

329

cvmUPLanguage, 92

data, 96
Data section, 37
dataBytes, 96
dataDeclSegmentAdr, 94
dec, 103
Declared Data Section, 37
declCode, 96
decsp, 103
disableevents, 103
div, 103
DivisionByZero, 42
Dynamic Popping, 35

elementary graphic shapes, 78
emulation mode, 89
enableevents, 104
ERROR, 129
Error, 58
error handling, 41
event code, 45
event codes, 49
event data, 45
event handling, 45
event parameters, 45
event queue, event buffer, 46
event registers, 47
event table, 48
event table structure, 48
event types, 49
event_enter, 51
EventExecute, 58
EventProcess, 58
EventProcessBuiltin, 58
EventTable, 223
eventtable, 96
Execute, 58

fcall, 224
fcall_l, 224
final instruction, 36
font, 228
fontAscent, 228
fontAscentPt, 229
fcCourier, 80
fcCourierBold, 80
fcCourierBoldItalic, 80
fcCourierItalic, 80

fontDescent, 228
fontDescentPt, 229
fcFixedItalic, 80
fcFixed, 80
fcFixedBold, 80
fcFixedStandard, 79
fcFixedStandardBold, 79
fcFixedStandardItalic, 79
fontHeight, 228
fontHeightPt, 229
fcHelvetica, 80
fcHelveticaBold, 80
fcHelveticaBoldItalic, 80
fcHelveticaItalic, 80
fcNewCenturySchoolbook, 80
fcNewCenturySchoolbookBold, 80
fcNewCenturySchoolbookBoldItalic, 80
fcNewCenturySchoolbookItalic, 80
fontPt, 228
fcSymbol, 81
fcTimesItalic, 81
fcTimes, 80
fcTimesBold, 80
fcTimesBoldItalic, 81
foreground color, 76
free, 104

GET, 130
getbp, 104
getDate, 84
getTime, 84
graphics primitives, 78
graphics state, 76

halt, 104
Heap section, 41
history buffer, 52
history buffer entry, 53
history_back, 50
history_forward, 50
history_reload, 50
hload, 104
Home Menu, 86
HomeMenu, 71, 86
hostAdr, 53, 56
hstore, 104

IllegalMemoryAddress, 43
ImageLoadFailure, 43

imgOrig, 139
imgScale, 139
imgTile, 139
immOperands, 98
in-between instruction, 35
inc, 104
incsp, 105
Init, 58
input_hostAdr, 50
Instruction Pointer, 37
Int, 33, 34
Int, 223
int1, int2, ..., 97
Int1, Int2, ..., 33
interval timer, 57
interval timer registers, 57
intz, 97
InvalidScreenSection, 43

je, jne, jl, jle, 105
jmp, 105

key_pressed, 51
key_pressed_enter, 51
key_pressed_escape, 51
key_released, 51
key_released_escape, 51
Keyboard module, 81

lenDataDecl, 96
lenInstructions, 96
lib, 105
libCode, 83
libFctCode, 83
line, 84
linehoriz, 105
linevert, 105
load, 224
loada, 105
loadc, 225
loadc1, loadc2, loadc3, loadc4, 106
loadc_0, loadc_1, loadc_m1, 106
loadcr, 225
loadcu1, loadcu2, loadcu3, 106
LoadCvmPacket, 58
loadep1, loadep2, loadep3, 106
loadr, 106
local variables, 39
low-level security, 98

macros, 224
magic, 94
MalformedCPTPMessage, 43
MalformedCVMPacket, 43
MalformedCVMProfile, 43
MalformedHomeMenu, 43
MAX, 229
measuring unit, 77
mem2screen, 106
mem[...], 36
menu_bookmarks, 51
menu_home, 52
message item, 127
MIN, 229
mouse double click, 52
Mouse module, 81
mouse wheel down, 52
mouse wheel up, 52
mouse_moved, 52
mouse_pressed, 52
mouse_pressed_left, 52
mouse_released, 52
mouse_released_left, 52
mul, 107

Nat, 33, 34
nat1, nat2, ..., 97
Nat1, Nat2, ..., 33
neg, 107
Network module, 81
NetworkError, 43
new, 107
newstackframe, 107
NoDNSLookup, 44
not, 107

oldstackframe, 107
opcode, 98
operand stack, 34
operation mode, 33
or, 107

page, 108
pageMemAdr, 53, 129
pageNo, 53, 56
pixmap, 85
pixmapFile, 229
pixmapgz, 85
pixmapHeight, 229

pixmapWidth, 229
png, 86
Point, 20, 77
pop, 108
printInt, 84
printIntBg, 85
printKeyName, 85
procedure parameters, 39
procedure stack frame, 40
PROFILE, 130
profileId, 89
profileItemCode, 89
profileItemValue, 89
pt, 20, 77
push, 108

R[...], 35
rcv, 108
rcvpage_a, 226
rcvpage, 225
rcvsvc, 226
rdup, 109
rect, rectfill, 109
rectRound, rectRoundFill, 85
regBgColorBlue, 76
regBgColorGreen, 76
regBgColorRed, 76
regBP, 37
regClipHeight, 76
regClipWidth, 76
regClipX, 76
regClipY, 76
regColorBlue, 76
regColorGreen, 76
regColorRed, 76
regErrorCode, 41
regEventCode, 47
regEventEnable, 47
regEventPar1, regEventPar2, regEventPar3, 47
regEventTableAdr, 48
regFontCode, 76
regFontSize, 77
regHTextLine, 77
regIP, 37
register stack, 34
Register Stack Pointer, 35
RegisterStackOverflow, 44
RegisterStackStaticOverflow, 44

RegisterStackUnderflow, 44
regLineWidth, 77
regMeasure, 77
regMouseFont, 82
regRSP, 35
regServiceNo, 83
regSessionId, 82
regSP, 38
regSS, 38
regState, 58
regTimerHandleAdr, 57
regTimerInterval, 57
regTimerSignal, 57
regXTextLine, 77
relative memory address, 36
rem, 109
rempty, 110
ret, 109
retload, 226
retstore, 226
return, 226
rgb, 149, 229
rskip, 110
rswap, 110

screen2mem, 110
sendrcv, 110
sendrcvpage_a, 227
sendrcvpage, 227
service number, 27
service variables, 145
serviceNo, 53, 56
sessionId, 53
setbgblue, 111
setbgcolor, 111
setbgcolor32, 111
setbggreen, 112
setbgred, 112
setblue, 112
setbp, 112
setclip, 112
setcolor, 112
setcolor32, 112
setDate, 84
seteventtableadr, 113
setfont, 113
setfont32, 113
setfontcode, 113

setfontsize, 113
setgreen, 113
sethtextline, 113
setlinewidth, 113
setmousefont, 114
setred, 114
setTime, 84
settimerhandleadr, 114
settimerinterval, 114
setxtextline, 114
shl, 114
shortcut events, 48
shr, 114
shrs, 115
sidzero, 115
sizeof, 229
special events, 48
stack frame, 40
stack machine code, 34
Stack Pointer, 38
Stack section, 38
Stack Segment, 38
StackOverflow, 44
stackSegmentAdr, 95
StackUnderflow, 44
State Register, 58
Static Popping, 35
store, 227
storea, 115
storer, 115
String, 33
String, 223
string, 97
stringBytes, 230
sub, 115

testsetbits, 115
text, textbg, 115
textBreakLines, 230
textBreakLinesPt, 231
textHeight, 231
textHeightPt, 231
textm, textmbg, 116
textp, textpbg, 116
textpm, textpmbg, 116
textWidth, 231
textWidthPt, 232
TimerExecute, 58

triangle, trianglefill, 85

Undeclared Data section, 37
UnexpectedCPTPMethodCode, 44
UnknownLibraryFunction, 45
UnknownFont, 44
UnknownMouseFont, 44
UnknownOpcode, 45
unsetbits, 116

Visual module, 75
VisualImage, 85
VisualMisc, 84
Void, 222

Wait, 58

xor, 116

VDM Verlagsservicegesellschaft mbH

Die VDM Verlagsservicegesellschaft sucht für wissenschaftliche Verlage abgeschlossene und herausragende

Dissertationen, Habilitationen, Diplomarbeiten, Master Theses, Magisterarbeiten usw.

für die kostenlose Publikation als Fachbuch.

Sie verfügen über eine Arbeit, die hohen inhaltlichen und formalen Ansprüchen genügt, und haben Interesse an einer honorarvergüteten Publikation?

Dann senden Sie bitte erste Informationen über sich und Ihre Arbeit per Email an *info@vdm-vsg.de*.

Sie erhalten kurzfristig unser Feedback!

VDM Verlagsservicegesellschaft mbH
Dudweiler Landstr. 99   Telefon +49 681 3720 174
D - 66123 Saarbrücken   Fax   +49 681 3720 1749
www.vdm-vsg.de

Die VDM Verlagsservicegesellschaft mbH vertritt

Printed by Books on Demand GmbH, Norderstedt / Germany